Essentials of
Programming Languages

Daniel P. Friedman
Mitchell Wand
Christopher T. Haynes

Foreword by Harold Abelson

Essentials of Programming Languages

The MIT Press
Cambridge, Massachusetts London, England

McGraw-Hill Book Company
New York St. Louis San Francisco Montreal Toronto

Third printing, 1992

This book was edited and produced by The MIT Press under a joint production-distribution arrangement with the McGraw-Hill Book Company.

Ordering Information:

North America
Text orders should be addressed to the McGraw-Hill Book Company. All other orders should be addressed to The MIT Press.

Outside North America
All orders should be addressed to The MIT Press or its local distributor.

This book was typeset by the authors using TEX 3.0. Camera-ready copy was generated off a L300 phototypesetter by Chiron, Inc.

This book was printed and bound in the United States of America.

Library of Congress Cataloging-in-Publication Data

Friedman, Daniel P.
    Essentials of programming languages / Daniel P. Friedman, Mitchell Wand, Christopher T. Haynes.
        p.   cm.
    Includes bibliographical references and index.
    ISBN 0-262-06145-7 (MIT Press) (hb)
    ISBN 0-07-022443-9 (McGraw-Hill)
    1. Programming languages (Electronic computers)
I. Wand, Mitchell. II. Haynes, Christopher Thomas. III. Title.
QA76.7.F73   1992
005.13—dc20   91-23373
                                                        CIP

Contents

1

Tools for Symbolic Programming   *1*

2

Induction, Recursion, and Scope   *31*

Contents

6

7

8

Contents

9

Continuation-Passing Interpreters *291*

10

Imperative Form and Stack Architecture *335*

11

Scanners and Parsers *375*

Contents

12

List of Figures

List of Figures

List of Figures

List of Figures

List of Figures

Foreword

This book brings you face-to-face with the most fundamental idea in computer programming:

> The interpreter for a computer language is just another program.

It sounds obvious, doesn't it? But the implications are profound. If you are a computational theorist, the interpreter idea recalls Gödel's discovery of the limitations of formal logical systems, Turing's concept of a universal computer, and von Neumann's basic notion of the stored-program machine. If you are a programmer, mastering the idea of an interpreter is a source of great power. It provokes a real shift in mindset, a basic change in the way you think about programming.

I did a lot of programming before I learned about interpreters, and I produced some substantial programs. One of them, for example, was a large data-entry and information-retrieval system written in PL/I. When I implemented my system, I viewed PL/I as a fixed collection of rules established by some unapproachable group of language designers. I saw my job not as to modify these rules, or even to understand them deeply, but rather to pick through the (very) large manual, selecting this or that feature to use. The notion that there was some underlying structure to the way the language was organized, and that I might want to override some of the language designers' decisions, never occurred to me. I didn't know how to create embedded sub-languages to help organize my implementation, so the entire program seemed like a large, complex mosaic, where each piece had to be carefully shaped and fitted into place, rather than as a cluster of languages, where the pieces could be flexibly combined. If you don't understand interpreters, you can still write programs; you can even be a competent programmer. But you can't be a master.

There are three reasons why as a programmer you should learn about interpreters.

First, you will need at some point to implement interpreters, perhaps not interpreters for full-blown general-purpose languages, but interpreters just the same. Almost every complex computer system with which people interact in flexible ways—a computer drawing tool or an information-retrieval system, for example—includes some sort of interpreter that structures the interaction. These programs may include complex individual operations—shading a region on the display screen, or performing a database search—but the interpreter is the glue that lets you combine individual operations into useful patterns. Can you use the result of one operation as the input to another operation? Can you name a sequence of operations? Is the name local or global? Can you parameterize a sequence of operations, and give names to its inputs? And so on. No matter how complex and polished the individual operations are, it is often the quality of the glue that most directly determines the power of the system. It's easy to find examples of programs with good individual operations, but lousy glue; looking back on it, I can see that my PL/I database program certainly had lousy glue.

Second, even programs that are not themselves interpreters have important interpreter-like pieces. Look inside a sophisticated computer-aided design system and you're likely to find a geometric recognition language, a graphics interpreter, a rule-based control interpreter, an object-oriented language interpreter, all working together. One of the most powerful ways to structure a complex program is as a collection of languages, each of which provides a different perspective, a different way of working with the program elements. Choosing the right kind of language for the right purpose, and understanding the implementation tradeoffs involved: that's what the study of interpreters is about.

The third reason for learning about interpreters is that programming techniques that explicitly involve the structure of language are becoming increasingly important. Today's concern with designing and manipulating class hierarchies in object-oriented systems is only one example of this trend. Perhaps this is an inevitable consequence of the fact that our programs are becoming increasingly complex—thinking more explicitly about languages may be our best tool for dealing with this complexity. Consider again the basic idea: the interpreter itself is just a program. But that program is written in some language, whose interpreter is itself just a program written in some language whose interpreter is itself . . .. Perhaps the whole distinction between program and programming language is a misleading idea, and that future programmers will see themselves not as writing programs in particular, but as creating new languages for each new application.

Friedman, Wand, and Haynes have done a landmark job, and their book will change the landscape of programming-language courses. They don't just *tell* you about interpreters; they *show* them to you. The core of the book is a tour de force sequence of interpreters starting with an abstract high-level language and progressively making linguistic features explicit until we reach a state-machine with a parser and compiler. You can actually run this code, study and modify it, change the way these interpreters handle scoping, parameter-passing, control structure.

Part of the reason for the appeal of this approach is that the authors have chosen a good tool—the Scheme language, which combines the uniform syntax and data-abstraction capabilities of Lisp, with the lexical scoping and block structure of Algol. The result is a language that is high-level enough so that an interpreter can be expressed in a single page of code, yet explicit enough to deal with control flow and register allocation. But a powerful tool becomes most powerful in the hands of masters. The sample interpreters in this book are outstanding models. Indeed, since they are *runnable* models, I'm sure that these interpreters will find themselves at the cores of many programming systems over the coming years.

This is not an easy book. Mastery of interpreters does not come easily, and for good reason. The language designer is a further level removed from the end user than is the ordinary application programmer. In designing an application program, you think about the specific tasks to be performed, and consider what features to include. But in designing a language, you consider the various applications people might want to implement, and the ways in which they might implement them. Should your language have static or dynamic scope, or a mixture? Should it have inheritance? Should it pass parameters by reference or by value? Should continuations be explicit or implicit? It all depends on how you expect your language to be used, on which kinds of programs should be easy to write, and which you can afford to make more difficult.

Also, interpreters really *are* subtle programs. A simple change to a line of code in an interpreter can make an enormous difference in the behavior of the resulting language. Don't think that you can just skim these programs—very few people in the world can glance at a new interpreter and predict from that how it will behave even on relatively simple programs. So study these programs. Better yet, *run* them—this is working code. Try interpreting some simple expressions, then more complex ones. Add error messages. Modify the interpreters. Design your own variations. Try to really master these programs, not just get a vague feeling for how they work.

If you do this, you will change your view of your programming, and your view of yourself as a programmer. You'll come to see yourself as a designer of languages rather than only a user of languages, as a person who chooses the rules by which languages are put together, rather than only a follower of rules that other people have chosen.

Hal Abelson
Cambridge, MA

Preface

The goal of this book is to give students a deep, hands-on understanding of the essential concepts of programming languages, using Scheme as an executable metalanguage. Because Scheme is a wide-spectrum language, it enables us to write both at the very high level needed to produce a concise, comprehensible interpreter and at the much lower level needed to understand how that interpreter might be coded in assembly language, or transformed into a compiler. Because of Scheme's excellent abstraction facilities, we can write substantial language-processing systems that are nevertheless compact enough for students to understand and manipulate with a reasonable amount of effort. This is a hands-on book: everything discussed in the book may be programmed by students.

Many texts are descriptive in nature and may be of use to the casual reader. Not this one. Our approach is analytic. Though we make little use of mathematical notation, our Scheme programs often play the same role. As with analytic texts in any discipline, this book requires careful reading with attention to detail. Before the material is mastered, it will frequently require rereading and reflection. Deep concepts are only absorbed with active participation. Their power must be experienced, not passively viewed.

Though we believe Scheme is an excellent metalanguage, this book is about the essentials of programming languages in general, *not* Scheme in particular. To emphasize this, we have given the interpreted language developed in this book a syntax very different from that of Scheme. This interpreted language is designed only for our pedagogic purposes and is not intended for other use. It is composed of a number of pieces, introduced throughout the text, which are not necessarily designed to form a coherent whole. Indeed, as we build new interpreters we often use the same concrete syntax with different semantics.

Beyond the use of Scheme, we use four major strategies:

1. The first strategy is the use of interpreters to explain the run-time behavior of programs in a given language. Interpreters express language design decisions in a manner that is both formal (unambiguous and complete) and executable. Furthermore, our interpreters are generally expressed in a fashion consistent with the principles of denotational semantics; they express key ideas of denotational semantics in a concrete way.

2. Instead of relying on mere descriptions, using English, diagrams, or some abstract notation, we present each principle using Scheme programs that implement it. The use of Scheme enables the student to understand these programs without drowning in a sea of irrelevant detail. The exercises allow the student to experiment with alternatives in design and implementation.

3. We emphasize the systematic derivation of low-level implementations from their high-level abstractions. We show how simple algebraic manipulation can be used to derive program properties and correctness-preserving program transformations. In particular, we use these techniques to derive stack-management protocols and to transform an interpreter into a compiler.

4. Finally, we use data abstraction, expressed as a modular coding style, to separate algorithms from the representation of the underlying quantities. In this way, we can change data representation without changing programs. In the case of interpreters, we use this technique to investigate different implementation strategies.

Through the use of these strategies, we are able to give students several working models, ranging from very high-level (almost formal semantics) to very low-level (almost assembly language), and to demonstrate a clear connection between these models.

Such depth must come at the expense of breadth. We make no attempt to survey existing languages, though we occasionally point out the design choices used in common languages. Although our approach is largely motivated by the developments in programming language semantics over the last 20 years, we do not address a number of important research areas, such as type checking and inference, logic programming, parallelism, and verification. We believe, however, that a command of the essentials will allow the student to study these topics. For example, an understanding of the mechanics of logic programming certainly requires understanding of continuations, dynamic binding, and the distinction between a variable's name, its binding, and the value of its binding.

Organization

The chart below represents the organizational structure of the book. The squares on the organizational chart represent chapters where syntax is introduced.

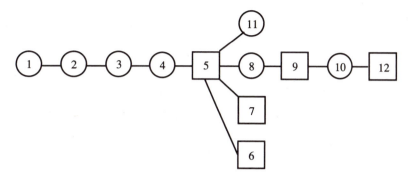

The first four chapters provide the foundations for a careful study of programming languages. Chapter 1 introduces most of the features of Scheme that are required in later chapters, along with some basic terminology. Readers who have prior experience with Scheme or other Lisp dialects may wish to skim this chapter and refer to it as necessary. Chapter 2 emphasizes the connection between inductive data specification and recursive programming, and introduces several notions related to the scope of variables. A set of exercises is provided to develop facility with recursive programming. Chapter 3 introduces some commonly used syntactic abstractions, including a variant record facility. This leads to a discussion of data abstraction and examples of representational transformations of the sort used in subsequent chapters. Chapter 4 introduces, in the context of the lambda calculus, several rewrite rules that are basic program transformations and provides a brief review of imperative programming.

The next three chapters show how these foundations may be used to describe the semantics of programming languages. Chapter 5 introduces interpreters as mechanisms for explaining the run-time behavior of languages and develops an interpreter for a simple, lexically scoped language with first-class procedures and variable assignment. This interpreter is the basis for most of the material in the remainder of the book. The chapter goes on to explore static and dynamic scoping and the implementation of recursion. Chapter 6 explores some parameter-passing mechanisms. Chapter 7 presents varieties of object-oriented facilities. These include several characterizations of inheritance and meta-classes. These two chapters can be studied in either order.

Chapters 8–10 show how the use of continuation-passing style enables us to transform our high-level interpreters into a flowchart-like form. Chapter 8 introduces continuation-passing style as a technique for expressing recursion by iteration. Using algebraic techniques, chapter 9 transforms our interpreter into continuation-passing style, and applies the techniques of chapter 3 to develop data structure representations of continuations. Data abstraction techniques then allow us to explore alternative representation strategies for the data manipulated by our interpreters. This includes the ability to make continuations accessible to the programmer as first-class objects of computation. In chapter 10 we complete the task of transforming our interpreter to a set of data structures manipulated by a finite-state controller. This gives us an interpreter that can be implemented in any low-level language. We then show how these data structures can be represented in a single stack with static and dynamic links. This development provides a solid understanding of stack-based language architectures, and also illustrates the power of algebraic reasoning techniques.

Finally, chapters 11 and 12 apply our techniques to the development of scanners, parsers, and compilers. Chapter 11 introduces lexical scanning and parsing techniques. Program transformations clarify the relationship between recursive descent and table-driven parsers. We show in chapter 12 how to start with a high-level functional specification of a language and, by choosing suitable representations of our data abstractions, derive both a virtual machine and a compiler that translates the high-level language to code for the virtual machine.

Chapters 5 through 10 are the heart of this book. The derivation of a sequence of interpreters ranging from very high- to very low-level does more than provide a solid, hands-on understanding of programming language semantics and a disciplined approach to language implementation. It also teaches an approach to programming that starts with a high-level operational specification, which also serves as a rapid prototype, and ends with what is effectively assembly language. We believe the programming transformation techniques used in this process should be in the toolbox of every computer scientist.

Usage

This text has been used in various forms to teach students from the sophomore to the graduate level, and in continuing education classes for professional programmers. It also has much to offer the dedicated computer scientist through self-study.

We assume the reader has at least one year of programming experience, including experience with a high-level language and assembly language and an introduction to data structures. Previous exposure to Lisp or Scheme is helpful but not required. This course might be followed by one in compiler construction or formal semantics of programming languages.

It is unlikely that all the material in this book can be covered in a single semester. Undergraduate students without some background in Scheme or Lisp will need to start with chapter 1 and can cover the material through chapter 5 or 6 in a semester. Undergraduate students who already know Scheme can quickly review the material in the first three chapters and cover chapters 4 through 10 in a semester. Well-prepared graduate students can reach chapter 12.

Not all of the material in each chapter need be covered. Much of the material in chapter 4, material at the end of chapters 5, 6, and 9, and all of chapters 7, 11, and 12 may be omitted as necessary. In chapter 8, a good introduction to the subject can be obtained by reading sections 8.1 and 8.2 and going through the examples in section 8.5.

The entire scanner, parser, and grammar for the interpreted language is given in the appendices. This facilitates the use of the syntax in exercises beginning with chapter 5, even though the parser technology is not developed until chapter 11. Those who prefer not to deal with the character syntax can use list structure syntax. This allows exercises to be done using the simple recursive descent parser, which is also given in the appendices. In order to study chapter 6, chapter 7, sections 9.3 through 9.6, or chapter 12, you need the appropriate parser for that chapter as well as the parser for the syntax of chapter 5.

Exercises are a vital part of the text and are scattered throughout. They range in difficulty from being trivial (if related material is understood) to requiring many hours of thought and programming work. We regard certain exercises as fundamental to mastery of the material. We introduce these with a bullet • instead of a circle ∘ and encourage readers to attempt them all.

Preface

Acknowledgments

Ten years ago, when we were all together at Indiana University, we decided to write a book based on the undergraduate programming languages course, C311. We had all taught it and felt that we had a way to unify its presentation. Eugene Kohlbecker, who had come to believe in our approach, was also an author. Eugene contributed many hours and hundreds of draft pages at the early stages, and without his taking charge in those early days, we would likely never have gotten started. We owe much to Eugene and use this forum to thank him. About the same time, Will Clinger arrived in Bloomington and he suggested that we change the course from using Lisp to using Scheme. He developed the Scheme 311 compiler, an ancestor of MacScheme, and the course has never been the same. For this and his time as an early author of the book, we thank him.

We very much appreciate having had the opportunity to course-test the book. We thank Claude Anderson, John Casey, Bruce Duba, Matthias Felleisen, Max Hailperin, Richard Kelsey, Dino Oliva, Jeff Perotti, and Richard Salter for trying out the book and for their comments. We particularly want to acknowledge Max for his insights, which greatly improved the material on parameter passing in chapter 6. We are grateful to Matthias for pointing out a bug in the implementation of recursive environments of chapter 5 and for his comments on chapter 4, which helped us improve the focus of that chapter. In addition, his concern for the lack of examples using continuations led to more material on them in chapter 9. We are grateful to Richard Kelsey for pointing out that chapter 11 should come after teaching continuation-passing style, rather than before understanding interpreters. His concern that it was too difficult for someone with little or no background using continuations helped us see the structure of the book more clearly.

We are grateful for the words of wisdom, criticism, and encouragement from Harold Abelson, Olivier Danvy, Kent Dybvig, Jim Miller, John Nienart, George Springer and Guy Steele. We particularly appreciate Hal for his suggestion of collecting the grammar rules in an appendix. This decision led to changes that significantly improved the book's overall clarity. In addition, Hal's criticism led to the inclusion of the implementation of the CPS algorithm in chapter 8 and to the inclusion of dynamic winding in chapter 9. We want to thank Kent for carefully reading the entire book and for making many suggestions that improved its clarity. Especially we want to thank him for his help in correcting our presentation of proper tail recursion. John's insight as a long-time practitioner of object-oriented programming led to what is now chapter 7. Without our discussions, it is unlikely that it would have its current, unified form. George taught us much about what freshmen could understand. This led to a clearer understanding of what sophomores and juniors should be able to understand. Furthermore, it helped clarify what it was that we really wanted to discuss in this book. We are also grateful to him for his words of encouragement. Jim Miller spent many hours of late-night phone conversations helping us conform to the Scheme standards. We thank all these hardy souls for their good suggestions; any mistakes or deficiencies are of course our own.

During the course of this book's development, it has been read by many students. In addition, some of the students helped solve some typesetting problems. We particularly appreciate the suggestions of David Boyer, Venkatesh Choppella, Peter Harlan, Bob Hieb, Haydn Huntley, Jim Marshall, Jacqueline Pulliam, Jon Rossie, Shing Shong (Bruce) Shei, Raja Thiagarajan, Sho-Huan (Simon) Tung, and Kiran Wagle. Jon discovered a subtle bug in an earlier version of our CPS algorithm. Venky's help on chapter 10 was greatly appreciated. David, Peter, and Haydn helped with their comments on chapter 12. Jacque and Raja rekindled our interest in inheritance in object-oriented programming. Simon commented on chapters 7 and 12, and Bob commented on chapter 8. Bruce and Kiran helped with some subtle aspects of typesetting.

We would like to thank Julia Lawall, Shinnder Lee, and John Simmons for their endless testing and retesting of the programs in this book. In addition, they have offered improvements at every step of the way. Julia's observation that our terminology in chapter 8 was inconsistent with her intuition led to major improvements in that chapter. Her efforts in chapter 12 enabled us to include a compiler that generated properly tail-recursive code. She also developed the streams solution of appendix F when we realized that conventional streams would not work for interactive systems. Julia, Shinnder, and John have uncovered the subtlest of errors and greatly improved the clarity of many of the programs in this book. For all of these contributions, we thank them.

Designing and drawing diagrams are difficult tasks. For helping design the diagrams, showing us how to use the drawing tool, and then drawing the actual diagrams, we would like to thank Venkatesh Choppella, Julia Lawall, John Simmons, and Kiran Wagle.

What wonderful software tools we have. These are especially impressive tools to those of us whose first programs used plugboards or punched cards. We would like to thank Richard Stallman and the Free Software Foundation for GNU Emacs, Donald Knuth for TEX, Gerald Sussman and Guy Steele for originating Scheme, Will Clinger for the Scheme 311 compiler, and Kent Dybvig for Chez Scheme. We are also grateful to the designers and implementors of the Internet who made it possible to work together across vast distances.

We are grateful to our respective academic homes, Indiana University and Northeastern University for encouraging us at every step of this project. We also want to thank the National Science Foundation for support of research that led to ideas presented in this book.

Working with Teresa Ehling at MIT Press has been a pleasure. She has made the process a most satisfying experience.

Every attempt has been made to acknowledge those who have helped us. We regret any oversight.

Last, we would like to thank those around us whose presence constantly reminds us of what is most important. They are our wives, Mary, Barbara and Janice, and our children, Brian, Robert, Rebecca, Jennifer, and Joshua. They deserve admiration for their patience, love, and understanding throughout the long gestation of this book.

Dan Friedman
Mitch Wand
Chris Haynes

Essentials of
Programming Languages

1   Tools for Symbolic Programming

You are about to begin the study of programming languages. It would be convenient if all the concepts behind programming languages could be explained using only natural language. Unfortunately, many aspects of programming languages require a high degree of precision, and natural language is not precise enough. In addition, we want to do more than just describe programming languages: we want to show how they are implemented. To fulfill these purposes, we use three different modes of expression:

1. For motivation and explanation, we use ordinary English.
2. When we need to be precise, we use the language of elementary mathematics: sets, functions, and elementary algebra.
3. When we need to display actual algorithms and implementations, we use the programming language Scheme.

The first two chapters of this book are designed to familiarize you with reading and writing Scheme programs. This includes a number of techniques for manipulating symbolic information of the kind found in programs and their run-time data structures. Particular emphasis is placed on techniques for *functional programming,* especially *recursion.* Along the way, we also introduce several fundamental concepts that allow us to talk precisely about programming languages. These are the basics you need to understand the rest of the book.

We begin in section 1.1 by introducing several basic ways of building Scheme expressions. Section 1.2 introduces a few primitive data types that taken together make Scheme especially suitable for symbolic programming. This is followed in section 1.3 by a discussion of procedures, which may be used with more flexibility in Scheme than in most other languages.

For every form of expression (or other component of a program) it is useful to distinguish between its *syntax,* which refers to rules governing how it is formed, and its *semantics,* which refers to rules that specify its meaning.

If you are already familiar with Scheme or another dialect of LISP, you may wish to skim this chapter quickly, taking note of any unfamiliar terminology (indicated by *italics*), and later refer to this chapter for specific information on Scheme. We introduce only those features of Scheme that are used later in this book.

1.1 Simple Expressions

A *statement* is a programming language construct that is evaluated only for its effect. Examples include assignment statements, input/output statements, and control statements (`while` loops, `if` statements, etc.). Programs in most languages are composed primarily of statements; such languages are said to be *statement oriented*.

Programming language constructs that are evaluated to obtain values are called *expressions*. Arithmetic expressions are the most common example. Expressions may occur as parts of statements, as in the right-hand side of an assignment statement. The data that may be returned as the values of expressions constitute the *expressed values* of a programming language. Expressions that are evaluated solely for their value, and not for any other effects of the computation, are said to be *functional*.

Some programming languages, such as Scheme, are *expression oriented:* their programs are constructed of definitions and expressions; there are no statements. This section reviews basic techniques for constructing expressions in Scheme.

1.1.1 Literals, Procedure Calls, and Variables

The simplest form of expression is a *literal* (or *constant*), which always returns the indicated value. For example, the result of evaluating the *numeral* 2 is a value denoting the number two, which has the printed representation 2. Other literals we shall have occasion to use include *strings,* such as "This is a string.", the *boolean* values #t (true) and #f (false), and *characters,* such as #\a and #\space. We discuss these and other Scheme data types in the next section.

The next simplest form of expression is a *variable reference*. The value of a variable reference is the value currently associated with, or *bound to,* the variable. A variable is said to *denote* the value of its *binding*. The data that can be bound to variables constitute the *denoted values* of a programming language. Since all variable references in Scheme are also expressions, and the value of any expression may be bound to a variable, the denoted values and the expressed values of Scheme are the same, at least in the absence of variable assignment (section 4.5).

Variables are represented by *identifiers*. As in most languages, sequences of letters and digits (not starting with a digit) may be used as identifiers, for example: `x`, `x3`, `foo`, and `longidentifier`. Scheme is more permissive than most languages in the use of special characters to form identifiers. For example, the following are all identifiers: `+`, `/`, `two+three`, `zero?`, `long_identifier`, `an-even-longer-identifier`. Some special characters, such as parentheses and spaces, are not allowed in identifiers. Digits may generally be used in identifiers, *e.g.* `x3`, but not as the first character. A few identifiers, such as `define` and `if`, are reserved for use as *keywords* and should generally not be used as variables.

Scheme provides standard bindings for a number of variables. For example, `+` is bound to the addition procedure and `zero?` is bound to a boolean procedure, or *predicate,* that tests whether its argument is zero. Other standard bindings will be introduced as they are needed. We call procedures that are the values of standard bindings *standard procedures.* (See appendix I.)

If a value is the binding of some variable, it is often convenient to refer to the value by the name of the variable. However, the distinction between the name of a variable and the value of its binding is very important. In this book we observe this distinction by using different fonts. When referring to the variable named "x" as a part of a program, we use the standard typewriter-style font: `x`. When referring to the value of the variable `x`, we use an italic font: x. Thus we use "*zero?*" instead of "the value of the variable `zero?`" when referring to the numeric zero predicate.

Statement-oriented languages usually distinguish between *functions,* which return values and are used in expressions, and *procedures,* which do not return values and are invoked by *procedure call* statements. Though function calls and procedure calls often look the same, syntactically they are distinct: function calls are expressions, while procedure calls are statements. However, since Scheme does not have statements, it does not make this distinction. In fact, Scheme functions are usually called procedures, and Scheme function calls are then referred to as procedure calls. We use the term "function" to refer only to abstract mathematical functions.

The syntax of procedure calls in Scheme is not typical of other programming languages. For example, a call to the procedure p with arguments 2 and 3 is written in Scheme as `(p 2 3)`, instead of `p(2,3)`. Parentheses surround the entire procedure call, and its components are separated by spaces. We say that the procedure p is *applied* to the arguments 2 and 3. Procedure (or function) calls are sometimes referred to as *applications* or *combinations.*

The general syntax of procedure calls is

$$(operator\ operand_1\ \ldots\ operand_n)$$

The ellipsis "..." indicates possible repetition. There may in general be any number of operands, or possibly none at all ($n = 0$). The *operator* and each *operand* are components that are themselves expressions. They are called *subexpressions*. The operator subexpression is evaluated to obtain a procedure, while the operand subexpressions are evaluated to obtain the *arguments* of the call before invoking the procedure. (Arguments are also referred to as *actual parameters,* or simply *parameters.*) In Scheme, the order in which the operator and operand subexpressions are evaluated is not specified, but in some languages it is guaranteed to be left to right and in others it is always right to left.

Any expression may be used as an operand in a procedure call. For example, the procedure call

```
(+ x (p 2 3))
```

contains the operand (p 2 3), which is itself a procedure call. If the value of (p 2 3) is 6 and x is 3, then (+ x (p 2 3)) is 9. (More precisely, "the value of (+ x (p 2 3)) is 9." Since a compound expression's value is not likely to be confused with the expression itself, in such cases we shall often omit the phrase "the value of.")

Operators may also be arbitrarily complex, as long as they return procedures. Thus if *g* were a procedure that when applied to 2 returned the addition procedure, then

```
((g 2) 3 4)
```

would return 7. Procedures that return procedures are called *higher-order procedures,* and expressions that return procedures are called *higher-order expressions.* They may be unfamiliar, but much will be accomplished with them later.

1.1.2 Definitions, Programs, and the Read-Eval-Print Loop

Most operations can be expressed as procedure calls. For those that cannot, a small number of *special forms* are required.

Consider the operation of binding the variable x to 3. We would like to accomplish this by saying

```
(define x 3)
```

The general definition syntax we use is

```
(define variable expression)
```

where *variable* and *expression* indicate an arbitrary variable and expression. If this were a procedure call, with the variable `define` bound to some procedure, *variable* would be evaluated as an argument and its value passed to the procedure. But *variable* may be unbound, in which case it cannot be evaluated. Even if the variable were already bound, say `x` was bound to 7, it still would not do to evaluate the variable. The special form `define` must modify the binding of `x`, which would not be possible if it were simply passed the value 7.

The solution is to declare that the above syntactic form is special—distinct from a procedure call. Each special form is indicated by an identifier, in this case `define`, that should not be used as a variable. These special form identifiers are called *keywords*. Each special form has its own sequencing rule, that is order of evaluation of subexpressions. In this case *expression* is evaluated first, and then *variable* is bound to the value of *expression*.

A Scheme program consists of a sequence of definitions and expressions that are executed in order by the Scheme system. These definitions and expressions are said to be at *top level*. We next discuss a few features of typical *programming environments* in which the Scheme language is used. It should be borne in mind that these are not features of the language itself.

Programs may be stored in a file for convenient loading, or they may be entered interactively. In the *interactive* mode, you enter a definition or expression, which is evaluated as soon as it is complete. When an expression is entered, its value is printed. The system then prints an input prompt and the cycle repeats. This repetitive action is often called the *read-eval-print loop*. The transcript of a brief interactive session follows.

```
> 3
3
> *      ; evaluates to the standard multiplication procedure
#<Procedure>
> (* 2 3)
6
> (define x 3)
> x
```

```
3
> (+ x (* 2 3))
9
```

In this case the Scheme prompt is ">." A semicolon ";" and anything following it on the same line is ignored by Scheme so that comments may be inserted in programs and transcripts. In general, procedures cannot be printed. Thus the system simply prints some indication that a procedure has been returned. In this book "#<Procedure>" is that indicator.

Following a definition, many Scheme systems print the name of the variable defined. As the transcript illustrates, however, we choose not to print anything following a definition. This emphasizes that, in general, definitions do not have values. In this respect they are like statements, but their use is more limited. In this book define is used only at top level.

A final note about definitions: the value of a variable may be *redefined*. That is, the value of an already defined variable may be changed with another definition.

```
> (define x 2)
> x
2
> (define x (+ 1 x))
> x
3
```

Redefinition is allowed simply to make software development more convenient. In Scheme the values of variables with standard bindings, such as +, can be redefined. This is occasionally useful, for example, if you wish to keep track of how many times + is invoked with a negative argument. Redefinition of standard procedures, however, is risky; others may depend on them in unexpected ways.

The interactive nature of Scheme aids program development. It is also helpful in learning Scheme, because it makes it easy to try things out if you wish to test your understanding or discover what will happen. Transcripts of interactions with Scheme are also a convenient way of providing examples. We use them frequently. You are urged to study our examples carefully to be sure you understand why Scheme behaves as it does. Sometimes definitions made in one transcript will be used in other transcripts that follow.

• *Exercise 1.1.1*
Start interacting with Scheme today! □

Tools for Symbolic Programming

Read-eval-print loops and redefinitions may not be appropriate in some programming environments. For example, a Scheme implementation might be designed to compile Scheme programs on one machine for execution at a later time on other machines. In this case a read-eval-print loop would be meaningless and redefinition would probably be undesirable. By making a clear distinction between a programming language and programming environments that support it, we treat the language itself as an abstraction. Such language abstraction is important, for it allows the same language to be used in many different environments.

1.1.3 Conditional Evaluation

We have seen that Scheme definitions cannot be expressed with an application, so a special form must be used. Conditional expressions are a second situation in which a special form is required. The basic conditional expression in Scheme has this syntax:

$$(\texttt{if} \;\; \textit{test-exp} \;\; \textit{then-exp} \;\; \textit{else-exp})$$

The expression *test-exp* is evaluated first. If its value is true, *then-exp* is evaluated, and its value is returned as the value of the entire if expression. If the value of *test-exp* is false, *else-exp* is evaluated to obtain the value of the if expression.

```
> (if #t 1 2)
1
> (zero? 5)
#f
> (if (zero? 5) 1 (+ 1 2))
3
> (define true #t)
> (define false #f)
> (if (zero? 0)
      (if false 1 2)
      3)
2
> (if (if true false true) 2 3)
3
```

The special form if cannot be implemented as a procedure. For one thing, only one of *then-exp* or *else-exp* should be evaluated, and it would be inefficient to evaluate both; but there is an even more compelling reason. An important use of conditionals is to prevent an expression from being evaluated when it is unsafe to do so. For example, we might write

```
(if (zero? a) 0 (/ x a))
```

to make sure that `a` is nonzero before dividing. In this situation, we say the test *guards* the division. Were `if` a procedure, its arguments would be evaluated before being applied, so the division-by-zero we were trying to avoid would be performed before it could be stopped.

Several other special forms will be introduced later as they are needed, but `define` and `if` are enough to get us started.

1.2 Data Types

In this section we explore some of the data types in Scheme. Scheme implementations vary somewhat in the range of data types they support, and the repertoire of operations on the data types also varies. We discuss only those data types and operations that are required in this book. They should be part of every implementation.

For each data type, we shall be concerned with three things:

1. The set of values of that type.
2. The procedures that operate on that type.
3. The representation of values of that type when they appear internally as literals in programs or externally as characters that are read or printed.

For example, in mathematics the data type of sets consists of the sets themselves, the well-defined operations on these sets (such as union, intersection, and set-difference), and the notation used to represent sets.

It is an error to pass a standard procedure a value that is not of the expected type. For example, it does not make sense to try to add a number to `#t`. *Type checking* is required to detect such *type errors*. If these checks are performed at run time when standard procedures are invoked, as is generally the case for Scheme implementations, we have *dynamic type checking*. In many languages, an analysis is performed at compile time to detect potential type errors. This analysis, which must be based only on the text of the program and not run-time values, is called *static type checking*. It has the advantage of catching errors earlier but requires more complicated and restrictive rules for determining if a program is correctly typed.

1.2.1 Numbers, Booleans, Characters, Strings, and Symbols

We have already used two data types: *number* and *boolean*. Numbers may be included in Scheme programs in the usual way. The operations on numbers include the standard arithmetic operations, such as +, -, *, and /. The type predicate *number?* takes an arbitrary value and returns true if its argument is a number and false otherwise. The equality predicate for numbers is =.

The boolean data type has only two values, true and false, represented by #t and #f, respectively. Booleans are used primarily in conditional expressions. The type predicate *boolean?* tests an arbitrary value to see if it is a boolean, boolean values may be compared for equality using the predicate *eq?*, and the standard procedure *not* performs logical negation.

```
> (eq? (boolean? #f) (not #f))
#t
```

Characters that are visible when they print are represented as literals by preceding them with #\, for example #\a and #\%. Some nonprinting characters also have literal representations, such as #\space and #\newline. The character type, equality, and order predicates are *char?*, *char=?*, and *char<?*, respectively, and *char->integer* takes a character and returns an integer representation of the character. The predicates *char-alphabetic?*, *char-numeric?*, and *char-whitespace?* are used to determine the class of a character. The predicate *char-whitespace?* returns true when its argument is a space, return or linefeed character.

```
> (char? #\$)
#t
> (char=? #\newline #\space)
#f
> (char<? #\a #\b)
#t
```

Strings are sequences of characters that are represented by surrounding the characters with double quote marks. The string type predicate is *string?*. The procedure *string-length* takes a string and returns an integer indicating the number of characters in the string. The procedure *string-append* concatenates its arguments to form a new string. The procedures *string->symbol*, *string->number*, and *string->list* convert a string into a symbol, number, and list of characters, respectively. (Symbols and lists will be discussed soon.) The procedure *string* takes any number of arguments, which must be characters, and returns a string of these characters. The procedure *string-ref* takes a string and a nonnegative integer less than the length of the string and returns the character indexed by the integer. Indexing is *zero based,* meaning that the characters are numbered starting with zero.

```
> (define s "This is a.")
> (define ss (string-append s "longer string"))
> (string? s)
#t
> (string-length s)
10
> (string-length ss)
23
> (string-ref s 2)
#\i
> (string #\a #\b)
"ab"
> (string->symbol "abc")
abc
> (string->list s)
(#\T #\h #\i #\s #\space #\i #\s #\space #\a #\.)
```

Programs that process other programs, such as many in this book, frequently manipulate identifiers. Identifiers are central to a number of other kinds of programming, such as artificial intelligence and database applications. In fact, identifiers play an important role in most programs that are not primarily concerned with manipulating numbers. When identifiers are treated as values in Scheme, they are called *symbols*. The manipulation of symbols is greatly facilitated by providing a distinct data type for them.

Just as strings must be surrounded with quote marks to distinguish them from the rest of a program, symbolic literals must be specially marked, for otherwise they would be indistinguishable from variable references. Thus another special form is needed to introduce symbols into programs:

(quote datum)

Here *datum* may be a symbol or any other standard external (printed) representation for Scheme data. The value of a quoted literal expression is the associated data value.

```
> (define x 3)
> x
3
> (quote x)
x
> 99
99
> (quote 99)
99
```

Such expressions are used so often that there is an abbreviation for them. The form (quote *datum*) may also be written

' *datum*

utilizing the single-quote character. Most languages have quoting mechanisms of some sort to avoid confusion between literals and other program elements. The only literals that are "self-quoting," meaning that they may be used directly as expressions without being enclosed in a quote expression, are numbers, booleans, strings, and characters.

Two basic operations on symbols are the symbol type predicate, *symbol?*, and the predicate for testing equality of two symbols, *eq?*.

```
> (define x 3)
> (number? x)
#t
> (symbol? x)
#f
> (number? 'x)
#f
> (symbol? 'x)
#t
> (eq? 'x 'x)
#t
> (eq? 'x 'y)
#f
> (define y 'apple)
> y
apple
> (eq? y (quote apple))
#t
> (eq? y 'y)
#f
```

1.2.2 Lists

A *list* is an ordered sequence of *elements,* which may be of arbitrary types. Lists are a flexible way of combining multiple values into a single *compound* object. Scheme provides convenient facilities for creating and manipulating lists. These facilities, along with most other Scheme data types, are derived from the much older language LISP. (The name stands for LISt Processing.)

A list is represented by surrounding representations of its elements with a pair of parentheses. For example, (a 3 #t) represents a list consisting of three elements: the symbol a, the number three, and the value true. Here are a few more lists

```
()              the empty list
(a)             a list of length 1
((b c d))       a list of length 1 that contains a list of length 3
```

Just as quote is necessary to distinguish between symbolic literals and variables, it is also necessary to avoid confusing literal lists with procedure calls or special forms. The expression (quote (a b c)) yields the list (a b c) as its value. However, the expression (a b c) is a procedure call whose value depends on the values of the variables a, b, and c; or perhaps it is a special form where a is a keyword.

There are several standard procedures that build new lists. Here we consider the most important ones, *list* and *cons*. The standard procedure *list* may be applied to any number of arguments. It forms a list of their values. (Most procedures take a fixed number of arguments, but *list*, *string* and *string-append* are exceptions.)

```
> (list 1 2 3)
(1 2 3)
> (define x 3)
> (define y 'apple)
> (list x y)
(3 apple)
> (define list-1 '())
> (define list-2 '(a))
> (define list-3 '((b)))
> (list list-1 list-2 list-3 '(((c))))
(() (a) ((b)) (((c))))
> (list)
()
```

The second important list-building procedure, *cons*, always takes two arguments. The first may be any Scheme value, and the second must (for the moment) be a list. If its first argument is the value v and its second argument is the list $(v_0\ v_1\ \ldots\ v_{n-1})$, then *cons* returns the list $(v\ v_0\ v_1\ \ldots\ v_{n-1})$. The returned list is always one longer than the second argument. The name cons stands for *cons*truct, because *cons* constructs a new compound object. (Actually *cons*'s second argument may be anything. But if it is not a list, the value returned will not be a list either. We discuss this further in section 1.2.3.) Study the following examples carefully; they illustrate several important features of *cons*.

```
> (cons 'a '(c d))
(a c d)
> (list 'a '(c d))
(a (c d))
> (cons '(a b) '(c d))
((a b) c d)
> (cons '() '(c d))
(() c d)
> (cons 'a '())
(a)
> (cons '(a b) '())
((a b))
> (define y 'apple)
> (cons y list-2)
(apple a)
> (define list-4 (cons list-1 list-2))
> list-4
(() a)
> (cons list-4 list-3)
((() a) (b))
```

Observe in these examples that if the first element to *cons* is a list, that list becomes an element of the value returned by *cons*. To add all elements of a list to the front of another list (in the same order), the procedure *append* should be used.

```
> (append '(a b) '(c d))
(a b c d)
> (append '() '(c d))
(c d)
> (append '(a b) '())
(a b)
```

Compare these results with those obtained by passing the same arguments to *cons*.

The simplest way to divide a list is between the first element and the rest of the list. For historical reasons, the first element of a list is known as its *car* and the rest of the list is known as its *cdr*. The standard procedures *car* and *cdr* select these components of a list. Thus if l is the list $(v_0 \ v_1 \ \ldots \ v_{n-1})$, then $(car \ l) = v_0$ and $(cdr \ l) = (v_1 \ \ldots \ v_{n-1})$. It is an error to call *car* or *cdr* with the empty list.

```
> (car '(a b c))
a
> (cdr '(a b c))
(b c)
> (car (cdr '(a b c)))
b
> (cdr '(a))
()
```

Clearly *car* and *cdr* undo what *cons* does. The exact relationship between *car*, *cdr*, and *cons* is expressed by the equations

$$(car \ (cons \ v \ l)) = v$$
$$(cdr \ (cons \ v \ l)) = l$$

where v is any value, l is any list, and $=$ indicates identical values.

Nested calls to *car* and *cdr* are so common that Scheme provides an assortment of procedures that take care of the more frequent cases. For example, the procedures *cadr* and *caddr* are defined such that

$$(cadr \ l) = (car \ (cdr \ l))$$
$$(caddr \ l) = (car \ (cdr \ (cdr \ l)))$$

The sequence of as and ds surrounded by c and r in the procedure name determines the cars and cdrs and their ordering. The rightmost a/d (car/cdr) is performed first, just as the innermost procedure call is done first.

```
> (cadr '(a b c))
b
> (cddr '(a b c))
(c)
> (caddr '(a b c))
c
```

Empty lists are always represented by the same object, called the *empty list*. (For historical reasons, it is sometimes called the *null* object.) The predicate `null?` tests if its argument is the empty list.

```
> (null? '())
#t
> (define list-2 (list 'a))
> list-2
(a)
> (null? list-2)
#f
> (null? (cdr list-2))
#t
```

○ *Exercise 1.2.1*

Fill in the blank lines of the following transcript.

```
> (define x '(a b ((3) c) d))
> (car (cdr x))

> (caddr x)

> (cdaddr x)

> (char? (car '(#\a #\b)))

> (cons 'x x)

> (cons (list 1 2) (cons 3 '(4)))

> (cons (list) (list 1 (cons 2 '())))
```

□

1.2.3 Pairs

Most of the time it is desirable to view lists abstractly as we have just done, however, it is sometimes necessary to understand how lists are constructed.

In Scheme, nonempty lists are represented as *pairs*. A pair (sometimes called a *dotted pair* or *cons cell*) is a structure with two fields, called *car* and *cdr*. The procedure *cons* creates a new pair with the car and cdr fields

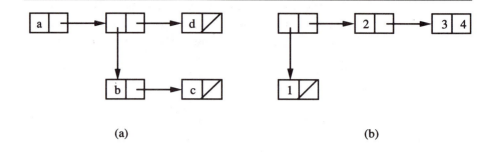

(a)   (b)

Figure 1.2.1 Box diagrams

initialized to the values of its first and second arguments, respectively. The procedures `car` and `cdr` access the two fields. This explains the behavior introduced in the last section. The type predicate for recognizing pairs is `pair?`.

The structure of values built from pairs is conveniently illustrated by diagrams in which pairs are represented by boxes. Each of these boxes has a left and a right half, representing the car and cdr fields, respectively. Each half contains a pointer to another box if the value of the corresponding field is another pair. If the field value is the empty list, this is represented by a slash through the box. Finally, if the field value is a symbol, number, or boolean, its printed representation is written in the corresponding half of the box. The list (a (b c) d) is represented in figure 1.2.1 (a).

If a list has length n, the result of taking the cdr of the list n times must be the empty list. Thus a list is represented by either the empty list or a chain of pairs, linked by their cdr fields, with the empty list in the cdr field of the last pair of the chain. A cdr-linked chain of cons cells that does not end in the empty list is called an *improper list,* even though it is not a list at all. Figure 1.2.1 (b) illustrates such a data structure. We can denote such data structures in a linear format by writing (*a* . *d*) for a pair whose car is *a* and whose cdr is *d*. (Hence the term *dotted pair.*) The data structures in figure 1.2.1 (a) and (b) might be written as

$$(a . ((b . (c . ()))) . (d . ()))$$

and

$$((1 . ()) . (2 . (3 . 4)))$$

respectively. Either of these might appear quoted in a Scheme program. This *dot notation* may be intermixed with conventional list notation, so the second structure might also be written

$$((1)\ 2\ 3\ .\ 4)$$

Dot notation is required only when writing improper lists.

The predicate *eq?* may be used to compare pairs as well as symbols. In fact, *eq?* may be used to test if any two objects are the same object. The behavior of *eq?* on symbols, booleans, characters, and the empty list is straightforward: if they have the same written representation, they are the same object. This is not necessarily true for numbers, pairs, and strings. The behavior of *eq?* on numbers is implementation dependent. If *eq?* is presented with two pairs (or strings), it returns true if and only if they are the *same* pair (or string). Since *cons* creates a new pair every time it is called, *eq?* must be used with caution on lists.

```
> (define a (cons 3 '()))
> (define b (cons 3 '()))
> a
(3)
> b
(3)
> (eq? a a)
#t
> (eq? a b)
#f
> (eq? (cons 1 2) (cons 1 2))
#f
> (eq? '() '())
#t
```

In this example a and b are different pairs, even though they both print as (3), so they are not "*eq* to each other." However, every reference to the variable a returns the same pair, so (eq? a a) is true.

Pairs may be *shared*. That is, the same pair may be referred to by different variable bindings and pair fields.

```
> b
(3)
> (define c b)
> (eq? b c)
```

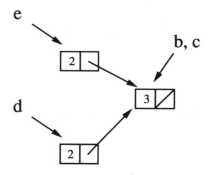

Figure 1.2.2 Box diagram with sharing

```
#t
> (define d (cons 2 c))
> (define e (cons 2 c))
> d
(2 3)
> e
(2 3)
> (eq? d e)
#f
> (eq? (cdr d) (cdr e))
#t
```

Here *b*, *c*, the cdr of *d*, and the cdr of *e* are all the same pair, though *d* and *e* are different pairs. Standard printed notation does not represent sharing, but box diagrams do, as figure 1.2.2 illustrates. The sharing of literals is not specified; for example, (eq? '(3) '(3)) could be true or false.

There are procedures for assigning new values to the car and cdr fields of an existing pair, which will be discussed in section 4.5. When a pair is modified by one of these procedures, the change is noted in all data structures that share the pair.

The only other way to detect sharing of pairs is by using *eq?*.

• *Exercise 1.2.2*
Fill in the blank lines of the following transcript.

```
> (define x1 '(a b))
> (define x2 '(a))
```

```
> (define x3 (cons x1 x2))
> x3

> (eq? x3 (cons x1 x2))

> (eq? (cdr x3) x2)

> (eq? (car x1) (car x2))

> (cons (cons 'a 'b) (cons 'c '()))

> (cons 1 (cons 2 3))
```

▯

1.2.4 Vectors

So far we have seen one means for building compound data objects in Scheme:
the cons cell. These cells may be used to construct lists of arbitrary length.
Lists are a *derived* data type because they are built using *primitive* data types:
the cons cell and the empty list. The advantage of lists is the ease with which
new lists may be formed by adding elements to the front of existing lists.
However, lists do not provide names for all their elements or random access to
them. Compositions of invocations of car and cdr, also called car/cdr chains,
are an awkward way of referring to the first few list elements. It is possible to
access list elements via an index number, but with conventional lists access
time increases linearly with the index, since to reach a given element it is
necessary to traverse the cdr pointers of all the elements that appear earlier
in the list.

Neither cons cells nor lists correspond to the two ways to build compound
data objects that are most commonly provided by programming languages:
records and arrays. Record elements are selected by *field names*. Records
are also *heterogeneous,* meaning that their elements may differ in their type.
Arrays, on the other hand, are *homogeneous,* in the sense that each of their
components must be of the same type, and array components are selected by
an index number (or multiple index numbers in the case of multidimensional
arrays). Both records and arrays provide *random access* to their components;
that is, each component may be accessed in the same amount of time.

Scheme does not provide arrays or records directly. Instead it supplies
vectors, which may be used in place of arrays and records. Vectors provide

random access via index numbers (like arrays) and may be heterogeneous (like records).

The standard procedure *vector* takes an arbitrary number of arguments, such as *list* and *string*, and constructs a vector whose elements contain the argument values. Vectors are written like lists, but with a hash (#) immediately preceding the left parenthesis. By convention, vectors must also be quoted when they appear in programs as literals.

```
> (define v1 (vector 1 2 (+ 1 2)))
> v1
#(1 2 3)
> (define v2 (quote #(a b)))
> v2
#(a b)
> (vector v1 v2)
#(#(1 2 3) #(a b))
> '#(#(a nested vector) (and a list) within a quoted vector)
#(#(a nested vector) (and a list) within a quoted vector)
```

The number of elements in a vector is its *length,* which may be determined with the standard procedure *vector-length*. The type predicate for vectors is *vector?*. The selector *vector-ref* takes a vector and a zero-based index and returns the value of the element indicated by the index. Thus the indices for a given vector are natural numbers in the range from zero through one less than the length of the vector. There are procedures, *vector->list* and *list->vector*, for transforming one compound data type into the other.

```
> (define v3 '#(first second last))
> (vector? v3)
#t
> (vector-ref v3 0)
first
> (vector-length v3)
3
> (vector-ref v3 (- (vector-length v3) 1))
last
> (vector-ref '#(another #((heterogeneous) "vector")) 1)
#((heterogeneous) "vector")
> (vector->list v3)
(first second last)
```

Of course it is an error to pass `vector-ref` an index number that is not a valid index for the given vector.

We use a data structure called a *cell*, a "one-element" vector. In addition to the procedure `make-cell`, which constructs a cell, there is a procedure for referencing a cell, `cell-ref` and one that determines if its argument is a cell, `cell?`. Cells will be useful in chapter 5 for characterizing languages with side effects and in chapter 6 for describing various parameter-passing mechanisms. See exercise 1.3.2 for an implementation of cells.

The procedure *eq?* may again be used to test whether two objects are the *same* vector. An assignment operation for changing the value of a vector element is introduced in section 4.5. As was the case with pairs, the sharing of vectors in data structures may be revealed using *eq?* or assignment.

○ *Exercise 1.2.3*
Fill in the blank lines of the following transcript

```
> (define v1 (vector (cons 1 2) 3))
> (define v2 (vector 'a v1))
> v2

> (define v3 '#(a #((1 . 2) 3)))
> (eq? v2 v3)

> (eq? v1 (vector-ref v2 1))

> (eq? (vector-ref v1 0)
       (vector-ref (vector-ref v2 1) 0))
```

□

1.3 Procedures

As you might expect, *procedure?* is a Scheme type predicate for procedures. The following transcript illustrates this as well as demonstrating that procedures can be treated as values.

```
> (procedure? 'car)
#f
> (procedure? car)
#t
```

```
> (procedure? (car (list cdr)))
#t
```

The first two examples distinguish between the symbol car and the procedure
car. The second and third illustrate passing a procedure as an argument to
another procedure. In the third, the procedure cdr is also stored in a data
structure and returned as the value of another procedure, car. Here are some
more complicated examples

```
> (if (procedure? 3) car cdr)
#<Procedure>
> ((if (procedure? 3) car cdr) '(x y z))
(y z)
> (((if (procedure? procedure?) cdr car)
     (cons car cdr))
   '(car in the car))
(in the car)
> (((if (procedure? procedure?) car cdr)
     (cons car cdr))
   '(x y z))
x
```

Procedures are normally called using the application form, as in (+ 1 2),
but sometimes we need to call a procedure with argument values that have
already been assembled into a list. The standard procedure apply is provided
for this purpose. It takes a procedure and a list and returns the result of calling
the procedure with the values given in the list.

```
> (apply + '(1 2))
3
> (define abc '(a b c))
> (apply cons (cdr abc))
(b . c)
> (apply apply (list procedure? (list apply)))
#t
```

1.3.1 lambda

We have seen that Scheme supplies a number of standard procedures. It is
also possible for the user to create new procedures, which may not be bound
to variables. The special form for creating new procedures is lambda. Its most
common syntax is

$$(\text{lambda } formals\ body)$$

Here *formals* is a (possibly empty) list of variables, and *body* is any expression. The listed variables are said to be *formal parameters,* or *bound variables,* of the procedure. In many languages, type information must be provided for formal parameters. However, Scheme automatically keeps track of types at run time, so type declarations are not required. (This is more flexible and simplifies code, but has the disadvantage that type errors are not detected until run time, increasing run-time overhead. We shall have more to say about types in chapter 3.) When the procedure is called, the formal parameters (if any) are first *bound to* (associated with) the arguments, and then the body is evaluated. Within the body, the argument values may be obtained by variables that correspond to the formal parameters. Lambda bindings are not accessible outside the body of the procedure: they are said to be *local* to the procedure's body.

For example, a procedure that adds two to its argument may be created by evaluating the expression:

$$(\text{lambda (n) (+ n 2))}$$

This expression does not give the procedure a name. Naming is accomplished by another expression, such as a define expression, if desired, however, a procedure may be applied immediately, passed as an argument, or stored in a data structure without ever being named.

```
> ((lambda (n) (+ n 2)) 4)
6
> (list (lambda (n) (+ n 2)) 6)
(#<Procedure> 6)
> (define add2 (lambda (n) (+ n 2)))
> (add2 6)
8
> (define select
    (lambda (b lst)
      (if b
          (car lst)
          (cadr lst))))
> (select #f '(a b))
b
> ((select #t (list cdr car))
   '(a b c))
(b c)
```

Procedures without names, which are not the binding of a variable, are said to be *anonymous*. In most other languages, procedures are never anonymous: they may be created only via declarations that name them. (Of course anonymity is relative to context: if an anonymous procedure is bound to a parameter via procedure call, it is not anonymous in the context of the called procedure.)

Anonymous procedures are often used as arguments. We illustrate this using the procedures `map` and `andmap`, which generally take two arguments: a procedure and a list. The list may be of any length, and the procedure must take one argument. The procedure `map` builds a new list whose elements are obtained by calling the procedure with the elements of the original list. The procedure `andmap` applies the procedure to each element of the list and returns true if all are true. Otherwise it returns false.

```
> (map (lambda (n) (+ n 2)) '(1 2 3 4 5))
(3 4 5 6 7)
> (define add2
    (lambda (n)
      (+ n 2)))
> (map add2 '(1 2 3 4 5))
(3 4 5 6 7)
> (andmap number? '(1 2 3 4 5))
#t
> (map null? '((a) () () (3)))
(#f #t #t #f)
> (andmap null? '((a) () () (3)))
#f
> (map car '((a b) (c d) (e f)))
(a c e)
> (map list '(a b c d))
((a) (b) (c) (d))
> (map (lambda (f) (f '(a b c d)))
       (list car cdr cadr cddr caddr))
(a (b c d) b (c d) c)
```

1.3.2 First-Class Procedures

A value is said to be *first class* if it may be passed to and returned from procedures and stored in data structures. In Scheme, *all* values are first class, including procedures. In other languages, simple values such as numbers are first class, compound values such as records and arrays are sometimes first class, and procedures are almost never first class. Though it is usually possible to pass procedures as arguments, it is often impossible to return them as values or store them in data structures. (See chapter 10 for a discussion of the implementation of such languages.) First class procedures contribute greatly to the expressive power of a language.

For an example of a procedure that takes procedural arguments and returns a procedural result, consider the problem of defining a procedure that performs functional composition. Assume that f and g are two functions of one argument such that $\text{Range}(g) \subseteq \text{Domain}(f)$. Then the *composition* of f and g, $f \circ g$, is defined by this equation:

$$(f \circ g)(x) = f(g(x)).$$

The assumption about the range of g and the domain of f ensures that every possible result from g is a possible argument to f. It is straightforward to define composition in Scheme.

```
> (define compose
    (lambda (f g)
      (lambda (x)
        (f (g x)))))
> (define add4 (compose add2 add2))
> (add4 5)
9
> ((compose car cdr) '(a b c d))
b
> ((compose list (compose cdr cdr))
   '(a b c d))
((c d))
```

● *Exercise 1.3.1*
What is unusual about the following expression?

```
((lambda (x)
   (list x (list (quote quote) x)))
 (quote (lambda (x)
          (list x (list (quote quote) x)))))
```

Try to figure out what it does without typing it into a Scheme system. Can similar behavior be achieved without using `list`? □

- *Exercise 1.3.2*

  Here is an implementation of cells.

  ```
  (define cell-tag "cell")

  (define make-cell
    (lambda (x)
      (vector cell-tag x)))

  (define cell?
    (lambda (x)
      (if (vector? x)
          (if (= (vector-length x) 2)
              (eq? (vector-ref x 0) cell-tag)
              #f)
          #f)))

  (define cell-ref
    (lambda (x)
      (if (cell? x)
          (vector-ref x 1)
          (error "Invalid argument to cell-ref:" x))))
  ```

  Fill in the values of the following transcript.

  ```
  > (define c (make-cell 5))
  > c

  > (cell? c)

  > (cell-ref c)
  ```

  □

- *Exercise 1.3.3*

  Consider two or three other languages you know or for which you can find documentation. What restrictions, if any, are imposed on procedures that keep them from being first class? Is it possible to create anonymous procedures? □

  Here is an example of a procedure that takes a numeric value and returns a procedure.

```
(define f
  (lambda (x)
    (lambda (y)
      (+ x y))))
```

When f is passed a number x it returns a procedure that takes a number and adds x to it.

```
> (define new-add2 (f 2))
> (new-add2 4)
6
```

Here *new-add2* has the same behavior as the *add2* procedure defined earlier. So what is the point of defining f? If a computation requires generating many of these add-n procedures for different values of n, or if the values of n are unknown at the time the program is written, then a procedure like f is called for.

```
> (define add3 (f (+ 1 2)))
> (add3 5)
8
> ((f 5) 6)
11
> (define g
    (lambda (a)
      (lambda (d)
        (cons a d))))
> ((g 'a) '(b c))
(a b c)
> (map (g 'a) '((b c) (1 2)))
((a b c) (a 1 2))
```

Having functions of more than one argument is certainly convenient, but it is not absolutely necessary. Using the technique just illustrated, any procedure p of $n \geq 2$ arguments can always be transformed into a procedure p' of one argument that returns a procedure of $n - 1$ arguments such that

$$((p'\, x_1)\, x_2\, \ldots\, x_n) = (p\, x_1\, \ldots\, x_n)$$

By repeating this transformation $n - 1$ times, we obtain a procedure p'' such that

$$(\ldots ((p''\, x_1)\, x_2)\, \ldots\, x_n) = (p\, x_1\, x_2\, \ldots\, x_n)$$

This transformation is known as *currying*. The procedures *f* and *g* above are curried versions of the addition and *cons* procedures, respectively. Of course if an existing procedure is to be replaced by a curried version, all calls to the procedure must be changed.

A curried version of a procedure normally takes the first argument first, but this is not always what is desired. The following example illustrates the use of a "reverse-curried" version of *cons*.

```
> (define h
    (lambda (d)
      (lambda (a)
        (cons a d))))
> ((h '(b c)) 'a)
(a b c)
> (map (h '(b c)) '(a 1 2))
((a b c) (1 b c) (2 b c))
```

• *Exercise 1.3.4*

Write a procedure *curry2* that takes a procedure of two arguments and returns a curried version of the procedure that takes the first argument and returns a procedure that takes the second argument. For example,

```
> (((curry2 +) 1) 2)
3
> (define consa ((curry2 cons) 'a))
> (consa '(b))
(a b)
```
☐

○ *Exercise 1.3.5*

Write a curried version of *compose*. Can you think of a use for it? ☐

○ *Exercise 1.3.6*

A language could be designed so that if a procedure is passed fewer arguments than it expects, it simply returns a procedure that takes the rest of the arguments. Thus procedures are "automatically" curried. What are the advantages and disadvantages of this feature? ☐

1.3.3 Variable Arity Procedures

The *arity* of a procedure is the number of arguments that it takes. Most procedures, including those that result from evaluating lambda expressions of the form introduced so far, have fixed arity. An error message results if a fixed arity procedure is invoked with the wrong number of arguments. Examples of procedures that can take a variable number of arguments are the standard procedures *list*, *vector*, and *string*. It is occasionally necessary to define new procedures of variable arity. This is accomplished with a lambda expression of the form

$$(\texttt{lambda } formal\ body)$$

where *formal* is a single variable. When the resulting procedure is invoked, this variable is bound to a list of the argument values. The simplest example is (lambda x x), which is equivalent to *list*. A more interesting example is the following procedure, which may be invoked with two or more arguments, in which case it behaves like +, or with one argument, in which case it behaves like a curried +.

```
> (define plus
    (lambda x
      (if (null? (cdr x))
          (lambda (y) (+ (car x) y))
          (apply + x))))
> (plus 1 2)
3
> ((plus 1) 2)
3
```

• *Exercise 1.3.7*
Define a version of compose that takes as arguments either two or three procedures (of one argument) and composes them. The composition of three procedures is specified by this equation:

$$(\texttt{compose f g h}) \Rightarrow (\texttt{compose f (compose g h)})$$

☐

1.4 Summary

Scheme programs consist mainly of expressions, which are evaluated for their value, rather than statements, which are evaluated only for their effect on the computation. Variable references and literals are the simplest forms of expression; they do not contain subexpressions, as other forms do. Procedure call expressions are the most common expressions in Scheme.

Programs are composed of definitions, introduced by the keyword `define`, and expressions. A read-eval-print loop provides a convenient interactive programming environment, but such programming environment features are generally not part of a language specification.

The special form `if` provides conditional evaluation. It cannot be a procedure, because it is improper to evaluate both its "then" expression and "else" expression.

Scheme supports a number of primitive data types, including numbers, booleans, characters, symbols, pairs, strings, and vectors. Pairs and vectors are compound data types that contain data elements. Lists are an important type derived from pairs and the empty list. New procedures are created by the `lambda` special form.

Procedures, and all other data objects in Scheme, are first class: they may be stored in data structures and returned from procedures as well as passed to procedures. They may also be anonymous: they need not be bound to a variable at the point of their creation.

2   Induction, Recursion, and Scope

This chapter introduces the fundamental technique of recursive programming, along with its relation to the mathematical technique of induction. The notion of scope, which plays a primary role in programming languages, is also presented. Finally, the material in this chapter will improve your facility with the tools introduced in chapter 1. Section 2.1 and section 2.2 introduce techniques for inductively specifying data structures and show how such specifications may be used to guide the construction of recursive programs. Section 2.3 then introduces the notions of variable binding and scope.

The programming exercises are the heart of this chapter. They provide experience that is essential for mastering the technique of recursive programming upon which the rest of this book is based.

2.1 Inductively Specified Data

We have already seen a number of data types in Scheme. What is a data type in general? For our purposes, it is enough to say that a data type consists of a set of values along with a set of operations on those values. Every time we decide to represent a certain set of quantities in a particular way, we are defining a new data type: the data type whose values are those representations and whose operations are the procedures that manipulate those entities.

When writing code for the operations on a new data type, it is important to know precisely what values may occur as members of the type. In this section we introduce formal techniques for specifying the set of values that belong to a data type.

2.1.1 Inductive Specification

Inductive specification is a powerful method of specifying a set of values. To illustrate this method, we use it to describe a certain subset of the natural numbers:

Define the set S to be the smallest set of natural numbers satisfying the following two properties:

1. $0 \in S$, and

2. Whenever $x \in S$, then $x + 3 \in S$.

"The smallest set" is the one that is a subset of all the sets satisfying properties 1 and 2.

Let us see if we can describe some partial information about S to arrive at a noninductive specification. We know that 0 is in S, by property 1. Since $0 \in S$, by property 2 it must be that $3 \in S$. Then since $3 \in S$, by property 2 we conclude that $6 \in S$, and so on. So we see that all the multiples of 3 are in S. If we let M denote the set of all multiples of 3, we can restate this conclusion as $M \subseteq S$. But the set M itself satisfies properties 1 and 2. Since S is a subset of every set that satisfies properties 1 and 2, it must be that $S \subseteq M$. So we deduce that $S = M$, the set of multiples of 3. This is plausible: we know all the multiples of 3 must be in S, and anything else is extraneous.

This is a typical inductive definition. To specify a set S by induction, we define it to be the smallest set satisfying two properties of the following form:

1. Some specific values must be in S.

2. If certain values are in S, then certain other values are also in S.

Sticking to this recipe guarantees that S consists precisely of those values inserted by property 1 and those values included by repeated application of property 2. As stated, this recipe is rather vague. It can be stated more precisely, but that would take us too far afield. Instead, let us see how this process works on some more examples.

The data type list-of-numbers is the smallest set of values satisfying the two properties:

1. The empty list is a list-of-numbers, and

2. If l is a list-of-numbers and n is a number, then the pair $(n \ . \ l)$ is a list-of-numbers.

From this definition we infer the following:

Induction, Recursion, and Scope

1. () is a list-of-numbers, because of property 1.

2. (14 . ()) is a list-of-numbers, because 14 is a number and () is a list-of-numbers.

3. (3 . (14 . ())) is a list-of-numbers, because 3 is a number and (14 . ()) is a list-of-numbers.

4. (-7 . (3 . (14 . ()))) is a list-of-numbers, because -7 is a number and (3 . (14 . ())) is a list-of-numbers.

5. Nothing is a list-of-numbers unless it is built in this fashion.

Converting from dot notation to list notation, we see that (), (14), (3 14), and (-7 3 14) are all members of list-of-numbers.

2.1.2 Backus-Naur Form and Syntactic Derivations

The previous example was fairly straightforward, but it is easy to imagine how the process of describing more complex data types might become quite cumbersome. To remedy this, a notation has been developed to express the same ideas more concisely: *Backus-Naur Form,* or *BNF*. We frequently use it to describe the structure of a data type. BNF is also widely used in specifying the syntax of programming languages.

BNF can be used to inductively define a number of sets at once. These sets are called *syntactic categories,* or sometimes *nonterminals,* and are customarily written with angle brackets around the name of the set: ⟨list-of-numbers⟩. (When no ambiguity results, we shall sometimes refer informally to syntactic categories without using angle brackets or dashes: "list of numbers.") Each syntactic category is defined by a finite set of *rules,* or *productions.* Each rule asserts that certain values must be in the syntactic category.

The BNF definition of list-of-numbers has two rules that correspond to the two properties.

⟨list-of-numbers⟩ ::= ()
⟨list-of-numbers⟩ ::= (⟨number⟩ . ⟨list-of-numbers⟩)

The first rule says that the empty list is in ⟨list-of-numbers⟩, and the second says that if n is in ⟨number⟩ and l is in ⟨list-of-numbers⟩, then $(n . l)$ is in ⟨list-of-numbers⟩.

Each rule begins by naming the syntactic category being defined, followed by ::= (read *is*). The right-hand side of each rule specifies a method for constructing members of the syntactic category in terms of other syntactic categories and *terminal symbols,* such as the left and right parentheses, and the period in the previous example.

Often some syntactic categories mentioned in a BNF rule are left undefined, such as ⟨number⟩. Defining all categories would needlessly complicate the rule if it is safe to assume the reader knows what some of the categories are.

BNF is often extended with a few notational shortcuts. One can write a set of rules for a single syntactic category by writing the left-hand side and ::= just once, followed by all the right-hand sides separated by the special symbol | (vertical bar, read *or*). A ⟨list-of-numbers⟩ can then be defined by

⟨list-of-numbers⟩ ::= () | (⟨number⟩ . ⟨list-of-numbers⟩)

Another shortcut is the *Kleene star,* expressed by the notation {…}*. When this appears in a right-hand side, it indicates a sequence of any number of instances of whatever appears between the braces. This includes the possibility of no instances at all. Using the Kleene star, the definition of ⟨list-of-numbers⟩ in list notation is simply

⟨list-of-numbers⟩ ::= ({⟨number⟩}*)

If there are zero instances, we get the empty list. A variant of the star notation is *Kleene plus* {…}$^+$, which indicates a sequence of *one* or more instances. Substituting $^+$ for * in the above example would define the syntactic category of nonempty lists of numbers. These notational shortcuts are just that—it is always possible to do without them by using additional BNF rules.

If a type is specified using BNF rules, a *syntactic derivation* may be used to prove that a given data value is a member of the type. Such a derivation starts with the nonterminal corresponding to the type. At each step, indicated by an arrow ⇒, a nonterminal is replaced by the right-hand side of a corresponding rule, or with a known member of its syntactic class if the class was left undefined. For example, the previous demonstration that (14 . ()) is a list of numbers may be formalized with the following syntactic derivation:

⟨list-of-numbers⟩
⇒ (⟨number⟩ . ⟨list-of-numbers⟩)
⇒ (14 . ⟨list-of-numbers⟩)
⇒ (14 . ())

The order in which nonterminals are replaced is not significant. Thus another possible derivation of (14 . ()) is

Induction, Recursion, and Scope

$\langle$list-of-numbers$\rangle$

$\Rightarrow$ ($\langle$number$\rangle$. $\langle$list-of-numbers$\rangle$)

$\Rightarrow$ ($\langle$number$\rangle$. ())

$\Rightarrow$ (14 . ())

o *Exercise 2.1.1*

Write a syntactic derivation that proves (-7 . (3 . (14 . ()))) is a list of numbers. ☐

2.1.3 Using BNF to Specify Data

The term *datum* refers to any literal data representation. BNF may be used to specify concisely the syntactic category of data in Scheme. We have seen that numbers, symbols, booleans, and strings all have literal representations, which we associate with the syntactic categories $\langle$number$\rangle$, $\langle$symbol$\rangle$, $\langle$boolean$\rangle$, and $\langle$string$\rangle$, respectively. Section 1.2 informally introduced representations for lists, improper lists (which end with dotted pairs), and vectors. These compound data types contain components that may be numbers, symbols, booleans, strings, or other lists, improper lists or vectors. This is formally specified by the following BNF rules

---

$\langle$list$\rangle$ ::= ({$\langle$datum$\rangle$}*)

$\langle$dotted-datum$\rangle$ ::= ({$\langle$datum$\rangle$}$^+$. $\langle$datum$\rangle$)

$\langle$vector$\rangle$ ::= #({$\langle$datum$\rangle$}*)

$\langle$datum$\rangle$ ::= $\langle$number$\rangle$ | $\langle$symbol$\rangle$ | $\langle$boolean$\rangle$ | $\langle$string$\rangle$
     | $\langle$list$\rangle$ | $\langle$dotted-datum$\rangle$ | $\langle$vector$\rangle$

These four syntactic categories are all defined in terms of each other. This is legitimate because there are some simple possibilities for data that are not defined in terms of the other categories.

To illustrate the use of this grammar, consider the following syntactic derivation proving that (#t (foo . ()) 3) is a datum.

$\langle$list$\rangle$

$\Rightarrow$ ($\langle$datum$\rangle$ $\langle$datum$\rangle$ $\langle$datum$\rangle$)

$\Rightarrow$ ($\langle$boolean$\rangle$ $\langle$datum$\rangle$ $\langle$datum$\rangle$)

$\Rightarrow$ (#t $\langle$datum$\rangle$ $\langle$datum$\rangle$)

$\Rightarrow$ (#t $\langle$dotted-datum$\rangle$ $\langle$datum$\rangle$)

$\Rightarrow$ (#t ({$\langle$datum$\rangle$}$^+$. $\langle$datum$\rangle$) $\langle$datum$\rangle$)
$\Rightarrow$ (#t ($\langle$symbol$\rangle$. $\langle$datum$\rangle$) $\langle$datum$\rangle$)
$\Rightarrow$ (#t (foo . $\langle$datum$\rangle$) $\langle$datum$\rangle$)
$\Rightarrow$ (#t (foo . $\langle$list$\rangle$) $\langle$datum$\rangle$)
$\Rightarrow$ (#t (foo . ()) $\langle$datum$\rangle$)
$\Rightarrow$ (#t (foo . ()) $\langle$number$\rangle$)
$\Rightarrow$ (#t (foo . ()) 3)

All three elements of the outer list were introduced at once. This shortcut was possible because the grammar uses a Kleene star. Of course, the Kleene star and plus notation could be eliminated by introducing new nonterminals and productions, and the three list elements would then be introduced with three derivation steps instead of one.

○ *Exercise 2.1.2*
Rewrite the $\langle$datum$\rangle$ grammar without using the Kleene star or plus. Then indicate the changes to the above derivation that are required by your grammar. □

○ *Exercise 2.1.3*
Write a syntactic derivation that proves (a "mixed" #(bag (of . data))) is a datum, using either the grammar in the book or your grammar from the last exercise. What can you say about (a . b . c)? □

Let us consider the BNF definitions of some other useful data types. Many symbol manipulation procedures are designed to operate on lists that contain only symbols and other similarly restricted lists. We formalize this notion with these rules:

$$\langle\text{s-list}\rangle ::= (\{\langle\text{symbol-expression}\rangle\}^*)$$
$$\langle\text{symbol-expression}\rangle ::= \langle\text{symbol}\rangle \mid \langle\text{s-list}\rangle$$

The literal representation of an s-list contains only parentheses and symbols. For example

```
(a b c)
(an (((s-list)) (with lots) ((of) nesting)))
```

A binary tree with numeric leaves and interior nodes labeled with symbols may be represented using three-element lists for the interior nodes as follows

$$\langle\text{tree}\rangle ::= \langle\text{number}\rangle \mid (\langle\text{symbol}\rangle \langle\text{tree}\rangle \langle\text{tree}\rangle)$$

Examples of such trees follow:

```
1
2
(foo 1 2)
(bar 1 (foo 1 2))
(baz (bar 1 (foo 1 2)) (biz 4 5))
```

BNF rules are said to be *context free* because a rule defining a given syntactic category may be applied in any context that makes reference to that syntactic category. Sometimes this is not restrictive enough. For example, a node in a binary search tree is either empty or contains a key and two subtrees

⟨bin-search-tree⟩ ::= () | (⟨key⟩ ⟨bin-search-tree⟩ ⟨bin-search-tree⟩)

This correctly describes the structure of each node but fails to mention an important fact about binary search trees: all the keys in the left subtree are less than (or equal to) the key in the current node, and all the keys in the right subtree are greater than the key in the current node. Such constraints are said to be *context sensitive,* because they depend on the context in which they are used.

Context-sensitive constraints also arise when specifying the syntax of programming languages. For instance, in many languages every identifier must be declared before it is used. This constraint on the use of identifiers is sensitive to the context of their use. Formal methods can be used to specify context-sensitive constraints, but these methods are far more complicated than BNF. In practice, the usual approach is first to specify a context-free grammar using BNF. Context-sensitive constraints are then added using other methods, usually prose, to complete the specification of a context-sensitive syntax.

2.1.4 Induction

Having described data types inductively, we can use the inductive definitions in two ways: to prove theorems about members of the data type and to write programs that manipulate them. Writing the programs is the subject of the next two sections; here we present an example of such a proof.

Theorem. *Let $s \in$ ⟨tree⟩. Then s contains an odd number of nodes.*

Proof. The proof is by induction on the size of s, where we take the size of s to be the number of nodes in s. The induction hypothesis, $IH(k)$, is that any tree of size $\leq k$ has an odd number of nodes. We follow the usual prescription for an inductive proof: we first prove that $IH(0)$ is true, and we then prove that whenever k is a number such that IH is true for k, then IH is true for $k + 1$ also.

i. There are no trees with 0 nodes, so $IH(0)$ holds trivially.

ii. Let k be a number such that $IH(k)$ holds, that is, any tree with $\leq k$ nodes actually has an odd number of nodes. We need to show that $IH(k+1)$ holds as well: that any tree with $\leq k+1$ nodes has an odd number of nodes. If s has $\leq k+1$ nodes, there are exactly two possibilities according to the BNF definition of ⟨tree⟩:

    a. s could be of the form n, where n is a number. In this case, s has exactly one node, and one is odd.

    b. s could be of the form (*sym* s_1 s_2), where *sym* is a symbol and s_1 and s_2 are trees. Now s_1 and s_2 must have fewer nodes than s. Since s has $\leq k+1$ nodes, s_1 and s_2 must have $\leq k$ nodes. Therefore they are covered by $IH(k)$, and they must each have an odd number of nodes, say $2n_1 + 1$ and $2n_2 + 1$ nodes, respectively. Therefore the total number of nodes in the tree, counting the two subtrees and the root, is

$$(2n_1 + 1) + (2n_2 + 1) + 1 = 2(n_1 + n_2 + 1) + 1$$

which is once again odd.

This completes the proof of the claim that $IH(k+1)$ holds and therefore completes the induction. □

The key to the proof is that the substructures of a tree s are always smaller than s itself. Therefore the induction might be rephrased as follows:

1. IH is true on simple structures (those without substructures).

2. If IH is true on the substructures of s, then it is true on s itself.

2.2 Recursively Specified Programs

In the previous section, we used the method of inductive definition to characterize complicated sets. Starting with simple members of the set, the BNF rules were used to build more and more complex members of the set. We now use the same idea to define procedures for manipulating those sets. First we define the simple parts of a procedure's behavior (how it behaves on simple inputs), and then we use this behavior to define more complex behaviors.

Imagine we want to define a procedure to find powers of numbers, *e.g.* $e(n, x) = x^n$, where n is a nonnegative integer and $x \neq 0$. It is easy to define a sequence of procedures that compute particular powers: $e_0(x) = x^0$, $e_1(x) = x^1$, $e_2(x) = x^2$:

$$e_0(x) = 1$$
$$e_1(x) = x \times e_0(x)$$
$$e_2(x) = x \times e_1(x)$$
$$e_3(x) = x \times e_2(x)$$

In general, if n is a positive integer,

$$e_n(x) = x \times e_{n-1}(x).$$

At each stage, we use the fact that the problem has already been solved for smaller n. We are using mathematical induction. Next the subscript can be removed from e by making it a parameter.

1. If n is 0, $e(n, x) = 1$.

2. If n is greater than 0, we assume it is known how to solve the problem for $n - 1$. That is, we assume that $e(n - 1, x)$ is well defined. Therefore, $e(n, x) = x \times e(n - 1, x)$.

To prove that $e(n, x) = x^n$ for any nonnegative integer n, we proceed by induction on n:

1. (Base Step) When $n = 0$, $e(0, x) = 1 = x^0$.

2. (Induction Step) Assume that the procedure works when its first argument is k, that is, $e(k, x) = x^k$ for some nonnegative integer k. Then we claim that $e(k + 1, x) = x^{k+1}$. We calculate as follows

$$
\begin{aligned}
e(k + 1, x) &= x \times e(k, x) & \text{(definition of } e) \\
&= x \times x^k & (\textit{IH at } k) \\
&= x^{k+1} & \text{(fact about exponentiation)}
\end{aligned}
$$

This completes the induction.

We can write a program to compute e based upon the inductive definition

```
(define e
  (lambda (n x)
    (if (zero? n)
        1
        (* x
           (e (- n 1) x)))))
```

The two branches of the if expression correspond to the two cases detailed in the definition.

If we can reduce a problem to a smaller subproblem, we can call the procedure that solves the problem to solve the subproblem. The solution it returns for the subproblem may then be used to solve the original problem. This works because each time we call the procedure, it is called with a smaller problem, until eventually it is called with a problem that can be solved directly, without another call to itself.

In the above example, we used induction on integers, so the subproblem was solved by recursively calling the procedure with a smaller value of n. When manipulating inductively defined structures, subproblems are usually solved by calling the procedure recursively on a substructure of the original.

When a procedure calls itself in this manner, it is said to be *recursively defined*. Such *recursive calls* are possible in Scheme and most other languages. The general phenomenon is known as *recursion*, and it occurs in contexts other than programming, such as inductive definitions. Later we shall study how recursion is implemented in programming languages.

2.2.1 Deriving Programs from BNF Data Specifications

Recursion is a powerful programming technique that is used extensively throughout this book. It requires an approach to programming that differs significantly from the style commonly used in statement-oriented languages. For this reason, we devote the rest of this section to this style of programming.

A BNF definition for the type of data being manipulated serves as a guide both to where recursive calls should be used and to which base cases need to be handled. This is a fundamental point: *when defining a program based on structural induction, the structure of the program should be patterned after the structure of the data.*

A typical kind of program based on inductively defined structures is a predicate that determines whether a given value is a member of a particular data type. Let us write a Scheme predicate, `list-of-numbers?` that takes a datum and determines whether it belongs to the syntactic category ⟨list-of-numbers⟩.

```
> (list-of-numbers? '(1 2 3))
#t
> (list-of-numbers? '(1 two 3))
#f
> (list-of-numbers? '(1 . 2))
#f
```

Recall the definition of ⟨list-of-numbers⟩:

⟨list-of-numbers⟩ ::= () | (⟨number⟩ . ⟨list-of-numbers⟩)

We begin by writing down the simplest behavior of the procedure: what it does when the input is the empty list.

```
(define list-of-numbers?
  (lambda (lst)
    (if (null? lst)
        ...
        ...)))
```

By definition, the empty list is a ⟨list-of-numbers⟩. Otherwise, *lst* is not a ⟨list-of-numbers⟩ unless it is a pair.

```
(define list-of-numbers?
  (lambda (lst)
    (if (null? lst)
        #t
        (if (pair? lst)
            ...
            #f))))
```

(Throughout this book, bars in the left margin indicate lines that have changed since an earlier version of the same definition.) If *lst* is a pair, there are two alternatives: either the first element is a number, or it is not. If not, the original value cannot be a list of numbers, so we write

```
(define list-of-numbers?
  (lambda (lst)
    (if (null? lst)
        #t
        (if (pair? lst)
            (if (number? (car lst))
                ...
                #f)
            #f))))
```

The only case left to consider is when the first element of the list in question passes the *number?* test. According to the definition of ⟨list-of-numbers⟩, a nonempty list belongs to ⟨list-of-numbers⟩ if and only if its first element is a number and its cdr belongs to ⟨list-of-numbers⟩. Since we already know that *lst* is nonempty and its car is a number, we can deduce that *lst* is a list of numbers if and only if its cdr is a list of numbers. Therefore we write

```
(define list-of-numbers?
  (lambda (lst)
    (if (null? lst)
        #t
        (if (pair? lst)
            (if (number? (car lst))
                (list-of-numbers? (cdr lst))
                #f)
            #f))))
```

To prove the correctness of *list-of-numbers?*, we would like to use induction on the length of *lst*. However, the argument to *list-of-numbers?* may not be a list at all. This prompts us to define the *list-size* of a datum to be zero if the datum is not a list and its length if it is a list. We now proceed by induction on the list-size:

1. *list-of-numbers?* works on data of list-size 0, since the only list of length 0 is the empty list, for which the correct answer, true, is returned, and if *list-of-numbers?* is not a list, the correct answer, false, is returned.

2. Assuming *list-of-numbers?* works on lists of length k, we show that it works on lists of length $k + 1$. Let *lst* be such a list. By the definition of ⟨list-of-numbers⟩, *lst* belongs to ⟨list-of-numbers⟩ if and only if its car is a number and its cdr belongs to ⟨list-of-numbers⟩. Since *lst* is of length $k + 1$, its cdr is of length k, so by the induction hypothesis we can determine the cdr's membership in ⟨list-of-numbers⟩ by passing it to *list-of-numbers?*. Hence *list-of-numbers?* correctly computes membership in ⟨list-of-numbers⟩ for lists of length $k + 1$, and the induction is complete.

The recursion terminates because every time *list-of-numbers?* is called, it is passed a shorter list. (This assumes lists are finite, which will always be the case unless the list mutation techniques introduced in section 4.5.3 have been used.)

As a second example, we define a procedure *nth-elt* that takes a list *lst* and a zero-based index *n* and returns element number *n* of *lst*.

Induction, Recursion, and Scope

```
> (nth-elt '(a b c) 1)
b
```

The procedure *nth-elt* does for lists what *vector-ref* does for vectors. (Actually, Scheme provides the procedure *list-ref*, which is the same as *nth-elt* except for error reporting, but we choose another name because standard procedures should not be tampered with unnecessarily.)

When n is 0, the answer is simply the car of *lst*. If n is greater than 0, then the answer is element $n - 1$ of *lst*'s cdr. Since neither the car nor cdr of *lst* exist if *lst* is the empty list, we must guard the *car* and *cdr* operations so that we do not take the car or cdr of an empty list.

```
(define nth-elt
  (lambda (lst n)
    (if (null? lst)
        (error "nth-elt: list too short")
        (if (zero? n)
            (car lst)
            (nth-elt (cdr lst) (- n 1))))))
```

The procedure *error* signals an error by printing its arguments, in this case a single string, and then aborting the computation. (*error* is not a standard Scheme procedure, but most implementations provide something of the sort. See appendix D and check your Scheme language reference manual for details.) If error checking were omitted, we would have to rely on *car* and *cdr* to complain about being passed the empty list, but their error messages would be less helpful. For example, if you receive an error message from *car*, you might have to look for uses of *car* throughout your program. Even this would not find the error if *nth-elt* were provided by someone else, so that its definition was not a part of your program.

Let us try one more example of this kind before moving on to harder examples. The standard procedure *length* determines the number of elements in a list.

```
> (length '(a b c))
3
> (length '((x) ()))
2
```

We write our own procedure, called *list-length*, to do the same thing. The length of the empty list is 0.

```
(define list-length
  (lambda (lst)
    (if (null? lst)
        0
        ...)))
```

The blank is filled in by observing that the length of a nonempty list is one
more than the length of its cdr.

```
(define list-length
  (lambda (lst)
    (if (null? lst)
        0
        (+ 1 (list-length (cdr lst))))))
```

○ *Exercise 2.2.1*

The procedures `nth-elt` and `list-length` do not check whether their arguments are of the expected type. What happens on your Scheme system if they
are passed symbols when a list is expected? What is the behavior of `list-ref`
and `length` in such cases? Write your own versions that guard against these
situations. Is it always necessary to signal errors when this occurs, or can a
sensible value sometimes be returned? When is it worth the effort to check
that arguments are of the right type? Why? □

2.2.2 Three Important Examples

In this section, we present three simple recursive procedures that will be used
as examples later in this book. As in previous examples, they are defined
so that (1) the structure of a program reflects the structure of its data and
(2) recursive calls are employed at points where recursion is used in the data
type's inductive definition.

The first procedure is *remove-first*, which takes two arguments: a symbol,
s, and a list of symbols, *los*. It returns a list with the same elements arranged
in the same order as *los*, except that the first occurrence of the symbol *s* is
removed. If there is no occurrence of *s* in *los*, then *los* is returned.

```
> (remove-first 'a '(a b c))
(b c)
> (remove-first 'b '(e f g))
(e f g)
```

```
> (remove-first 'a4 '(c1 a4 c1 a4))
(c1 c1 a4)
> (remove-first 'x '())
()
```

Before we start on the program, we must complete the problem specification by defining the data type ⟨list-of-symbols⟩. Unlike the s-lists introduced in the last section, these lists of symbols do not contain sublists.

⟨list-of-symbols⟩ ::= () | (⟨symbol⟩ . ⟨list-of-symbols⟩)

A list of symbols is either the empty list or a list whose car is a symbol and whose cdr is a list of symbols. If the list is empty, there are no occurrences of s to remove, so the answer is the empty list.

```
(define remove-first
  (lambda (s los)
    (if (null? los)
        '()
        ...)))
```

If los is nonempty, is there some case where we can determine the answer immediately? If $los = (s \ s_1 \ ... \ s_{n-1})$, the first occurrence of s is as the first element of los. So the result of removing it is just $(s_1 \ ... \ s_{n-1})$.

```
(define remove-first
  (lambda (s los)
    (if (null? los)
        '()
        (if (eq? (car los) s)
            (cdr los)
            ...))))
```

If the first element of los is not s, say $los = (s_0 \ s_1 \ ... \ s_{n-1})$, then we know that s_0 is not the first occurrence of s. Therefore the first element of the answer must be s_0. Furthermore, the first occurrence of s in los must be its first occurrence in $(s_1 \ ... \ s_{n-1})$. So the rest of the answer must be the result of removing the first occurrence of s from the cdr of los. Since the cdr of los is shorter than los, we may recursively call *remove-first* to remove s from the cdr of los. Thus using (cons (car los) (remove-first s (cdr los))), the answer may be obtained. With this, the complete definition of *remove-first* follows.

```
(define remove-first
  (lambda (s los)
    (if (null? los)
        '()
        (if (eq? (car los) s)
            (cdr los)
            (cons (car los) (remove-first s (cdr los)))))))))
```

- *Exercise 2.2.2*

  In the definition of *remove-first*, if the inner if's alternative (cons ...) were replaced by (remove-first s (cdr los)), what function would the resulting procedure compute? □

The second procedure is *remove*, defined over symbols and lists of symbols. It is similar to *remove-first*, but it removes all occurrences of a given symbol from a list of symbols, not just the first.

```
> (remove 'a4 '(c1 a4 d1 a4))
(c1 d1)
```

Since *remove-first* and *remove* work on the same input, their structure is similar. If the list *los* is empty, there are no occurrences to remove, so the answer is again the empty list. If *los* is nonempty, there are again two cases to consider. If the first element of *los* is not *s*, the answer is obtained as in *remove-first*.

```
(define remove
  (lambda (s los)
    (if (null? los)
        '()
        (if (eq? (car los) s)
            ...
            (cons (car los) (remove s (cdr los)))))))
```

If the first element of *los* is the same as *s*, certainly the first element is not to be part of the result. But we are not quite done: all the occurrences of *s* must still be removed from the cdr of *los*. Once again this may be accomplished by invoking *remove* recursively on the cdr of *los*.

Induction, Recursion, and Scope

```
(define remove
  (lambda (s los)
    (if (null? los)
        '()
        (if (eq? (car los) s)
            (remove s (cdr los))
            (cons (car los) (remove s (cdr los)))))))
```

• *Exercise 2.2.3*

In the definition of *remove*, if the inner if's alternative (cons ...) were replaced by (remove s (cdr los)), what function would the resulting procedure compute? ☐

The last of our examples is *subst*. It takes three arguments: two symbols, *new* and *old*, and an s-list, *slst*. All elements of *slst* are examined, and a new list is returned that is similar to *slst* but with all occurrences of *old* replaced by instances of *new*.

```
> (subst 'a 'b '((b c) (b d)))
((a c) (a d))
```

Since *subst* is defined over s-lists, its organization reflects the definition of s-lists

$$\langle\text{s-list}\rangle ::= (\{\langle\text{symbol-expression}\rangle\}^*)$$
$$\langle\text{symbol-expression}\rangle ::= \langle\text{symbol}\rangle \mid \langle\text{s-list}\rangle$$

If the list is empty, there are no occurrences of *old* to replace.

```
(define subst
  (lambda (new old slst)
    (if (null? slst)
        '()
        ...)))
```

If *slst* is nonempty, its car is a member of ⟨symbol-expression⟩ and its cdr is another s-list. Thus the program branches on the type of the symbol expression in the car of *slst*. If it is a symbol, we need to ask whether it is the same as the symbol *old*. If it is, the car of the answer is *new*; if not, the car of the answer is the same as the car of *slst*. In either case, to obtain the answer's cdr, we need to change all occurrences of *old* to *new* in the cdr of *slst*. Since the cdr of *slst* is a smaller list, we may use recursion.

```
(define subst
  (lambda (new old slst)
    (if (null? slst)
        '()
        (if (symbol? (car slst))
            (if (eq? (car slst) old)
                (cons new (subst new old (cdr slst)))
                (cons (car slst) (subst new old (cdr slst))))
            ...)))))
```

In the final case to be considered the car of *slst* is a list. Since the car and cdr of *slst* are both lists, the answer is obtained by invoking *subst* on both and consing the results together.

```
(define subst
  (lambda (new old slst)
    (if (null? slst)
        '()
        (if (symbol? (car slst))
            (if (eq? (car slst) old)
                (cons new (subst new old (cdr slst)))
                (cons (car slst) (subst new old (cdr slst))))
            (cons (subst new old (car slst))
                  (subst new old (cdr slst)))))))
```

This definition has been completed by following the structure of ⟨s-list⟩ and then ⟨symbol-expression⟩ and checking for *old* when dealing with symbols.

The subexpression (subst new old (cdr slst)) appears three times in the above definition. This redundancy can be eliminated by noting that when *slst* is nonnull, the answer's car and cdr may be independently computed and then combined with *cons*. The answer's cdr is obtained by invoking *subst* on the cdr of *slst*. The answer's car is obtained by substituting *new* for *old* in the car of *slst*, but the type of *slst*'s car is ⟨symbol-expression⟩, not ⟨s-list⟩, so *subst* cannot be used directly. The solution is to make a separate procedure for handling substitutions on members of ⟨symbol-expression⟩.

```
(define subst
  (lambda (new old slst)
    (if (null? slst)
        '()
        (cons (subst-symbol-expression new old (car slst))
              (subst new old (cdr slst))))))
```

```
(define subst-symbol-expression
  (lambda (new old se)
    (if (symbol? se)
        (if (eq? se old) new se)
        (subst new old se))))
```

Since we have strictly followed the BNF definition of ⟨s-list⟩ and ⟨symbol-expression⟩, this recursion is guaranteed to halt. Observe that *subst* and *subst-symbol-expression* call each other recursively. Such procedures are said to be *mutually recursive*.

• *Exercise 2.2.4*

In the last line of `subst-symbol-expression`, the recursion is on *se* and not a smaller substructure. Why is the recursion guaranteed to halt? □

• *Exercise 2.2.5*

Write *subst* using *map*. □

The decomposition of *subst* into two procedures, one for each syntactic category, is an important technique. It allows us to think about one syntactic category at a time, which is important in more complicated situations.

There are many other situations in which it may be helpful or necessary to introduce auxiliary procedures to solve a problem. Always feel free to do so. In some cases the new procedure is necessary in order to introduce an additional parameter. As an example, we consider the problem of summing all the values in a vector.

Since vectors require a program structure that differs from the ones we have used for lists, let us first solve the problem of summing the values in a list of numbers. This problem has a natural recursive solution because nonempty lists decompose naturally into their car and cdr components. We return 0 as the sum of the elements in the empty list.

```
(define list-sum
  (lambda (lon)
    (if (null? lon)
        0
        (+ (car lon)
           (list-sum (cdr lon))))))
```

It is not possible to proceed in this way with vectors, because they do not decompose as readily. Sometimes the best way to solve a problem is to solve a more general problem and use it to solve the original problem as a special case. For the vector sum problem, since we cannot decompose vectors, we generalize the problem to compute the sum of part of the vector. We define *partial-vector-sum*, which takes a vector of numbers, *von*, and a number, *n*, and returns the sum of the first *n* values in *von*.

```
(define partial-vector-sum
  (lambda (von n)
    (if (zero? n)
        0
        (+ (vector-ref von (- n 1))
           (partial-vector-sum von (- n 1))))))
```

Observe that *von* does not change. In the next chapter we shall see how the conceptual overhead of passing such parameters may be avoided. Since *n* decreases steadily to zero, a proof of correctness for this program would proceed by induction on *n*. It is now a simple matter to solve our original problem

```
(define vector-sum
  (lambda (von)
    (partial-vector-sum von (vector-length von))))
```

○ *Exercise 2.2.6*
Prove the correctness of *partial-vector-sum* with the following assumption: $0 \leq n < length(von)$. □

Getting the knack of writing recursive programs involves practice. Thus we conclude this section with a number of exercises.

● *Exercise 2.2.7*
Define, test, and debug the following procedures. Assume that *s* is any symbol, *n* is a nonnegative integer, *lst* is a list, *v* is a vector, *los* is a list of symbols, *vos* is a vector of symbols, *slst* is an s-list, and *x* is any object; and similarly *s1* is a symbol, *los2* is a list of symbols, *x1* is an object, etc. Make no other assumptions about the data unless further restrictions are given as part of a particular problem. You do not have to check that the input matches the description; for each procedure, assume that its input values are members of the specified data types.

To test your procedures, at the very minimum try all of the given examples. You should also use other examples to test your procedures, since the given examples are not adequate to reveal all possible errors.

1. (duple n x) returns a list containing n copies of x.

```
> (duple 2 3)
(3 3)
> (duple 4 '(ho ho))
((ho ho) (ho ho) (ho ho) (ho ho))
> (duple 0 '(blah))
()
```

2. (invert lst), where lst is a list of 2-lists (lists of length two), returns a list with each 2-list reversed.

```
> (invert '((a 1) (a 2) (b 1) (b 2)))
((1 a) (2 a) (1 b) (2 b))
```

3. (list-index s los) returns the zero-based index of the first occurrence of s in los, or −1 if there is no occurrence of s in los.

```
> (list-index 'c '(a b c d))
2
> (list-ref '(a b c) (list-index 'b '(a b c)))
b
```

4. (vector-index s vos) returns the zero-based index of the first occurrence of s in vos, or −1 if there is no occurrence of s in vos.

```
> (vector-index 'c '#(a b c d))
2
> (vector-ref '#(a b c) (vector-index 'b '#(a b c)))
b
```

5. (ribassoc s los v fail-value) returns the value in v that is associated with s, or fail-value if there is no associated value. If the first occurrence of s in los has index n, the value associated with s is the nth value in v. There is no associated value for s if s is not a member of los. You may assume that los and v are the same length.

```
> (ribassoc 'b '(a b c) '#(1 2 3) 'fail)
2
> (ribassoc 'c '(a b foo) '#(3 squiggle bar) 'fail)
fail
> (ribassoc 'i '(a i o i) '#(fx (fz) () (fm fe)) 'fail)
(fz)
```

6. (filter-in p lst), where *p* is a predicate, returns the list of those elements in *lst* that satisfy the predicate.

```
> (filter-in number? '(a 2 (1 3) b 7))
(2 7)
> (filter-in symbol? '(a (b c) 17 foo))
(a foo)
```

7. (product los1 los2) returns a list of 2-lists that represents the Cartesian product of *los1* and *los2*. The 2-lists may appear in any order.

```
> (product '(a b c) '(x y))
((a x) (a y) (b x) (b y) (c x) (c y))
```

8. (swapper s1 s2 slst) returns a list the same as *slst*, but with all occurrences of *s1* replaced by *s2* and all occurrences of *s2* replaced by *s1*.

```
> (swapper 'a 'd '(a b c d))
(d b c a)
> (swapper 'x 'y '((x) y (z (x))))
((y) x (z (y)))
```

9. (rotate los) returns a list similar to *los*, except that the last element of *los* becomes the first in the returned list.

```
> (rotate '(a b c d))
(d a b c)
> (rotate '(notmuch))
(notmuch)
> (rotate '())
()
```

☐

- *Exercise 2.2.8*

  These are a bit harder.

  1. (down lst) wraps parentheses around each top-level element of *lst*.

     ```
     > (down '(1 2 3))
     ((1) (2) (3))
     > (down '(a (more (complicated)) object))
     ((a) ((more (complicated))) (object))
     ```

  2. (up lst) removes a pair of parentheses from each top-level element of *lst*. If a top-level element is not a list, it is included in the result, as is. The value of (up (down lst)) is equivalent to *lst*, but (down (up lst)) is not necessarily *lst*.

     ```
     > (up '((1 2) (3 4)))
     (1 2 3 4)
     > (up '((x (y)) z))
     (x (y) z)
     ```

  3. (count-occurrences s slst) returns the number of occurrences of *s* in *slst*.

     ```
     > (count-occurrences 'x '((f x) y (((x z) x))))
     3
     > (count-occurrences 'w '((f x) y (((x z) x))))
     0
     ```

  4. (flatten slst) returns a list of the symbols contained in *slst* in the order in which they occur when *slst* is printed. Intuitively, *flatten* removes all the inner parentheses from its argument.

     ```
     > (flatten '(a b c))
     (a b c)
     > (flatten '((a b) c (((d)) e)))
     (a b c d e)
     > (flatten '(a b (() (c))))
     (a b c)
     ```

  5. (merge lon1 lon2), where *lon1* and *lon2* are lists of numbers that are sorted in ascending order, returns a sorted list of all the numbers in *lon1* and *lon2*.

```
> (merge '(1 4) '(1 2 8))
(1 1 2 4 8)
> (merge '(35 62 81 90 91) '(3 83 85 90))
(3 35 62 81 83 85 90 90 91)
```
□

- *Exercise 2.2.9*

  These are harder still:

  1. (path n bst), where *n* is a number and *bst* is a binary search tree that
     contains the number *n*, returns a list of Ls and Rs showing how to find the
     node containing *n*. If *n* is found at the root, it returns the empty list.

     ```
     > (path 17 '(14 (7 () (12 () ()))
                     (26 (20 (17 () ())
                             ())
                         (31 () ()))))
     (R L L)
     ```

  2. (car&cdr s slst errvalue) returns an expression that, when evaluated,
     produces the code for a procedure that takes a list with the same struc-
     ture as *slst* and returns the value in the same position as the leftmost
     occurrence of *s* in *slst*. If *s* does not occur in *slst*, then *errvalue* is
     returned.

     ```
     > (car&cdr 'a '(a b c) 'fail)
     (lambda (lst) (car lst))
     > (car&cdr 'c '(a b c) 'fail)
     (lambda (lst) (car (cdr (cdr lst))))
     > (car&cdr 'dog '(cat lion (fish dog) pig) 'fail)
     (lambda (lst) (car (cdr (car (cdr (cdr lst))))))
     > (car&cdr 'a '(b c) 'fail)
     fail
     ```

  3. (car&cdr2 s slst errvalue) is like the previous exercise, but it generates
     procedure compositions.

     ```
     > (car&cdr2 'a '(a b c) 'fail)
     car
     > (car&cdr2 'c '(a b c) 'fail)
     (compose car (compose cdr cdr))
     > (car&cdr2 'dog '(cat lion (fish dog) pig) 'fail)
     (compose car (compose cdr (compose car (compose cdr cdr))))
     > (car&cdr2 'a '(b c) 'fail)
     fail
     ```

Induction, Recursion, and Scope

4. (compose p1 ... pn), where *p1*, ..., *pn* is a sequence of zero or more procedures of one argument, returns the composition of all the procedures. The
   composition of zero procedures is the identity procedure, the composition
   of one procedure is the procedure itself, and the composition of two or more
   procedures is specified by this equation:

$$((\text{compose p1 p2 ...}) \ x) \Rightarrow (\text{p1} \ ((\text{compose p2 ...}) \ x))$$

```
> ((compose) '(a b c d))
(a b c d)
> ((compose car) '(a b c d))
a
> ((compose car cdr cdr) '(a b c d))
c
```

5. (sort lon) returns a list of the elements of *lon* in increasing order.

```
> (sort '(8 2 5 2 3))
(2 2 3 5 8)
```

6. (sort predicate lon) returns a list of elements determined by the predicate.

```
> (sort < '(8 2 5 2 3))
(2 2 3 5 8)
> (sort > '(8 2 5 2 3))
(8 5 3 2 2)
```
[]

2.3 Static Properties of Variables

Those properties of a program that can be determined by analyzing the text
of a program are said to be *static*, as opposed to the *dynamic* properties that
are determined by run-time inputs. It is important to determine if a property
is static, because static properties can be analyzed by a compiler to detect
errors before run time and to improve the efficiency of object code.

In Scheme, as in most other languages, the relation between a variable
reference and the formal parameter to which it refers is a static property. In
this section we focus on this relation and some of its important consequences.

2.3.1 Free and Bound Variables

In order to focus on variable binding with a minimum of distraction, we initially study it in the most abstract context possible. For this purpose we introduce a language that has only variable references, lambda expressions with a single formal parameter, and procedure calls.

⟨exp⟩ ::= ⟨varref⟩
    | (lambda (⟨var⟩) ⟨exp⟩)
    | (⟨exp⟩ ⟨exp⟩)

This language is called the *lambda calculus*. Although quite concise, its concepts generalize easily to most programming languages. For these reasons, the lambda calculus is the formal basis for much of the theory of programming languages.

The traditional syntax for procedures in the lambda calculus uses the Greek letter λ (lambda), replacing the second alternative in the above grammar with

$$\lambda\langle\text{var}\rangle \, . \, \langle\text{exp}\rangle$$

We use the keyword lambda and the extra parentheses so that these expressions look like Scheme expressions. Furthermore, since elements of ⟨exp⟩ are lists, it is convenient to write programs that manipulate them.

A variable reference is said to be *bound* in an expression if it refers to a formal parameter introduced in the expression. A reference that is not bound to a formal parameter in the expression is said to be *free*. Thus in

$$((\text{lambda (x) x) y}) \qquad\qquad (*)$$

the reference to x is bound and the reference to y is free. A variable is said to *occur bound* in an expression if the expression contains a bound reference to the variable. Similarly, a variable is said to *occur free* in an expression if the expression contains a free reference to the variable.

All variable references must have some associated value when they are evaluated at run time. If they are bound to a formal parameter, they are said to be *lexically bound*. Otherwise, they must either be bound at top level by definitions or be supplied by the system. In this case, they are said to be *globally bound*. It is an error to reference a variable that is neither lexically nor globally bound.

Induction, Recursion, and Scope

The value of an expression depends only on the values associated with the variables that occur free within the expression. The context that surrounds the expression must provide these values. For example, the value of (*) depends on the value of the free variable y. If (*) were embedded in the body of a lambda expression with formal parameter y, as in

$$\text{(lambda (y) ((lambda (x) x) y))},\qquad (**)$$

then the binding of this parameter would provide the value for the reference to variable y. Thus a variable reference that is free in one context, such as (*), may be bound in a larger surrounding context, such as (**).

The value of an expression is independent of bindings for variables that do not occur free in the expression. For example, the value of (*) is independent of any bindings that might exist for x at the time that (*) is evaluated. By the time the free occurrence of x in the body of (lambda (x) x) is evaluated, it will have a new binding (in (*), the value associated with y).

The meaning of (lambda (x) x) is always the same: it is the identity function that returns whatever value it is passed. Other lambda expressions without free variables also have fixed meanings. For example, the value of

```
(lambda (f)
  (lambda (x)
    (f x)))
```

is a procedure that takes a procedure, f, and returns a procedure that takes a value x, applies f to it, and returns the result. Lambda expressions without free variables are called *combinators*. A few combinators, such as the identity function and the above application combinator, are useful programming tools. We shall use more elaborate combinators in the procedural representation of data types, beginning in section 3.6.

Free and bound occurrences may be defined formally as follows:

A variable x *occurs free* in an expression E if and only if

1. E is a variable reference and E is the same as x; or

2. E is of the form $(E_1\ E_2)$ and x occurs free in E_1 or E_2; or

3. E is of the form (lambda $(y)\ E'$), where y is different from x and x occurs free in E'.

A variable x *occurs bound* in an expression E if and only if

1. E is of the form $(E_1\ E_2)$ and x occurs bound in E_1 or E_2; or
2. E is of the form (lambda $(y)\ E'$), where x occurs bound in E' or x and y are the same variable and y occurs free in E'.

No variable occurs bound in an expression consisting of just a single variable.

- *Exercise 2.3.1*

  Write a procedure `free-vars` that takes a list structure representing an expression in the lambda calculus syntax given above and returns a set, a list without duplicates, of all the variables that occur free in the expression. Similarly, write a procedure `bound-vars` that returns a set of all the variables that occur bound in its argument.

  Hint: The definitions of occurs free and occurs bound are recursive and based on the structure of an expression. Your program should have a similar structure. □

- *Exercise 2.3.2*

  Write predicates `free?` (respectively, `bound?`) that determines if an expression contains a free (respectively, bound) instance of a particular variable. □

- *Exercise 2.3.3*

  Give an example of a lambda calculus expression in which the same variable occurs both bound and free. □

- *Exercise 2.3.4*

  Give an example of a lambda calculus expression in which a variable occurs free but which has a value that is independent of the value of the free variable. □

○ *Exercise 2.3.5*

  Scheme `lambda` expressions may have any number of formal parameters, and Scheme procedure calls may have any number of operands. Modify the definitions of occurs free and occurs bound to allow `lambda` expressions with any number of formal parameters and procedure calls with any number of operands. □

○ *Exercise 2.3.6*

  Extend the formal definitions of occurs free and occurs bound to include `if` expressions. □

Induction, Recursion, and Scope

○ *Exercise 2.3.7*

What effect does `quote` have on the set of free and bound variables? □

2.3.2 Scope and Lexical Address

Associated with each declaration of a variable (as in a formal parameter list) is a *region* of text within which the declaration is effective. The region depends on the form of declaration. For example, in Scheme the region of a formal parameter is the body of the lambda expression, and the region of a top-level definition is the entire program (all text entered at top level). The *scope* of a variable declaration is the text within which references to the variable refer to the declaration. Alternatively, we may speak of the declarations that are *visible* at the point of a variable reference, meaning those that contain the variable reference within their scope. The region and scope of a variable may be the same, but we shall see that the scope does not include the entire region.

Declarations have a limited scope so that the same variable name may be used for different purposes in different parts of a program. For example, in this chapter we have repeatedly used `1st` as a formal parameter, and in each case its scope was limited to the body of the corresponding lambda expression.

In most languages, including Scheme, a declaration's region and scope can be determined statically. Such languages are said to be *lexically* or statically scoped. Most modern languages allow regions to be *nested* within each other, as when one lambda expression appears in the body of another. Regions are sometimes called *blocks,* and such languages are said to be *block structured*.

Block-structured languages do not allow declarations that use the same variable name to be associated with the same region. For example, the expression `(lambda (x x) ...)` is illegal. Declarations using the same variable name, however, may be nested. In this case the intention is clearly that the inner declaration supersedes the outer one. Thus the inner one creates a *hole* in the scope of the outer one. For example, consider

```
> (define x
    (lambda (x)
      (map (lambda (x) (+ x 1)) x)))
> (x '(1 2 3))
(2 3 4)
```

The region of the x declared on the first line is the read-eval-print loop's top level, which includes the body of the definition: however, its scope does not include the body of the defined procedure. The scope of the formal parameter x in the third line is the lambda expression's body, (+ x 1). This formal parameter creates a hole in the scope of the formal parameter x in the second line. The scope of the x in the second line includes the reference to x as the second argument to map, but not the reference to x as the first argument to +. The inner declarations of x *shadow* the outer declarations of x.

Thus the scope of a declaration is the region of text associated with the declaration, excluding any inner regions associated with declarations that use the same variable name. Put another way, the declaration of a variable v has a scope that includes all references to v that *occur free* in the region associated with the declaration. Those references to v that *occur bound* in the region associated with its declaration are shadowed by inner declarations.

There is a simple algorithm for determining to which declaration a variable reference refers. Search the regions enclosing the reference, starting with the innermost. As each successively larger region is encountered, check whether a declaration of the given variable is associated with the block. If one is found, that is the declaration of the variable. If not, proceed to the next enclosing region. If the outermost (top-level or global) region is reached and no declaration is found, the variable reference is unbound.

• *Exercise 2.3.8*

In the following expressions, draw an arrow from each variable reference to its associated formal parameter declaration.

```
(lambda (x)
  (lambda (y)
    ((lambda (x)
       (x y))
     x)))

(lambda (z)
  ((lambda (a b c)
     (a (lambda (a) (+ a c)) b))
   (lambda (f x)
     (f (z x)))))
```

☐

○ *Exercise 2.3.9*

Repeat the above exercise with programs written in another block-structured language. ☐

Induction, Recursion, and Scope

It is sometimes more helpful to picture the borders of regions, rather than the interiors of regions. These borders are called *contours*. Execution of the above algorithm may then be viewed as a journey outward from a variable reference. In this journey a number of contours may be crossed before arriving at the associated declaration. The number of contours crossed is called the *lexical* (or *static*) *depth* of the variable reference. For example, in

```
(lambda (x y)
  ((lambda (a)
     (x (a y)))
   x))
```

the reference to x on the last line and the reference to a both have lexical depth zero, while the references to x and y in the third line both have lexical depth one.

The declarations associated with a region may be numbered in the order of their appearance in the text. Each variable reference may then be associated with two numbers: its lexical depth and the position of its declaration in the declaring contour (its *declaration position*). Taken together, these two numbers are the *lexical address* of the variable reference.

To illustrate lexical addresses, we may replace every variable reference v in an expression by

$$(v : d\ p)$$

where d is its lexical depth and p is its declaration position. Using zero-based indexing for both d and p, the above example becomes

```
(lambda (x y)
  ((lambda (a)
     ((x : 1 0) ((a : 0 0) (y : 1 1))))
   (x : 0 0)))
```

Since the lexical address completely specifies each variable reference, variable names may be considered superfluous! That is, variable references could be replaced by expressions of the form (: $d\ p$), and formal parameter lists could be replaced by their length, as in

```
(lambda 2
  ((lambda 1
     ((: 1 0) ((: 0 0) (: 1 1))))
   (: 0 0)))
```

Variable names are certainly a great help in understanding programs, but they are not absolutely necessary in writing programs.

Compilers routinely calculate the lexical address of each variable reference. Once this has been done, the variable names may be discarded unless they are required to provide debugging information.

● *Exercise 2.3.10*

Consider the subset of Scheme specified by the BNF rules

⟨exp⟩ ::= ⟨varref⟩
    | (if ⟨exp⟩ ⟨exp⟩ ⟨exp⟩)
    | (lambda ({⟨var⟩}*) ⟨exp⟩)
    | ({⟨exp⟩}⁺)

Observe that a `lambda` expression can have zero formal parameters.

Write a procedure *lexical-address* that takes any expression and returns the expression with every variable reference v replaced by a list $(v : d\ p)$, as above. If the variable refers to a free variable, like `eq?` and `cons`, imagine that the entire expression is wrapped within a lambda that binds it. In the example below, it would be (lambda (eq? cons) (lambda (a b c) ...)).

```
> (lexical-address '(lambda (a b c)
                       (if (eq? b c)
                           ((lambda (c)
                              (cons a c))
                            a)
                           b)))
(lambda (a b c)
  (if ((eq? : 1 0) (b : 0 1) (c : 0 2))
      ((lambda (c)
         ((cons : 2 1) (a : 1 0) (c : 0 0)))
       (a : 0 0))
      (b : 0 1)))
```
□

● *Exercise 2.3.11*

What is wrong with the following lexical-address expression?

```
(lambda (a)
  (lambda (a)
    (a : 1 0)))
```
□

• *Exercise 2.3.12*
Write a Scheme expression that is equivalent to the following lexical-address expression from which variable names have been removed.

```
(lambda 1
  (lambda 1
    (: 1 0)))
```
☐

o *Exercise 2.3.13*
Write the procedure `un-lexical-address`, which takes lexical-address expressions with formal parameter lists and with variable references of the form (: *d p*), and returns an equivalent expression formed by substituting standard variable references for the lexical address information, or `#f` if no such expression exists.

```
> (un-lexical-address '(lambda (a)
                          (lambda (b c)
                            ((: 1 0) (: 0 0) (: 0 1)))))
(lambda (a) (lambda (b c) (a b c)))
> (un-lexical-address '(lambda (a) (lambda (a) (: 1 0))))
#f
```
☐

2.3.3 Renaming Variables

Since variable names are not strictly necessary, as we have just seen, the behavior of a procedure must surely be independent of the choice of its formal parameter names. Thus (lambda (*var*) *var*) is the identity combinator, regardless of what identifier *var* is chosen for its formal parameter.

From this observation we wish to obtain a general program transformation rule. (Other transformation rules will be introduced in chapter 4.) The general idea is that the meaning of a lambda expression is unchanged if the name of a formal parameter is changed along with all references to the parameter, however, there are two difficulties that must be avoided. First, the new variable name should not conflict with any other variable names used in that part of the program. Such a conflict occurs exactly in those cases where the new name is the same as the name of a variable that occurs free in the body of the original lambda expression. For example,

```
(lambda (x) (cons x '()))
```

is not the same as

```
(lambda (cons) (cons cons '()))
```

In this case the new binding of cons is said to *capture* the existing reference to another binding of cons.

The second difficulty occurs if an inner formal parameter declaration creates a hole in the scope of the outer formal parameter: the references to the inner declaration should not be changed. For example,

```
(lambda (x)
  ((lambda (x) (cons x '()))
   (cons x '())))
```

might be transformed to

```
(lambda (y)
  ((lambda (x) (cons x '()))
   (cons y '())))
```

but should not become

```
(lambda (y)
  ((lambda (x) (cons y '()))
   (cons y '())))
```

The result of substituting an expression y for all free occurrences of a variable x in an expression exp is written $exp[y/x]$ (or by some authors $[y/x]exp$ or $exp[x \leftarrow y]$), and may be read "exp with y for x." With this notation the general variable renaming rule for lambda expressions with one formal parameter may be expressed as

$$(\text{lambda } (var) \; exp) = (\text{lambda } (var') \; exp[var'/var])$$

where var' is any variable that does not occur free in exp. In the lambda calculus this is called α-*conversion*. Generalizing this rule to procedures with multiple formal parameters is straightforward.

Induction, Recursion, and Scope

∘ *Exercise 2.3.14*

Write a procedure `rename` that takes a lambda calculus expression *exp* and two variables `var1` and `var2` and returns *exp*[*var1*/*var2*] if `var1` does not occur free in *exp* and `#f` otherwise.

```
> (rename '(lambda (b) (b a)) 'c 'a)
(lambda (b) (b c))
> (rename '((lambda (x) x) x) 'y 'x)
((lambda (x) x) y)
> (rename '(a b) 'a 'b)
#f
```
☐

∘ *Exercise 2.3.15*

Use `rename` to write a procedure `alpha-convert` that takes a lambda expression *exp* of the form (lambda (*var*) *exp*), and a variable *v*, and returns (lambda (*v*) *exp*[*v*/*var*]), or `#f` if *v* occurs free in *exp*.

```
> (alpha-convert '(lambda (a) (lambda (b) (b a))) 'c)
(lambda (c) (lambda (b) (b c)))
> (alpha-convert '(lambda (x) ((lambda (x) x) x)) 'y)
(lambda (y) ((lambda (x) x) y))
> (alpha-convert '(lambda (x) (y x)) 'y)
#f
```
☐

2.4 Summary

Induction provides a powerful tool for specifying data. Backus-Naur Form, or BNF, is a convenient shorthand for expressing context-free inductive definitions. The structure of data can often be expressed concisely using BNF, as can the structure of programs. Structural induction is a technique for basing proofs on inductive data specifications.

Procedures may contain calls to themselves. Such procedures are said to be recursive. Many recursive procedures may be derived systematically from inductive specifications of their data. The structure of recursion in such procedures matches the inductive structure of the data definitions. Three examples, `remove-first`, `remove`, and `subst`, illustrate the use of inductive specifications, and will be the basis for later examples.

A variable reference may either be free in the context of a particular expression, or it may be bound to some formal parameter in the expression. Associated with each declaration is a region within which it has effect and a scope within which variable references using the same name refer to the variable introduced by the declaration. Regions may be nested in block-structured languages. The boundary of a region is called its contour.

Each variable reference is completely characterized by its lexical address. This consists of its lexical depth, the number of contours that separate it from its associated declaration, and the position of the declaration among others of the same contour.

Variable names may be systematically changed without changing the meaning of a program, provided the new name does not conflict with variables occurring free in the region of the renamed variable, and only references in the scope of the renamed variable are changed. This is called α-conversion.

3   Syntactic Abstraction and Data Abstraction

In this chapter we present several special forms that are precisely equivalent to syntactic patterns that are expressible in terms of existing forms. They are examples of *syntactic abstraction,* since they abstract common syntactic patterns. They are informally known as *syntactic sugar,* since they make a language more pleasant to use but add nothing of substance. First we introduce syntactic abstractions that are useful for creating local bindings and performing multi-way branches. We then present a record facility for Scheme that may be implemented via two more syntactic abstractions.

Our implementation of records hides details of how records are implemented. This provides an example of *data abstraction* and leads to a general discussion of *abstract data types.* These data types allow the development of programs that are independent of how their data is represented. One of the benefits of such *representation independence* is that data that is first represented, for simplicity, as first-class procedures may later be represented, for efficiency, as records or other more specialized data representations. The last section illustrates such transformations of data representation, which are extensively used throughout the rest of this book.

3.1   Local Binding

So far we have seen two ways to create bindings in Scheme. Definitions, as we use them, create *top-level* bindings whose region is the entire program. Lambda expressions, which yield procedures, create local bindings for their parameters when invoked. The region of these bindings is restricted to the body of the procedure. There is frequently a need to create local bindings for immediate use, rather than for use when a procedure is invoked. This section introduces two special forms for creating such bindings.

3.1.1 let

Consider the `if` expression of the first *subst* definition in section 2.2.2.

```
(define subst
  (lambda (new old slst)
    ...
    (if (symbol? (car slst))
        (if (eq? (car slst) old)
            (cons new (subst new old (cdr slst)))
            (cons (car slst) (subst new old (cdr slst))))
        (cons (subst new old (car slst))
              (subst new old (cdr slst))))
    ... ))
```

The expression (subst new old (cdr slst)) appears three times, and its value is always needed if *slst* is not null. It would be clearer if this value could be computed and bound to a variable, say cdr-result, before the expression is evaluated and then simply referred to by this name. Since this binding has no significance outside of this expression, the binding should be local to the expression. One way to accomplish this is to use a lambda expression whose body is the expression and invoke the resulting procedure immediately.

```
((lambda (cdr-result)
   (if (symbol? (car slst))
       (if (eq? (car slst) old)
           (cons new cdr-result)
           (cons (car slst) cdr-result))
       (cons (subst new old (car slst))
             cdr-result)))
 (subst new old (cdr slst)))
```

We treat (car slst) similarly, since it appears four times.

```
((lambda (car-value cdr-result)
   (if (symbol? car-value)
       (if (eq? car-value old)
           (cons new cdr-result)
           (cons car-value cdr-result))
       (cons (subst new old car-value)
             cdr-result)))
 (car slst)
 (subst new old (cdr slst)))
```

The original expression has now been simplified considerably. Furthermore, in the original expression (car slst) is evaluated two or three times (depending on which if branches are taken), whereas in the version above it is evaluated only once. This illustrates another advantage of local bindings: they can reduce the amount of computation. In our example, the amount of computation involved in taking the car of *slst* is small enough that this is of little significance, however, sometimes expressions that appear repeatedly involve a great deal of computation.

You probably sense the problem with the approach taken above: it is difficult for the eye to match the formal parameters with their associated operands. Looking at the expression above, it is not obvious that *cdr-result* is the value of (subst new old (cdr slst)). The let special form is provided to solve this problem. Using let, the definition of *subst* becomes

```
(define subst
  (lambda (new old slst)
    (if (null? slst)
        '()
        (let ((car-value (car slst))
              (cdr-result (subst new old (cdr slst))))
          (if (symbol? car-value)
              (if (eq? car-value old)
                  (cons new cdr-result)
                  (cons car-value cdr-result))
              (cons (subst new old car-value)
                    cdr-result))))))
```

In general, let expressions have the form

$$
\begin{array}{l}
\texttt{(let ((}var_1\ exp_1\texttt{)} \\
\qquad \ldots \\
\qquad \texttt{(}var_n\ exp_n\texttt{))} \\
\quad body\texttt{)}
\end{array}
$$

The region associated with the declarations of $var_1, \ldots, var_n$ is *body*. Each of the expressions $exp_1, \ldots, exp_n$ is evaluated, the variables $var_1, \ldots, var_n$ are bound to their values, and finally the expression *body* is evaluated and its value is returned. Thus the above form is precisely equivalent to

$$
\begin{array}{l}
\texttt{((lambda (}var_1\ \ldots\ var_n\texttt{)}\ body\texttt{)} \\
\quad exp_1\ \ldots\ exp_n\texttt{)}
\end{array}
$$

In fact, when some Scheme compilers see a `let` expression, they immediately translate it into this form. (They also typically implement `let` or the equivalent form efficiently by avoiding the creation of a procedure, as in figure 5.3.2.)

Sometimes when two local bindings are required, the value of one of them depends on the value of the other. In this case nested `let` expressions must be used. For example,

```
(let ((x 3))
  (let ((y (+ x 4)))
    (* x y)))
```

is *not* equivalent to

```
(let ((x 3)
      (y (+ x 4)))
  (* x y))
```

since in the latter expression the region of the new declaration of x is the body of the `let` expression and does *not* include the expression (+ x 4) used to define y. The `let` expression is equivalent to this lambda expression:

```
((lambda (x y) (* x y))
 3
 (+ x 4))
```

It is clear that (+ x 4) is not in the scope of the formal parameter x. Nested `let` expressions may also be used to create bindings for the same variable:

```
(let ((x 3))
  (let ((x (* x x)))
    (+ x x)))
```

Here the inner `let` creates a *hole* in the scope of the outer binding of x, but the hole does not include the expression (* x x). Thus the expression has value 18. If this is not clear, try replacing each `let` expression by the equivalent application of a procedure created by `lambda`.

• *Exercise 3.1.1*

What are the values of the following two expressions?

Syntactic Abstraction and Data Abstraction

```
(let ((x 5) (y 6) (z 7))
  (let ((x 13) (y (+ x y)) (z x))
    (- (+ x z) y)))

(let ((x 5) (y 6) (z 7))
  (+ (let ((z (+ x z))) (* z (+ z x)))
     (let ((z (* x y))) (+ z (* z (- z y))))))
```

▯

○ *Exercise 3.1.2*

Write `let->application`, which takes a `let` expression (represented as a list)
and returns the equivalent expression, also represented as a list: an application
of a procedure created by a `lambda` expression. Your solution should not
change the body of the `let` expression.

```
> (let->application '(let ((x 4) (y 3))
                       (let ((z 5))
                         (+ x (+ y z)))))
((lambda (x y)
   (let ((z 5))
     (+ x (+ y z))))
 4 3)
```

▯

3.1.2 `letrec`

Frequently it is desirable to bind procedures locally. For example, in
section 2.2 we defined the procedure *partial-vector-sum* for use by
vector-sum. If a procedure is not likely to be of use in other contexts, it
is good practice to restrict the scope of its binding to the section of code
where it is needed. Thus within the definition of *vector-sum* we would like
to use something like

```
(let ((partial-vector-sum
        (lambda (von n)
          (if (zero? n)
              0
              (+ (vector-ref von (- n 1))
                 (partial-vector-sum von (- n 1)))))))
  (partial-vector-sum von (vector-length von)))
```

but this does not work. Recall that the region of a `let` binding is restricted to the body of the `let`. The difficulty is that in *partial-vector-sum* the recursive call (`partial-vector-sum von (- n 1)`) is not within the scope of the binding for *partial-vector-sum*. The same difficulty arises whenever there is a need to bind a recursive procedure locally.

Scheme provides the special form `letrec` to make local recursive definitions. The general form follows:

$$\text{(letrec } ((var_1 \ exp_1)$$
$$\dots$$
$$(var_n \ exp_n))$$
$$body)$$

This is similar to `let`, except that the region of the declarations $var_1, \dots, var_n$ is the entire `letrec` expression, including the expressions $exp_1, \dots, exp_n$. Thus $exp_1, \dots, exp_n$ may define mutually recursive procedures. In most uses of `letrec`, $exp_1, \dots, exp_n$ are lambda expressions, but this is not required. It is required, however, that no reference be made to $var_1, \dots, var_n$ during the evaluation of $exp_1, \dots, exp_n$. For example,

```
(letrec ((x 3)
         (y (+ x 1)))
    y)
```

is illegal. This restriction is necessary because the bindings of $var_1, \dots, var_n$ cannot have values until $exp_1, \dots, exp_n$ have been evaluated. The requirement is easily met if these are lambda expressions, because references to variables within the body of a lambda expression are evaluated only when the resulting procedure is invoked, not when the lambda expression is evaluated. Thus

```
(letrec ((x 3)
         (y (lambda () (+ x 1))))
    (y))
```

is legal and evaluates to 4.

Using `letrec`, *vector-sum* may be defined as in figure 3.1.1. We no longer need to pass *von* to *partial-vector-sum*, since *von* does not change and the reference to *von* in the *vector-ref* call is within the scope of *vector-sum*. A simple example of mutual recursion using `letrec` is shown in the program of figure 3.1.2, where the procedures *even?* and *odd?* are defined for nonnegative integers.

There are several advantages to using `letrec`, or `let` for procedures, rather than using `define`:

Figure 3.1.1   The procedure `vector-sum` using `letrec`

```
(define vector-sum
  (lambda (von)
    (letrec ((partial-vector-sum
               (lambda (n)
                 (if (zero? n)
                     0
                     (+ (vector-ref von (- n 1))
                        (partial-vector-sum (- n 1)))))))
      (partial-vector-sum (vector-length von)))))
```

Figure 3.1.2   Example of mutual recursion

```
(letrec ((even? (lambda (n)
                  (if (zero? n)
                      #t
                      (odd? (- n 1)))))
         (odd? (lambda (n)
                  (if (zero? n)
                      #f
                      (even? (- n 1))))))
  (even? 3))
```

1. When studying a procedure call, finding a local definition is easier than finding a global one.

2. The code that could be affected by a modification to a procedure is limited to the scope of a local declaration.

3. Frequently the number of arguments required is reduced when a local declaration is used, because some bindings are provided by the context (as with `von` in the `vector-sum` example above).

4. By reducing the number of global definitions, the chance of a conflict occurring because the same name is used for more than one global definition is reduced. In large programs to which many people contribute code, this last point is very important. We shall have more to say about this in chapter 7.

We have seen that Scheme allows any expression to contain local definitions. Some languages allow local procedure declarations only in certain contexts, such as at the head of procedure declarations or even larger units such as files.

- *Exercise 3.1.3*

  Rewrite *subst* using `letrec`. □

○ *Exercise 3.1.4*

  The special forms `let` and `letrec` are both binding forms. Extend the definitions of *occurs free* and *occurs bound* to accommodate `let` and `letrec` expressions. Augment your programs *free-vars* and *bound-vars* to take your new rules into account. □

○ *Exercise 3.1.5*

  Extend the language of exercise 2.3.10 to include `let` and `letrec` expressions. Adapt your program *lexical-address* so that it recognizes `letrec` expressions. □

3.2 Logical Connectives

Most programming languages provide a means for expressing the *conjunction* of expressions with the connective *and*, which forms a logical expression that is true if and only if *all* its subexpressions are true. Similarly, logical *disjunction* may be expressed with the connective *or*, which forms an expression that is true if *any* of its subexpressions are true.

In some languages, *and* and *or* are provided as procedures. In this case, all the subexpressions of a conjunction or disjunction are always evaluated, since operands are evaluated prior to a procedure call. This may be unnecessary. As soon as a false subexpression of a conjunction is found, it is known that the entire expression is false, and when a true subexpression of a disjunction is found, true may be returned immediately. Evaluation of all the subexpressions of a conjunction or disjunction not only may result in wasted computation, but also restricts the way in which they may be used. For example, consider this conjunction:

```
(and (pair? x) (number? (car x)))
```

Since `car` may only be passed a pair, the second subexpression may be evaluated only if it is known that the first is true. Thus it would be an error to write such an expression if `and` were a procedure.

Therefore in many languages, including Scheme, logical conjunction and disjunction are implemented as special forms that evaluate their subexpressions from left to right and do not evaluate subexpressions unnecessarily. There is one more factor that complicates the special forms and and or in Scheme. Any value other than #f is treated as true, so when a value has been computed and found to be true, it may still be useful to return it as the result of an and or or expression. Thus and returns the value of its *last* subexpression if all its subexpressions are true, and or returns the value of its *first* true subexpression (or #f if none are true).

```
> (and 3 (number? #t))
#f
> (and #t (number? 3) 4)
4
> (or (number? #t) 3 4)
3
```

The special form and may be specified inductively. Defining (and *test*) to be equivalent to *test* provides the basis of the induction. The induction step specifies that

$$(\text{and } test_1 \ test_2 \ \ldots \ test_n)$$

is equivalent to

```
(if test₁
    (and test₂ ... testₙ)
    #f)
```

The special form or may also be specified inductively. Defining (or *test*) to be equivalent to *test* provides the basis. In the induction step, we are careful to record the value of the first subexpression so it may be returned without reevaluation if it is true. We specify that

$$(\text{or } test_1 \ test_2 \ \ldots \ test_n)$$

is equivalent to

```
(let ((*value* test₁))
  (if *value*
      *value*
      (or test₂ ... testₙ)))
```

where it is assumed that *value* does not occur free in $test_2, \ldots, test_n$.

○ *Exercise 3.2.1*

Write boolean procedures `and-proc` and `or-proc` as variable arity procedures. Can you think of any uses for these procedures where `and` and `or` could not be used? □

3.3 Branching

So far we have used only one built-in branching mechanism, `if`, which performs a two-way branch based on a single test. In this section we introduce the special forms `cond` and `case`, which perform multi-way branching based on multiple tests.

3.3.1 cond

The special form `cond` performs a multi-way branch based on a series of test expressions. Its syntax follows:

```
(cond
  (test₁ consequent₁)
  ...
  (testₙ consequentₙ)
  (else alternative))
```

Here `else` is a keyword that is part of the syntax of `cond`. The test expressions are evaluated in the order in which they occur until one returns true. The associated consequent expression is then evaluated, and its value is the value of the `cond` expression. If none of the test expressions are true, the alternative expression is evaluated and its value returned. Such `cond` expressions are thus equivalent to a nested series of `if` expressions of this form:

```
(if test₁
    consequent₁
    ...
      (if testₙ
          consequentₙ
          alternative) ...)
```

A `cond` expression with a single consequent is equivalent to a single `if` expression, in which case the `if` expression is generally preferred.

The (`else` *alternative*) clause is optional. If none of the test expressions are true and there is no `else` clause, the value of a `cond` expression is unspecified.

Using `cond`, we can rewrite our original version of `subst` as follows

```
(define subst
  (lambda (new old slst)
    (cond
      ((null? slst) '())
      ((symbol? (car slst))
       (if (eq? (car slst) old)
           (cons new (subst new old (cdr slst)))
           (cons (car slst) (subst new old (cdr slst)))))
      (else (cons (subst new old (car slst))
                  (subst new old (cdr slst)))))))
```

An `if` is still used in this example because both the consequent and alternative of the `if` expression are to be evaluated only if `(symbol? (car slst))` is true. If we started with this version of `subst` and then wished to use `let` as in the last section, we would first need to convert the `cond` expression into its corresponding nested `if` expression.

○ *Exercise 3.3.1*
Write a procedure `if->cond` that takes an if expression and returns the corresponding cond expression (but does not expand consequent expressions). What does this procedure do with `(if else 1 2)`? In addition, write a procedure `cond->if` that takes a cond expression as its argument and returns the corresponding if expression.

```
> (if->cond '(if a b c))
(cond (a b) (else c))

> (if->cond '(if a b (if c d (if e f g))))
(cond (a b) (c d) (e f) (else g))

> (if->cond '(if a (if x b c) (if d e f)))
(cond (a (if x b c)) (d e) (else f))

> (cond->if '(cond (a b) (c d) (else e)))
(if a b (if c d e))
```
▢

○ *Exercise 3.3.2*
Extend the language of exercise 2.3.10 to include cond expressions. Adapt your `lexical-address` program so that it recognizes cond expressions. ▢

3.3.2 `case`

A common form of multi-way branch involves comparison of a value with a fixed set of symbols or numbers. In Scheme this is facilitated by the special form `case` with the following syntax:

```
(case key
  (key-list₁  consequent₁)
  . . .
  (key-listₙ  consequentₙ)
  (else alternative))
```

where each *key-list* is a list of symbols, numbers, booleans, or characters, and the else clause is optional. The expression *key* is evaluated, and its value is compared with the key list elements. The *consequent* corresponding to the first matching key list element is then evaluated and its value returned. If no match is found, *alternative* is evaluated and its value returned, unless the else clause is omitted, in which case the value of the `case` expression is unspecified.

A `case` expression can always be transformed into an equivalent expression using `let` and `cond` as follows

```
(let ((*key* key))
  (cond
    ((memv *key* 'key-list₁) consequent₁)
    . . .
    ((memv *key* 'key-listₙ) consequentₙ)
    (else alternative)))
```

where the variable `*key*` does not occur free within the consequent or alternative expressions and the standard procedure `memv` takes a key and a list and returns true if the key is equal to an element of the list (using `eq?`, `=`, or `char=?`, as appropriate for the type of the key). Here, `let` is used so that *key* is only evaluated once. If *key* is simply a variable, the `let` could be omitted and the references to `*key*` replaced by this variable.

○ *Exercise 3.3.3*
Transcribe the following `case` expression into a `let` and `cond` expression.

```
(case (get-position-of item)
  ((one first 1) (car lst))
  ((two second 2) (cadr lst))
  (else (error "Invalid position")))
```

□

Transcribe the following `cond` expression into a `case` expression

```
(cond
  ((memv color '(red pink mauve)) 'reddish)
  ((memv color '(white off-white cream)) 'whiteish)
  ((memv color '(blue azure navy)) 'blueish)
  (else (error "Invalid color" color)))
```

☐

In the next section we introduce a third form for multi-way dispatch, called `variant-case`.

3.4 Records

So far we have seen two methods of creating compound data in Scheme: pairs (with which lists are made) and vectors. Elements of these structures are accessed by their position in the structure. Most programming languages support data structures, called *records* (or *structures*), whose elements are accessed by name. This section presents a record facility for Scheme that we use extensively in this book. (Though records are not a standard feature of Scheme, this facility may be implemented without difficulty in any Scheme system with a syntactic extension facility. See appendix A for details.)

3.4.1 `define-record`

Each type of record has a type name and a set of field names. Our record facility only supports the definition of new record types at top level using the special form `define-record`. Definitions have this general form:

$$(\texttt{define-record}\ name\ (field_1\ \ldots\ field_n))$$

This defines a procedure for creating records of type *name*, a predicate for identifying records of this type, and an accessing procedure for each field. The creation procedure, called `make-`*name*, takes n arguments and returns a new record of the given type with *field$_i$* containing the ith argument value. The type predicate, called *name*`?`, returns true only when passed records of the new type. The accessing procedures, called *name*`->`*field$_i$*, for $1 \leq i \leq n$, take a record of the new type and return the value of the indicated field.

For example, consider the representation of binary trees used in section 2.1:

⟨tree⟩ ::= ⟨number⟩ | (⟨symbol⟩ ⟨tree⟩ ⟨tree⟩)

Here a record type, call it `interior`, could be used with advantage to represent interior nodes. This allows us to assign names, say `symbol`, `left-tree`, and `right-tree`, to the three components of an interior node.

```
> (define-record interior (symbol left-tree right-tree))
> (define tree-1 (make-interior 'foo (make-interior 'bar 1 2) 3))
> (interior? tree-1)
#t
> (interior->symbol tree-1)
foo
> (interior->right-tree (interior->left-tree tree-1))
2
```

We now define *leaf-sum*, which sums the leaves of a tree.

```
(define leaf-sum
  (lambda (tree)
    (cond
      ((number? tree) tree)
      ((interior? tree) (+ (leaf-sum (interior->left-tree tree))
                           (leaf-sum (interior->right-tree tree))))
      (else (error "leaf-sum: Invalid tree" tree)))))
```

In general, a distinct record type may be used to represent each alternative of a BNF specification. Each nonterminal within an alternative is recorded in a field of the associated type of record. Using this approach, we require an additional record type to represent trees. We provide it with

```
(define-record leaf (number))
```

This makes it possible to distinguish a tree that consists of a single leaf from a number.

● *Exercise 3.4.1*
Redefine *leaf-sum* for trees with `leaf` records. ☐

Syntactic Abstraction and Data Abstraction

3.4.2 Variant Records and `variant-case`

A type that combines two or more other types as alternatives is called a *union* type. The tree type is a union of records of type `leaf` or `interior`. A union type all of whose alternatives are records is called a *variant record* type. Many languages provide support for unions or variant records. Though Scheme does not provide explicit means for declaring type unions, they may be used implicitly, as in the tree example above. The alternatives of the union can be distinguished using the predicates provided for each type.

In this book we shall make frequent use of variant records, so it is convenient to have a special facility for branching on the type of the record. Furthermore, when the type has been identified, it is helpful to bind some or all of its field values to variables named after the fields. The special form `variant-case` performs both of these services. Its syntax is

$$
\begin{array}{l}
(\texttt{variant-case}\ \textit{record-expression} \\
\quad (\textit{name}_1\ \textit{field-list}_1\ \textit{consequent}_1) \\
\quad \cdots \\
\quad (\textit{name}_n\ \textit{field-list}_n\ \textit{consequent}_n) \\
\quad (\texttt{else}\ \textit{alternative}))
\end{array}
$$

where for $1 \leq i \leq n$, *field-list*$_i$ is a list of fields for records of type *name*$_i$. (Each record type should be distinct, as should the field names within a given field name list.) First, *record-expression* is evaluated, resulting in some value v. If v is not a record of one of the indicated types, *alternative* is evaluated and its value returned. If v is a record of type *name*$_i$, each of the names in *field-list*$_i$ is bound to the value of the field of v with the same name. Then *consequent*$_i$ is evaluated within the region of these bindings and its value returned.

For example, using `variant-case`, it is easy to define *leaf-sum* for a tree built from records of the type defined above.

```
(define leaf-sum
  (lambda (tree)
    (variant-case tree
      (leaf (number) number)
      (interior (left-tree right-tree)
        (+ (leaf-sum left-tree) (leaf-sum right-tree)))
      (else (error "leaf-sum: Invalid tree" tree)))))
```

The `symbol` field of the record type `interior` is not used, so it need not be mentioned. This is equivalent to

```
(define leaf-sum
  (lambda (tree)
    (let ((*record* tree))
      (cond
        ((leaf? *record*)
         (let ((number (leaf->number *record*)))
           number))
        ((interior? *record*)
         (let ((left-tree (interior->left-tree *record*))
               (right-tree (interior->right-tree *record*)))
           (+ (leaf-sum left-tree) (leaf-sum right-tree))))
        (else (error "leaf-sum: Invalid tree" tree))))))
```

In this case the outer let expression is clearly unnecessary because the *record expression* is simply the variable tree. As in the expansion of case, however, the outer let expression is in general necessary since *record-expression* should only be evaluated once. Care must also be taken, as in the case expansion, that the variable introduced by this let expression does not appear free in any of the expansions of the *alternative* or *consequent* expressions.

- *Exercise 3.4.2*
  Use variant-case to write *max-interior*, which takes a binary tree of numbers with at least one interior node and returns the symbol associated with an interior node with a maximal leaf sum.

  ```
  > (define tree-a (make-interior 'a (make-leaf 2) (make-leaf 3)))
  > (define tree-b (make-interior 'b (make-leaf -1) tree-a))
  > (define tree-c (make-interior 'c tree-b (make-leaf 1)))
  > (max-interior tree-b)
  a
  > (max-interior tree-c)
  c
  ```

  The last invocation of *max-interior* might also have returned a, since both the a and c nodes have a leaf sum of 5. Your program should not perform more additions than necessary, which means that *leaf-sum* cannot be used. Instead, use an auxiliary procedure that is similar to *max-interior* but returns both the symbol of a maximal sum node and the value of the maximal sum. Use a new type of record to contain both the symbol and the sum. Returning multiple values in this way is another important use of records. □

3.4.3 Abstract Syntax and its Representation Using Records

Programs that process other programs, such as interpreters or compilers, are usually *syntax directed*. What is done with each part of a program is guided by knowledge of the grammar rules associated with the part, and any subparts corresponding to nonterminals in the grammar rules should also be readily accessible. For example, when processing the lambda calculus expression `(lambda (x) (f (f x)))`, we must first recognize it as a lambda expression, corresponding to the BNF rule

⟨exp⟩ ::= (lambda (⟨var⟩) ⟨exp⟩)

Then the formal parameter is `x` and the body is `(f (f x))`. The body must in turn be recognized as an application, and so on.

An *abstract syntax* is a representation that identifies the syntactic rule associated with each syntactic component and provides ready access to subcomponents. Syntax that is designed for human consumption is *concrete syntax*.

In designing an abstract syntax for a given concrete syntax, we must name each production of the concrete syntax and each occurrence of a nonterminal in each production. The same nonterminal occurrence name may not be used twice in the same production. For the lambda calculus syntax introduced in the last chapter we might choose the names given on the right below, where the nonterminal occurrence names in parentheses are listed in the order of their appearance in the production. This grammar also differs from the previous one, since we include numbers.

⟨exp⟩ ::= ⟨number⟩	`lit (datum)`
| ⟨varref⟩	`varref (var)`
| (lambda (⟨var⟩) ⟨exp⟩)	`lambda (formal body)`
| (⟨exp⟩ ⟨exp⟩)	`app (rator rand)`

The symbols `lit`, `varref`, `app`, `rator`, and `rand` abbreviate *literal, variable reference, application, operator,* and *operand,* respectively.

The abstract syntax representation of an expression is most readily viewed as an *abstract syntax tree*. For example, see figure 3.4.1 for the abstract syntax tree of the lambda calculus expression `(lambda (x) (f (f x)))`. Each node of the tree corresponds to a step in a syntactic derivation of the expression, with internal nodes labeled with their associated production name. Edges are labeled with the name of the corresponding nonterminal occurrence. Leaves

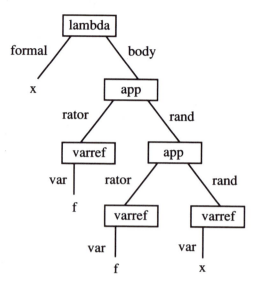

Figure 3.4.1   Abstract syntax tree for (lambda (x) (f (f x)))

correspond to terminal strings. (Leaves associated with terminals such as parentheses, which convey no information, are usually omitted from abstract syntax.)

○ *Exercise 3.4.3*
Generate a syntactic derivation and associated abstract syntax tree for the lambda calculus expression ((lambda (a) (a b)) c). □

In programs, abstract syntax is best represented by variant records. A record type is associated with each production name, and the fields are named after the corresponding nonterminal occurrences. Thus for the lambda calculus with numbers we use the following record definitions:

```
(define-record lit (datum))
(define-record varref (var))
(define-record lambda (formal body))
(define-record app (rator rand))
```

If a program is represented as a string of characters, it may be a complex business to derive the corresponding abstract syntax tree. This task, which is called *parsing*, is unrelated to whatever we may wish to do with the abstract syntax tree. Thus the job of parsing is best performed by a separate program, called a *parser*. Since abstract syntax trees are produced by parsers, they are also known as *parse trees*. Chapter 11 provides a general introduction to parsers.

If the concrete syntax of a language happens also to be list structures (including symbols and numbers), the parsing process is greatly simplified. For example, every expression specified by the previous lambda calculus grammar is also a list structure. Thus the Scheme `read` routine automatically parses these expressions into lists and symbols. It is still of value to parse these list structures into abstract syntax trees based on the record types previously defined. This is easily accomplished as follows:

```
(define parse
  (lambda (datum)
    (cond
      ((number? datum) (make-lit datum))
      ((symbol? datum) (make-varref datum))
      ((pair? datum)
       (if (eq? (car datum) 'lambda)
           (make-lambda (caadr datum) (parse (caddr datum)))
           (make-app (parse (car datum)) (parse (cadr datum)))))
      (else (error "parse: Invalid concrete syntax" datum)))))
```

If we would like to view an expression represented in abstract syntax, it is useful to be able to "unparse" it. We need only convert it back to the list and symbol representation, and the Scheme print routines will then display it in its concrete syntax. This is performed by the following procedure.

```
(define unparse
  (lambda (exp)
    (variant-case exp
      (lit (datum) datum)
      (varref (var) var)
      (lambda (formal body)
        (list 'lambda (list formal) (unparse body)))
      (app (rator rand) (list (unparse rator) (unparse rand)))
      (else (error "unparse: Invalid abstract syntax" exp)))))
```

A version of *free-vars* (exercise 2.3.1) that takes a parsed expression may be defined as follows.

```
(define free-vars
  (lambda (exp)
    (variant-case exp
      (lit (datum) '())
      (varref (var) (list var))
      (lambda (formal body) (remove formal (free-vars body)))
      (app (rator rand)
        (union (free-vars rator) (free-vars rand))))))
```

where `union` appends two lists of symbols and removes duplicates. A comparison of this definition with your solution to exercise 2.3.1 illustrates the utility of abstract syntax and `variant-case`.

○ *Exercise 3.4.4*
The procedure `parse` above does not detect several possible syntactic errors, such as `(a b c)`, and aborts with inappropriate error messages for other expressions, such as `(lambda)`. Modify `parse` so that it will accept any list structure and issue an appropriate error message if it does not represent a lambda calculus expression. □

• *Exercise 3.4.5*
Write a predicate `free?` that takes a variable, v, and a lambda calculus expression in abstract syntax and indicates whether v occurs free in it. Also rewrite the procedure *bound-vars* of exercise 2.3.1 using *parse*.

```
> (free? 'x (parse '(lambda (y) (x (x y)))))
#t
> (free? 'y (parse '(lambda (y) (x (x y)))))
#f
```
□

Where a Kleene star or plus is used in concrete syntax, it is most convenient to use a *list* of associated subtrees when constructing an abstract syntax tree. For example, consider a variant of the exercise 2.3.10 syntax:

$\langle exp \rangle ::= \langle number \rangle$	lit (datum)
$\| \langle varref \rangle$	varref (var)
$\| (if \langle exp \rangle \langle exp \rangle \langle exp \rangle)$	if (test-exp then-exp else-exp)
$\| (lambda (\{\langle var \rangle\}^*) \langle exp \rangle)$	lambda (formals body)
$\| (\langle exp \rangle \{\langle exp \rangle\}^*)$	app (rator rands)

Here `formals` and `rands` are associated with lists of formal parameters and operand expressions, respectively.

○ *Exercise 3.4.6*

Define the record types and parse procedure for the above grammar. Then implement `lexical-address` of exercise 2.3.10 using abstract syntax. It will be helpful to extend the abstract syntax with this definition:

```
(define-record lex-info (var distance position))
```

These records represent the lexical distance and position information of a given variable reference. The value returned by `lexical-address` may then be generated using an unparse procedure that takes an abstract syntax tree of the form indicated by the above grammar, but with `lex-info` records in place of `varref` records. □

3.4.4 An Implementation of Records

As we have presented them so far, records are *abstract* in the sense that we have not committed to a specific representation of records. They could be represented as vectors, or lists, or even binary trees built with pairs, or they might be provided by a Scheme implementation in a form distinct from all other types. We shall have more to say shortly about the importance of such data abstraction.

To conclude this section, we present one possible implementation of records, in which they are represented as vectors. In many cases this is the most efficient representation in terms of both storage space and field access time. The first element of the vector that represents a record is a symbol identifying the record type. The remaining elements contain the field values in the order in which the fields appeared in the type's `define-record` statement. For example,

```
> (parse '(lambda (x) (y x)))
#(lambda x #(app #(varref y) #(varref x)))
```

From now on we assume this representation of records when record values are printed. Given this representation, the tree leaf record definition

```
(define-record leaf (number))
```

would produce definitions equivalent to

```
(define make-leaf
  (lambda (number)
    (vector 'leaf number)))

(define leaf?
  (lambda (obj)
    (and (vector? obj)
         (= (vector-length obj) 2)
         (eq? (vector-ref obj 0) 'leaf))))

(define leaf->number
  (lambda (obj)
    (if (leaf? obj)
        (vector-ref obj 1)
        (error "leaf->number: Invalid record" obj))))
```

○ *Exercise 3.4.7*
Assuming this vector representation of records, directly define the five procedures that result from this record definition:

```
(define-record interior (symbol left-tree right-tree))
```
☐

3.5 Data Abstraction

Data representations are often complex, so we do not want to be concerned with their details when we can avoid them. For example, a table might be stored as a balanced binary search tree, but we need not be concerned with the details of maintaining and searching a balanced tree when invoking procedures that update or access the table. We may also decide to change the representation of the data. The most efficient representation is often a lot more difficult to implement, so we may wish to develop a simple implementation first and only change to a more efficient representation if it proves critical to the overall performance of a system. For example, unbalanced binary trees, or even a simple list, may provide adequate performance as representations of tables, and they are much easier to implement than balanced trees. It is also frequently not known which representation will be most efficient until considerable experience has been obtained with a system, perhaps including experimentation with alternative representations. If we decide to change the representation of some data for any reason, we must be able to locate all parts of a program that are dependent on the representation.

Details of the representation of data should be isolated, both so details of the representation do not complicate our understanding of a program and so the representation can be readily changed. This is accomplished using *data abstraction* techniques. The approach is to define a small set of procedures that create and operate on a given type of data and allow only these procedures direct access to the data. This set of procedures and the chosen data representation constitute an *abstract data type,* or *ADT*. Since access to data of an ADT is only possible through the procedures of the ADT, the rest of a program is independent of the representation chosen for the data. This property is *representation independence*. It ensures that if the representation is changed, only the procedures of the ADT are affected.

The properties of an ADT may be specified in ways that are independent of the representation, and only these properties are of concern when using the procedures of the ADT. Such specifications provide an *interface* between the ADT and the rest of the program. ADT specifications may take the form of equations relating the procedures of the type. The study of formal equational specification techniques is beyond the scope of this book, but whether the specification technique is formal or informal, the data abstraction principle on which the specification is based is of primary importance.

The record mechanism introduced in the last section is an example of data abstraction. The procedures defined by `define-record` are in effect an ADT for a new record type, however, this abstraction mechanism is flawed. There is nothing to prevent procedures other than those created by `define-record` from being applied to records in ways that expose, or even corrupt, the representation we have chosen. We have already seen one example of this: the representation is exposed when records are printed. The following transcript reveals other difficulties.

```
> (interior? tree-1)
#t
> (vector? tree-1)
#t
> (vector-ref tree-1 0)
interior
```

In some systems, types are *disjoint,* that is, each value is of one and only one type. The predicate calls in this transcript demonstrate that `tree-1` has both type *interior* and type *vector,* however, so vector and record types are not disjoint. Furthermore, the *vector-ref* call above reveals that records are represented as vectors with the record name in the first element.

If the representation of a type is hidden, so it cannot be exposed by any operation (including printing), the type is said to be *opaque*. Otherwise, it is said to be *transparent*. The *primitive* (built-in) types in Scheme are procedure, number, pair, vector, character, symbol, string, boolean, and empty list. These types are mutually disjoint and opaque. Lists are a *derived* type consisting of pairs and the empty list. No attempt at abstraction is made with the list type, since it shares the construction and selection procedures `cons`, `car`, and `cdr` with the pair type. The empty list is a *singleton* type with only one element, which is tested for with the type predicate `null?`.

We would like records to be opaque types, but there is no standard mechanism in Scheme for creating new opaque types. (The ability to define new opaque types is problematic. Opaque types are hard to debug, since you cannot see inside them.) Thus we settle for the intermediate level of abstraction provided by our record facility. As long as no procedures other than those created by `define-record` are used to create, identify, and access records, our programs will be independent of the representation chosen for records. Though we do not use a formal mechanism for defining new abstract types, we informally define a number of types in this book. Representation independence is maintained provided that only the procedures associated with the type are used to create and access elements of the type.

In section 7.1 we consider language mechanisms that encapsulate the data and operations of an ADT in an opaque object.

- *Exercise 3.5.1*
Define the procedures of the `interior` and `leaf` record types in the last section such that records are represented as lists rather than vectors. Verify that `leaf-sum` works without modification using the new procedures. □

3.6 From Procedural to Data Structure Representations

In the last section we saw that when data abstraction is used, programs have the property of representation independence: programs are independent of the particular representation used to implement an abstract data type. It is then possible to change the representation by redefining the small number of procedures belonging to the ADT. In later chapters we shall frequently exploit representation independence. Initially we represent data as procedures. This "high-level" representation concisely conveys the intended semantics of the data type. (Another advantage of using procedures to represent a new type is that the representation is in a way opaque, since procedures are themselves usually opaque. For instance, when printing them, we can see that they are procedures, but no more.) We then convert to the record representation, which is usually more efficient and can be implemented in a straightforward manner in low-level languages (including assembly language) that do not support first-class procedures.

3.6.1 Procedural Representation

In this section we illustrate the transformation from procedural to record representation using a data type for *finite functions*. A finite function associates a value with each element of a finite set of symbols. There are many uses for finite functions. One example is an *environment*, which associates variables with their values in a programming language implementation. A *symbol table*, which among other things may associate variables with lexical address information at compile time, is another example (see exercise 12.4.12).

The simplest way of creating finite functions is to have a representation of the empty finite function, which makes no associations, and a way of adding a new symbol/value association to an existing finite function. This motivates the interface of our finite-function ADT, which consists of three procedures:

1. `create-empty-ff` is a procedure of no arguments that returns the empty finite function, which makes no associations.

2. `extend-ff` takes a symbol, `sym`, a value, `val`, and a finite function, `ff`, and returns a new finite function that preserves the associations of `ff` and also associates `sym` with `val`. Any association with `sym` that might already exist in `ff` is ignored by the new finite function.

3. `apply-ff` takes a finite function and a symbol and returns the value associated with the symbol.

In mathematics a finite function is generally represented as a set of pairs, such as $\{(d, 6), (x, 7), (y, 8)\}$, which may be constructed and accessed as follows.

```
> (define dxy-ff
    (extend-ff 'd 6
      (extend-ff 'x 7
        (extend-ff 'y 8
          (create-empty-ff)))))
> (apply-ff dxy-ff 'x)
7
```

A finite function may be represented as a Scheme procedure that takes a symbol and returns the associated value. With this representation, the finite-function interface may be defined as follows:

```
(define create-empty-ff
  (lambda ()
    (lambda (symbol)
      (error "empty-ff: no association for symbol" symbol))))

(define extend-ff
  (lambda (sym val ff)
    (lambda (symbol)
      (if (eq? symbol sym)
          val
          (apply-ff ff symbol)))))

(define apply-ff
  (lambda (ff symbol)
    (ff symbol)))
```

The empty finite function, created by invoking *create-empty-ff*, indicates with an error message that the given symbol is not in its domain. The procedure *extend-ff* returns a new procedure that represents the extended finite function. Finally, the procedure *apply-ff* simply performs procedure application.

3.6.2 Record Representation

This procedural representation is easy to understand, but it requires that procedures be first-class objects. We can systematically transform this representation into one using records by noting the information that is contained in each of the finite-function procedures. There are only two kinds of finite-function procedures: the ones returned by creating an empty finite function and those returned by *extend-ff*. The specification of what is to be done when one of these procedures is invoked is given by the bodies of their respective (lambda (symbol) ...) expressions. Since these bodies do not change, the finite functions themselves need only contain an indication of which kind of procedure they represent so that the appropriate actions may be taken when *apply-ff* is invoked. But in the (lambda (symbol) ...) lambda expression of *extend-ff*, the variables sym, val, and ff occur free. A procedure created by evaluating a lambda expression must record the values of all variables that occur free in the body of the lambda expression. The values recorded must be the bindings that are in effect *at the time the procedure is created.*

We conclude that we can capture the information that is unique to each finite-function procedure with two record types:

```
(define-record empty-ff ())
(define-record extended-ff (sym val ff))
```

We can implement the finite-function abstraction by redefining *create-empty-ff* and *extend-ff* to build the appropriate records and by redefining *apply-ff* to interpret the information in these records and perform the actions specified by the body of the appropriate (lambda (symbol) ...) expression. The definition of the finite-function ADT using this new representation follows:

```
(define create-empty-ff
  (lambda ()
    (make-empty-ff)))

(define extend-ff
  (lambda (sym val ff)
    (make-extended-ff sym val ff)))

(define apply-ff
  (lambda (ff symbol)
    (variant-case ff
      (empty-ff ()
        (error "empty-ff: no association for symbol" symbol))
      (extended-ff (sym val ff)
        (if (eq? symbol sym)
            val
            (apply-ff ff symbol)))
      (else (error "apply-ff: Invalid finite function" ff)))))
```

Observe that the consequent expressions of the variant-case expression are *exactly* the same as the bodies of the respective (lambda (symbol) ...) expressions in the procedural representation. Also, the definitions above could be replaced by these two:

```
(define create-empty-ff make-empty-ff)
(define extend-ff make-extended-ff)
```

With this representation, the last transcript might continue as follows.

```
> dxy-ff
#(extended-ff d 6 #(extended-ff x 7 #(extended-ff y 8 #(empty-ff))))
```

The importance of the technique illustrated above for transforming a procedural representation into a record representation is its generality. It may be applied to *any* set of procedures that represents an ADT, provided that these procedures are always invoked by an apply procedure that is specific to the data type. The key steps in the transformation follow:

1. Identify the lambda expressions whose evaluation yields values of the type, and create a distinct record type for each of these expressions.

2. Identify the free variables in these lambda expressions whose values are distinct for each element, and allocate a field of the corresponding record type for each of these variables.

3. Define the apply procedure for the type using a `variant-case` expression with one case per record type, where the variable list of each case lists the free variables identified in (2) and the consequent expression of each case is the body of the corresponding lambda expression.

Suppose we wish to define a procedure *extend-ff** that takes a list of symbols, *sym-list*, a list of values, *val-list*, and a finite function, *ff*, and returns a new finite function that associates each symbol of *sym-list* with the value in the corresponding position in *val-list*, as well as maintaining the associations of *ff* for symbols other than those in *sym-list*. It happens that *extend-ff** can be defined entirely in terms of existing elements of the finite-function interface.

```
(define extend-ff*
  (lambda (sym-list val-list ff)
    (if (null? sym-list)
        ff
        (extend-ff (car sym-list) (car val-list)
          (extend-ff* (cdr sym-list) (cdr val-list) ff)))))
```

Sometimes, however, new procedures on a data type can be defined only in terms of the underlying representation of the type, so the procedure must be added to the interface of the type. In other cases it may be desirable to extend the interface for reasons of efficiency. To illustrate how such situations may be handled, we employ the technique introduced above to add *extend-ff** to the finite-function interface. We always begin extensions of an ADT by returning to the original procedural representation and then repeating the transformation to other representations with whatever modifications are necessary to accommodate the new addition.

Thus we first define *extend-ff** to directly return a new procedure representing a finite function. This is simplified by making use of the procedure *ribassoc* of exercise 2.2.7.

```
(define extend-ff*
  (lambda (sym-list val-list ff)
    (lambda (symbol)
      (let ((val (ribassoc symbol
                  sym-list (list->vector val-list) '*fail*)))
        (if (eq? val '*fail*)
            (apply-ff ff symbol)
            val)))))
```

(We assume the symbol **fail** is not in the range of the finite function.) Since the value returned by (list->vector val-list) is always the same for a given finite-function procedure, a let expression may be used to compute this vector only once and bind its value in the newly created finite-function procedure. We have

```
(define extend-ff*
  (lambda (sym-list val-list ff)
    (let ((val-vector (list->vector val-list)))
      (lambda (symbol)
        (let ((val (ribassoc symbol sym-list val-vector '*fail*)))
          (if (eq? val '*fail*)
              (apply-ff ff symbol)
              val))))))
```

The free variables in the (lambda (symbol) ...) expression above that vary from one evaluation to the next are sym-list, val-vector, and ff. This motivates two new definitions and an extension of our earlier definition of *apply-ff*.

```
(define-record extended-ff* (sym-list val-vector ff))

(define extend-ff*
  (lambda (sym-list val-list ff)
    (make-extended-ff* sym-list (list->vector val-list) ff)))
```

```
(define apply-ff
  (lambda (ff symbol)
    (variant-case ff
      (empty-ff ()
        (error "empty-ff: no association for symbol" symbol))
      (extended-ff (sym val ff)
        (if (eq? symbol sym)
            val
            (apply-ff ff symbol)))
      (extended-ff* (sym-list val-vector ff)
        (let ((val (ribassoc symbol sym-list val-vector '*fail*)))
          (if (eq? val '*fail*)
              (apply-ff ff symbol)
              val)))
      (else (error "apply-ff: Invalid finite function" ff)))))
```

```
> (define ff1 (extend-ff* '(d x y) '(6 7 8) (create-empty-ff)))
> (define ff2 (extend-ff* '(a b c) '(1 2 3) ff1))
> (apply-ff ff2 'd)
6
> ff2
#(extended-ff* (a b c) #(1 2 3)
   #(extended-ff* (d x y) #(6 7 8) #(empty-ff)))
> (define ff3 (extend-ff* '(d e) '(4 5) ff2))
> (apply-ff ff3 'd)
4
> (apply-ff ff3 'a)
1
> ff3
#(extended-ff* (d e) #(4 5)
   #(extended-ff* (a b c) #(1 2 3)
      #(extended-ff* (d x y) #(6 7 8) #(empty-ff))))
```

3.6.3 Alternative Data Structure Representations

As mentioned above, the transformation from procedure to record representation is completely general, so we can always use it as a first step in deriving
data structure representations. In many cases we can exploit patterns in the

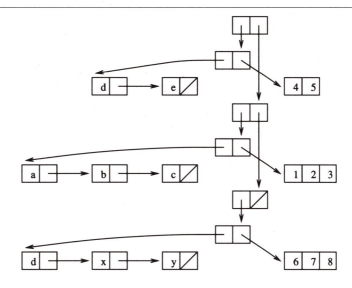

Figure 3.6.1   Ribcage environment structure

record representations to obtain further simplifications. Assume for example that **extend-ff** is no longer part of the finite-function interface.

In this case all finite functions are built by starting with the empty finite function and applying **extend-ff*** n times, for some $n \geq 0$. Thus the resulting representations are always of the form

$$\texttt{\#(extended-ff*}\ \textit{sym-list}_n\ \textit{val-vector}_n$$
$$\cdots$$
$$\texttt{\#(extended-ff*}\ \textit{sym-list}_1\ \textit{val-vector}_1$$
$$\texttt{\#(empty-ff))}\ \cdots)$$

where $\textit{sym-list}_i$ and $\textit{val-vector}_i$ were contributed by the ith application of **extend-ff***. The information in this record structure can be represented in other ways, which may be more convenient or efficient. One natural representation would be as a list of pairs, where the ith pair joins $\textit{sym-list}_i$ and $\textit{val-vector}_i$. The resulting general form would be

$$((\textit{sym-list}_n\ \ .\ \ \textit{val-vector}_n)$$
$$\cdots$$
$$(\textit{sym-list}_1\ \ .\ \ \textit{val-vector}_1))$$

This list may be pictured as a ribcage, where each *sym-list/val-vector* pair is a pair of ribs joined by a cons cell (see figure 3.6.1). The procedure `ribassoc` was named with this picture in mind.

- *Exercise 3.6.1*
  Define the finite-function ADT using the ribcage representation. ☐

○ *Exercise 3.6.2*
  Write `extend-ff` in terms of `extend-ff*`. ☐

○ *Exercise 3.6.3*
  Another way for `ribassoc` to handle its error condition is to return a *list* containing the associated value as its only element, or `#f` if there is no associated value. Thus if the associated value is `#f`, then `(#f)` is returned, and `#f` ≠ `(#f)`. Of course the `errvalue` argument to `ribassoc` is no longer needed. Implement `ribassoc` and `apply-ff` using this technique. ☐

3.7 Summary

Some important patterns of usage are not expressible as procedures. Some of these are encapsulated as syntactic abstractions. These include the local binding forms `let` and `letrec`, the logical connectives `and` and `or`, and the multi-way branching forms `cond` and `case`. The syntactic abstractions `define-record` and `variant-case` provide an interface for manipulating variant records. Abstract syntax represents the syntactic structure of an expression as a tree.

An abstract data type, or ADT, establishes an interface to a class of data. It is then possible to change the representation of this data by changing only the procedures that implement the interface. Programs that use the interface need not be modified. This is the principle of data abstraction.

Frequently it is convenient to initially represent data as procedures. Such a representation can then be transformed systematically into one based on records, in which each record contains the same dynamic information in the corresponding procedure, with the static information collected in a single procedure that interprets the records.

4   Reduction Rules and Imperative Programming

In this chapter we first introduce transformation rules for reasoning about procedures. These rules are studied, for simplicity, in the context of the lambda calculus. We next show how an evaluation mechanism for the lambda calculus may be obtained from these transformation rules and survey the main features of this mechanism.

In the second part of this chapter we introduce assignment and evaluation sequencing, along with a few facilities for input/output. A simple approach to object-oriented programming is presented as an example of the interaction between environment sharing and assignment. Finally, we use these techniques to provide several implementations of an abstract data type for streams. These are useful for representing input sequences when experimenting with programming language implementations developed in later chapters.

4.1   Reasoning about Procedures

In chapter 1 we informally introduced procedures as they are created and used in Scheme. In this section we consider procedures in a more formal light to isolate some simple rules for reasoning about programs.

To determine the result of a procedure call, we must look at the body of the procedure being called. When a reference to one of the procedure's formal parameters is encountered in the body, we can imagine the corresponding argument from the call as appearing in place of the variable. For example, given the definition

```
(define foo
  (lambda (x y)
    (+ (* x 3) y)))
```

and the procedure call

```
(foo (+ 4 1) 7)
```

we might obtain the result by evaluating (+ (* (+ 4 1) 3) 7), yielding 22.

The rule we have used here may be stated informally as follows:

> The result of a procedure call may be obtained by substituting the call's operands for the corresponding variables in the procedure's body.

As we shall see, we shall need some restrictions (to be spelled out in section 4.3.1) to make this rule an accurate description of what happens in most languages (including Scheme), but in cases where it applies, it is a valuable tool for reasoning about programs.

We can express this kind of reasoning by writing a derivation in which at each step some subexpression is replaced by an equivalent subexpression. For example, we can record the reasoning above with this derivation:

```
    (foo (+ 4 1) 7)

⇒ ((lambda (x y) (+ (* x 3) y))
    (+ 4 1)
    7)

⇒ (+ (* (+ 4 1) 3) 7)

⇒ 22
```

For brevity, we sometimes omit steps of the first kind, in which a reference to a defined procedure is replaced by the definition of the procedure.

Alternatively, we might first find the arguments of the call by evaluating the operands, and then substitute literal representations of these arguments for occurrences of the corresponding formal parameters in the body of the procedure. The following derivation applies this kind of reasoning to the same example:

```
    (foo (+ 4 1) 7)

⇒ (foo 5 7)

⇒ (+ (* 5 3) 7)

⇒ (+ 15 7)

⇒ 22
```

We obtained the final answer by replacing calls to standard procedures with literal operands by a literal representing the value of the call.

As another example, the result of the call ((c+ 5) 3) using the curried procedure

```
(define c+
  (lambda (n)
    (lambda (m)
      (+ n m))))
```

can be obtained by the following derivation:

```
    ((c+ 5) 3)

⇒ ((lambda (m) (+ 5 m)) 3)

⇒ (+ 5 3)

⇒ 8
```

We saw in the last chapter that some special forms, such as let, are just syntactic sugar for other forms. Sugaring rules can also be expressed as transformations. For example,

$$(\text{let } ((var_1 \ exp_1) \ \ldots \ (var_n \ exp_n))$$
$$body)$$

$$\Rightarrow ((\text{lambda } (var_1 \ \ldots \ var_n) \ body)$$
$$exp_1 \ \ldots \ exp_n)$$

Such rules may be used in conjunction with procedure call substitutions of the type introduced in this section to derive the value of this complex expression:

```
    (let ((x 3)
          (add5 (c+ 5)))
      (add5 x))

⇒ (let ((x 3)
          (add5 (lambda (m) (+ 5 m))))
      (add5 x))
⇒ ((lambda (x add5) (add5 x))
     3
     (lambda (m) (+ 5 m)))
```

```
⇒ ((lambda (m) (+ 5 m)) 3)

⇒ (+ 5 3)

⇒ 8
```

In the preceding discussion, we have used the phrase "literal representation of a value" several times. We cannot put values themselves in expressions. The examples above have used only numeric literals, so it may be difficult to see the difference. The difference becomes clear when the values include lists. We mark the literal representation of a list with `quote`.

```
(let ((second (lambda (x) (car (cdr x)))))
  (second (list 1 2 3)))

⇒ ((lambda (second) (second (list 1 2 3)))
   (lambda (x) (car (cdr x))))

⇒ ((lambda (x) (car (cdr x)))
   (list 1 2 3))

⇒ ((lambda (x) (car (cdr x)))
   '(1 2 3))

⇒ (car (cdr '(1 2 3)))

⇒ (car '(2 3))

⇒ 2
```

In this example, if we had used the list (1 2 3) itself in the expression (car (cdr (1 2 3))), we would have had an application of the number 1 to some arguments, which is not what was intended. The use of `quote` marks the occurrence of the literal representation of the list in the expression.

4.2 The Lambda Calculus and β-Conversion

In order to study these transformation rules with a minimum of distraction, we initially study it in the most abstract context possible. This is the language of the *lambda calculus*, which was introduced in section 2.3.1. This language has only variable references, `lambda` expressions with a single formal parameter, and procedure calls. It is given by the following grammar:

$\langle exp \rangle ::= \langle varref \rangle$
$\qquad | \text{ (lambda } (\langle var \rangle) \text{ } \langle exp \rangle))$
$\qquad | \text{ (}\langle exp \rangle \text{ } \langle exp \rangle))$

Constants are frequently added to the lambda calculus. They make it more convenient to express intuitive examples. We use numbers as constants.

$\langle exp \rangle ::= \langle number \rangle$

This does not affect the theoretical properties of the lambda calculus.

In this language, the transformation rule applies to calls of the form

$$((\text{lambda } (var) \text{ } exp) \text{ } rand)$$

The basic idea is that such an expression is equivalent to the expression obtained by replacing references to *var* in *exp* by *rand*. Using the notation introduced to define variable renaming in chapter 2, this replacement can be expressed concisely as *exp*[*rand*/*var*]. As with variable renaming, however, care must be taken to avoid conflicts due to different uses of the same variable name. In this case the difficulty is that free variables in *rand* may be captured by bindings of *var* in the lambda expression, or by other lambda expressions in *exp*. For example, it would be incorrect to transform

```
((lambda (x)
   (lambda (y) (x y)))
 (y w))
```

into

```
(lambda (y) ((y w) y))
```

The reference to `y` in `(y w)` should remain free, but it has been captured by the inner lambda expression. This is wrong, because the `y` in `(y w)` refers to the current value of `y` in the original expression (perhaps `c+` defined above), but in the transformed expression it refers to the value of the `y` to which the resulting procedure will be applied. Admittedly this example is contrived, but this sort of thing can easily happen in much more complicated expressions, where it might go undetected unless care is taken.

The solution is to change the name of the inner variable `y` to some name, say `z`, that does not occur free in the argument `(y w)`:

```
((lambda (x)
   (lambda (z) (x z)))
 (y w))
```

This expression is equivalent, by the α-conversion rule, to our original example. Now we can perform the substitution without capturing the reference to y, obtaining

```
(lambda (z) ((y w) z))
```

So, in order to make our procedure-application rule precise, we need to formalize the substitution process in a way that avoids variable capture.

We inductively define the substitution of M for x in E, written $E[M/x]$. The induction is based on the form of E, with separate rules for each form of expression in the lambda calculus. If E is the variable x, the result is M.

$$x[M/x] = M.$$

If E is any other variable, y, or a constant, c, the result is simply that variable or constant

$$y[M/x] = y,$$
$$\text{where } y \text{ is distinct from } x.$$
$$c[M/x] = c$$

If E is an application of the form $(F\ G)$, we simply perform the substitution on F and G.

$$(F\ G)[M/x] = (F[M/x]\ G[M/x]).$$

The interesting case is when E is of the form (lambda (y) E'). If y is the same as x (the variable we are replacing), no further replacements should be done, since there are no free occurrences of x in (lambda (x) E'). The lambda creates a hole in the scope of the outer x.

$$(\text{lambda } (x)\ E')[M/x] = (\text{lambda } (x)\ E').$$

Also, no further replacement is required if x does not occur free in E'.

$$(\text{lambda } (y)\ E')[M/x] = (\text{lambda } (y)\ E'),$$
$$\text{where } x \text{ does not occur free in } E'.$$

If $y \neq x$ and y does not occur free in M, then we can perform the substitution on E'.

$$(\text{lambda } (y) \ E')[M/x] = (\text{lambda } (y) \ E'[M/x]),$$

where y does not occur free in M.

The only case left is the most interesting one: $y \neq x$, x occurs free in E', and y occurs free in M. This is the situation in which accidental capture will occur. The solution is to rename y (using α-conversion) to some other name, say z, that does not occur free in E' or M

$$(\text{lambda } (y) \ E')[M/x] = (\text{lambda } (z) \ (E'[z/y])[M/x]),$$

where z does not occur free in E' or M.

Given this rigorous definition of substitution, the rule we have been seeking for procedure calls is simply

$$((\text{lambda } (x) \ E) \ M) = E[M/x].$$

This is called *β-conversion* (β is pronounced "beta".) An expression of the form

$$((\text{lambda } (x) \ E) \ M)$$

to which this rule may be applied is called a *β-redex*.

When the β-conversion rule is used in the left-to-right direction to transform a β-redex, it is called *β-reduction*. As we shall see, the term "reduction" is appropriate because β-reduction may be used to reduce expressions to their "simplest" form.

The β-conversion rule may also be used in the right-to-left direction. This is what is done when `let` is introduced into a program to avoid repetition of some expression. For example,

```
((f (a (b c))) (a (b c)))
```

$\Rightarrow$ `((lambda (x) ((f x) x))`
`(a (b c)))`

$\Rightarrow$ `(let ((x (a (b c))))`
`((f x) x))`

- *Exercise 4.2.1*

Use β-reductions to simplify the following expressions as much as possible.

1.   ```
     ((lambda (x) (x (y x)))
      z)
     ```

2.   ```
     ((lambda (x) (x y))
      (lambda (y) (x y)))
     ```

3.   ```
     ((lambda (x)
        (lambda (y) ((x y) z)))
      (lambda (a) y))
     ```

4.   ```
     ((lambda (x)
        (lambda (y)
          ((lambda (x) (z x))
           (lambda (y) (z y)))))
      (lambda (y) y))
     ```

◻

o *Exercise 4.2.2*

Write a predicate `beta-redex?` that takes a parsed lambda calculus expression and indicates whether it is a β-redex. Use a parser like the one in section 3.4.3 to test `beta-redex?`.

```
> (beta-redex? (parse '(lambda (x) (y z))))
#f
> (beta-redex? (parse '((lambda (x) (y x)) z)))
#t
> (beta-redex? (parse '(lambda (x) ((lambda (x) (y x)) z))))
#f
```

◻

o *Exercise 4.2.3*

Write a procedure `substitute`, that takes two expressions, *e* and *m*, and a variable *x*, and returns $e[m/x]$. The definition of this procedure should closely follow the inductive definition of substitution given above. When α-conversion is required, it is necessary to obtain a variable that does not occur free either in the body of the lambda expression or in the operand that is being substituted. Most systems include the procedure *gensym*, which generates a new symbol guaranteed to be distinct from all other symbols. If *gensym* is not available, see exercise 4.6.3 for a simplified one, which we call `next-symbol`.

```
> (unparse (substitute (parse '(a b)) (parse 'c) 'b))
(a c)
> (unparse (substitute (parse '(lambda (a) (a b))) (parse 'a) 'b))
(lambda (g01234) (g01234 a))
```

The symbol g01234 is typical of those produced by **gensym**. □

- *Exercise 4.2.4*
  Write a procedure `beta-reduce` that takes a parsed β-redex and returns the result of applying the β-reduction rule.

  ```
  > (unparse (beta-reduce (parse '((lambda (x) (y x)) z))))
  (y z)
  > (unparse (beta-reduce (parse '((lambda (x) (lambda (y) (x y)))
                                   (y w)))))
  (lambda (g01235) ((y w) g01235))
  ```

  What would happen if `beta-reduce` were called with

  ```
  (parse '((lambda (x) (x x)) (lambda (x) (x x))))
  ```

  and why? □

  We noted earlier in section 3.6 that

  ```
  (define extend-ff
    (lambda (sym val ff)
      (make-extended-ff sym val ff)))
  ```

  was equivalent to

  ```
  (define extend-ff make-extended-ff)
  ```

Since the first version simply passes its arguments along unchanged to **make-extended-ff**, it behaves in exactly the same way as **make-extended-ff**, so it might as well be **make-extended-ff**.

This is an application of a general rule, which when simplified (so it applies only to procedures with a single operand) may be stated as

$$(\text{lambda } (x) \ (E \ x)) = E$$

where E denotes a function of one variable and x does not occur free in E.

In the lambda calculus this is known as η-*conversion* (η is pronounced "eta"), or when applied only from left to right, η-*reduction*. An expression on the left-hand side of this equation is an η-*redex* if x does not occur free in E. Though not as fundamental as β-conversion, this is at times a useful optimization.

Write a predicate **eta-redex?** that takes a parsed lambda calculus expression
and indicates whether it is an η-redex.

```
> (eta-redex? (parse '(lambda (x) (y x))))
#t
> (eta-redex? (parse '(lambda (x) ((lambda (y) y) x))))
#t
> (eta-redex? (parse '((lambda (x) (y x)) z)))
#f
> (eta-redex? (parse '(lambda (x) ((lambda (y) x) x))))
#f
```

□

○ *Exercise 4.2.6*

Write a procedure **eta-reduce** that takes a parsed η-redex and returns the
result of applying the η-reduction rule.

```
> (unparse (eta-reduce (parse '(lambda (x) ((lambda (y) y) x)))))
(lambda (y) y)
```

□

○ *Exercise 4.2.7*

Write a procedure **eta-expand** that takes a parsed expression **exp** (that may
be presumed to denote a function of one argument) and returns a parsed
expression of the form (for some x not free in **exp**)

$$(\text{lambda } (x) (exp \ x))$$

```
> (unparse (eta-expand (parse '(lambda (y) y))))
(lambda (g01236) ((lambda (y) y) g01236))
> (unparse (eta-expand (parse '((lambda (v) (lambda (y) (v y)))
                                (lambda (x) x)))))
(lambda (g01238)
  (((lambda (v) (lambda (y) (v y)))
    (lambda (x) x))
   g01238))
```

□

4.3 Reduction Strategies

We have seen how β-reduction can be used to model the effect of evaluating an application. We need more information, however, before we can use this model to transform expressions to their answers. The problem is that a lambda expression may have more than one redex, so there may be more than one way to reduce the expression. We saw that in the very first example in this chapter, where in

```
((lambda (x y) (+ (* x 3) y))
 (+ 4 1)
 7)
```

we could reduce either the β-redex or the (+ 4 1). In that example, we were lucky: both reduction sequences gave the same answer, 22.

This leads to an important question: *Can an expression be reduced to more than one constant?* Fortunately, no. This is not at all obvious, since an expression may have many redexes and nothing has been said about the order in which reductions are performed. There is an important theorem, however, called the *Church-Rosser theorem,* which says that if an expression E can be reduced to either $E1$ or $E2$, using different reduction sequences, then there is some expression N that can be reached from both $E1$ and $E2$. This is called the *Church-Rosser, confluence,* or *diamond* property. The latter term refers to the figure below, in which arrows represent reduction sequences.

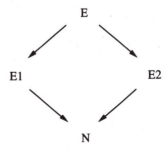

Figure 4.3.1   Diamond Property

How does this theorem answer our question? If an expression reduced to two different constants, then the Church-Rosser theorem says that there would have to be some other term N to which both constants reduced. But constants cannot be reduced! So there could not have been two different constants to which our expression is reducible.

This is helpful, but does the Church-Rosser theorem tell us that we can apply β-reduction blindly and be guaranteed to find an answer? No, because not every expression is reducible to a constant. Consider

```
((lambda (x) (x x))
 (lambda (x) (x x)))
```

This expression is a β-redex, but β-reduction results in the same expression. (Try it.)

Perhaps a weaker result holds: does the Church-Rosser theorem tell us that if an answer exists, we can find it by blindly applying β-reduction? Again, the answer is no. Some expressions reduce to a constant, but still have infinite reduction sequences in which the computation could get lost. Consider this example:

```
((lambda (y) 3)
 ((lambda (x) (x x))
  (lambda (x) (x x))))
```

The whole expression is a β-redex, which reduces immediately to 3, since y does not occur free in the body of the first lambda expression. However, the operand of this application is just the expression we used above as an example of an expression that does not reduce to a constant. Therefore a reduction sequence that repeatedly reduced the operand expression would never find the answer for the whole expression. So different strategies for reducing an expression may differ in whether or not they find an answer, but they will always agree on the constant they find.

4.3.1 Applicative-Order Reduction

We began studying the lambda calculus because we wanted to reason about procedures in Scheme. Therefore the next question is: *What reduction strategy best models the behavior of Scheme?* It is a strategy called *applicative-order reduction*. For applicative-order reduction, an *answer* is either a constant, a variable, or an abstraction (a lambda expression): anything but an application. In applicative-order reduction, β-reduction may be applied only if both the operator and operand are already answers. If they are not, then either the operator or the operand can be reduced. A redex in the body of an abstraction is never reduced, and η-reduction is never applied. This variation is sometimes called the *lambda-value calculus*.

We can now rephrase a version of the β rule to be accurate for Scheme:

$$((\texttt{lambda } (x)\ E)\ M) = E[M/x]$$

where M is an answer.

Let us develop a procedure *reduce-once-appl* that takes a (parsed) lambda calculus expression and reduces the first redex it finds according to applicative-order reduction, if there is such a redex, and returns the entire reduced expression. If the expression is a constant, a variable, or a lambda-expression, it cannot be reduced. If the expression is an applicative β-redex, we simply perform the reduction (using `beta-reduce` from exercise 4.2.4) and return the result. If it is an application but not a β-redex, we first try to reduce the operator. If this fails (the operator is already an answer), then we try to reduce the operand. Whenever we succeed in reducing a subexpression, we must construct a new expression that contains the reduced form of the subexpression.

Somehow we must indicate whether a call to *reduce-once-appl* succeeds in performing a reduction or fails. One way to do this would be to return a special value indicating failure, as was done with *ribassoc* in exercise 2.2.7. This is somewhat awkward, for every time *reduce-once-appl* is called, the value it returns must be recorded using `let`, and then this value must be tested, since the way the computation continues depends on whether a reduction was performed. Here we use another approach. We pass *reduce-once-appl* two additional arguments: a procedure *succeed* that is passed the reduced expression in the event of success, and a procedure *fail* of no arguments that is invoked if the reduction fails.

Thus the specification for *reduce-once-appl* is

(reduce-once-appl exp succeed fail) =
    (*succeed exp′*) if *exp* contains an applicative β-redex, in which case *exp′*
       is the result of performing one applicative-order reduction on *exp*, or
    (*fail*) if *exp* has no applicative β-redex.

The procedures *succeed* and *fail* are called *continuations*, because they indicate how the computation is to continue in the event of success or failure. The technique of passing one or more continuations to a procedure is of use in a number of contexts. Chapter 8 is devoted to a study of continuations, and they are used extensively in chapters 8–11. For another example, see exercise 4.3.3.

Figure 4.3.2   `reduce-once-appl` for the lambda calculus

```
(define answer?
  (lambda (exp)
    (not (app? exp))))

(define reduce-once-appl
  (lambda (exp succeed fail)
    (variant-case exp
      (lit (datum) (fail))
      (varref (var) (fail))
      (lambda (formal body) (fail))
      (app (rator rand)
        (if (and (beta-redex? exp) (answer? rand))
            (succeed
              (beta-reduce exp))
            (reduce-once-appl rator
              (lambda (reduced-rator)
                (succeed
                  (make-app reduced-rator rand)))
              (lambda ()
                (reduce-once-appl rand
                  (lambda (reduced-rand)
                    (succeed
                      (make-app rator reduced-rand)))
                  fail)))))))
```

Using this approach, the `reduce-once-appl` procedure may now be defined as in figure 4.3.2. Note that if reduction of an application's `rator` fails, `fail` tries to reduce the `rand`. When `reduce-once-appl` is called with the `rand` there is nothing else to try if the reduction fails, so `fail` is passed as the failure continuation. The next two exercises are easily solved by invoking `reduce-once-appl` with the appropriate success and failure continuations.

- *Exercise 4.3.1*
Write a procedure `reduce-history` that takes an unparsed lambda calculus expression, `exp`, and a positive integer, `n`, and returns a list of unparsed expressions indicating a (perhaps incomplete) reduction history of `exp`. The last element in the list is the answer, or the result of the nth reduction if the answer cannot be obtained in n reductions. For example,

```
> (reduce-history '((lambda (x) (x ((lambda (x) y) z))) w) 5)
((w ((lambda (x) y) z))
 (w y))
> (reduce-history '((lambda (x) (x x)) (lambda (x) (x x))) 3)
(((lambda (x) (x x)) (lambda (x) (x x)))
 ((lambda (x) (x x)) (lambda (x) (x x)))
 ((lambda (x) (x x)) (lambda (x) (x x))))
```
[]

- *Exercise 4.3.2*

  Write a procedure *reduce∗* that takes an unparsed lambda calculus expression, *exp*, and a positive integer, *n*, and returns the answer for *exp* if it can be obtained by *n* or fewer applicative-order reductions, and #f otherwise.

  ```
  > (reduce* '((lambda (x) (x ((lambda (x) y) z))) w) 5)
  (w y)
  > (reduce* '((lambda (x) (x x)) (lambda (x) (x x))) 100)
  #f
  ```
  []

- *Exercise 4.3.3*

  Write *ribassoc* using success and failure continuations and use it to rewrite *apply-ff* with the ribcage representation. []

o *Exercise 4.3.4*

  Modify *reduce-once-appl* so it can deal with standard procedures like +. []

4.3.2 Leftmost Reduction

Applicative-order reduction is a good model of Scheme's behavior on procedures, but we have seen that it may fail to find an answer, even if one exists. For example, applicative order fails on

```
((lambda (y) 3)
 ((lambda (x) (x x)) (lambda (x) (x x))))
```

because it will be caught in an infinite loop trying to reduce the operand to an answer. The next question is: *Is there a reduction strategy which is guaranteed to find the answer if it exists?* Yes, it is called *leftmost* reduction, and it is the strategy of reducing the β-redex whose left parenthesis comes first.

In fact, leftmost reduction does better than just finding constants. Let us say that a lambda expression is in *normal form* if it contains no β-redexes. If an expression is in normal form, then no further reduction is possible. For example, (lambda (x) x) is in normal form, but is not a constant. By the same argument we used above, the Church-Rosser theorem leads us to the conclusion that an expression can have at most one normal form. It can be shown that leftmost reduction will always find the normal form of an expression, if one exists. For this reason, leftmost reduction is sometimes called *normal order* reduction.

Leftmost reduction obtains this generality, however, at the expense of efficiency. For example, consider the following leftmost reduction sequence, in which the operand ((lambda (w) w) z) is reduced twice:

```
    ((lambda (x) (x (x y)))
     ((lambda (w) w) z))

⇒  (((lambda (w) w) z)
    (((lambda (w) w) z)
     y))

⇒  (z (((lambda (w) w) z) y))

⇒  (z (z y))
```

If the operand ((lambda (w) w) z) is reduced before calling the procedure (lambda (x) (x (x y))), one less reduction is required to obtain the normal form.

```
    ((lambda (x) (x (x y)))
     ((lambda (w) w) z))

⇒  ((lambda (x) (x (x y)))
    z)

⇒  (z (z y))
```

In general, applicative-order reduction is more efficient than leftmost reduction. Therefore, most modern programming languages use some variation on applicative-order reduction. There are a few languages that use leftmost reduction to guarantee that a normal form will be found whenever one exists. Compilers for these languages typically do an extensive analysis (called strictness analysis) to find those places where it is safe to use applicative-order reduction. (See section 6.5 for related strategies.)

We can easily modify the procedure of figure 4.3.2 to do leftmost reduction. If the expression is a variable or a constant, it cannot be reduced. If the expression is a `lambda` expression, then the leftmost redex, if it exists, must be in the expression's body, so we can call the reduction procedure recursively to perform the reduction. If the expression is a β-redex, we simply perform the reduction (using `beta-reduce` from exercise 4.2.4) and return the result. If it is an application but not a β-redex, we first try to reduce the leftmost redex in the operator. If this fails, then we try to reduce the operand. Whenever we succeed in reducing a subexpression, we must construct a new expression that contains the reduced form of the subexpression.

- *Exercise 4.3.5*
  Modify *reduce-once-appl* to obtain a procedure *reduce-once-leftmost* that implements one step of leftmost reduction. ☐

○ *Exercise 4.3.6*
  Modify *reduce-once-leftmost* to use η-reduction as well as β-reduction. ☐

4.4 Defining Recursive Procedures in the Lambda Calculus

We conclude our discussion of the lambda calculus by considering the problem of expressing recursive procedures. The lambda-calculus, unlike Scheme, does not have a `letrec` or `define` mechanism. So how are we to define a recursive procedure in the lambda calculus?

Assume *exp* is a lambda expression defining a recursive procedure, where recursion is performed by reference to a variable, say *g*, that occurs free in *exp*. That is, *g* is supposed to be a name for the same procedure as *exp*. The variable *g* must itself be introduced by a lambda expression, such as

$$(\text{lambda } (g) \ exp)$$

For example, to define a procedure that computes the factorial function, we might write something like

```
(lambda (g)
  (lambda (n)
    (if (zero? n) 1 (* n (g (- n 1))))))
```

where we are assuming the lambda calculus is extended with if, zero?, *, -
and 1, and where g is intended to be bound to the factorial function. Call
this expression f. How can it be turned into the recursive factorial function?

We need to write a procedure, called Y, such that (Y f) is the desired recursive procedure. The assumption that recursion may be obtained by reference
to g may be satisfied by binding g to (Y f) with the application (f (Y f)).
But since f also returns the recursive procedure, we conclude that Y should
satisfy this equation:

$$(Y\ f)\ =\ (f\ (Y\ f))$$

Can Y be written as a lambda expression, or must it be added to the lambda
calculus as a special feature? Remarkably, Y can be defined as

```
(lambda (f)
  ((lambda (x) (f (x x)))
   (lambda (x) (f (x x)))))
```

This is called the *Y combinator,* since it has no free variables. Notice that the
Y combinator has no normal form.

• *Exercise 4.4.1*
Verify, by β-conversion, that the Y combinator satisfies the equation (Y f) =
(f (Y f)). ☐

This version of Y does not work when applicative order reduction is used.
Reduction of the subexpression (x x) results in divergence. This may be
prevented by η-expanding the (x x) subexpressions to obtain the *applicative
order Y combinator.*

```
(lambda (f)
  ((lambda (x) (f (lambda (y) ((x x) y))))
   (lambda (x) (f (lambda (y) ((x x) y))))))
```

This also demonstrates that η-conversion can affect termination under applicative order reduction. In the most common cases in which it is used,
however, where the simpler form is merely a variable reference, termination
is not a problem.

• *Exercise 4.4.2*
Use the applicative order Y combinator to define the factorial function in
Scheme. ☐

Here we have considered the definition of only a single recursive procedure. Mutual recursion is also possible using the Y combinator, but it presents added technical difficulties. The general approach is to pass Y a procedure that represents a record structure containing all the mutually recursive procedures, which refer to each other by selecting the appropriate fields of the record. (All manner of data structures can be represented as lambda expressions using appropriate tricks.)

○ *Exercise 4.4.3*
Implement mutual recursion using the Y combinator and test it using `even?` and `odd?` of section 3.1.2. □

We are able to touch on only the highlights of the lambda calculus. Though the syntax and evaluation rules of the lambda calculus are very simple, the calculus provides an extraordinarily rich framework for the study of programming languages (as well as issues in mathematical logic, for which it was invented). For example, it is possible to translate numbers and other data objects into lambda calculus expressions and implement customary operators such as addition in terms of other expressions in the lambda calculus. In fact, *any* algorithm can be translated into the lambda calculus. Of particular interest to the study of programming languages, many programming language features, and sometimes entire languages, are conveniently defined by specifying methods for translating them into the lambda calculus. The simplicity of the lambda calculus then makes it easier to prove theoretical results. Fascinated readers are urged to explore the references suggested at the end of the book.

4.5 Sequencing and Imperative Programming

The subset of Scheme introduced so far is purely *functional*—every expression is evaluated just for its value. No other effects of evaluation need be considered. We have seen that many problems can be solved in a straightforward manner using only functional programming. This is especially true when procedures are first class. We have also seen that we can reason about functional programs using simple, yet powerful, rules.

Yet in some situations the purely functional style is awkward or inefficient. Therefore most programming languages, including Scheme, support *imperative* operations that are performed not to obtain a value but rather for some *side effect* on the computation. These may be broadly characterized as assignment and input/output operations. When operations perform side effects, the order of their evaluation is critical. This introduces the need for *sequencing* mechanisms.

Though imperative programming sometimes allows problems to be solved in a more efficient and straightforward way than is possible using functional programming, imperative programs are often more complicated and more difficult to reason about than equivalent functional programs. In particular, the β-conversion and η-conversion rules presented in the last section are *not* applicable when imperative operations are involved. For example, consider a case in which an operand is not fully reduced before multiple copies of it are made in a β-reduction step. If further reduction of these copies involves side effects, they will occur multiple times—once for each copy. On the other hand, with applicative order reduction the side effects would occur only once. But the result of a computation should be the same regardless of the reduction order (providing the reduction sequence terminates).

In this section we introduce those imperative operations and sequencing mechanisms that will be required later. A few applications of these operations are introduced by way of example. Special attention is given to one application: the development of several implementations of a *stream* ADT. Streams provide a convenient way of connecting and interacting with the program analysis and evaluation procedures developed in chapter 5. We do not attempt a careful study of when the functional or imperative styles of programming are most appropriate. For this, the interested reader is urged to consult the suggested readings mentioned at the end of this book.

4.5.1 Sequencing

Sequencing refers to the order in which side effects are performed. In statement-oriented languages, sequencing is indicated simply by the ordering of statements. In an expression-oriented language, sequencing is required only for expressions that result in side effects. For these, Scheme provides this special form:

$$(\texttt{begin } exp_1 \; exp_2 \; \ldots \; exp_n)$$

The expressions $exp_1, exp_2, \ldots, exp_n$ are evaluated in order, and the value of exp_n is the value of the entire begin expression. The values of the other expressions are discarded. (We shall sometimes informally use the term *statement* when referring to expressions that are evaluated entirely for their side effects. With this usage, $exp_1, exp_2, \ldots, exp_{n-1}$ are statements.)

For our examples, we use two output procedures: *display*, which prints its argument (omitting the quotes when printing strings), and *newline*, which has no arguments and simply forces further output to begin on a new line. As with most standard procedures that produce side effects, the values returned by these procedures are not specified. Implementations may return anything, so programs should never rely on the value returned.

The following example illustrates the use of begin and some peculiarities of output programming.

```
> (begin (display "Two plus two = ") (display (+ 2 2)))
Two plus two = 44
>
```

Where did the extra 4 come from? It is the unspecified value that happened to be returned by the second call to *display*, which was printed as the value of the begin expression by the read-eval-print loop. It is on the same line as the displayed output because we forgot to print a newline at the end of the line. A different value might be returned by *display* in another system or even in the same system at another time.

```
> (begin (display "Two plus two = ") (display (+ 2 2)) (newline))
Two plus two = 4
()
>
```

Here the empty list was returned by *newline*. Henceforth when top-level expressions return unspecified values, our transcripts will not display the value.

Recall that *map* generally takes a procedure, *proc*, and a list, *lst*, and returns a new list with values obtained by applying *proc* to each element of *lst*. Though the order of elements in the new list is determined, the order in which *proc* is invoked on elements of *lst* is not specified. (For example, the new list might be built from left to right or right to left or any other sequential order) A related procedure, *for-each*, is useful for procedures that perform side effects. It takes the same arguments as *map*, but it always invokes *proc* on elements of *lst* in left-to-right order. It is not specified what *for-each* returns. It could be defined by

```
(define for-each
  (lambda (proc lst)
    (if (null? lst)
        'done
        (begin
          (proc (car lst))
          (for-each proc (cdr lst))))))
```

The procedure *for-each* may be used to define a procedure that displays its arguments in order, followed by a newline.

```
> (define displayln
    (lambda lst
      (begin
        (for-each display lst)
        (newline))))
> (displayln 2 "+" 2 "=" (+ 2 2))
2+2=4
>
```

Sequences of expressions may also appear in several places other than begin expressions, including the bodies of lambda, let, and letrec expressions and the consequents of cond, case, and variant-case expressions. All of these are treated as if the sequence of expressions were contained in a begin expression. For example,

```
(lambda lst
  (begin
    (for-each display lst)
    (newline)))
```

may be simplified to

```
(lambda lst
  (for-each display lst)
  (newline))
```

and

```
(case skip-amount
  ((1 one) (newline))
  ((2 two) (begin (newline) (newline)))
  (else (begin (newline) (newline) (newline))))
```

is equivalent to

```
(case skip-amount
  ((1 one) (newline))
  ((2 two) (newline) (newline))
  (else (newline) (newline) (newline)))
```

Reduction Rules and Imperative Programming

One advantage of *implicit* begin is that it becomes easier to add output statements to expressions for debugging purposes.

```
> (define fact
    (lambda (n)
      (displayln "Entering fact with n = " n)
      (let ((ans (if (zero? n)
                     1
                     (* n (fact (- n 1))))))
        (displayln "Returning from fact with " ans)
        ans)))
> (fact 3)
Entering fact with n = 3
Entering fact with n = 2
Entering fact with n = 1
Entering fact with n = 0
Returning from fact with 1
Returning from fact with 1
Returning from fact with 2
Returning from fact with 6
6
```

Most Scheme implementations have a debugging facility that provides this sort of procedure tracing. Even in such systems, however, debugging statements are often useful for other purposes.

4.5.2 More Input-Output

We have seen that sequencing becomes important when input and output are considered. The output procedures *display* and *newline* have already been introduced. We shall also use the output procedure *write*. It is similar to *display*, but it prints objects in their standard literal representation. Thus *write* prints strings with quotation marks and characters with the #\ prefix.

```
> (begin
    (write "written string")
    (display " displayed string ")
    (write #\x)
    (display #\space)
    (display #\x)
    (display #\newline))
"written string" displayed string #\x x
>
```

Input may be done either a character at a time, using *read-char*, or an entire datum at a time, using *read*. Both of these standard procedures take no arguments and return the character or other value read. If an end of file condition is encountered when either input procedure is called, an object is returned for which the standard predicate *eof-object?* returns #t. It returns #f for any value that can be read by *read* or *read-char*. An error is signaled if an end of file is encountered while *read* has read an incomplete datum.

By default, input is typically from the keyboard or terminal and output is typically to the screen or terminal. The standard input and output procedures may optionally take a port argument to allow input and output to files.

Most Scheme implementations provide the procedure *eval*. It takes a value, whose printed representation should be a Scheme expression, and returns the value of this expression. This procedure has a long tradition, dating from early versions of Lisp, and has been much overused. Implementing a read-eval-print loop is one application for which it is appropriate.

```
> (define read-eval-print
    (lambda ()
      (display "--> ")
      (write (eval (read)))
      (newline)
      (read-eval-print)))
> (read-eval-print)
--> (+ 1 2)
3
--> (car (cons "foo" 'foo))
"foo"
--> (cdr 3)
Error: Invalid argument to cdr: 3
>
```

The use of *write* rather than *display* allows us to distinguish between the values of "foo" and 'foo. For variety, we used a different prompt, -->. Errors typically cause all user procedures to be aborted, with control returning to the system read-eval-print loop. By using alternative *eval* procedures, read-eval-print loops for other languages may easily be obtained. These are convenient when testing language evaluation procedures, such as those developed in later chapters.

○ *Exercise 4.5.1*
Write a read-eval-print loop for the lambda calculus using *reduce** of exercise 4.3.2 instead of *eval*. □

Reduction Rules and Imperative Programming

4.5.3 Data Structure Mutation

Another kind of side-effect that requires the use of sequencing is data structure *mutation*. For example, the car and cdr fields of pairs and the elements of vectors are locations whose contents may be changed.

Mutation of pairs is performed by the standard procedures *set-car!* and *set-cdr!*, respectively. Each takes two arguments, the pair to be mutated and the new value to be assigned. As with all assignments, the value returned is not specified.

```
> (define 1st (list 1 2))
> (set-car! 1st 3)
> 1st
(3 2)
> (set-cdr! 1st (list 4 5))
> 1st
(3 4 5)
> (set-cdr! 1st 6)
> 1st
(3 . 6)
```

Using *set-cdr!* it is possible to define the procedure *reverse!*, which reverses a list "in place" by destroying the original list. The first pair of the original list becomes the last pair of the new list, and the last pair of the original list is returned as the first pair of the new list.

```
> (define reverse!
    (letrec ((loop
                (lambda (last ls)
                  (let ((next (cdr ls)))
                    (set-cdr! ls last)
                    (if (null? next)
                        ls
                        (loop ls next)))))))
        (lambda (ls)
          (if (null? ls)
              ls
              (loop '() ls)))))
> (define ls (list 1 2 3))
> (reverse! ls)
(3 2 1)
> ls
(1)
```

○ *Exercise 4.5.2*

After (`reverse!` a) below, what value is printed for a, b, c, **x**, **y**, and **z**?

```
> (define c (cons 3 '()))
> (define b (cons 2 c))
> (define a (cons 1 b))
> (define x (cons 4 a))
> (define y (cons 5 b))
> (define z (cons 6 c))
> (reverse! a)
```
☐

Mutation of vectors is accomplished with the standard procedure *vector-set!*, which takes a vector, a valid index for that vector, and an arbitrary value, and assigns the given value to the location of the indicated element of the vector.

```
> (define v (vector 1 2 3))
> (vector-set! v 1 4)
> v
#(1 4 3)
```

Data elements that may be changed are said to be *mutable,* as are data objects that contain mutable elements. Pairs created by `cons` and `list`, vectors created by `make-cell` (see exercise 4.5.5) and `vector`, and strings created by `string` are mutable, but symbols and numbers are *immutable.* Pairs and vectors that result from evaluating `quote` expressions may be immutable, so an attempt to mutate them is an error.

○ *Exercise 4.5.3*

Consider the following:

```
> (define p (cons 1 '()))
> (begin (set-cdr! p p) 'done)
done
```

Describe *p* after its mutation. Why did we avoid returning the result of the *set-cdr!* expression to the read-eval-print loop? Hint: In some systems *set-cdr!* returns the mutated pair. ☐

Figure 4.5.1 Cell ADT

```
(define cell-tag "cell")

(define make-cell
  (lambda (x)
    (vector cell-tag x)))

(define cell?
  (lambda (x)
    (and (vector? x)
         (= (vector-length x) 2)
         (eq? (vector-ref x 0) cell-tag))))

(define cell-ref
  (lambda (x)
    (if (cell? x)
        (vector-ref x 1)
        (error "Invalid argument to cell-ref:" x))))

(define cell-set!
  (lambda (x value)
    (if (cell? x)
        (vector-set! x 1 value)
        (error "Invalid argument to cell-set!:" x))))

(define cell-swap!
  (lambda (cell-1 cell-2)
    (let ((temp (cell-ref cell-1)))
      (cell-set! cell-1 (cell-ref cell-2))
      (cell-set! cell-2 temp))))
```

○ *Exercise 4.5.4*

Implement the procedures of figure 4.5.1 using cons cells instead of vectors. □

○ *Exercise 4.5.5*

Using the definitions of figure 4.5.1, fill in the following transcript:

```
> (define c (make-cell 3))
> c

> (define c1 (make-cell 100))
> (cell-set! c 8)
> (cell-ref c)

> (cell-swap! c c1)
> (cell-ref c)
```

□

4.6 Variable Assignment and Sharing

So far, we have thought of variables as being bound directly to values. To introduce variable assignment, we instead think of variables as being bound to *locations*. Variable references now refer to the values contained in these locations. Variable assignment is performed with the special form

$$(\texttt{set!}\ \textit{var}\ \textit{exp})$$

which evaluates expression *exp*, places its value in the location that is the binding of variable *var*, and returns an unspecified value. In Scheme, operations that involve assignment generally have names that end with an exclamation mark, read "bang." The bang signals danger, since it is hard to reason about programs that use assignments. A few examples follow.

```
> (define x 1)
> (set! x 2)
> x
2
> (let ((y 3))
    (set! y 4)
    (+ y 1))
5
```

If a global binding for a variable does not exist, one must be created using define before assigning to it using set!. The first meaningful value for a binding may be an assignment that is not at top level. In such cases we initially bind the variable to some arbitrary value. For example,

```
> (define a '*)
> (let ((b 'not-three))
    (displayln "b is " b)
    (set! a 3)
    (if (= a 3) (set! b 'three))
    b)
b is not-three
three
> a
3
```

Variables appearing on the left-hand side of assignment statements (*var* in the above syntax for set!) denote locations, not the values of locations. The denoted values in Scheme, which are locations, are distinct from the expressed values, which can never be locations.

In order to understand the effect of set!, we must understand how bindings are shared. For example, the following implements a simple stack.

```
> (define push! '*)
> (define pop! '*)
> (define top '*)
> (let ((stk '()))
    (set! empty?
      (lambda ()
        (null? stk)))
    (set! push!
      (lambda (x)
        (set! stk (cons x stk))))
    (set! pop!
      (lambda ()
        (if (empty?)
            (error "Stack empty")
            (set! stk (cdr stk)))))
    (set! top
      (lambda ()
        (if (empty?)
            (error "Stack empty")
            (car stk)))))
```

```
> (push! 1)
> (push! 2)
> (top)
2
> (pop!)
> (top)
1
> (pop!)
```

The procedures *empty?*, *push!*, *pop!*, and *top* share the same *stk* binding. Because this binding is not accessible elsewhere, the stack is a data abstraction. For instance, the definitions could be changed to represent the stack as a vector rather than as a list. The limited scope of the *stk* binding prevents this change from being detected elsewhere. Actually, this abstraction is flawed because the value returned by the set! operation in *push!* is unspecified and might be the stack itself. The *stk* binding itself would still be secure, but the nature of its value would be exposed and could even be modified using the mutation operations introduced in section 4.5.3. This flaw could be fixed by modifying *push!* to return some meaningless value or perhaps the value pushed.

A related use of set! is to modify a binding that is local to a single procedure. For example, consider an implementation of a stack as a procedure that takes a symbolic argument, where the argument is interpreted as a message requesting some service based on its local binding. Using this technique, the stack example becomes the program of figure 4.6.1. The transcript shows an interactive session with *stack*.

```
> ((stack 'push!) 1)
> ((stack 'push!) 2)
> ((stack 'top))
2
> ((stack 'pop!))
> ((stack 'top))
1
> ((stack 'pop!))
```

Note that the let, which introduces the *stk* binding, contains the lambda expression that evaluates to the stack procedure. If the let expression were inside this lambda expression, a new stack would be created each time the procedure was invoked, which would be inconsistent with our intentions.

Only one stack is provided above. We can easily define a procedure for generating many stacks as in figure 4.6.2. A transcript follows.

Figure 4.6.1 A simple stack

```
(define stack
  (let ((stk '()))
    (lambda (message)
      (case message
        ((empty?) (lambda ()
                    (null? stk)))
        ((push!) (lambda (x)
                   (set! stk (cons x stk))))
        ((pop!) (lambda ()
                  (if (null? stk)
                      (error "Stack empty")
                      (set! stk (cdr stk)))))
        ((top) (lambda ()
                 (if (null? stk)
                     (error "Stack empty")
                     (car stk))))
        (else (error "stack: Invalid message" message))))))
```

```
> (define s1 (make-stack))
> (define s2 (make-stack))
> ((s1 'push!) 1)
> ((s2 'push!) 2)
> ((s1 'top))
1
> ((s2 'top))
2
```

Each time *make-stack* is invoked, a new stack procedure, with its own *stk* binding, is returned. Thus, *make-stack* implements an abstract data type, with the push!, pop!, and top messages corresponding to the operations of the ADT.

If a procedure has bindings that have been modified by assignment or whose values have been mutated, it is said to have *state*. When message passing is used to access this state, these procedures are often called *objects*. We have sketched here one approach to a style of programming in which many or all values used in a computation may be objects. When this is combined with the concept of *inheritance,* the resulting style is known as as *object-oriented programming,* In section 7.2 we discuss inheritance and develop a non-procedural representation for objects.

Figure 4.6.2   A simple stack maker

```
(define make-stack
  (lambda ()
    (let ((stk '()))
      (lambda (message)
        (case message
          ((empty?) (lambda ()
                      (null? stk)))
          ((push!) (lambda (x)
                     (set! stk (cons x stk))))
          ((pop!) (lambda ()
                    (if (null? stk)
                        (error "Stack empty")
                        (set! stk (cdr stk)))))
          ((top) (lambda ()
                   (if (null? stk)
                       (error "Stack empty")
                       (car stk))))
          (else (error "stack: Invalid message" message)))))))
```

○ *Exercise 4.6.1*
Modify `make-stack` to take a positive integer n, indicating the maximum size of the stack, and return an object that represents the stack as a vector of length n. ☐

○ *Exercise 4.6.2*
Implement the finite function ADT of section 3.6 with a procedure `make-ff` that returns a new object that responds to the messages `empty?`, `extend`, and `apply`. New procedures must be returned in response to the `extend` and `apply` messages to receive additional arguments. ☐

● *Exercise 4.6.3*
Below is a definition of `next-symbol`. When invoked, it generates the next symbol in the sequence g1, g2, etc.

```
(define next-symbol
  (let ((c 0))
    (lambda ()
      (set! c (+ c 1))
      (string->symbol (string-append "g" (number->string c))))))
```

What is displayed in the following transcript, and why?

```
> (eq? (next-symbol) 'g1)

> (eq? (next-symbol) 'g1)

> (eq? (next-symbol) (next-symbol))
```


Variable assignment makes it possible to implement `letrec` via the following syntactic transformation.

$$(\text{letrec } ((var_1 \; exp_1) \; \ldots \; (var_n \; exp_n))$$
$$\quad body)$$

$$\Rightarrow (\text{let } ((var_1 \; \text{'*}) \; \ldots \; (var_n \; \text{'*}))$$
$$\quad (\text{set! } var_1 \; exp_1)$$
$$\quad \ldots$$
$$\quad (\text{set! } var_n \; exp_n)$$
$$\quad body)$$

The `let` expression first introduces variable bindings that initially contain some irrelevant value. The expressions $exp_1, \ldots, exp_n$ are then evaluated in the scope of these bindings, and their values assigned to the bindings. Finally, *body* is evaluated in the scope of the bindings. This implementation fixes a specific order for the evaluation of $exp_1, \ldots, exp_n$, though in general this order is unspecified. In section 5.6 we present another version of `letrec` that solves the order of evaluation problem. In some implementations, `letrec` may be implemented directly (not as a syntactic transformation) using techniques similar to those introduced later.

4.7 Streams

A *stream* is a possibly infinite sequence of values that allows access, if need be, to initial values while later ones are still being generated. For example, the characters typed in an interactive session may be represented as a stream. The number of characters is potentially infinite (no bound can be given on the length of a session), and it is often necessary to process initial input while later characters have yet to be typed.

We present several implementations of an ADT for streams that may be used with programs developed in later chapters. The stream interface consists of the following procedures:

1. *stream-car* takes a nonempty stream and returns the first element in the stream.

2. *stream-cdr* takes a nonempty stream and returns a stream that contains the same values as the given stream, in the same order, less the first value.

3. *make-stream* takes a value, *v*, and a procedure of no arguments, *p*, and returns a new stream *s* such that (stream-car *s*) is *v* and (stream-cdr *s*) is the stream obtained by invoking *p*.

4. *the-null-stream* is the empty stream.

5. *stream-null?* is the predicate for recognizing empty streams.

The key difference between the stream interface and the list interface is that the second argument to *make-stream* is not the rest of the stream but rather a procedure of no arguments that returns the rest of the stream. This delays the formation of the rest of the stream until it is required by *stream-cdr*. Procedures of no arguments that are used in this way to delay evaluation are called *thunks*.

The following is a version of *for-each* for streams.

```
(define stream-for-each
  (lambda (proc stream)
    (letrec ((loop (lambda (stream)
                     (if (not (stream-null? stream))
                         (begin
                           (proc (stream-car stream))
                           (loop (stream-cdr stream)))))))
      (loop stream))))
```

A simple use of *stream-for-each* follows.

```
(define display-stream
  (lambda (stream)
    (stream-for-each display stream)
    (newline)))
```

The next procedure takes a string and returns a stream containing its characters.

```
(define string->stream
  (lambda (string)
    (let ((string-len (string-length string)))
      (letrec
        ((loop (lambda (cursor)
                 (if (= cursor string-len)
                     the-null-stream
                     (make-stream
                       (string-ref string cursor)
                       (lambda ()
                         (loop (+ cursor 1))))))))
        (loop 0)))))
```

For finite streams, we can define a procedure *stream->list* that takes a stream and returns the corresponding list.

```
(define stream->list
  (lambda (stream)
    (if (stream-null? stream)
        '()
        (cons (stream-car stream)
          (stream->list (stream-cdr stream))))))
```

Another useful procedure is *stream-filter*, which takes a predicate *pred* and a stream *stream*, and produces a stream consisting of those values from *stream* that satisfy *pred*. Using it, we can easily produce a stream of even positive integers from a stream of positive integers.

```
(define stream-filter
  (lambda (pred stream)
    (cond
      ((stream-null? stream) the-null-stream)
      ((pred (stream-car stream))
       (make-stream (stream-car stream)
         (lambda ()
           (stream-filter pred (stream-cdr stream)))))
      (else (stream-filter pred (stream-cdr stream))))))

(define even-positive-integers
  (stream-filter even? positive-integers))
```

Another useful procedure returns a (possibly infinite) stream of characters read from the terminal.

```
(define make-input-stream
  (lambda ()
    (let ((char (read-char)))
      (if (eof-object? char)
          the-null-stream
          (make-stream char make-input-stream)))))
```

This may be used to construct a read-print loop.

```
(define read-print
  (lambda ()
    (display "--> ")
    (display-stream (make-input-stream))
    (read-print)))
```

In the following *read-print* transcript, <eof> indicates entry of an end-of-file.

```
> (read-print)
--> A line of input<eof>
a line of input
--> This input is
three lines
long.<eof>
This input is
three lines
long.
-->
```

In chapter 5 and appendix F we present several approaches to read-eval-print loops.

○ *Exercise 4.7.1*
Your Scheme system may not allow an end-of-file to be generated from the keyboard, or you may prefer a different input terminator, such as two carriage returns in a row. Modify *make-input-stream* to use another input terminator and test it with *read-print*. □

Because streams and lists are so similar, an obvious implementation strategy is to represent a stream as the list of its elements. This only works for finite streams.

```
(define stream-car car)

(define stream-cdr cdr)

(define make-stream
  (lambda (value thunk)
    (cons value (thunk))))

(define the-null-stream '())

(define stream-null?
  (lambda (stream)
    (eq? stream the-null-stream)))
```

If we do not know whether the stream is finite or infinite, then we cannot represent the stream as a list. In this case, the stream can be represented as a pair with the car containing the first element and the cdr containing a thunk that returns the rest of the stream. Unlike the case of a list or pair, in which the car and cdr are both computed before the pair is built, this representation defers computation of the rest of the stream until *stream-cdr* is invoked. The thunk is a finite representation of the possibly infinite stream. Streams based on thunks may be obtained by changing the definitions of *stream-cdr*, *make-stream*, and *the-null-stream* above to

```
(define stream-cdr
  (lambda (stream)
    ((cdr stream))))

(define make-stream
  (lambda (value thunk)
    (cons value thunk)))

(define the-null-stream
  (make-stream "end-of-stream" (lambda () the-null-stream)))
```

Streams of this kind are sometimes called *lazy lists*. They are lazy because they delay generating their cdr as long as possible.

This definition works when the rest of the same stream is never taken twice. If evaluation of the thunk involves a side-effect, however, then taking *stream-cdr* of a stream twice will perform the side-effect twice. This is unpleasant, especially if the side-effect is an input/output operation.

We can solve this problem by using mutation to build streams. When asked for the rest of a stream, we check if the cdr contains a procedure. If so, we invoke the procedure (a thunk) and then install the value returned in the cdr of the stream. Henceforth if we are asked for the rest of the same stream, we notice that the cdr contains a pair, not a procedure, and we simply return the pair. (The procedure `make-stream` is unchanged.)

```
(define stream-cdr
  (lambda (stream)
    (if (pair? (cdr stream))
        (cdr stream)
        (let ((s ((cdr stream))))
          (set-cdr! stream s)
          s))))
```

This illustrates a general technique that is an important use of assignment. The first time a value is computed, it is recorded using some form of assignment. If it is required again, it can then be returned without recomputation. This is known as *memoizing* or *caching*. In general usage, the term *stream* often refers to streams in which the `stream-cdr` operation is memoized. Variations are possible in the implementation technique. For example, rather than testing the type of the cdr field, the stream data structure may include a boolean flag indicating whether a suspension is present.

○ *Exercise 4.7.2*
Sometimes it may not be possible or desirable to generate the head of a stream before the stream is created. In that situation the stream mechanism presented here cannot be used. This problem may be overcome by memoizing the car, as well as the cdr, of the stream. Implement two versions of such *fully lazy* streams, one that memoizes `stream-car`, and one that does not. Your implementations may memoize `stream-cdr` or not, as you choose. ☐

4.8 Summary

The β-conversion rule of the lambda calculus is a powerful rule for reasoning about functional programs. By repeatedly applying this rewrite rule in one direction only, expressions in the lambda calculus may be reduced to answers. The Church-Rosser theorem implies that each expression may be reduced to at most one constant. The order in which the reductions are performed may affect the termination of the reduction process, but not the answer obtained if the process terminates. Leftmost reduction terminates whenever possible, while applicative order reduction is usually more efficient and is used in most programming languages. Recursive procedures may be defined directly in the lambda calculus.

Imperative programming techniques, which involve side effects, are sometimes useful. If they are used, however, it becomes more difficult to reason about programs. Sequencing mechanisms control the order in which side effects are performed. Data structure mutation involves assignment to locations in data. Variable assignment involves mutation of locations that are bindings of variables. Assignment in combination with lexical scope gives a simple model of object-oriented programming.

Streams allow potentially infinite sequences of data to be represented. Infinite streams must be lazy, that is, they must be generated on demand. Procedures of no arguments, called thunks, may be used to construct lazy streams. Memoization uses assignment to store results so they need not be recomputed.

5   Interpreters

We now have the necessary background to study the semantics of programming languages via *interpreters*. These are procedures that take the abstract syntax tree of a program and perform the indicated computation.

An interpreter is a program that looks at a data structure and performs some actions that depend on its structure. We have already developed several such data- or table-driven procedures. These include the parser and unparser of section 3.4.3 and `apply-` procedures that interpret data structures derived from procedures in section 3.6, as well as the lambda calculus reducer of section 4.3.1. Each of these procedures took data in the form of variant records and performed some action determined by the type of record.

The interpreters developed in this chapter reveal the semantics of a language with sufficient clarity that they are often suitable for specifying the semantics of programming languages. Indeed, they will be our major tool for understanding the semantics of the programming language features we wish to study.

5.1 A Simple Interpreter

In this section we develop a simple interpreter. It reflects the fundamental semantics of many modern programming languages and is the basis for most of the material in the rest of this book. We build this interpreter in stages, starting with the simplest forms: literals, variables, and applications. Then we add other forms one at a time.

An important part of the specification of any programming language is the set of values that the language manipulates. In chapter 1, we introduced two sets of values that are associated with a programming language: the *expressed values* and the *denoted values*. The expressed values are the possible values of expressions, and the denoted values are the values bound to variables. In Scheme, for example, there are many kinds of expressed values, such as numbers, pairs, characters, and strings, but there is only one kind of denoted value: cells containing expressed values.

For simplicity, our language has only two types of expressed values: integers and procedures. For the moment, the denoted values will be the same as the expressed values. We write this as follows:

$$\text{Expressed Value} = \text{Number} + \text{Procedure}$$

$$\text{Denoted Value} = \text{Number} + \text{Procedure}$$

We use equations like this as informal reminders of the expressed and denoted values for each of our interpreters.

We also need to distinguish two languages: the *defined language,* which is the language we are specifying with our interpreter, and the *defining language,* which is the language in which we write the interpreter. In our case the defining language is Scheme. The equations above describe the expressed and denoted values of the defined language.

We start with the following concrete and abstract syntax

⟨exp⟩ ::= ⟨integer-literal⟩	lit (datum)
| ⟨varref⟩	
| ⟨operator⟩ ⟨operands⟩	app (rator rands)
⟨operator⟩ ::= ⟨varref⟩ | (⟨exp⟩)	
⟨operands⟩ ::= ( ) | (⟨operand⟩ {,⟨operand⟩}*)	
⟨operand⟩ ::= ⟨exp⟩	
⟨varref⟩ ::= ⟨var⟩	varref (var)

Typical expressions in our language follow:

```
3
n
+(3, n)
add1(+(3, n))
(add1)(+(3, n))
```

The abstract syntax trees are built, as before, of records with type definitions based on the abstract syntax names given with the grammar.

```
(define-record lit (datum))
(define-record varref (var))
(define-record app (rator rands))
```

Figure 5.1.1   A simple interpreter using `variant-case`

```
(define eval-exp
  (lambda (exp)
    (variant-case exp
      (lit (datum) datum)
      (varref (var) (apply-env init-env var))
      (app (rator rands)
        (let ((proc (eval-exp rator))
              (args (eval-rands rands)))
          (apply-proc proc args)))
      (else (error "Invalid abstract syntax: " exp)))))

(define eval-rands
  (lambda (rands)
    (map eval-exp rands)))
```

The `rands` field of an `app` record contains a list of abstract syntax trees for the application's operands. The abstract syntax tree for the third or fourth example above is

```
#(app
  #(varref add1)
  (#(app
     #(varref +)
     (#(lit 3) #(varref n)))))
```

Our first interpreter is shown in figure 5.1.1. The main procedure, *eval-exp*, is passed the abstract syntax tree of an expression and returns the value of the expression. It follows a familiar pattern, dispatching on the type of record at the root of the tree. The first case is easy: If *exp* is a literal, the datum is returned.

If *exp* is a node that represents a variable, the value of the expression should be the value bound to that variable. Now we need to decide from where we should retrieve this value. We need to supply an *environment*: a finite function that takes a symbol and returns the associated denoted value. This environment is consulted to find the value of any variable in the language. In this language, there is (at least for the moment) only one environment, the initial environment *init-env*.

We define an ADT for environments by borrowing the finite function ADT.

```
(define the-empty-env (create-empty-ff))
(define extend-env extend-ff*)
(define apply-env apply-ff)
```

Since we follow the principle of data abstraction, we may use any implementation of finite functions that supports *extend-ff**, which simultaneously adds multiple bindings to the environment. The ribcage implementation of section 3.6.3 is a good choice.

When evaluating a variable, the interpreter need only look up its binding in *init-env*. Thus we have the following variant-case clause in *eval-exp*:

```
(varref (var) (apply-env init-env var))
```

This leaves the case of an application. Since the operator may be any expression, we must evaluate it to obtain the procedure to be called. This is easily done with the recursive call (eval-exp rator) in figure 5.1.1. As with most languages, including Scheme, the language we are interpreting uses applicative-order evaluation: the operands of an application are evaluated before calling the procedure. The auxiliary procedure *eval-rands* is called to evaluate the list of operands and returns a list of arguments (operand values). It uses *map* to recursively invoke *eval-exp* on each operand.

How application is performed depends on the representation of procedures. We isolate dependence on this representation within the procedure *apply-proc*, allowing *eval-exp* to be completed as in figure 5.1.1.

We now turn to the representation of procedures. Initially we shall have only one kind of procedure: *primitive procedures* that are supported directly by the underlying implementation. To be precise, we use a BNF grammar to specify the data that *apply-proc* must manipulate:

⟨procedure⟩ ::= ⟨prim-op⟩	prim-proc (prim-op)
⟨prim-op⟩ ::= ⟨addition⟩	+
| ⟨subtraction⟩	-
| ⟨multiplication⟩	*
| ⟨increment⟩	add1
| ⟨decrement⟩	sub1

This specification says that there is only one kind of procedure, a primitive procedure, and that there are five of these: addition, subtraction, multiplication, increment (adding 1), and decrement (subtracting 1). Furthermore, such procedures are represented by records specified by

```
(define-record prim-proc (prim-op))
```

Later this will allow us to easily distinguish them from other types of procedures. The only item stored in a `prim-proc` record is the symbol naming the operator. The procedures *make-prim-proc* and *apply-proc* define an ADT for procedures.

All that *apply-proc* does at this point is verify that its first argument is a primitive procedure and then invoke *apply-prim-op*.

```
(define apply-proc
  (lambda (proc args)
    (variant-case proc
      (prim-proc (prim-op) (apply-prim-op prim-op args))
      (else (error "Invalid procedure:" proc)))))

(define apply-prim-op
  (lambda (prim-op args)
    (case prim-op
      ((+) (+ (car args) (cadr args)))
      ((-) (- (car args) (cadr args)))
      ((*) (* (car args) (cadr args)))
      ((add1) (+ (car args) 1))
      ((sub1) (- (car args) 1))
      (else (error "Invalid prim-op name:" prim-op)))))
```

We could have represented primitive operators in any convenient way that would allow *apply-prim-op* to do its work. We have chosen to represent each primitive operator by a symbol: the same symbol that the initial environment will use as a name for that primitive operator. Hence we can build the initial environment as follows:

```
(define prim-op-names '(+ - * add1 sub1))

(define init-env
  (extend-env
    prim-op-names
    (map make-prim-proc prim-op-names)
    the-empty-env))
```

This completes our first interpreter. Before we can conveniently test our interpreter, however, we need a front end that parses expressions and invokes *eval-exp*. There are several approaches to building such a front end.

One approach is to ignore, for the moment, the details of the concrete syntax at the beginning of this section, and to write our expressions as list structures, as we did in section 4.1. Thus, instead of writing add1(+(3, n)), we might write (add1 (+ 3 n)). For this approach, all we need is a procedure *parse*, which takes a Scheme list, symbol, or number and returns the corresponding abstract syntax tree. Our interpreter can then be tested easily; see appendix G and appendix H.

```
> (define run
    (lambda (x)
      (eval-exp (parse x))))
> (run '5)
5
> (run '(add1 2))
3
```

o *Exercise 5.1.1*

Write *parse*. See section 3.4.3. □

A read-eval-print loop may also be defined for our interpreter.

```
(define read-eval-print
  (lambda ()
    (display "-->")
    (write (eval-exp (parse (read))))
    (newline)
    (read-eval-print)))
```

This provides a more convenient interface if a number of tests are to be made.

```
> (read-eval-print)
--> 5
5
--> (add1 2)
3
--> (* (add1 2) (- 6 4))
6
```

From now on, if the prompt --> appears in a transcript, it indicates that the current version of *eval-exp* is performing the evaluation.

This approach is simple, but may lead to confusion between the defined language and the defining language. Alternatively, by using the code of appendix D and appendix E, we can write a character string parser.

```
> (define parse character-string-parser)
> (run "5")
5
> (run "add1(2)")
3
```

By using appendix F, we can have a read-eval-print loop for ⟨exp⟩. In this case, we need to terminate each top-level expression to be evaluated with a semicolon, so we can distinguish between add1 and add1(2). For example,

```
> (read-eval-print)
--> 5;
5
--> add1(2);
3
--> *(add1(2),-(6,4));
6
```

- *Exercise 5.1.2*
Implement *eval-exp* and test it using both *run* and a read-eval-print loop. You may use either a list structure or a character string parser. ☐

- *Exercise 5.1.3*
Extend the initial environment with the operator minus, which takes one argument, n, and returns $-n$.

```
--> minus(+(minus(5), 9));
-4
```
☐

- *Exercise 5.1.4*
Add list processing features to *init-env*, including *cons*, *car*, *cdr*, *list*, and a new variable, *emptylist*, which is bound to the empty list. (Since there is no support for symbols, lists can contain only numbers and other lists.)

```
--> list(1, 2, 3);
(1 2 3)
--> car(cons(4, emptylist));
4
```
☐

Another way to represent procedures in our interpreter is to represent them as procedures of the defining language. For example, + would be bound in `init-env` to the Scheme addition procedure. We could then say

```
(define apply-proc apply)
```

Rewrite the interpreter of this section to use this procedure representation. □

5.2 Conditional Evaluation

To study the semantics and implementation of a wide range of programming language features, we now begin adding these features to our defined language. For each feature, we add a production to the grammar of ⟨exp⟩, specify an abstract syntax for that production, and then include an appropriate `variant-case` line in *eval-exp* to handle the new type of abstract syntax tree node.

First we add a conditional expression with the concrete and abstract syntax,

---

⟨exp⟩ ::= if ⟨exp⟩ then ⟨exp⟩ else ⟨exp⟩   if (test-exp then-exp else-exp)

---

and then we define the record type that supports its abstract syntax.

```
(define-record if (test-exp then-exp else-exp))
```

To avoid adding booleans as a new type of expressed value, we let zero represent false and any other value represent true and use the procedure *true-value?*, which abstracts this decision:

```
(define true-value?
  (lambda (x)
    (not (zero? x))))
```

If the value of the `test-exp` subexpression is a true value, the value of the entire `if` expression should be the value of the `then-exp` subexpression; otherwise it should be the value of the `else-exp` subexpression. For example,

```
--> if 1 then 2 else 3;
2
--> if -(3, +(1, 2)) then 2 else 3;
3
```

This behavior is obtained by adding the following clause in *eval-exp*

```
(if (test-exp then-exp else-exp)
  (if (true-value? (eval-exp test-exp))
      (eval-exp then-exp)
      (eval-exp else-exp)))
```

This code uses the `if` special form of the defining language to define the `if` form of the defined language. This illustrates how we are dependent on our understanding of the defining language: if we did not know what Scheme's `if` did, this code would not help us understand the new language. In this case, of course, we do understand Scheme's `if`, and our code provides some additional information on the defined language's conditional expression as it considers any nonzero value to be true.

● *Exercise 5.2.1*
Test `if` forms by extending the interpreter of figure 5.1.1. Use either the string syntax given above or this list syntax:

⟨exp⟩ ::= (if ⟨exp⟩ ⟨exp⟩ ⟨exp⟩)

▯

● *Exercise 5.2.2*
Add the numeric equality, zero-testing, and order predicates `equal`, `zero`, `greater` and `less` to the initial environment. These predicates should use 1 to represent true.

```
--> equal(3, 3);
1
--> zero(sub1(5));
0
--> if greater(2, 3) then 5 else 6;
6
```
▯

● *Exercise 5.2.3*
Extend exercise 5.1.4 by adding the predicate `null`. ▯

5.3 Local Binding

Next we address the problem of creating new variable bindings in the context of a `let` form. We add to the interpreted language a syntax in which the keyword `let` is followed by a series of declarations, the keyword `in`, and the body. For example,

```
let x = 5;
    y = 6
in +(x, y)
```

The entire `let` form is an expression, as is its body, so `let` expressions may be nested. The usual lexical scope rules for block structure apply: the binding region of a `let` declaration is the body of the `let` expression, and inner bindings create holes in the scope of outer bindings. Thus in

```
let x = 3
in let x = *(x, x)
   in +(x, x)
```

the references to `x` in the first application refer to the outer declaration, whereas the references to `x` in the second application refer to the inner declaration, and hence the value of the entire expression is 18.

The concrete syntax of the `let` form is

⟨exp⟩ ::= `let` ⟨decls⟩ `in` ⟨exp⟩	`let (decls body)`
⟨decls⟩ ::= ⟨decl⟩ {`;` ⟨decl⟩}*	
⟨decl⟩ ::= ⟨var⟩ `=` ⟨exp⟩	`decl (var exp)`

The abstract syntax uses the following record types:

```
(define-record let (decls body))
(define-record decl (var exp))
```

The `decls` field of a `let` record is associated with a ⟨decl⟩ nonterminal that may be repeated zero or more times (indicated by the Kleene star). Thus it contains a list of `decl` records.

The body of a `let` expression should be evaluated in an environment in which the declared variables are bound to the values of the expressions on

Figure 5.3.1   Interpreter with explicit environment-passing

```
(define eval-exp
  (lambda (exp env)
    (variant-case exp
      (lit (datum) datum)
      (varref (var) (apply-env env var))
      (app (rator rands)
        (let ((proc (eval-exp rator env))
              (args (eval-rands rands env)))
          (apply-proc proc args)))
      (if (test-exp then-exp else-exp)
        (if (true-value? (eval-exp test-exp env))
            (eval-exp then-exp env)
            (eval-exp else-exp env)))
      (else (error "Invalid abstract syntax:" exp)))))

(define eval-rands
  (lambda (rands env)
    (map (lambda (rand) (eval-exp rand env))
         rands)))
```

the right-hand sides of the declarations, whereas other bindings should be obtained from the environment in which the entire let expression is evaluated.

With the introduction of let, different expressions may be evaluated using different environments. This is a significant change, because so far our interpreter evaluated all expressions with respect to a single environment, *init-env*. Therefore, we first rewrite *eval-exp* to take two arguments: an expression and an environment. The new *eval-exp* evaluates the given expression with respect to the given environment. The resulting interpreter is shown in figure 5.3.1. It looks up variables using the environment *env*, rather than *init-env*, and we are careful to pass the environment on each call to *eval-exp*. This requires that the environment be passed to *eval-rands*.

When a let expression is evaluated, the subexpressions on the right-hand side of its declarations are evaluated first. Since the scope of these declarations is restricted to the let expression's body, the right-hand side subexpressions are evaluated in *env*, the environment of the entire let expression. The body is then evaluated in an environment obtained by extending *env* to bind the declared variables to the values of their right-hand subexpressions. We obtain this behavior by adding the let clause in figure 5.3.2. First the variable names

Figure 5.3.2 Interpreter with `let`

```
(define eval-exp
  (lambda (exp env)
    (variant-case exp
      (lit (datum) datum)
      (varref (var) (apply-env env var))
      (app (rator rands)
        (let ((proc (eval-exp rator env))
              (args (eval-rands rands env)))
          (apply-proc proc args)))
      (if (test-exp then-exp else-exp)
        (if (true-value? (eval-exp test-exp env))
            (eval-exp then-exp env)
            (eval-exp else-exp env)))
      (let (decls body)
        (let ((vars (map decl->var decls))
              (exps (map decl->exp decls)))
          (let ((new-env (extend-env vars
                            (eval-rands exps env)
                            env)))
            (eval-exp body new-env))))
      (else (error "Invalid abstract syntax:" exp)))))
```

and expressions are extracted from the declaration records. Then `eval-rands` is used to evaluate the declaration expressions in the environment `env`. Finally, the body is evaluated in a new environment obtained by extending the current environment with bindings that associate the declared variables with the values of their right-hand side expressions.

In accordance with our expectation for a lexically-scoped language, a fixed region of text, *body*, is associated with the new environment bindings. Also, if *extend-env* creates a binding for an already bound variable, the new binding takes precedence over the old. Inner declarations thus shadow, or create holes in the scope of, outer declarations. For example, in

```
let x = 1
in let x = +(x, 2)
   in add1(x)
```

the subexpression `add1(x)` is evaluated in a new environment obtained by extending an environment binding `x` to 1 with a binding of `x` to 3. Since the binding of x to 3 takes precedence, the reference to x in add1(x) yields 3 and the final value is 4. This satisfies the lexical scope rule associated with block-structured languages: a variable reference is associated with the nearest lexically enclosing binding of the variable.

- *Exercise 5.3.1*

  Test the let form of the interpreter of figure 5.3.2. The parser may accept either the syntax of let used in this section or the syntax of Scheme's let. The procedure *run* must also be modified to pass *init-env* to *eval-exp*. ☐

o *Exercise 5.3.2*

  Extend exercise 5.1.4 by adding the primitive procedure eq, which should correspond to the Scheme procedure *eq?*. Why could this predicate not be adequately tested until now? ☐

5.4 Procedures

So far our language has only the procedures that were included in the initial environment. For our interpreted language to be at all useful, we must allow new procedures to be created. We use the following syntax:

$\langle exp \rangle ::= $ proc $\langle varlist \rangle \langle exp \rangle$ proc (formals body)

$\langle varlist \rangle ::= $ ( ) | ($\langle vars \rangle$)

$\langle vars \rangle ::= \langle var \rangle \; \{ , \langle var \rangle \}^*$

Thus we can write programs like

```
let f = proc (y, z) *(y, -(z, 5))
in f(2, 8)
```

Since the proc form may be used anywhere an expression is allowed, we can also write

```
(proc (y, z) *(y, -(z, 5)))(2, 8)
```

This is the application of the procedure proc (y, z) *(y, -(z, 5)) to the literals 2 and 8.

When a procedure is applied, its body is evaluated in an environment that binds the formal parameters of the procedure to the arguments of the application. Variables occurring free in the procedure should also obey the lexical scope rule. This requires that they retain the bindings that were in force *at the time the procedure was created*. Consider the following example:

```
let x = 5
in let f = proc (y, z) *(y, -(z, x));
       x = 28
   in f(2, 8)
```

When f is called, its body should be evaluated in an environment that binds y to 2, z to 8, and x to 5. Recall that the scope of the inner declaration of x does not include the procedure declaration. Thus from the position of the reference to x in the procedure's body, the nearest lexically enclosing declaration of x is the outer declaration, which associates x with 5.

A first-class procedure may be passed to and returned from other procedures and stored in data structures. As a result, it may be invoked at a place in the program that is distant from the place at which the procedure was created. This is also true of the "second-class" procedures found in many languages, which may be passed as arguments to procedures but not returned as values or stored in data structures. We shall have more to say about this in chapter 10.

In order for a procedure to retain the bindings that its free variables had at the time it was created, it must be a *closed* package, independent of the environment in which it is used. Such a package is called a *closure*. In order to be self-contained, a closure must contain the procedure body, the list of formal parameters, and the bindings of its free variables. It is convenient to store the entire creation environment, rather than just the bindings of the free variables. We sometimes say the procedure is *closed over* or *closed in* its creation environment. We represent closures as records.

```
(define-record closure (formals body env))
```

In a compiled implementation, where lexical address calculations have been performed (as in section 2.3), only the number of formal parameters need be recorded in a closure, along with free variable bindings and a reference to the compiled code of its body.

We now modify `apply-proc` to recognize closures. We may write down the data that `apply-proc` needs to recognize with this equation:

$$\text{Procedure} = \text{Primitive Procedure} + \text{Closure}$$

The procedure `apply-proc` first checks to see what kind of procedure it was passed. If it was a closure, it simply invokes the body of the closure in an appropriately extended environment.

```
(define apply-proc
  (lambda (proc args)
    (variant-case proc
      (prim-proc (prim-op) (apply-prim-op prim-op args))
      (closure (formals body env)
        (eval-exp body (extend-env formals args env)))
      (else (error "Invalid procedure:" proc)))))
```

When a proc expression is evaluated, all that is done is to build a closure
and return it immediately.

```
(define eval-exp
  (lambda (exp env)
    (variant-case exp
      (proc (formals body)
        (make-closure formals body env))
      ...)))
```

The body of the procedure is not evaluated here: it cannot be evaluated until
the values of the formal parameters are known, when the closure is applied to
some arguments. The interpreter is shown in figure 5.4.1.

- *Exercise 5.4.1*
Test user-defined procedures with the interpreter of figure 5.4.1. The parser
may accept either the character string or the list structure syntax. ☐

- *Exercise 5.4.2*
In exercise 5.1.5, primitive operators are represented as procedures of the
defining language, allowing *apply-proc* to be *apply*. To pursue this approach, closures must also be represented as procedures of the defining language. Define *make-closure* for this representation of closures. Hint: Use an
expression of the form (lambda args ...). ☐

o *Exercise 5.4.3*
As a variation on the previous exercise, we can define *apply-proc* to be
(lambda (f args) (f args)). Redefine *make-closure* and primitive operations using this variation. Hint: Use the form (lambda (args) ...). For example, bind the symbol + to (lambda (args) (+ (car args) (cadr args))).
☐

Figure 5.4.1   Interpreter with user-defined procedures

```
(define eval-exp
  (lambda (exp env)
    (variant-case exp
      (lit (datum) datum)
      (varref (var) (apply-env env var))
      (app (rator rands)
        (let ((proc (eval-exp rator env))
              (args (eval-rands rands env)))
          (apply-proc proc args)))
      (if (test-exp then-exp else-exp)
        (if (true-value? (eval-exp test-exp env))
            (eval-exp then-exp env)
            (eval-exp else-exp env)))
      (let (decls body)
        (let ((vars (map decl->var decls))
              (exps (map decl->exp decls)))
          (let ((new-env (extend-env vars
                            (eval-rands exps env)
                            env)))
            (eval-exp body new-env))))
      (proc (formals body)
        (make-closure formals body env))
      (else (error "Invalid abstract syntax:" exp)))))

(define apply-proc
  (lambda (proc args)
    (variant-case proc
      (prim-proc (prim-op) (apply-prim-op prim-op args))
      (closure (formals body env)
        (eval-exp body (extend-env formals args env)))
      (else (error "Invalid procedure:" proc)))))
```

We saw in section 3.1 that a `let` expression is equivalent to an application in which the operator is a `proc` (or `lambda`) expression. This equivalence can be verified in our interpreter by observing that in either case the result is obtained by evaluating the `let` or `proc` body in the same environment. The only difference is that the application creates a closure, whereas the `let` does not. Since `let` can be treated as an abbreviation for the equivalent application, we omit it from subsequent interpreters.

Write a procedure *syntax-expand* that takes a syntax tree for the language
of this section and returns a syntax tree with every `let` record replaced by
a semantically equivalent app record with a `proc` record in its `rator` field.
Use this procedure to process the output of the parser before it is passed
to *eval-exp*. The `let` clause may now be removed from *eval-exp*, while
retaining `let` in the language. □

5.5 Variable Assignment

Next we wish to add variable assignment (:=) to our interpreter. First we
must change our environment abstraction, since it currently does not provide a
means for modifying the value bound to a variable. At present, environments
bind each variable directly to its associated expressed value (the value of
some expression). Thus denoted values (the values of variable bindings) and
expressed values are the same.

Our approach is to introduce a level of indirection between variable bindings
and expressed values. In the new arrangement, variables will be bound to
locations in memory, and it is the contents of these locations that are modified
by variable assignment. Thus denoted values are locations or cells whose
contents are expressed values:

$$\text{Denoted Value} = \text{Cell (Expressed Value)}.$$

Scheme does not allow the programmer to mutate (modify, or assign to) arbitrary memory locations. Instead it provides procedures, such as *set-cdr!*,
that allow changes to mutable data structure elements. We use cells as developed in exercise 4.5.5 for modeling abstract memory locations. The collection
of all locations, including mutable data structure fields, is called the *store*.

We next modify the interpreter to use the cells as denoted values. This
requires two changes. First, when a closure is invoked (in *apply-proc*), the
new bindings must be cells that contain the arguments. This is accomplished
by writing

```
(extend-env formals
  (map make-cell args)
  env)
```

instead of (extend-env formals args env). Second, when variables are referenced, it is necessary to dereference their bindings, since the bindings are now cells. Thus in *eval-exp* we have the variant-case clause

```
(varref (var) (cell-ref (apply-env env var)))
```

instead of

```
(varref (var) (apply-env env var))
```

This design, in which formal parameters are bound to fresh cells containing the values of the operands, is known as call-by-value. Call-by-value is the most commonly used form of parameter passing, and is the standard against which other parameter passing mechanisms are usually compared.

- *Exercise 5.5.1*
  Add cells to the interpreter of figure 5.3.2. In addition to the changes mentioned above, you will have to alter the let clause and add cells to the initial environment. □

To add assignment to the interpreter, we choose the concrete syntax

---

$\langle exp \rangle ::= \langle var \rangle := \langle exp \rangle$ varassign (var exp)

---

and an abstract syntax based on records defined by

```
(define-record varassign (var exp))
```

To implement assignment, we add the following variant-case clause to *eval-exp*:

```
(varassign (var exp)
  (cell-set! (apply-env env var) (eval-exp exp env)))
```

Cells or locations, such as the cells passed to *cell-set!*, are sometimes called *L-values*. This reflects their association with variables appearing on the left-hand side of assignment statements. Analogously, expressed values, such as the values of the right-hand side expressions of assignment statements, are known as *R-values*. See figure 5.5.1 for the complete interpreter with variable assignment.

Figure 5.5.1   eval-exp with variable assignment call-by-value

```
(define eval-exp
  (lambda (exp env)
    (variant-case exp
      (lit (datum) datum)
      (varref (var) (cell-ref (apply-env env var)))
      (app (rator rands)
        (let ((proc (eval-exp rator env))
              (args (eval-rands rands env)))
          (apply-proc proc args)))
      (if (test-exp then-exp else-exp)
        (if (true-value? (eval-exp test-exp env))
            (eval-exp then-exp env)
            (eval-exp else-exp env)))
      (proc (formals body)
        (make-closure formals body env))
      (varassign (var exp)
        (cell-set! (apply-env env var) (eval-exp exp env)))
      (else (error "Invalid abstract syntax: " exp)))))

(define apply-proc
  (lambda (proc args)
    (variant-case proc
      (prim-proc (prim-op) (apply-prim-op prim-op args))
      (closure (formals body env)
        (eval-exp body
          (extend-env
            formals
            (map make-cell args)
            env)))
      (else (error "Invalid procedure:" proc)))))
```

○ *Exercise 5.5.2*

In the ribcage representation of environments (figure 3.6.1), the values are stored in vectors. We can use the fact that vector elements are mutable in Scheme to avoid introducing cells. To do this, let the binding associated with the nth variable be the nth location of the vector. Thus, using **vector-set!**, we can directly mutate the binding of a variable. Implement this idea. □

The following definition of `apply-proc` no longer assumes that `args` will be bound to a list of expressed values but will be bound to a list of denoted values. This means that `args` will be bound to a list of cells. Redefine `eval-rands` of figure 5.3.1 to use this version of `apply-proc`.

```
(define denoted->expressed cell-ref)

(define apply-proc
  (lambda (proc args)
    (variant-case proc
      (prim-proc (prim-op)
        (apply-prim-op prim-op (map denoted->expressed args)))
      (closure (formals body env)
        (eval-exp body
          (extend-env formals args env)))
      (else (error "Invalid procedure:" proc)))))
```
▯

● *Exercise 5.5.4*

Now that we have introduced side effects into the language, it is natural to introduce a form for sequencing expressions.

⟨exp⟩ ::= **begin** ⟨exp⟩ ⟨compound⟩   begin (exp1 exp2)
⟨compound⟩ ::= {;⟨exp⟩}* **end**

A `begin` expression may contain an arbitrary number of subexpressions separated by semicolons. These are evaluated in order and the value of the last is returned. For example,

```
--> let x = 3
    in begin
         x := add1(x);
         x := +(x, x);
         +(x, 2)
       end;
  10
```

The abstract syntax of `begin` contains only two subexpressions. A `begin` expression containing more than two subexpressions generates a nested `begin` internally. A `begin` expression containing only one subexpression generates the abstract syntax of that expression. Thus, the above example parses to

```
#(let (#(decl x #(lit 3)))
   #(begin
       #(varassign x #(app #(varref add1) (#(varref x))))
       #(begin
           #(varassign x #(app #(varref +) (#(varref x) #(varref x))))
           #(app #(varref +) (#(varref x) #(lit 2)))))))
```

Extend the interpreter to implement the `begin` form. □

- *Exercise 5.5.5*
Define a *form* to be a *definition* or expression. Modify the parser for the
following abstract and concrete syntax

⟨form⟩ ::= `define` ⟨var⟩ = ⟨exp⟩   `define (var exp)`
       | ⟨exp⟩

This syntax intentionally prevents definitions (as opposed to local declarations) from appearing inside expressions.

Modify the read-eval-print loop so that it reads a sequence of forms, with
definitions performed and expressions evaluated as they are encountered. A
definition is performed by first evaluating the given expression in the initial
environment. If the given variable is not bound in the initial environment, the
initial environment should be extended to bind the variable to a cell containing
the expression's value. If the initial environment already contains a binding
for the given variable, the expression's value is assigned to this binding as
if by a top-level assignment. After performing a definition, the next prompt
is printed without printing any value. After evaluation of an expression, the
value of the expression should be printed, as usual, before prompting for the
next definition or expression.

```
--> define x = 3;
--> +(x, 1);
4
--> define x = 5;
--> x;
5
--> begin
       x := 6;
       x
     end;
6
```

```
--> let x = 3
    in begin
          define y = 4;
          +(x, y)
       end;
Error: Invalid parse-exp token: #3(token define *)
```
☐

○ *Exercise 5.5.6*

Typically the value of an expression such as assignment, whose purpose is
to perform a side effect, is unspecified. In our interpreter this value will be
whatever value the procedure *cell-set!* returns (which is, of course, unspecified in Scheme, since it is defined with *vector-set!*). Extend the parser to
include assignment expressions and modify the interpreter in figure 5.5.1 so
that the symbol *unspecified* is returned when the assignment expression is
evaluated.

```
--> let x = 3
    in x := 4;
*unspecified*
```
☐

○ *Exercise 5.5.7*

In the interpreter of figure 5.5.1, all variable bindings are mutable (as in
Scheme). Another alternative is to allow both mutable and immutable variable bindings:

Denoted Value = Cell (Expressed Value) + Expressed Value

Then variable assignment works only when the variable to be assigned to has
a mutable binding.

One approach to supporting both mutable and immutable variable bindings
is to add a letmutable form for introducing mutable bindings. For example,
we could use a syntax similar to the let form.

⟨exp⟩ ::= letmutable ⟨decls⟩ in ⟨exp⟩   letmutable (decls body)

Modify the parser and interpreter so that the letmutable form is just the
same as the let form, except that it introduces mutable bindings to the environment, whereas let bindings remain immutable. ☐

○ *Exercise 5.5.8*

Local variable binding need be mutable only if there is an assignment expression to the variable somewhere within its scope. Process the output of the parser and modify the interpreter so that only bindings for variables that might change their values are mutable, while all other bindings remain immutable. □

○ *Exercise 5.5.9*

Our understanding of assignment, as expressed in this interpreter, depends on the semantics of side effects in Scheme. In particular, it depends on *when* these effects take place. If we could model assignment without using Scheme's side-effecting operations, our understanding would not be dependent on Scheme in this way. We can do this by modeling the store not as a collection of cells but as a finite function. The domain of the store function is some arbitrary set of addresses (say the nonnegative integers) that represents locations or cells, and its range is the set of expressed values. Mutation of a location in the store is then modeled by extending this finite function to associate the location with the new value. This new association supersedes any earlier associations for the same cell.

In order for the new store to be used in subsequent evaluation, it is passed as an additional argument to all interpreter procedures that might need it (`eval-exp`, `eval-rands`, `apply-proc`, etc.). For example,

```
(define eval-exp
  (lambda (exp env store)
    (variant-case exp
      (varref (var) (apply-store store (apply-env env var)))
      ...)))
```

Every procedure that might modify the store will return not just its usual value but a pair consisting of the value and a new store. The trickiest interpreter procedure to modify is *eval-rands*. It can no longer just use map. Instead, it must evaluate the operands in some specific order, with the store resulting from each evaluation being used in the next evaluation. We can evaluate the operands from left to right and accumulate the partial answers in reverse order.

```
(define-record interp-result (value store))

(define eval-rands
  (lambda (rands env store)
    (letrec
      ((loop
         (lambda (rands ans store)
           (if (null? rands)
               (make-interp-result (reverse ans) store)
               (let ((first-result
                       (eval-exp (car rands) env store)))
                 (loop
                   (cdr rands)
                   (cons (interp-result->value first-result) ans)
                   (interp-result->store first-result)))))))
      (loop rands '() store))))
```

Modify the rest of the interpreter according to this design. Be sure to define your store ADT explicitly. Then rewrite *eval-rands* so it does not use the accumulator variable ans. □

5.6 Recursion

The last issue that must be addressed to complete our simple interpreter is recursion. We have already seen two approaches to implementing recursion in section 4.4. The first approach, the Y combinator, is of theoretical importance because it requires only the ability to create and apply first-class procedures. We could write the applicative-order Y combinator directly in our defined language and use it to define recursive procedures. In most implementations, however, an approach like this is too inefficient for routine use.

The second approach is frequently used to implement letrec in Scheme. A letrec expression is syntactically transformed into an expression that first uses let to create an environment with dummy variable bindings. Recursive procedures are closed in this environment, after which variable assignment is used to store the closures in the cells bound to the associated variables. The transformation that accomplishes this is similar to the equation for letrec, which was presented in section 4.6. This equation, however, maintains the property that the order of evaluation of the exp_i is left undetermined.

```
    (letrec ((var₁ exp₁) ... (varₙ expₙ))
      body)
```

$\Rightarrow$
```
    (let ((var₁ '*) ... (varₙ '*))
      (let ((v₁ exp₁) ... (vₙ expₙ))
        (set! var₁ v₁)
        ...
        (set! varₙ vₙ)
        'unspecified)
      body)
```

Here $v_1, \ldots, v_n$ are fresh variables that appear nowhere else in the letrec expression. The inclusion of 'unspecified is to guarantee that the inner let always has a body, even when there are no definitions.

In this way recursive procedures are created by closing them in an environment that includes the variables to which they will be bound. Note that an attempt to dereference one of the variables var_i in any of the exp_j may lead to strange results, but after the set!'s are done all the cells will contain the right values. If each exp_i is a lambda, then we are guaranteed that none of the letrec variables will be prematurely dereferenced, and that the order of evaluation of the exp_i is not important.

In Scheme, letrec can be used even when the exp_i are not lambda expressions. This generality is rarely needed but is important in some applications such as streams.

Top-level definitions may also be used to create recursive procedures in a similar way. This works because procedures defined at the top level of the read-eval-print loop (see exercise 5.5.5) will be closed in the initial environment, and the initial environment will include the new definition. This is the way top-level recursive procedures are defined in Scheme.

This approach implements recursion by introducing cycles in the data structure representing the run-time environment. For example, the local environment created by

```
(letrec ((fact (lambda (n)
                 (if (zero? n)
                     1
                     (* n (fact (- n 1)))))))
  ...)
```

contains a circularity. The environment contains a binding that points to a closure that in turn contains a reference to the environment (see figure 5.6.1).

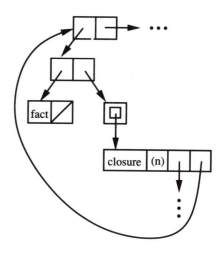

Figure 5.6.1   Circular environment for `fact`

In most languages only procedures may be defined recursively, and circular environments are created by the same mechanism that creates recursive procedures. We look now at how recursion may be added directly to an interpreter *without* circularity.

We use a variation on the `letrec` syntax that restricts the right-hand side of recursive declarations to `proc` expressions. The concrete and abstract syntax is described by this grammar:

⟨exp⟩ ::= `letrecproc` ⟨procdecls⟩   `letrecproc (procdecls`
          `in` ⟨exp⟩   `body)`
⟨procdecls⟩ ::= ⟨procdecl⟩ {`;`⟨procdecl⟩}*
⟨procdecl⟩ ::= ⟨var⟩ ⟨varlist⟩ `=` ⟨exp⟩   `procdecl (var formals body)`

The left-hand side of a recursive declaration is the name of the recursive procedure and a list of formal parameters. To the right of the `=` is the procedure body. For example,

```
letrecproc
  fact(x) = if zero(x) then 1 else *(x, fact(sub1(x)))
in fact(6)
```

Figure 5.6.2   Environment ADT without circular closures

```
(define-record extended-rec-env (vars vals old-env))

(define extend-rec-env
  (lambda (procdecls env)
    (make-extended-rec-env
      (map procdecl->var procdecls)
      (list->vector
        (map (lambda (procdecl)
               (make-proc
                 (procdecl->formals procdecl)
                 (procdecl->body procdecl)))
             procdecls))
      env)))

(define apply-env
  (lambda (env var)
    (variant-case env
      (extended-rec-env (vars vals old-env)
        (let ((p (ribassoc var vars vals '*fail*)))
          (if (eq? p '*fail*)
              (apply-env old-env var)
              (make-closure (proc->formals p) (proc->body p) env))))
      ...)))
```

or

```
letrecproc
  even(x) = if zero(x) then 1 else odd(sub1(x));
  odd(x)  = if zero(x) then 0 else even(sub1(x))
in odd(13)
```

In some languages, variables that are referenced before they are defined must first be declared using a *forward* declaration. For example, in the body of even, it would be necessary to declare odd to be forward. This is not necessary in Scheme or our interpreter, since all the variables in a mutually recursive declaration are identified before analyzing the procedure bodies.

To add letrecproc to the interpreter, we first introduce a new operator to the environment ADT. This operator, called *extend-rec-env*, extends the environment with a set of mutually recursive procedures. The letrecproc variant-case clause in *eval-exp* is similar to the `let` clause, except that *extend-rec-env* is used instead of *extend-env* to create the environment in which the body is evaluated.

```
(letrecproc (procdecls body)
  (eval-exp body (extend-rec-env procdecls env)))
```

We assume for the time being that this clause is being added to figure 5.4.1, and not figure 5.5.1, so that environment bindings are not cells.

An environment ADT with *extend-rec-env* may be implemented in many ways. We do so in a manner that does not involve the use of side effects. We cannot build a recursive closure directly, since the only way to build a cyclic structure is to use side effects. Instead, we store all the information contained in the recursive closure, *except* the environment, in a `proc` record. Before a value is returned from the environment, we build a complete closure by adding the environment. This is possible because the environment is available at the time we *build* the closure. Using this approach, the environment ADT is defined as in figure 5.6.2

- *Exercise 5.6.1*
  Add `letrecproc` to the interpreter of figure 5.4.1 using the environment ADT given above. □

○ *Exercise 5.6.2*
  The use of *make-proc* in the definition of *extend-rec-env* may seem a bit odd. We can avoid this by introducing a new form `letrec`, whose abstract syntax is much like that of `let`.

⟨exp⟩ ::= letrec ⟨decls⟩ in ⟨exp⟩   letrec (decls body)

The `decls` is a list of `decls` and each `decl` is composed of a `var` and an `exp`. The `exp` of the `decl`, however, must be a `proc` record. Replace `letrecproc` by `letrec` and redefine *extend-rec-env* to utilize `letrec`'s abstract syntax. □

○ *Exercise 5.6.3*
  The environment ADT of figure 5.6.2 can be made compatible with the interpreter of figure 5.5.1, in which bindings are cells, by wrapping recursive closures in cells before *apply-env* returns them. If this were done, what would happen if := were used to assign a variable bound by a `letrecproc` expression? □

It is somewhat inefficient to build a new closure each time a variable bound to a recursive procedure is referenced. Modify the environment ADT of figure 5.6.2 to build a single recursive closure for each recursive procedure. As in implementations of `letrec` via syntactic extension, begin by building an environment with bindings that are cells containing dummy values. Then build the closures and use *cell-set!* to install them in the environment. Use this new ADT to add `letrecproc` to the interpreter of figure 5.5.1. Then write a program in the defined language that behaves differently with this environment ADT than it does with the environment ADT of figure 5.6.2. Hint: Extend the predicate `eq` of exercise 5.3.2 to test equality of procedures as well as of lists. ☐

We have seen that `letrec` (or `letrecproc`), like `let`, can be implemented as a syntactic extension into expressions using only forms that are already supported by the interpreter. Thus, as with `let`, we shall not include `letrec` (or `letrecproc`) in subsequent interpreters.

○ *Exercise 5.6.5*
Extend *syntax-expand* of exercise 5.4.4 to replace all `letrecproc` records with syntactically equivalent `let` records, as indicated by the syntactic transformation for `letrec` given above. Be sure that *syntax-expand* also expands these `let` records. Then `letrecproc` may be used with the interpreter of figure 5.5.1. ☐

5.7 Dynamic Scope and Dynamic Assignment

In this section we present two different approaches to dynamically rearranging information in an environment. The first approach, dynamic scope, is a kind of binding mechanism that adds additional expressiveness at the cost of making programs far more difficult to understand. The second approach, dynamic assignment, provides most of the expressiveness of dynamic scope without abandoning the clarity of lexical scope.

5.7.1 Dynamic Scope

We have emphasized that when a procedure is applied, it is the environment in which the procedure was *created* that is used to evaluate the procedure's body. This is necessary for variables to be lexically scoped, but it requires that a new closure be formed each time a proc expression is evaluated. It would seem simpler to evaluate the body in the environment of application. We now explore this alternative.

Consider this program:

```
let a = 3
in let p = proc (x) +(x, a);
       a = 5
   in *(a, p(2))
```

By the lexical scope rule, the reference to a in the body of *p* refers to the first binding of a, yielding 3, and the entire expression yields 25. This is achieved by closing *p* in the environment established by the outer let. If instead the body of *p* were evaluated in the environment of its application, this reference to a would refer to the call-time binding of a, yielding 5, and the entire expression would yield 35. The scope of the inner binding of a changed with the application to *p* so that the body of *p* was included in the scope. The scope of variables is now dynamic, not lexical: it changes with each application. This is referred to as *dynamic binding* and obeys the following rule:

> A dynamic binding is *extant* during the evaluation of the body associated with the binding form. References to a dynamically-bound variable refer to the *most recent* extant binding of that variable.

As we shall see later in this section, dynamic scoping is more difficult to reason about than lexical scoping, but it is often easier to implement. Since procedures are not closed over their creation environment, the only information that needs to be recorded in a procedure is the formal parameter list and body. This is exactly the information in a proc abstract syntax record. Thus when evaluating a proc expression, rather than building a new data structure to represent the dynamic procedure, we can simply return the proc record. The proc clause of the variant-case in *eval-exp* is simply

```
(proc (formals body) exp)
```

Dynamic scope makes the evaluation of proc expressions particularly simple and efficient, which was at least in part responsible for its early popularity in some programming languages, including Lisp.

When apply-proc receives a proc record, it must extend the *current* environment to obtain the environment in which to evaluate the body. This

Figure 5.7.1   Interpreter with dynamic scope

```
(define eval-exp
  (lambda (exp env)
    (variant-case exp
      (lit (datum) datum)
      (varref (var) (cell-ref (apply-env env var)))
      (app (rator rands)
        (let ((proc (eval-exp rator env))
              (args (eval-rands rands env)))
          (apply-proc proc args env)))
      (if (test-exp then-exp else-exp)
        (if (true-value? (eval-exp test-exp env))
            (eval-exp then-exp env)
            (eval-exp else-exp env)))
      (proc (formals body) exp)
      (varassign (var exp)
        (cell-set! (apply-env env var) (eval-exp exp env)))
      (else (error "Invalid abstract syntax:" exp)))))

(define apply-proc
  (lambda (proc args current-env)
    (variant-case proc
      (prim-proc (prim-op) (apply-prim-op prim-op args))
      (proc (formals body)
        (eval-exp body
          (extend-env formals (map make-cell args) current-env)))
      (else (error "Invalid procedure:" proc)))))
```

requires that the current environment be passed as an additional argument to *apply-proc*. The resulting interpreter is shown in figure 5.7.1.

With dynamic scope, when a binding is added to the environment, it remains in effect (is extant) until all subsequent bindings are removed. In other words, the environment obeys a last-in-first-out, or stack, discipline. We take advantage of this by modifying the interpreter of figure 5.7.1 to use a single global environment stack, rather than passing the environment between the procedures of the interpreter. See figure 5.7.2, where a new environment ADT is used. This ADT has procedures *push-env!*, *pop-env!*, *lookup-in-env*, and *initialize-env!* that perform the expected stack operations on the global environment stack. Here *eval-exp* uses the global environment stack instead of an environment argument. When *eval-exp* returns, it must leave the global environment stack in the same state that it found it. Therefore, *apply-proc* calls *push-env!* to add a new set of bindings to the environment, evaluates the procedure body, and then calls *pop-env!* to restore the environment stack.

- *Exercise 5.7.1*
  Implement the interpreter of figure 5.7.1. ☐

- *Exercise 5.7.2*
  With dynamic scope, recursive procedures may be bound by `let`; no special mechanism is necessary for recursion. This is of historical interest, because in the early years of programming language design other approaches to recursion, such as `letrec` and the Y combinator, were not widely understood. To demonstrate recursion via dynamic scope, define and test the factorial procedure for your interpreter. Do this by expanding a `let` expression that binds `fact` into its equivalent application with a `proc` expression as the operator. ☐

- *Exercise 5.7.3*
  Implement the interpreter of figure 5.7.2. ☐

- *Exercise 5.7.4*
  Modify the results of exercise 5.4.3, in which procedures are represented as procedures in the defining language, so that variables are dynamically scoped. Hint: Use an expression of the form `(lambda (args env) ...)`. ☐

The structure of the stack environment cannot be determined statically. There is no way of knowing in advance how "deep" the binding of a variable may be in the environment. Since a linear search of the stack is required for each variable reference, this approach to storing dynamic bindings, called *deep binding*, is characterized by inefficient variable reference. Another approach, called *shallow binding*, maintains a separate stack for each variable name. The environment maps variable names to their associated stacks. When a variable is bound, the binding is pushed onto the stack associated with its name, and when it is *unbound* (no longer extant), its stack is popped. There is exactly one stack per variable, so a compiler can make the association between variable references and stacks at compile time. Since the current binding is always at the top of the stack, variable reference is more efficient. If the procedure has several formal parameters, however, entry and exit is less efficient than with deep binding, because a separate stack must be pushed and popped for each formal parameter.

Figure 5.7.2   Interpreter with dynamic scope and environment stack

```
(define eval-exp
  (lambda (exp)
    (variant-case exp
      (lit (datum) datum)
      (varref (var) (cell-ref (lookup-in-env var)))
      (app (rator rands)
        (let ((proc (eval-exp rator))
              (args (eval-rands rands)))
          (apply-proc proc args)))
      (if (test-exp then-exp else-exp)
        (if (true-value? (eval-exp test-exp))
            (eval-exp then-exp)
            (eval-exp else-exp)))
      (proc (formals body) exp)
      (varassign (var exp)
        (cell-set! (lookup-in-env var) (eval-exp exp)))
      (else (error "Invalid abstract syntax:" exp)))))

(define eval-rands
  (lambda (rands)
    (map (lambda (exp) (eval-exp exp))
         rands)))

(define apply-proc
  (lambda (proc args)
    (variant-case proc
      (prim-proc (prim-op) (apply-prim-op prim-op args))
      (proc (formals body)
        (push-env! formals (map make-cell args))
        (let ((value (eval-exp body)))
          (pop-env!)
          value))
      (else (error "Invalid procedure:" proc)))))
```

```
let a = 3
in let p = proc () +(x, a);
       f = proc (x, y) *(p(), y);
       a = 5
   in *(a, f(let a = 2 in a, 1))
```

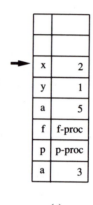

(a)

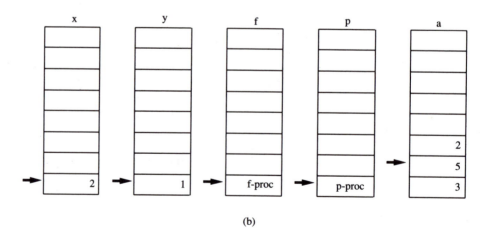

(b)

Figure 5.7.3 Example of dynamic scope and environments when *p* is called

Interpreters

To get a better feeling for dynamic scope and binding techniques, consider the program in figure 5.7.3. The deep and shallow binding environments at the time the reference to a in the body of p is evaluated are given in figure 5.7.3 (a) and (b), respectively. Here stacks grow in an upward direction. At this time a will have been most recently bound to 2 in the innermost let. however, this binding is no longer extant, since evaluation of the body of the innermost let is completed before p (or f) is called. The most recent extant binding is that of the second let. The evaluation of its body is not complete until the entire expression has been evaluated. Therefore the reference to a in the body of p yields 5. The binding of the first let is extant at the time p is called, but it is not the most recent binding. The reference to x in the body of p yields 2, since the binding of x created when f was called is still extant, and hence the entire expression yields 35.

o *Exercise 5.7.5*
Modify the interpreter of figure 5.7.1 to use a shallow-bound environment. Create a stack ADT with *push!*, *pop!*, *top*, and *make-stack* operations. See figure 4.6.2. The procedure *make-stack* takes no arguments and returns a newly created empty stack. For convenience, you may use a globally bound finite function to associate variable names with stacks. □

A number of program transformation techniques that are supported by lexical scope rules, such as α-, β-, and η-conversion, are not valid when dynamic scope is used. For example, consider the effect of α-converting y to a in the program of figure 5.7.3, so that the declaration of f becomes

```
f = proc (x, a) *(p(), a)
```

The reference to a in the body of p then refers to the binding established by f, with value 1, instead of to the inner binding established by the inner let, with value 5. Thus parameter names must be chosen in such a way as to avoid possible conflicts with other parameters declared at very distant points in a program. Binding variables with dynamic scope may have *global* effect, whereas binding variables with lexical scope has *local* effect.

If all of this gives you the impression that it is difficult to reason about programs that use dynamic scope, you are right. Imagine the problem of locating the most recent extant binding in a program of, say, 100,000 lines. It is natural to ask, "Are there any good uses for dynamic scope?" There are a few. We shall review them briefly after considering another form of dynamic binding.

• *Exercise 5.7.6*

What is the value of the following expression if variables are dynamically scoped?

```
let x = 1;
    f = proc (x) +(x, y);
    g = proc (y) f(+(z, x));
    z = 2
in g(+(x, z))
```
▯

5.7.2 Dynamic Assignment

The interpreters we have been examining have introduced bindings with lexical scope. These bindings also have *indefinite extent*: they are retained as long as they are needed. Bindings recorded in a closure are maintained as long as the closure is accessible. We then saw how bindings were created with dynamic scope, and we saw that these bindings had dynamic extent. Now we explore yet another alternative: assignments with dynamic extent to bindings that have lexical scope. This is also called "fluid binding."

In the defined language we express dynamic assignment using a form with concrete and abstract syntax given by

---

⟨exp⟩ ::= ⟨var⟩ := ⟨exp⟩ during ⟨exp⟩   `dynassign (var exp body)`

The effect of

$$var := exp \text{ during } body$$

is to temporarily assign the value of *exp* to *var*, evaluate *body*, reassign *var* to its original value, and return the value of *body*. For example, in

```
let x = 4
in let p = proc (y) +(x, y)
   in +(x := 7 during p(1),
        p(2))
```

the value of x, which is free in procedure *p*, is 7 in the call p(1), but is reset to 4 in the call p(2), so the value of the expression is $8 + 6 = 14$.

This may be implemented by adding the following `variant-case` clause to figure 5.5.1.

```
(dynassign (var exp body)
  (let ((a-cell (apply-env env var))
        (b-cell (make-cell (eval-exp exp env))))
    (cell-swap! a-cell b-cell)
    (let ((value (eval-exp body env)))
      (cell-swap! a-cell b-cell)
      value)))
```

• *Exercise 5.7.7*

If the dynamic assignment x := 7 during p(1) of the preceding example were
replaced by let x = 7 in p(1), what would be the value of this new expression? ▢

○ *Exercise 5.7.8*

Dynamic assignment may change the values of several variables at one time.
Use the following syntax, which allows multiple variables to be dynamically
set, and modify figure 5.5.1 to include letdynamic.

⟨exp⟩ ::= letdynamic ⟨decls⟩ in ⟨exp⟩   letdynamic (decls body)

For example,

```
--> define x = 1;
--> define y = 2;
--> define p = proc (x, a) +(a, *(x, y));
--> letdynamic
        x = +(x, y);
        y = +(x, 3)
    in p(x, y);
16
--> p(x, y);
4
```

▢

○ *Exercise 5.7.9*

Include dynassign in the procedure *syntax-expand* of exercise 5.4.4. Replace
instances of dynassign in the syntax tree by instances of varassign and let.
State any assumptions you make about variables not occurring free in the *exp*
or *body* parts. ▢

One of the most common uses of dynamic binding or assignment is the redirection of input and output. I/O operations usually use "standard" input and output ports (connected, say, to a keyboard and the display), unless a specific port is indicated. But we may want all the output generated as a result of invoking a particular procedure call, such as p(1, 2), to be directed to a port associated with a new file, say port (instead of the standard output port). If the variable standardoutput were bound to the default standard output port, this could be accomplished by

```
standardoutput := port
during p(1, 2)
```

Or in a language with dynamic scope, we could use

```
let standardoutput = port
in p(1, 2)
```

which is equivalent to

```
(proc (standardoutput) p(1, 2))(port)
```

In the absence of dynamic binding or assignment, it would be necessary to pass the new port as an argument to p. This might not be a problem, but p would also have to pass the port unaltered to all the procedures it calls that do output, and these procedures would have to do the same. Some of these procedures may not do any output directly, but they must still receive and pass on the output port if any procedure they call does output, either directly or by calling other procedures.

In any situation in which a change must be made dynamically, that is, from the beginning to the end of the time required to evaluate an expression, dynamic binding or assignment may eliminate the need for much parameter passing. For example, in addition to the output port, there are often a number of formatting parameters that affect the generation of output, such as line length. It is frequently convenient to set these dynamically. For this reason, all binding is dynamic in some text formatting languages (such as TeX, with which this book was typeset).

Another common use of dynamic assignment or binding is in dealing with *exceptions,* that is, situations, such as errors, that must be handled outside of the program's normal flow of control. In some programming languages, it is possible to build *exception handlers:* procedures that are invoked by the system in the event that an exception is detected while the program executes.

It is frequently desirable to dynamically assign or bind exception handlers. For example, it may be that during the call to a particular procedure, it is desired that all divide-by-zero exceptions result in the largest possible number being returned as the result of the division, whereas at most times the response to this exception is to abort the program. This is easily accomplished with dynamic assignment.

The ability to use dynamic assignment or binding may also, in a sense, make procedures more abstract. For example, in the situation above it may be that not only does p not do any direct output, the programmer may not know whether any of the procedures it calls produce output. Furthermore, the writer of procedure p and its users may not even care whether output occurs while p executes. It is counter to the notion of abstraction for p to take an output port as a parameter and pass it to the procedures it calls just in case they might need it.

Dynamic assignment avoids most of all the difficulties of dynamic scope. For example, α-conversion is valid. Dynamic assignment does, however, share the problems of other forms of assignment. For example, procedures do not behave functionally: the value they return may be dependent on more than the values of their parameters. The advantage of dynamic assignment is that it can be used in a lexically-scoped language. The difficulties associated with dynamic behavior are then restricted to the few cases where dynamic assignment or scope is advantageous. For more discussion on dynamic assignment, see section 9.3.

5.8 Summary

An interpreter takes an abstract syntax tree representing a program and performs the computation directed by that program. Interpreters give a high-level, comprehensible specification of the action of a phrase in a programming language.

The expressed values of a language are the possible values of expressions. The denoted values are the possible values of variables.

Local bindings and user-defined procedures require that new environments be created and passed around within the interpreter. Variable assignment requires that denoted values be mutable cells containing expressed values, rather than the values themselves.

Recursive procedures can be defined either by building a circular environment or by building a specialized contour that closes the procedures at the time they are retrieved.

Dynamically-scoped binding is useful for applications such as changing output routine parameters and exception handlers during the evaluation of an expression. Pure dynamic scoping allows a simplified implementation, since procedures do not have to close over their creation environment. This simplicity is deceptive, however, since dynamic scope makes understanding programs much more difficult. Dynamic assignment to lexical variables is of use in the same contexts as dynamic scope, but retains the advantages of lexical scope.

6   Parameter Passing

In the last chapter we explored the semantics of language features that are to be found in most programming languages, though sometimes in restricted forms. In this chapter we explore a number of semantic variations that are commonly found in programming languages. Once more, we find interpreters to be valuable tools in the study of programming language semantics. By modifying these interpreters to express each semantic alternative, we obtain precise specifications of each alternative and highlight their essential differences.

In this chapter, we explore several areas of language design. In section 6.1, we look at two models of arrays and similar data structures. In sections 6.2–6.5, we study different mechanisms for the transmission of parameters to procedures. Along the way, in section 6.4, we look at some of the implications of our choice of expressed and denoted values. Finally, in section 6.6 we explore optional parameters and keyword arguments.

6.1 Adding Arrays

Most programming languages include data structures composed of multiple elements, such as arrays and records. Such structures are called *aggregates*. The introduction of aggregates brings with it new choices in language design.

The primitive aggregate data types of Scheme are vectors, pairs, and strings. Values of these types are typically represented by consecutive memory locations that contain their elements. When an aggregate value is passed to a procedure, what is passed is a pointer to the first memory location of the structure. We call this an *indirect* representation, since the values of aggregate elements are obtained indirectly, by reference to the aggregate's pointer. Later, we shall see what a direct representation of aggregates might mean.

A characteristic feature of this design is that when an aggregate value is passed to a procedure, the procedure and its caller both see the same memory locations. This sharing is visible when the procedure assigns a new value to one of the aggregate elements. Then the caller sees the change in the aggregate value. For example,

```
> (let ((p (lambda (b) (set-car! b 3)))
        (a (cons 1 2)))
    (p a)
    (car a))
  3
```

To illustrate these ideas, we add arrays to the defined language. Other types of aggregate values may be treated the same as arrays for parameter-passing purposes.

To support arrays, we extend the language with special forms for creating array bindings, accessing array elements, and assigning to array elements. We use the following concrete and abstract syntax:

⟨form⟩ ::= definearray ⟨var⟩ [⟨exp⟩]	definearray (var dim-exp)
⟨exp⟩ ::= letarray ⟨arraydecls⟩ in ⟨exp⟩	letarray (arraydecls body)
| ⟨array-exp⟩ [⟨exp⟩]	arrayref (array index)
| ⟨array-exp⟩ [⟨exp⟩] :=	arrayassign (array index
⟨exp⟩	exp)
⟨array-exp⟩ ::= ⟨exp⟩	
⟨arraydecls⟩ ::= ⟨arraydecl⟩ {;⟨arraydecl⟩}*	
⟨arraydecl⟩ ::= ⟨var⟩ [⟨exp⟩]	decl (var exp)

An array is a sequence of cells containing expressed values. We write this as

$$\text{Array} = \text{Cell*(Expressed Value)}$$

The asterisk is meant to suggest the Kleene star (section 2.1). For our Scheme implementation, arrays are built from vectors, which provide a sequence of mutable elements; see figure 6.1.1.

The defined language's expressed values include arrays, and its denoted values are still simply cells containing expressed values as in section 5.5.

$$\text{Expressed Value} = \text{Number} + \text{Procedure} + \text{Array}$$

$$\text{Denoted Value} = \text{Cell (Expressed Value)}$$

Array indexing is zero based, so a[0] refers to the first element of array a. For example, with indirect arrays we obtain

Figure 6.1.1   Array ADT

```
(define-record aggregate (vector))

(define make-array
  (lambda (dimension)
    (make-aggregate (make-vector dimension))))

(define array? aggregate?)

(define array-ref
  (lambda (array index)
    (vector-ref (aggregate->vector array) index)))

(define array-set!
  (lambda (array index value)
    (vector-set! (aggregate->vector array) index value)))

(define array-copy
  (lambda (array)
    (make-aggregate (list->vector (vector->list (aggregate->vector array))))))
```

```
--> define p = proc (b) b[0] := 3;
--> letarray a[2]
    in begin
        a[0] := 1; a[1] := 2;
        p(a);
        a[0]
    end;
3
```

much as we did with the Scheme example above.

Figure 6.1.2 shows the core of an interpreter for handling arrays. In *eval-exp*, the letarray, arrayref, and arrayassign cases are, of course, new. The procedure *apply-proc* now expects args to be a list of denoted values, so it is the responsibility of *eval-rands*, not *apply-proc*, to call *make-cell* (as in exercise 5.5.3.) The procedure *eval-rands* now maps *eval-rand* across the operands. We introduce *eval-rator*, whose definition starts out as *eval-exp*. The lit, if, proc, and begin cases in *eval-exp* are omitted in figure 6.1.2, for they are the same as those we have seen in chapter 5, as are auxiliary procedures such as *apply-env*.

Figure 6.1.2   Interpreter for illustrating parameter-passing variations

```
(define eval-exp
  (lambda (exp env)
    (variant-case exp
      (varref (var) (denoted->expressed (apply-env env var)))
      (app (rator rands)
        (apply-proc (eval-rator rator env) (eval-rands rands env)))
      (varassign (var exp)
        (denoted-value-assign! (apply-env env var) (eval-exp exp env)))
      (letarray (arraydecls body)
        (eval-exp body
          (extend-env (map decl->var arraydecls)
            (map (lambda (decl)
                   (do-letarray (eval-exp (decl->exp decl) env)))
                 arraydecls)
            env)))
      (arrayref (array index)
        (array-ref (eval-array-exp array env)
          (eval-exp index env)))
      (arrayassign (array index exp)
        (array-set! (eval-array-exp array env)
          (eval-exp index env)
          (eval-exp exp env)))
      ...)))

(define eval-rator
  (lambda (rator env)
    (eval-exp rator env)))

(define eval-rands
  (lambda (rands env)
    (map (lambda (rand) (eval-rand rand env)) rands)))

(define eval-rand
  (lambda (exp env)
    (expressed->denoted (eval-exp exp env))))

(define apply-proc
  (lambda (proc args)
    (variant-case proc
      (prim-proc (prim-op) (apply-prim-op prim-op (map denoted->expressed args)))
      (closure (formals body env) (eval-exp body (extend-env formals args env)))
      (else (error "Invalid procedure:" proc)))))
```

Figure 6.1.3   Auxiliaries for call-by-value with indirect arrays

```
(define denoted->expressed cell-ref)

(define denoted-value-assign! cell-set!)

(define do-letarray (compose make-cell make-array))

(define eval-array-exp eval-exp)

(define expressed->denoted make-cell)
```

Figure 6.1.2 introduces five new procedures that are not defined there. These are *denoted->expressed*, *denoted-value-assign!*, *do-letarray*, *eval-array-exp*, and *expressed->denoted*. By varying the definitions of these procedures, we can model a variety of parameter-passing mechanisms.

For the indirect representation of arrays, the code for these auxiliary procedures is shown in figure 6.1.3. A denoted value is a cell, so to convert a denoted value to an expressed value we simply take the contents of the cell, and to assign to a denoted value, we use *cell-set!*. The procedure *do-letarray* first makes an array and then places it in a new cell. This cell can then be bound to a variable. Since arrays are expressed values, *eval-array-exp* can simply be *eval-exp*. Last, *expressed->denoted* just creates a cell containing the expressed value.

• *Exercise 6.1.1*
Implement this interpreter and run some examples. ☐

○ *Exercise 6.1.2*
Replace the letarray construct by a new primitive procedure makearray that takes one argument, the dimension of the array, and returns an array of the specified size. ☐

Scheme and C both use the indirect model of arrays. Some other languages, like Pascal, use a different model of arrays, in which an array is a sequence of expressed values, not a sequence of cells:

$$\text{Array} = (\text{Expressed Value})^*$$

Figure 6.1.4   Auxiliaries for call-by-value with direct arrays

```
(define denoted->expressed
  (lambda (den-val)
    (let ((exp-val (cell-ref den-val)))
      (if (array? exp-val) (array-copy exp-val) exp-val))))

(define eval-array-exp
  (lambda (exp env)
    (variant-case exp
      (varref (var) (let ((exp-val (cell-ref (apply-env env var))))
                      (if (array? exp-val)
                          exp-val
                          (error "Expecting an array:" exp-val))))
      (else (eval-exp exp env)))))
```

In this model, when an array is passed by value, the formal parameter is bound to a cell containing a *copy* of the sequence of values in the original array. Then, if the procedure performs array assignment, we know that only the local copy of the array is modified, just as in ordinary parameter passing. We call this the *direct* model of arrays.

Modeling direct arrays in Scheme is somewhat tricky because Scheme uses the indirect model. The simplest way to do this is to model an array with a vector, as in the indirect case, but to copy it when it is returned as a value. We can do this by redefining *denoted->expressed* as in figure 6.1.4. Values other than arrays do not need to be copied because Scheme already copies them. In an array reference or array assignment, however, we don't want to copy the array, so we modify *eval-array-exp* so that the array is returned without copying whenever possible. See figure 6.1.4.

The difference between indirect and direct models of arrays is illustrated by figure 6.1.5. For the indirect version, x and u are both bound to cells that point at the first location of an array containing 5, 6, and 4 and v is bound to a cell that points to the first location of an array containing 3 and 8. Executing the assignment x[1] := 7 changes the 6 to a 7. Then executing x := v changes the x cell to point at the same array as v does. Finally, executing x[1] := 9 then changes the 8 to a 9. See figure 6.1.6 (a). For the direct version, x is bound to a cell that contains an array just like u's. Executing x[1] := 7 changes the 6 in x's array to a 7. The assignment x := v replaces the contents of x's cell by a copy of v's array. See figure 6.1.6 (b).

Figure 6.1.5   Example illustrating direct and indirect array models

```
letarray u[3]; v[2]
in begin
    u[0] := 5; u[1] := 6; u[2] := 4; v[0] := 3; v[1] := 8;
    let p = proc (x)
              begin
                x[1] := 7;
                x := v;
                x[1] := 9
              end
    in p(u)
  end
```

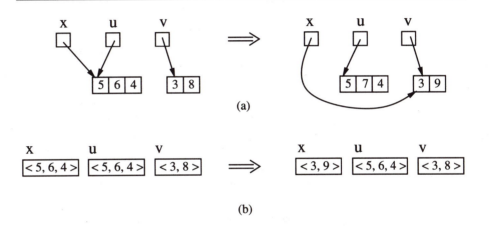

(a)

(b)

Figure 6.1.6   Effect of figure 6.1.5 using call-by-value

○ *Exercise 6.1.3*

Is it true that using direct arrays, call-by-value parameter passing in a procedure really prevents side-effects from being visible to the caller? □

○ *Exercise 6.1.4*

Do the interpreters presented in this section do the right thing when an array element contains another array? Modify the direct array interpreter to behave correctly in this case. □

6.2 Call-by-Reference

When an operand is a variable and the called procedure assigns to the corresponding formal parameter, is this visible to the caller as a change in the binding of its variable? The indirect model of arrays provides such visibility for arrays modified by array assignment, but for ordinary variables, with modification by variable assignment, the answer to this question has been no. If an assignment is made to a procedure's call-by-value parameter, it affects only the binding made when the procedure was called. For example, in

```
let p = proc (x) x := 5
in let a = 3;
       b = 4
   in begin
         p(a);
         p(b);
         +(a, b)
      end
```

on each call to procedure p, the variable x is bound to a fresh cell. Therefore the assignment to x does not affect a or b, and so the expression yields 7. The effect of an assignment is always restricted to the scope of the assigned variable. This is generally desirable, especially given the difficulties inherent in understanding assignment. It is clear what code needs to be examined to understand the effect of an assignment.

There are times, however, when it is necessary or convenient for a procedure to be capable of assigning a binding passed by its caller, even though the procedure may not be defined within the scope of the associated variable. For example, it may be intended above that a and b both be set to 5, in which case the expression should yield 10.

This may be accomplished by a different parameter-passing technique in which the arguments passed to p are the bindings of a and b, not their corresponding expressed values. This form of parameter passing is known as *call-by-reference*.

Call-by-reference allows us to write some procedures that cannot be written using call-by-value. The classic example is a procedure that swaps the contents of its arguments. For example, using call-by-reference we can write

```
--> define swap =
    proc (x, y)
       let temp = 0
       in begin temp := x; x := y; y := temp end;
--> define c = 3;
--> let b = 4
    in begin
         swap(c, b);
         b
       end;
3
--> c;
4
```

○ *Exercise 6.2.1*

Why doesn't this work under call-by-value? □

In most languages with call-by-reference, references can be array elements as well as variable bindings. If an array element is passed by reference to a procedure and the procedure assigns to its corresponding formal parameter, the effect is to assign a new value to the array element. Thus *swap* may be used to exchange the values of array elements.

```
--> define b = 2;
--> letarray a[3]
    in begin
         a[1] := 5;
         swap(a[1], b);
         a[1]
       end;
2
--> b;
5
```

In some languages, call-by-reference operands may be expressions other than variable or data structure references (such as applications). In these languages the value of the operand is placed in a new location, and assignments to this location by the called procedure have no effect that is visible to the caller. For example, consider

```
--> define c = 3;
--> define p = proc (x) x := 5;
--> begin
       p(add1(c));
       c
    end;
3
```

Here c refers to a location that initially contains 3. The assignment changes the value of the binding of x from 4 to 5 but does not affect the binding of c. In such cases call-by-value and call-by-reference behave the same way.

More than one call-by-reference parameter may refer to the same location:

```
--> let b = 3;
       p = proc (x, y)
              begin
                 x := 4;
                 y
              end
    in p(b, b);
4
```

The reason this yields 4 is that x and y both refer to the cell that is the binding of b. This phenomenon is known as *aliasing*. Here x and y are aliases (names) for the same location. Aliasing makes it very difficult to understand programs. Generally, we do not expect an assignment to one variable to change the value of another. Virtually all rules for reasoning formally about programs are invalid in the presence of aliasing.

If references to array elements are passed as arguments, then in general it is impossible to detect aliasing without costly run-time checks. For example, swap(a[1], a[f(b)]) results in aliasing if and only if f(b) yields 1, which may be impossible to predict.

The preceding definition of *swap* happens to work even if its parameters are aliased, but aliasing can provide unpleasant surprises. The following version of swap cleverly avoids the use of a temporary variable by assuming that its arguments are integers.

```
--> define swap2 =
    proc (x, y)
      begin
        x := +(x, y); y := -(x, y); x := -(x, y)
      end;
```

```
--> define b = 1;
--> define c = 2;
--> swap2(b, c);
--> b;
2
--> c;
1
--> swap2(b, b);
--> b;
0
```

The first call to *swap2* works correctly. In the second call, however, x and y are aliases for b, so b is assigned $2 + 2 = 4$, and then $4 - 4 = 0$. Clearly *swap2* works only if its arguments are not aliased.

How is call-by-reference to be modeled? The clue is that the denoted values of the caller are the same as the denoted values of the procedure. Thus, if the operand is a variable, we can pass its binding directly to the procedure, rather than copying its contents to a new cell, as we did in call-by-value. So we can obtain a simple version of call-by-reference by changing the production

$$\langle operand \rangle ::= \langle exp \rangle$$

to

$$\langle operand \rangle ::= \langle varref \rangle$$

and changing *eval-rand* to

```
(define eval-rand
  (lambda (rand env)
    (variant-case rand
      (varref (var) (apply-env env var))
      (else (error "Invalid operand:" rand)))))
```

What other forms can operands take? We have seen that when an array reference appears as an operand in call-by-reference, we must pass a reference to the array element, not the value of the array element. In a typical implementation, a reference to an array element is simply a pointer to the element. Since it is not possible in Scheme to obtain a pointer directly to a vector element, we represent array elements by the ae record type, which records the array and the index of an element within the array's vector.

```
(define-record ae (array index))
```

So in general, an L-value in the language is either a cell or an array element; in either case the contents of the L-value is an expressed value. We write this as

$$\text{L-value} = \text{Cell (Expressed Value)} + \text{Array Element (Expressed Value)}$$

$$\text{Denoted Value} = \text{L-value}$$

Later we introduce denoted values that are not L-values.

We have explored two possibilities for call-by-reference operands: variables and array references. We could restrict call-by-reference operands to these two forms, but instead we adopt the more common design alternative, suggested earlier in this section, that arbitrary expressions be allowed as call-by-reference operands, with their values passed to the procedure in fresh cells as in call-by-value. Hence we write the grammar for operands as

⟨operand⟩ ::= ⟨varref⟩
     | ⟨array-exp⟩ [⟨exp⟩]   `arrayref (array index)`
     | ⟨exp⟩

To obtain an interpreter for call-by-reference, we start off with the interpreter for call-by-value and modify the auxiliary procedures that deal with operands and denoted values, since those are the ones that change.

If we start with an interpreter for call-by-value with indirect arrays, we get the auxiliary procedures shown in figure 6.2.1. Corresponding to the grammar for operands, `eval-rand` has three cases. If the operand is a variable or an array reference, the corresponding L-value should be passed directly to the procedure; otherwise the expression should be evaluated and copied into a new cell, as for call-by-value.

Since we have changed the set of denoted values (or at least the set of representations of denoted values), we need to change the procedures that deal with denoted values. There are only two of these: `denoted->expressed` and `denoted-value-assign!`. We modify each of them to check what kind of denoted value they are given and to do the right thing in each case. In this interpreter, the error lines in each of these two procedures should never be executed, but they allow for extension later.

The distinction between direct and indirect parameter passing is orthogonal to the distinction between call-by-value and call-by-reference. The former concerns allocation and sharing of aggregate values, which are mutated through array assignment, whereas the latter concerns allocation and sharing of variable bindings, which are mutated through variable assignment.

Figure 6.2.1   Auxiliaries for call-by-reference with indirect arrays

```
(define eval-rand
  (lambda (rand env)
    (variant-case rand
      (varref (var) (apply-env env var))
      (arrayref (array index)
        (make-ae (eval-array-exp array env) (eval-exp index env)))
      (else (make-cell (eval-exp rand env))))))

(define denoted->expressed
  (lambda (den-val)
    (cond
      ((cell? den-val) (cell-ref den-val))
      ((ae? den-val) (array-ref (ae->array den-val) (ae->index den-val)))
      (else (error "Can't dereference denoted value:" den-val)))))

(define denoted-value-assign!
  (lambda (den-val val)
    (cond
      ((cell? den-val) (cell-set! den-val val))
      ((ae? den-val) (array-set! (ae->array den-val) (ae->index den-val) val))
      (else (error "Can't assign to denoted value:" den-val)))))
```

The combination of direct parameter passing and call-by-reference is used, for example, when arrays are bound to var parameters in Pascal. Though the combination of indirect parameter passing and call-by-reference is less common, it is occasionally used, as in Modula-2, when passing an aggregate value whose type is "hidden."

Figure 6.2.2 shows the effect of executing the program in figure 6.1.5 under both the indirect and direct models. In the indirect model, both x and u are bound to a cell containing a pointer to the first location in the array containing the sequence 5, 6, and 4. The assignment x := v mutates that cell, so that now u and x both point to the other array. (See figure 6.2.2 (a).) In the direct model, x and u are both bound to the same cell, which contains the sequence $<5, 6, 4>$. The assignment x := v mutates that cell, so it contains the same contents as the other array. Since we are using the direct model, this means the sequence of numbers $<3, 8>$, rather than a sequence of cells containing them, so we are forced to copy the array. The final assignment x[1] := 9 mutates the copied array, so at the end of the procedure x and u

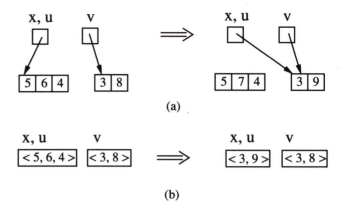

(a)

x, u   v

| < 5, 6, 4 > | | < 3, 8 > | ⟹ | < 3, 9 > | | < 3, 8 > |

(b)

Figure 6.2.2 Effect of figure 6.1.5 using call-by-reference

are both bound to a cell containing the sequence <3, 9>, and v is bound to a cell containing the sequence <3, 8>. (See figure 6.2.2 (b).)

One advantage of call-by-reference is that it allows a procedure to "return" more than one value by side-effecting some of its parameters. For example, a procedure may take a call-by-reference parameter to which it assigns a status code indicating what sort of exception, if any, it may have encountered. This allows the procedure to return normal results in the usual way without danger of confusion with error codes. There are other ways of returning multiple results using call-by-value (for example, continuation-passing style as in exercise 11.4.4 or variant records as used in exercise 5.5.8).

As we saw in section 6.1, passing structured objects such as arrays by value requires copying the object. For reasons of efficiency structured objects may be passed by reference, even when other arguments are passed by value. Another alternative when call-by-value is used by default is to provide specific declarations that force certain parameters to be passed by reference. If such a declaration is forgotten when passing an array, an inefficient copy may be performed without the programmer's knowledge. Of course, assignments to elements of an array are visible to the caller if the array has been passed by reference, but not if it has been copied. Heap-allocated objects, including Scheme's cons cells and vectors, are always accessed via references. They are not copied when these references to them are passed by value.

Figure 6.2.3   Program for exercise 6.2.4

```
letarray u[3]; v[2]
in begin
    u[0] := 5; u[1] := 6; u[2] := 4; v[0] := 3; v[1] := 8;
    let p = proc (x, y)
              begin
                write(y);
                x[1] := 7;
                write(y);
                x := v;
                x[1] := 9;
                write(y)
              end
    in begin
        p(u, u[1]);
        write(u[1])
      end
```

• *Exercise 6.2.2*

Modify this interpreter to use the direct model of arrays rather than the indirect model. What does it mean to pass an array element by reference in the direct model? ☐

• *Exercise 6.2.3*

Implement the call-by-reference interpreters for both direct and indirect arrays. Test them using *swap* and *swap2*. Also verify that only with indirect arrays can the caller of a procedure notice assignments made by the procedure to array elements. ☐

○ *Exercise 6.2.4*

Draw appropriate diagrams and describe how the program in figure 6.2.3, whose parameter passing protocol uses call-by-reference with indirect arrays, prints 6779. ☐

6.3 Call-by-Value-Result and Call-by-Result

It is often possible for compilers to allocate memory (cells) for call-by-value parameters of a procedure in locations that the procedure's code can access directly. This contrasts with call-by-reference parameters, the locations of which are not known until the procedure is called. This usually makes variable references less efficient when call-by-reference is used. The *call-by-value-result* parameter-passing technique combines the variable reference efficiency of call-by-value with the ability, provided by call-by-reference, to return information to the caller through parameters. The trick is to pass a pointer to the caller's cell, as in call-by-reference, and then to copy the contents of the cell in a location local to the called procedure. The called procedure then uses the local cell just as it would with call-by-value. Then, just before the procedure returns, the contents of the local cell is copied back into the caller's cell.

Call-by-value-result achieves more efficient variable reference than call-by-reference at the expense of less efficient procedure call and return. In this respect it is superior only if variables are referenced many times in a typical call, as in a loop. Even in such cases, a compiler may be able to eliminate the indirection of call-by-reference using optimization techniques that are beyond the scope of this book.

There may, however, be other reasons to prefer call-by-value-result over call-by-reference. One is that call-by-value-result does not suffer from the aliasing problems of call-by-reference. For example, *swap2* is correct if parameters are passed by value-result. Given the difficulties that aliasing poses for formal proof and other approaches to reasoning carefully about programs, call-by-value-result may be preferred when attempting to write highly reliable programs.

In the absence of aliasing, call-by-value-result has the same effect as call-by-reference. Therefore, some language specifications allow the use of either call-by-reference or call-by-value-result. The compiler is then free to choose for each parameter the passing technique that is optimum under the circumstances of the call. The danger is that if aliasing does occur, the results are unpredictable. This may have serious consequences. For example, though a program may at times alias two arguments, it might still work correctly because the compiler happens to choose call-by-value-result for one or both of the arguments. If the program is then compiled using a different compiler, or even using the same compiler after the program has been changed in ways that affect optimization of the call, call-by-reference may be used for both arguments. This exposes an error in a program that may have performed correctly for some time. To make matters worse, the error may not actually cause damage for a long time, since the arguments may be array elements that are aliased only under run time conditions that rarely occur.

Call-by-reference and call-by-value-result allow information to be passed both to and from a called procedure. The *call-by-result* parameter-passing technique is appropriate when a parameter is used only to pass information from a procedure to its caller. It is simply a variation on call-by-value-result in which the local L-value of a parameter is uninitialized. It may be used, for example, to return an error code to the caller.

Call-by-value, call-by-value-result, and call-by-result are sometimes known collectively as *call-by-copy,* since they all involve making a copy of a variable binding when the operand is a variable reference.

- *Exercise 6.3.1*
Modify the parameter-passing of the call-by-reference with indirect arrays interpreter so that parameters are passed by value-result. □

- *Exercise 6.3.2*
Write a program (without using *swap2*) in which call-by-value, call-by-reference, and call-by-value-result all yield different results. □

6.4 Expressed or Denoted Values?

The languages we have developed follow the tradition of Scheme and similar languages in that they have a rich set of expressed values, but the denoted values are comparatively simple: they are always cells containing expressed values. Having a rich set of expressed values is important, because the primary way in which computed information is returned is as the value of a procedure: an expressed value.

In traditional imperative languages, however, expressions occur primarily inside assignment statements, so the set of expressed values corresponds roughly to the set of values that are *storable* in a memory location. In such languages, the set of expressed values is generally simple, but the set of denoted values is quite rich. In Pascal, for example, the expressed values are scalars, such as integers and characters, but the denoted values include arrays and procedures. We shall now see how this change in perspective is reflected in our interpreters.

The next language has the simplest possible set of expressed values:

$$\text{Expressed Value} = \text{Number}$$

but we make the set of denoted values much richer:

$$\text{Denoted Value} = \text{L-value} + \text{Array} + \text{Procedure}$$

So arrays and procedures are denoted values but not expressed values. This does not cause much problem for arrays, since arrays are already introduced with `letarray`, but procedures are more complicated. The fact that procedures are expressed values is built into our syntax and interpreters. Procedures are created as expressed values by `proc`, and retrieved as expressed values when *eval-exp* evaluates the operator portion of an application.

So our first task is to change the language's syntax. Since a procedure (or array) can exist only as the binding of a variable, we make ⟨operator⟩ (or ⟨array-exp⟩) be a variable. In addition, we need to introduce a form, like `let`, that allows us to introduce variables, without using procedure application. To do this, we delete the productions

---

⟨exp⟩ ::= `proc` ⟨varlist⟩ ⟨exp⟩   `proc (formals body)`
⟨operator⟩ ::= ⟨exp⟩
⟨array-exp⟩ ::= ⟨exp⟩

---

and replace them by the productions

⟨exp⟩ ::= `letproc` ⟨procdecls⟩ `in`   `letproc (procdecls`
          ⟨exp⟩   `body)`
        ╎ `local` ⟨decls⟩ `in` ⟨exp⟩   `local (decls body)`
⟨operator⟩ ::= ⟨varref⟩
⟨array-exp⟩ ::= ⟨varref⟩

In order to have something interesting to pass to these procedures, we use call-by-reference. Our starting point is the call-by-reference interpreter of section 6.2, shown in figure 6.1.2 and figure 6.2.1. Figure 6.4.1 shows the resulting interpreter. There are only two changes in the code of figure 6.4.1. First, we replace *eval-rator*, which was *eval-exp*, with code that uses `apply-env`, since the `rator` is known to be a variable reference.

Figure 6.4.1   Interpreter with denoted procedures and arrays

```
(define eval-exp
  (lambda (exp env)
    (variant-case exp
      (letproc (procdecls body)
        (let ((vars (map procdecl->var procdecls))
              (closures (map (lambda (decl)
                               (make-closure
                                 (procdecl->formals decl)
                                 (procdecl->body decl)
                                 env))
                             procdecls)))
          (let ((new-env (extend-env vars closures env)))
            (eval-exp body new-env))))
      (local (decls body)
        (let ((vars (map decl->var decls))
              (exps (map decl->exp decls)))
          (let ((new-env (extend-env vars
                           (map (lambda (exp)
                                  (make-cell (eval-exp exp env)))
                                exps)
                           env)))
            (eval-exp body new-env))))
      ...)))

(define eval-rator
  (lambda (rator env)
    (let ((den-val (apply-env env (varref->var rator))))
      (if (closure? den-val)
          den-val
          (denoted->expressed den-val)))))
```

The second change is the new construction letproc. The code for letproc
builds a list of closures, and then evaluates the body in a new environment
in which each of the names is bound to the corresponding closure. See figure 6.4.1.

Since the set of denoted values has changed, we also need to review the auxiliary procedures introduced in section 6.1, which manipulate denoted values.
The results are shown in figure 6.4.2. The procedures *denoted->expressed*
and *denoted-value-assign!* can be the same as for the call-by-reference

Figure 6.4.2   Procedures for call-by-reference with denoted indirect arrays

```
(define denoted->expressed
  (lambda (den-val)
    (cond
      ((cell? den-val) (cell-ref den-val))
      ((ae? den-val) (array-ref (ae->array den-val) (ae->index den-val)))
      (else (error "Can't dereference denoted value:" den-val)))))

(define denoted-value-assign!
  (lambda (den-val val)
    (cond
      ((cell? den-val) (cell-set! den-val val))
      ((ae? den-val) (array-set! (ae->array den-val) (ae->index den-val) val))
      (else (error "Can't assign to denoted value:" den-val)))))

(define do-letarray make-array)

(define eval-array-exp
  (lambda (array-exp env)
    (apply-env env (varref->var array-exp))))
```

case, since they already contain checks to make sure that only legal L-values are dereferenced or mutated. Similarly, *expressed->denoted* and *eval-rand* remain unchanged. In letarray, the variables are bound directly to the arrays, rather than to cells pointing to the arrays, so *do-letarray* need not call *make-cell*. Since array expressions must be variables, *eval-array-exp* can be simplified to use *apply-env*. This completes the interpreter.

Typically, languages that use a stack as their basic run-time structure (see section 10.4) allocate their environments on the stack, so denoted values are restricted to values that are storable on the stack. These typically include single-word quantities, such as small integers and pointers, but may also include quantities that take up several words on the stack. In Pascal, for example, even arrays are allocated on the stack, and are copied when they are passed by value, an expensive operation. Denoted values typically include cells, since these are represented by pointers, which are easily stored on the stack. In section 10.4, we study the issue of stack allocation and the representation of various values on the stack in much more detail.

Imperative languages typically equate expressed values with those values that are storable in a memory cell. Therefore the set of expressed values is restricted to those that fit into a single machine word, such as small integers and pointers. Languages vary in the specification of what values are storable, particularly when those values are pointers. In Pascal, for example, pointers refer to heap-allocated data structures, similar to cons cells in Scheme. C, on the other hand, allows pointers to almost any type of value, including procedures.

Scheme has a rich set of expressed values, as do a number of other functional and almost-functional languages, including ML. Since Scheme uses an indirect model of aggregates, most values are represented as pointers. Cells (L-values) are not expressed values in Scheme. This is reflected in our need to define a `cell` ADT, and in our simulation of array element pointers. Scheme's denoted values are just cells. ML, on the other hand, does not support variable assignment. Instead, assignment is accomplished by explicit operations on cells, just as we have used the cell ADT in our interpreters. Expressed values then include cells. Since there is no variable assignment, there is no reason to require denoted values to differ from expressed values, and therefore denoted and expressed values are the same in ML.

We have only touched upon the study of the value structures of programming languages. Studying the denoted and expressed values of a language provides deep insight into its structure. A language's value structure determines a great deal of its expressive power and affects its efficiency and implementation strategies. For example, when procedures are not expressed values, many functional programming techniques (such as currying) are not possible. On the other hand, when procedures are expressed values, they must at times be heap allocated, which is generally less efficient than stack allocation. Clever compilers are, however, often able to avoid apparent inefficiencies. If, for example, a Scheme procedure is bound directly using `let` and every reference to it is in the operator position of an application, then it could be stack allocated.

● *Exercise 6.4.1*
Implement the interpreter of this section and test it with several programs. ▯

○ *Exercise 6.4.2*
The interpreter of this section, like our earlier ones, assumes that the initial environment consists of cells containing primitive procedures. These cells can thus be modified by variable assignment. Modify the interpreter to prevent this by having the initial environment contain procedures rather than cells. ▯

- *Exercise 6.4.3*

  Modify this interpreter to use call-by-value instead of call-by-reference. □

o *Exercise 6.4.4*

  Modify this interpreter to pass structures directly, rather than indirectly. □

o *Exercise 6.4.5*

  Modify this interpreter so that `letproc` defines its procedures recursively, as `letrecproc` does. □

o *Exercise 6.4.6*

  Several times during the course of this chapter we have presented a grammar rule that weakens the expressiveness of the language. For example, ⟨array-exp⟩ was any expression and now it can be only a variable. Modify the parser or the interpreter to support these restrictions. □

6.5 Call-by-Name and Call-by-Need

In section 4.3, we saw that lambda calculus expressions may be evaluated using β-reduction. In this model, procedures are called by performing the body of the procedure after the operands are substituted for each reference to the corresponding variable. This substitution may require (α-conversion) to avoid capturing of variable references that occur free in the operands. Such rewriting techniques, which require manipulation of program text during evaluation, are heavily used in the theoretical study of programming languages. In general, however, they are too inefficient for practical use.

β-reduction does have one characteristic that is sometimes of practical importance and is not shared by the parameter-passing techniques discussed so far: the possibility of delaying (through normal order reduction) the evaluation of operands until their values are needed. This may avoid unnecessary, or even nonterminating computation.

The price paid for avoiding non-termination is that if there are repeated references to the same parameter, then the associated operand is reevaluated with each reference. Another subtlety of this evaluation scheme is that the index subexpression of an array reference is not evaluated until the time of assignment. In the following example, the delay of array index evaluation is critical.

```
--> define p = proc (x)
                begin
                    i := 1;
                    x := 2
                end;
--> define i = 0;
--> letarray a[2]
    in begin
        a[0] := 1;
        p(a[i]);
        writeln(a[0], a[1])
    end;
1 2
```

Delayed evaluation and assignment do not combine well, since it is hard to understand the effect of assignment if it is unclear when the assignment will happen. Nevertheless, this combination is supported by some languages, notably Algol 60, and there are times when it is useful. A classic example is Jensen's device (exercise 6.5.4). Nevertheless, parameter-passing mechanisms that use delayed evaluation are used in some programming languages, so they are worth studying.

To delay operand evaluation without program rewriting, it is tempting simply to pass a reference to some representation such as an abstract syntax tree (or compiled code) of the operand. However, it is necessary to prevent free variables in the operand from being captured by declarations in the called procedure. We have already encountered the variable capture problem when creating procedures, and the solution is the same: close the operand in the calling environment. We do this by forming a data structure that includes both some representation of the text of the operand and also the bindings of all variables that occur free in the operand. Closures created to delay evaluation are called *thunks*. For example, in section 4.5.2, we saw how thunks (created as procedures of no arguments) may be used to delay evaluating a stream's tail.

Parameter passing in which argument evaluation is delayed using thunks that are reevaluated with every variable reference is called *call-by-name*. To develop an implementation for a call-by-name interpreter employing indirect parameter passing, we first identify the expressed and denoted values. We begin with the language of section 6.1. For this language we had

$$\text{Expressed Value} = \text{Number} + \text{Procedure} + \text{Array}$$

What should the denoted values be? As suggested above, these values should include thunks that encapsulate an operand and its environment. But what kind of value should invocation of such a thunk return? Since a formal parameter may appear on the left-hand side of a variable assignment, the only safe answer is that invocation of a thunk must return an L-value. We write this as

$$\text{Thunk} = () \rightarrow \text{L-value}$$

meaning that a thunk is a procedure of no arguments, which returns an L-value when called. We represent a thunk, containing an operand and an environment, using the following record type:

```
(define-record thunk (exp env))
```

As in the case of call-by-reference, the possible L-values include array elements:

$$\text{L-value} = \text{Cell (Expressed Value)} + \text{Array Element (Expressed Value)}$$

Since these L-values are the same as in section 6.2, we can use most of the same auxiliary procedures.

We would also like to have local variables, either scalars or arrays, in procedure bodies. It is unnecessary and inefficient to use the thunk mechanism for these variables, so we can represent them in the usual way. Thus, the denoted values are either L-values or thunks:

$$\text{Denoted Value} = \text{L-value} + \text{Thunk}$$

We can continue to use *eval-exp* from figure 6.1.2, which we extend with local in figure 6.5.1. The call-by-name interpreter contains one big difference: *eval-rands* does not evaluate the operands. Instead, it merely packages them in thunks.

A thunk is evaluated when the variable to which it is bound is evaluated. Since the body of a thunk is an operand, *eval-rand* is used to evaluate the thunk body. Since invocation of a thunk returns an L-value, we cannot use *eval-exp* here. Instead, we use a grammar for operands that recognizes the special case of an operand that is a variable or array reference. In this case we can pass the corresponding L-value directly. This is the same situation as in call-by-reference.

Figure 6.5.1   Call-by-name interpreter

```
(define eval-exp
  (lambda (exp env)
    (variant-case exp
      (local (decls body)
        (let ((vars (map decl->var decls))
              (exps (map decl->exp decls)))
          (let ((new-env (extend-env vars
                            (map (lambda (exp)
                                   (make-cell (eval-exp exp env)))
                                 exps)
                            env)))
            (eval-exp body new-env))))
      (app (rator rands)
        (apply-proc (eval-rator rator env) (eval-rands rands env)))
      (varref (var) (denoted->expressed (apply-env env var)))
      (varassign (var exp)
        (denoted-value-assign! (apply-env env var) (eval-exp exp env)))
      (letarray (arraydecls body)
        (eval-exp body
          (extend-env (map decl->var arraydecls)
            (map (lambda (decl)
                   (do-letarray (eval-exp (decl->exp decl) env)))
                 arraydecls)
            env)))
      (arrayref (array index)
        (array-ref (eval-array-exp array env) (eval-exp index env)))
      (arrayassign (array index exp)
        (array-set!
          (eval-array-exp array env)
          (eval-exp index env)
          (eval-exp exp env)))
      ...)))

(define eval-rands
  (lambda (rands env)
    (map (lambda (rand) (make-thunk rand env)) rands)))
```

Figure 6.5.2 Auxiliaries for call-by-name interpreter

```
(define eval-rand
  (lambda (rand env)
    (variant-case rand
      (varref (var) (denoted->L-value (apply-env env var)))
      (arrayref (array index)
        (make-ae (eval-array-exp array env) (eval-exp index env)))
      (else (make-cell (eval-exp rand env))))))

(define denoted->L-value
  (lambda (den-val)
    (if (thunk? den-val)
        (eval-rand (thunk->exp den-val) (thunk->env den-val))
        den-val)))

(define denoted->expressed
  (lambda (den-val)
    (let ((l-val (denoted->L-value den-val)))
      (cond
        ((cell? l-val) (cell-ref l-val))
        ((ae? l-val)
         (array-ref (ae->array l-val) (ae->index l-val)))
        (else (error "Can't dereference denoted value:" l-val))))))

(define denoted-value-assign!
  (lambda (den-val exp-val)
    (let ((l-val (denoted->L-value den-val)))
      (cond
        ((cell? l-val) (cell-set! l-val exp-val))
        ((ae? l-val) (array-set! (ae->array l-val) (ae->index l-val) exp-val))
        (else (error "Can't assign to denoted value:" l-val))))))

(define expressed->denoted make-cell)

(define do-letarray (compose make-cell make-array))

(define eval-array-exp eval-exp)

(define eval-rator eval-exp)
```

We write the grammar for operands as

$$\langle operand \rangle ::= \langle varref \rangle$$
$$| \ \langle array\text{-}exp \rangle \ [\langle exp \rangle] \qquad\qquad \texttt{arrayref (array index)}$$
$$| \ \langle exp \rangle$$

and we invoke thunks with a slightly modified version of the call-by-reference `eval-rand`, shown in figure 6.5.2. If the thunk contains a variable or an array reference, the corresponding L-value is returned. The invocation (`apply-env env var`) may return another thunk rather than an L-value, so `denoted->L-value` is called, which in turn invokes that thunk. If the thunk contains a more complex expression, the best we can do is to evaluate it and put it in a new cell. Because this mechanism tries to return an L-value rather than copying its contents, call-by-name often coincides with call-by-reference.

All that remains is to define the auxiliary procedures used in figure 6.5.1. Since these L-values are the same as in the call-by-reference case, we can do this by adapting them to invoke thunks when necessary; see figure 6.5.2.

The procedure `denoted->expressed` first coerces its denoted value to an L-value by using `denoted->L-value` to invoke the thunk if necessary. It then dereferences the L-value, just as it did in the call-by-reference case. The procedure `denoted-value-assign!` works similarly. Since arrays are expressed but not denoted, we use the version of `do-letarray` that calls `make-cell`. Furthermore, since arrays are expressed values, array expressions may be arbitrary expressions, and `eval-array-exp` must be `eval-exp`. Similarly, `eval-rator` must be `eval-exp`. This completes the procedures that need to be defined for the interpreter.

- *Exercise 6.5.1*
Since call-by-name is so much like call-by-reference, you might expect *swap* to work under call-by-name. One example of an unpleasant surprise provided by the interaction between delayed array index evaluation and assignment is that *swap* may fail. What values are printed by the following expression?

```
letarray a[2]
in local i = 0
   in begin
       a[0] := 1; a[1] := 0;
       swap(i, a[i]);
       writeln(a[0], a[1])
     end
```
□

- *Exercise 6.5.2*

  What values are returned when these two program terminate?

  ```
  let p = proc (x)
          begin
              x := 3; x := +(x, 5); x := +(x, 5)
          end
  in local a = 10
     in begin p(a); a end


  local a = 10
  in let p = proc (x)
             begin
                a := 3; a := +(x, 5); a := +(x, 5)
             end
     in begin p(+(a, a)); a end
  ```

  What values are returned if the `local` is replaced by `let`? Remember that `let` is syntactic sugar for procedure application. ▯

- *Exercise 6.5.3*

  Write an interpreter that implements procedure calling by substituting the operands for the formal parameters of the procedures. What difficulties do you encounter? ▯

- *Exercise 6.5.4*

  Although the combination of assignment and delayed evaluation is problematic, there are times when it is useful. The classic example is a procedure that computes integral approximations. Write a procedure `int` that takes an integrand expression E, an integration parameter x (a variable occurring free in the integrand expression E), lower and upper bounds a and b, and an increment δ, and returns an approximation to the integral using the rectangular rule. That is,

  $$\text{int}(E\ x\ a\ b\ \delta) = \left(\sum_{\substack{x=a,a+\delta,\ldots,\\ a+\lceil (b-a)/\delta \rceil \delta}} E \right) \approx \int_a^b E\, dx$$

  For example, assuming arithmetic operations are defined on floating point numbers (written with decimal points) as well as integers, and a primitive division procedure has been added to the initial environment, we could obtain a rough approximation of $\int_1^5 2x\, dx$ as follows.

```
--> define x = 0;
--> int(*(x, 2), x, 1, 5, quotient(1, 2))
35.0
--> x;
5.0
```

(Here we have assumed that the numbers in the defined language include real numbers under suitable arithmetic operations, but for this example we can avoid real-number literals). The variable x could have been initialized to any value. Assignments to x performed by `int` leave it with the value of the upper bound (or a bit more). The trick of assigning to an argument that is the binding of a variable occurring free in another argument is called *Jensen's device*. How should `int` be written using first-class procedures? ☐

When side effects are not involved, a delayed argument yields the same value each time it is referenced. Repeated evaluation of such arguments is a waste of effort. By saving the value obtained the first time such an argument is needed, it is possible to avoid redundant computation. This is *call-by-need*. A similar technique, memoization, was used in section 4.5.2 to avoid repeated evaluation of a stream's tail.

We can turn the call-by-name interpreter into a call-by-need interpreter by memoizing the result of invoking a thunk, so that later evaluations of the same variable will see the result instead of the thunk. To do this, we must change the set of denoted values slightly:

$$\text{Denoted Value} = \text{L-value} + \text{Memo}$$

$$\text{Memo} = \text{Cell (Thunk} + \text{L-value)}$$

so that a denoted value is either an L-value or a memo, which is a cell containing either a thunk or its resulting L-value. We represent a memo as a record type:

```
(define-record memo (cell))
```

To incorporate this into the interpreter, we need change only `eval-rands`, to produce memos, and `denoted->L-value`, to actually do the memoization. The procedure `denoted->L-value` looks to see if its denoted value is a memo. If not, it must be an L-value, so it is returned directly. Otherwise, it looks at the contents of the cell. If the cell contains an L-value, it returns that L-value. If not, the cell contains a thunk, so the thunk is invoked with `eval-rand`, returning an L-value. This L-value is put in the cell, and then returned; see figure 6.5.3.

Figure 6.5.3   Auxiliaries for call-by-need interpreter

```
(define eval-rands
  (lambda (rands env)
    (map (lambda (rand)
           (make-memo (make-cell (make-thunk rand env))))
         rands)))

(define denoted->L-value
  (lambda (den-val)
    (if (memo? den-val)
        (let ((cell (memo->cell den-val)))
          (let ((contents (cell-ref cell)))
            (if (thunk? contents)
                (let ((l-val (eval-rand
                               (thunk->exp contents)
                               (thunk->env contents))))
                  (cell-set! cell l-val)
                  l-val)
                contents)))
        den-val)))
```

○ *Exercise 6.5.5*

What do call-by-name and call-by-need print for this program?

```
local a = 10
in let p = proc (x) +(x, x)
   in p(+(begin write(a); a end, a))
```
☐

6.6 Optional and Keyword Arguments

In most languages, procedures usually require a fixed number of arguments, and an exception is raised if they are called with the wrong number. If a given argument is the same in most calls to a procedure, it is convenient to omit this argument from these calls. This is possible if there is provision for *optional* arguments. If an optional argument is omitted from a call, the corresponding formal parameter is associated with a *default* value that is specified by the called procedure. For example, it is usually possible to supply a port to an output procedure so that output may be directed to a chosen file. In most cases, however, there is a "standard output port" to which most output is directed, such as the terminal in an interactive system. Thus the port argument of an output procedure is often optional and defaults to the standard output port.

Procedures may have several optional arguments. Usually optional parameters must follow required parameters in formal parameter lists. If there are n required parameters and m optional parameters, the procedure may be called with i arguments, where $n \leq i \leq n + m$, and the last $n + m - i$ parameters assume their default values. Arguments that it would most often be convenient to omit should be placed last, since omission of an argument requires omission of all the following arguments. Scheme input and output procedures take optional port arguments in this way.

Scheme procedures with optional arguments may be created using a syntax in which an improper list is used to specify the formal parameters.

$$(\texttt{lambda} \ (var_1 \ \ldots \ var_n \ . \ opt) \ body)$$

When a procedure created with this syntax is invoked with $m \geq n$ arguments, opt is bound to a (possibly empty) list of arguments $n + 1$ through m. This generalizes the Scheme expression of the form ($\texttt{lambda}$ var $body$) discussed in section 1.3, which may be used to create procedures in which all arguments are optional.

The Scheme optional-argument form does not allow the specification of default values for optional arguments. We can characterize this feature by a translation into Scheme as follows:

```
(lambda-opt  (var_1 ... var_n (opt_1 exp_1) ... (opt_k exp_k))
    body)

⇒ (lambda (var_1 ... var_n . opts)
     (let ((len-opts (length opts)))
       (let ((opt_1 (if (< len-opts 1) exp_1 (list-ref opts 0)))
             ...
             (opt_k (if (< len-opts k) exp_k (list-ref opts k-1))))
         body)))
```

This translation highlights some design decisions about the default values. The expressions exp_i appear inside the scope of the var_j, but they could have been placed outside that scope. Furthermore, the exp_i are evaluated each time the procedure is called. Even if the exp_i were not in the scope of the var_j, we might get different values because of side-effects.

- *Exercise 6.6.1*

  Modify the parser to accept the following extended syntax for ⟨varlist⟩.

  ⟨varlist⟩ ::= ( )
        | (⟨vars⟩ {,⟨keydecl⟩}*)
        | (⟨keydecls⟩)
  ⟨keydecls⟩ ::= ⟨keydecl⟩ {,⟨keydecl⟩}*
  ⟨keydecl⟩ ::= :⟨var⟩ = ⟨exp⟩   `decl (var exp)`

  Then modify the interpreter of figure 5.5.1 to support optional arguments. When a procedure with optional formals is called, the expressions associated with optional arguments are evaluated in the scope outside the procedure to obtain their default values before evaluating the procedure body. It is a run-time error to omit an argument that has not been given a default value.

  ```
  --> (proc (x, :a = 1) +(x, a))(100);
  101
  --> let y = 3
      in (proc (x, :a = 1, :b = +(2, y))
             +(x, +(a, b)))
         (100, 10);
  115
  ```
  □

- *Exercise 6.6.2*

  The default values may appear inside or outside the scope of the non-optional formals var_j, and they may be evaluated at procedure creation time or at procedure call time. This gives two design decisions, for a total of four possible designs. Are all of them sensible? Give examples to show how the same program would give different answers in each possible design. Modify the equation for `lambda-opt` to express each design. □

  In most languages, formal parameters are associated with arguments by *position*: the value of the nth operand of an application is associated with the nth variable in the procedure's formal parameter list. It is also possible to make this association by pairing operands with *keywords* that name the corresponding formal parameter. It then does not matter in what order these operands appear. In Lisp dialects that support keyword parameters, these keywords are typically indicated with a colon followed by the associated variable name. For example, a procedure `make-window` with keyword parameters named `height` and `width` might be called with

```
make-window(:height = 1, :width = +(2, 3)),
```

which is the same as

```
make-window(:width = +(2, 3), :height = 1).
```

Some languages use only keyword operands. In others, both positional and keyword operands may be used in the same call, with the positional operands occurring first. With keyword operands, the programmer must remember the name but not the operand's position, whereas for positional operands it is the position, not the name, that matters.

Keyword operands add significantly to the visual complexity of applications, unless they allow the number of operands to be significantly reduced. This is the case when they are used in combination with optional operands. Then any collection of optional operands may be used in a call. An optional operand identified by a keyword is especially useful when the behavior of a procedure is determined by a large number of parameters whose default values are suitable most of the time. There may be many optional parameters that a programmer does not even know exist, but a rarely needed parameter may be specified using the appropriate keyword. Operating system commands often use some form of keyword parameter mechanism.

o *Exercise 6.6.3*
Modify the parser and interpreter of exercise 6.6.1 to support keyword parameters by extending the grammar of ⟨operands⟩.

⟨operands⟩ ::= ( )
     | (⟨exps⟩ {,⟨keydecl⟩}*)
     | (⟨keydecls⟩)
  ⟨exps⟩ ::= ⟨exp⟩ {,⟨exp⟩}*

For example,

```
--> (proc (x, y) -(x, y)) (:y = 3, :x = 2);
-1
--> (proc (x, :a = 1, :b = +(2, 3))
        +(x, +(a, b)))
    (100, :b = 2);
103
```
□

6.7 Summary

In the indirect model of arrays, an array is a sequence of cells, so when an array is passed by value, the procedure and its caller both see the same cells. In the direct model, an array is a sequence of values, so the procedure and its caller see different copies of the same sequence.

Call-by-reference allows a procedure to return information to its caller by assigning new values to its parameters. This is made possible by parameters that are references to variable bindings or data structure elements belonging to the caller. With call-by-reference it is possible for two parameters to refer to the same location. This phenomenon, known as aliasing, makes it difficult to understand programs. Call-by-value-result also allows information to be returned to the caller through variables but avoids the aliasing problem.

Analysis of the expressed and denoted values of our languages play an important role in the design of all these alternatives. Some languages are rich in expressed values but poor in denoted values, and others have the opposite mix.

Call-by-name delays evaluation of arguments until their values are needed, as with leftmost evaluation in the lambda calculus. This is achieved by passing thunks that close arguments over the calling environment. Call-by-name in combination with assignment is dangerous, since it may be difficult to predict just when assignments will take place. Call-by-need is a memoized variation on call-by-name. It avoids the inefficiency of repeatedly evaluating the same argument, but in combination with assignment it may not yield the same results as call-by-name.

Optional arguments and keyword operands are useful when a procedure has many parameters. With keyword operands the programmer need not remember the order of the arguments, and optional arguments may be omitted when a default value supplied by the procedure is appropriate.

7   Object-Oriented Languages

In this chapter we review the essential principles of object-oriented languages. This chapter is divided into three sections. The first discusses simple classes and objects, the second extends classes to include inheritance, and the last presents meta-classes. The interpreters of this section build from the interpreters of chapter 5.

7.1   Objects and Classes

In chapter 3 we introduced the notion of an abstract data type, or ADT. A data type is *abstract* when information about its representation is restricted to a designated set of procedures associated with the type. The techniques we use for implementing ADTs in Scheme are simple and adequate for our purposes. These techniques rely on our programming style, rather than on a language mechanism, to enforce data abstraction. We must be careful not to violate the abstraction of a data type by making any assumptions about a chosen representation except in the procedures that implement the ADT.

Data abstraction is aided by *modularity* mechanisms that group all the procedures that operate on elements of an ADT. Modularity facilities usually enforce *information hiding,* which ensures that only the procedures of an ADT operate on its values. When dynamic (or *latent*) type checking is used (as with Scheme's opaque primitive types) representation information is hidden by attaching to each value a tag indicating its type, and by requiring that all procedures check these tags before operating on values. Type tags are not needed if analysis prior to evaluation can prove that values are accessed only by appropriate operations. (Type checkers perform this job in statically-typed languages.) In either case, a fixed set of operations is associated with each type and adding support for user-defined data types may be difficult.

A more flexible approach to information hiding is to represent values as *objects*. An object is a set of operations that share a *state*. The state consists of one or more values that may be viewed and modified only by operations belonging to the object. These operations are often called *methods*. The operations supply the interface of the ADT to which the object belongs. Associating operations directly with the representation of a value makes it easy to create new data types. It also allows two objects of the same ADT to be represented differently, as long as their operations implement that same abstract interface. Extensive use of objects, particularly in conjunction with inheritance (discussed in the next section), characterizes a programming style called *object-oriented programming*.

Objects that share the same methods are said to be of the same *class*. In object-oriented programming, a typical style is to specify a set of methods (a class), and then to create objects that use those methods. The objects are then said to be *instances* of the class. A class is not the same as an ADT: one might have several different classes that give different implementations of the same ADT. Since the operations are associated directly with the object, it is possible to invoke the operation, which is in the interface, directly on the object without knowing which implementation it uses.

We shall see that it is useful for classes to be objects themselves, in which case creation of an instance is just another operation of the object that represents the class.

In languages with first class procedures, it is possible to represent objects as procedures. The simplest approach is to use a *message passing* protocol: a procedure representing an object is passed a message that selects the operation to be performed on the object. We have already seen one example of this approach in the `stack` and `make-stack` procedures of section 4.6. In this section we review this approach briefly and then present an interpreter that represents classes and instances as records. This interpreter gives a better understanding of techniques that may be employed to implement objects, and is extended further in the next section to reflect additional principles of object-oriented programming.

The `make-stack` procedure of figure 7.1.1 extends that of section 4.6. This procedure represents a class; each time it is invoked it returns a new instance of a stack object. These instances take a symbol representing a message and return a procedure that takes any additional arguments required by the operation and then performs the operation.

Each instance and class may have its own state, which is maintained as the bindings of one or more *instance variables* and *class variables,* respectively. In figure 7.1.1 there are two instance variables, `stk` and `local-pushed`, and one

Figure 7.1.1   Procedural stack class

```
(define make-stack
  (let ((pushed 0))
    (lambda ()
      (let ((stk '()) (local-pushed 0))
        (lambda (message)
          (case message
            ((empty?) (lambda () (null? stk)))
            ((push!) (lambda (x
                        (set! pushed (+ pushed 1))
                        (set! local-pushed (+ local-pushed 1))
                        (set! stk (cons x stk))))
            ((pop!) (lambda ()
                        (if (null? stk)
                            (error "Stack: Underflow")
                            (begin
                              (set! pushed (- pushed 1))
                              (set! local-pushed (- local-pushed 1))
                              (set! stk (cdr stk))))))
            ((top) (lambda ()
                        (if (null? stk)
                            (error "Stack: Underflow")
                            (car stk))))
            ((local-pushed) (lambda () local-pushed))
            ((pushed) (lambda () pushed))
            (else (error "Stack: Invalid message" message))))))))
```

class variable, *pushed*. Class variables maintain information that is common
to *all* instances of a class, whereas each instance of a class has its own value
for every instance variable. The following transcript illustrates the use of
local-pushed and *pushed*.

```
> (define s1 (make-stack))
> (define s2 (make-stack))
> ((s1 'push!) 13)
> ((s2 'push!) 14)
> ((s2 'push!) 15)
> ((s1 'local-pushed))
1
> ((s2 'local-pushed))
2
```

```
> ((s1 'pushed))
3
> ((s2 'pushed))
3
```

We now turn to modeling objects with an interpreter. The interpreted
language includes the following concrete and abstract syntax.

$\langle$exp$\rangle$ ::= $\langle$instance-var$\rangle$
 | $\langle$class-var$\rangle$
 | $\langle$instance-var$\rangle$:= $\langle$exp$\rangle$ `i-varassign (var exp)`
 | $\langle$class-var$\rangle$:= $\langle$exp$\rangle$ `c-varassign (var exp)`
 | `method` $\langle$varlist$\rangle$ $\langle$exp$\rangle$ `method (formals body)`
 | `$`$\langle$var$\rangle$ ($\langle$exps$\rangle$)   `meth-app (name rands)`
 | `simpleinstance` $\langle$exp$\rangle$ `new-simpleinst (class-exp)`
 | `simpleclass` $\langle$varlist$\rangle$ `new-simpleclass (c-vars`
        $\langle$varlist$\rangle$ $\langle$methdecls$\rangle$ $\langle$exp$\rangle$ `i-vars methdecls init-exp)`
$\langle$instance-var$\rangle$ ::= `&`$\langle$var$\rangle$ `i-varref (var)`
  $\langle$class-var$\rangle$ ::= `&&`$\langle$var$\rangle$ `c-varref (var)`
$\langle$methdecls$\rangle$ ::= ( )
 | ($\langle$decls$\rangle$)

References to instance and class variables are distinguished by the prefixes
`&` and `&&`, respectively. Method declarations are composed of two parts: the
method name and an expression that evaluates to an *open method*. When open
methods are supplied in a class declaration as the values of method declaration
expressions, they are incorporated into the class and become *closed* methods.
(Though open methods usually appear in method declarations, they do not
have to; open methods are first-class values, like procedures.) The components
of a simple class definition are lists of class and instance variables (without
prefix), a series of method declarations, and an expression that is evaluated
when the class is created. This expression is typically used to initialize class
variables.

The transcript in figure 7.1.2 illustrates how a stack class, similar to that of
figure 7.1.1, may be defined and used in the concrete syntax of our language of
objects. We assume the initial environment supports the usual list operations.
The `simpleinstance` form is used to create instances. We reserve the keywords
`class` and `instance` for use in the next sections. Method calls have the syntax
of procedure calls, preceded by a dollar sign. The name of the method to be
invoked appears in the operator position (as if it were a variable reference),

Figure 7.1.2   Stack class definition transcript

```
--> define stackclass =
    simpleclass (pushed) (stk, localpushed)
    (initialize = method ()
                      begin
                          &localpushed := 0;
                          &stk := emptylist
                      end;
      empty = method () null(&stk);
      push = method (x)
                  begin
                      &&pushed := +(&&pushed, 1);
                      &localpushed := +(&localpushed, 1);
                      &stk := cons(x, &stk)
                  end;
      pop = method ()
                  if null(&stk)
                  then error()
                  else begin
                          &&pushed := -(&&pushed, 1);
                          &localpushed := -(&localpushed, 1);
                          &stk := cdr(&stk)
                       end;
      top = method ()
                  if null(&stk)
                  then error()
                  else car(&stk);
      pushed = method () &&pushed;
      localpushed = method () &localpushed)
    &&pushed := 0;
--> define stack = simpleinstance(stackclass);
--> $push(stack, 7);
--> $top(stack);
7
```

the first operand of the application is evaluated to obtain the current object of the call, and any remaining operands supply arguments to the selected method.

We are now ready to describe the interpreter, which will reveal additional elements of the interpreted language's semantics. First we consider its environments. Class and instance variable environments associate class and instance variable names with their values. Since all instances of a particular class have the same instance variable names, we split the instance variable environment, storing an instance variable list in the class record and an instance value vector in the instance record. The only other information in an instance record is a pointer to its class, which will include all the other information needed to process a message sent to the instance.

```
(define-record instance (class i-vals))
```

All instances of a particular class share the same set of methods, which are recorded in the class's method environment. Given an instance, the appropriate method environment can be found using the class field of the instance record and the m-env field of the class record. Thus a class record contains four fields: one for each half of the class variable environment, one for the variable list of the instance variable environment, and one for the method environment.

```
(define-record class (c-vars c-vals i-vars m-env))
```

The interpreter also employs the usual lexical variable environment.

The interpreter for this language is shown in figure 7.1.3. The current class and instance are now passed to *eval-exp* for use in variable lookup. Although the current class may be easily obtained from the current instance, we pass both in anticipation of developments in the next section.

Instance and class variable lookup and assignment is performed by the procedure *cell-lookup* (see figure 7.1.4), which takes the variable being looked up, the variable list, and its value vector, and returns the associated cell. See the i-varref, c-varref, i-varassign, and c-varassign clauses of *eval-exp* in figure 7.1.3.

Since instance and class variables are assignable, their environments bind variables to cells that contain the binding values. Each instance and class variable environment is represented as a single rib consisting of a list of symbols and a vector of value cells. These cells are stored in an order that is the *reverse* of the corresponding symbols list. This anticipates developments in the next section.

Figure 7.1.3   Interpreter for language of objects

```
(define eval-exp
  (lambda (exp env class inst)
    (variant-case exp
      (i-varref (var) (lookup var (class->i-vars class) (instance->i-vals inst)))
      (c-varref (var) (lookup var (class->c-vars class) (class->c-vals class)))
      (i-varassign (var exp)
        (let ((value (eval-exp exp env class inst)))
          (assign var value (class->i-vars class) (instance->i-vals inst))))
      (c-varassign (var exp)
        (let ((value (eval-exp exp env class inst)))
          (assign var value (class->c-vars class) (class->c-vals class))))
      (method (formals body)
        (let ((new-formals (cons 'self formals)))
          (lambda (class-thunk)
            (lambda (args)
              (eval-exp body (extend-env new-formals (map make-cell args) env)
                (class-thunk)
                (car args))))))
      (meth-app (name rands)
        (let ((args (map (lambda (rand) (eval-exp rand env class inst)) rands)))
          (meth-call name (instance->class (car args)) args)))
      (new-simpleinst (class-exp)
        (let ((inst-class (eval-exp class-exp env class inst)))
          (let ((new-inst (make-instance inst-class
                            (make-vals (class->i-vars inst-class)))))
            (meth-call 'initialize inst-class (list new-inst))
            new-inst)))
      (new-simpleclass (c-vars i-vars methdecls init-exp)
        (let ((open-methods
                (map (lambda (decl)
                       (eval-exp (decl->exp decl) env class inst))
                     methdecls)))
          (letrec ((new-class
                     (make-class c-vars (make-vals c-vars) i-vars
                       (extend-env (map decl->var methdecls)
                         (map (lambda (open-method)
                                (open-method (lambda () new-class)))
                              open-methods)
                         init-meth-env))))
            (eval-exp init-exp env new-class inst)
            new-class)))
      ...)))
```

Figure 7.1.4 Auxiliary definitions for the language of objects interpreter

```
(define lookup
  (lambda (var vars vals)
    (cell-ref (cell-lookup var vars vals))))

(define assign
  (lambda (var value vars vals)
    (cell-set! (cell-lookup var vars vals) value)))

(define cell-lookup
  (lambda (var vars vals)
    (letrec ((loop (lambda (vars c)
                     (cond
                       ((null? vars) (error "Unassigned variable:" var))
                       ((eq? (car vars) var) (vector-ref vals c))
                       (else (loop (cdr vars) (- c 1)))))))
      (loop vars (- (length vars) 1)))))

(define meth-call
  (lambda (name class args)
    (let ((method (meth-lookup name class)))
      (method args))))

(define meth-lookup
  (lambda (name class)
    (apply-env (class->m-env class) name)))

(define make-vals
  (lambda (vars)
    (list->vector (map make-empty-cell vars))))

(define init-meth-env
  (extend-env '(initialize)
    (list (lambda (args) "Not initialized"))
    the-empty-env))

(define init-env
  (extend-env '(classof)
    (list (make-cell (make-prim-proc 'instance->class)))
    base-env))
```

In the first line of the method clause, the variable `self` is added to the front of the list of formals that are used to extend the lexical environment of the method at the time of method call. This is appropriate, since the first argument to a method is always the current instance of the call. By referring to the object bound to `self`, the methods of an instance may call each other as if they were mutually recursive. For example, the expression `null(&stk)` in the pop and `top` methods of figure 7.1.2 could be replaced by `$empty(self)`.

Evaluation of method expressions simply involves returning an open method procedure that is closed over the current lexical environment (*env*). When an open method is incorporated into a class, it is supplied with a *class thunk*. When the method is called, this class thunk is invoked to obtain the identity of the class to which it belongs. It might be preferable to put a reference to the class directly in the method when it is incorporated into the class. Unfortunately, this is impossible because at that time the class has not yet been fully formed. The best we can do at method-incorporation time is to put in the method a thunk that will evaluate at method-application time to the right class. This is similar to the technique we used in section 5.6 to implement `letrecproc` without circular environments. In that case we needed to construct procedures whose bodies were evaluated in an environment in which the procedures themselves were contained. In this case we construct methods that must refer to the class in which they are contained.

Method application uses the auxiliary procedure `meth-call`. It is straightforward, based on the calling convention for methods.

When a `simpleinstance` expression is evaluated its subexpression is first evaluated to obtain the class of the new instance. A new instance record is then formed that contains a reference to the class and an instance value vector that associates instance variables with cells that initially contain unspecified values. The `initialize` method of the new class is then called, and finally the new instance is returned.

When creating a new class, a new method environment must be formed (see figure 7.1.3). The expressions of the method declarations are evaluated to obtain open methods. These open methods are then closed in the class by being passed a class thunk. Note the circularity introduced by the `letrec` in the code. Method environments have only one rib, so the environment that is extended is always a trivial environment. After the method environment is created it is included in a new class record, along with class and instance variable lists and a vector of class value bindings. These bindings are cells whose values are initially unspecified. The initialization expression of the class expression is then evaluated with the newly created class as the current class. Thus references to class variables in the initialization expression refer to the variables of the new class, allowing them to be assigned meaningful values. The `inst` argument that is passed to `eval-exp` is useless, since there are no instances of the newly created class.

The remaining clauses of `eval-exp` are the same as those in earlier interpreters, except that the new class and instance arguments must be passed to `eval-exp`. The programmer is given access to the class of any instance via the primitive procedure `classof` supplied in the initial environment. See `init-env` in figure 7.1.4. It is assumed that `base-env` provides bindings for primitive procedures and values.

○ *Exercise 7.1.1*

We have said that object-oriented programming allows an ADT to have multiple implementations that coexist in a single program. Extend the example of figure 7.1.2 by defining a second implementation of the stack ADT. Write a procedure in the defined language to count the number of elements on a stack. Show that it behaves correctly with either kind of stack object as an argument. ☐

● *Exercise 7.1.2*

Some object-based languages do not syntactically distinguish applications and method calls (as we do using a dollar sign). In such a language, if the first argument of an application is an object and the operator names one of the object's methods, the application is actually a method call. Modify the interpreter of figure 7.2.4 to support this calling convention by removing the `meth-app` clause and redefining the `app` clause. ☐

○ *Exercise 7.1.3*

In section 5.6 we saw that another approach to the implementation of `letrec` is to use assignment, which effectively forms a circular data structure. Modify the interpreter of figure 7.1.3 to avoid the use of class thunks by the introduction of side-effects. ☐

○ *Exercise 7.1.4*

Since in the interpreter of figure 7.1.3 the current class is always the class of the current instance, the `class-thunk` variable is not necessary. Rewrite `eval-exp` of figure 7.1.3 without using the `class-thunk` variable. ☐

● *Exercise 7.1.5*

The syntax of our defined language requires that all the methods associated with a class be specified at the time the class is created. Modify the defined language and the interpreter of figure 7.1.3 to allow methods to be added to or deleted from a class at any time. □

○ *Exercise 7.1.6*

Redefine the Scheme procedure `make-stack` of figure 7.1.1 so that the lexical variable `self` is bound to the current instance in the scope of the class operations. For example, in the `pop!` and `top` operations this would allow the expression (null? stk) to be replaced by (self 'empty?). □

○ *Exercise 7.1.7*

We have chosen to make `self` a lexical variable. It could be an instance variable instead. In that case it could be installed permanently in the instance variable environment when the instance is made. Of course, this requires a side-effect. Modify the interpreter so that `self` is an instance variable and not a variable of the method's lexical environment. □

○ *Exercise 7.1.8*

At the time open methods are included in a class, instance variable addresses (locations in the corresponding instance value vector) can be statically determined. Write a procedure that takes a method expression and a list of instance variables and replaces each instance variable reference and assignment record by a new record that contains an address rather than a variable symbol. Then rewrite instance variable lookup to support these variable references. Remember that the instance value vector is treated as if it were reversed, so for example, the address of b in (a b c d e) is 3. □

● *Exercise 7.1.9*

The decision to require an `&` to precede an instance variable is arbitrary. We could instead allow instance variables to appear like lexical variables within method bodies. We would then have to decide which would have precedence. We arbitrarily decide that instance variables within method bodies shadow free lexical variables of the same name. Modify the interpreter to support this behavior. □

7.2 Inheritance

Large object-oriented programs typically use many classes. Frequently a class is similar to another class in the same program in that it requires some of the same variables and methods, but it supports some additional or modified methods, and perhaps requires additional class or instance variables.

For example, a program might require a class of bounded stacks, as well as a class of simple stacks. The bounded-stack class supports all the methods of the simple-stack class, plus an additional method for setting a limit on the size of the stack and a modified method for pushing elements on the stack, which checks that the limit is not exceeded. Of course the bounded-stack class also requires an additional instance variable to record the limit.

The techniques of inheritance and delegation allow similar objects to share common methods and variables. This sharing has advantages at many points in the software development process. It simplifies program specification, speeds coding, and eases program maintenance, as well as encouraging the development of libraries of general purpose classes that may easily be extended to meet specific needs.

The range of opportunities for code sharing, and the scope of its benefits, are striking. An adequate appreciation of the utility of inheritance and delegation can be obtained only by studying a number of examples drawn from a variety of programming contexts. It is not our purpose to provide such examples, which may be found in a number of object-oriented programming books. We are concerned rather with understanding the programming language mechanisms that support this style of programming.

Delegation refers to code sharing that is determined by the organization of objects. In delegation, if an object receives a message that it does not know how to handle, it simply passes the message on to another object, thereby delegating authority for handling the message. *Inheritance,* on the other hand, refers to code sharing that is determined by the organization of classes. Each class may have one or more *parent* classes from which methods and variables are inherited.

In the procedural model of objects, it is easy to implement delegation. Consider the bounded-stack class mentioned above, which extends the previous stack class with a new `set-bound!` method and modifies the `push!` method (see figure 7.2.1). The class *make-bounded-stack* has two instance variables, `bound` and `stack`. The latter is an instance of the simple stack class of figure 7.1.1, to which `empty?`, `pop!`, `top`, `pushed`, and `local-pushed` messages are delegated. The `push!` message is also delegated to the simple stack if the number of elements in the stack is less than the bound. The bound is 10

Figure 7.2.1   Bounded stack with delegation

```
(define make-bounded-stack
  (lambda ()
    (let ((bound 10) (stack (make-stack)))
      (lambda (message)
        (case message
          ((push!) (if (< ((stack 'local-pushed)) bound)
                       (stack 'push!)
                       (error "Bounded stack: bound exceeded")))
          ((set-bound!) (lambda (x) (set! bound x)))
          (else (stack message)))))))
```

by default. Alternatively, we could have made the bound an argument to *make-bounded-stack*.

Delegation is more dynamic than inheritance, and hence more flexible. It is possible, for example, for an object to determine when and how to delegate responsibility for a given message based on the state of the system at the time of method call. Patterns of inheritance, on the other hand, are the same for all instances of a class and are determined at the time of class creation. Inheritance is the more common method of code sharing, since the flexibility of delegation often comes at the expense of efficiency, and the added flexibility is seldom required. Also, unnecessary flexibility may be a liability, since flexible program behavior is often harder to understand. If necessary, delegation may even be simulated with inheritance by creating classes dynamically.

Inheritance may be either *single,* if each class has just one parent, or *multiple,* when classes are permitted to have more than one parent. With single inheritance, the class structure of a program may be represented as a tree. Such hierarchical organizations are natural in a great many contexts. A method inherited by a class is supplied by the nearest ancestor of the class that supplies the method.

Multiple inheritance results in a less structured class organization that may be represented as a directed acyclic graph. Locating an inherited method with multiple inheritance is more complicated than the linear search through ancestor classes that suffices for single inheritance. Since two parent classes may in turn inherit (directly or indirectly) from a common ancestor, we must be careful that the method search does not visit some classes more than once. Some languages impose the restriction that methods of the same name may not belong (either directly or by inheritance) to multiple parents of a

Figure 7.2.2 Bounded-stack class

```
define boundedstackclass =
 class stackclass, () (bound)
  (initialize = method ()
                    begin
                       &bound := 10;
                       $initialize(super)
                    end;
   push = method (x)
             if less(&localpushed, &bound)
             then $push(super, x)
             else error();
   setbound = method (x) &bound := x)
  noop
```

class. This makes multiple inheritance relatively simple to understand and implement. If a class is allowed to have two parents that each supply a method with the same name, which method is to be called, or should both methods be somehow called? One approach is to use the first method of a given name that is encountered in a depth-first search of the ancestors of a class. A variety of other approaches are possible, but they are beyond the scope of this text.

We now extend the interpreted language of the last section to model single inheritance. There are two changes to the syntax of our interpreted language. First, we replace the simpleclass form with the class form that is similar but includes an expression that is evaluated to obtain the parent of the new class. Second, we provide a special form for *super* method application. This provides access to inherited methods that would otherwise be inaccessible by virtue of being "shadowed" by other methods of the same name. Its syntax is the same as that of ordinary method application but with the variable name super as the first operand.

$\langle\text{exp}\rangle ::=$ `class` $\langle\text{exp}\rangle$ `,` $\langle\text{c-vars}\rangle$ `new-class (parent-exp c-vars`
      $\langle\text{i-vars}\rangle$ $\langle\text{methdecls}\rangle$ $\langle\text{exp}\rangle$ `i-vars methdecls init-exp)`
   $|$ `$`$\langle\text{var}\rangle$ $\langle\text{super-rands}\rangle$ `super-meth-app (name rands)`
$\langle\text{super-rands}\rangle ::=$ `(super)`
       $|$ `(super,` $\langle\text{exps}\rangle$`)`

Figure 7.2.3   Count class

```
define countclass =
 class baseobject, (classinstcount) ()
  (initialize = method () &&classinstcount := +(&&classinstcount, 1);
   howmany = method () &&classinstcount)
  &&classinstcount := 0
```

For example, figure 7.2.2 shows the definition of a bounded-stack class that inherits from a stack class. The stack class may be defined as in figure 7.1.2 but with `simpleclass ...` replaced by `class baseobject ...`, where `baseobject` is a primitive object used as the parent of a class that does not need to inherit from another class. Instances of `boundedstackclass` support not only the methods `setbound` and `push`, but also (by inheritance) those of `stackclass` other than `push`. The instance variable `localpushed` is also inherited from `stackclass`. In general, a class inherits all the instance and class variables of its ancestors. Since there are no class variables, the class initialization expression does nothing (indicated by a variable `noop` that may be bound to any value). In this example two uses of super method application are required to invoke the initialization and push methods of the stack class, since both of these methods are also defined by the bounded-stack class.

Most often a new class inherits from an existing class, as in the bounded-stack example. It is also possible to create a new class that is to be inherited by several classes in order to support some behavior that they all have in common. For example, `countclass` of figure 7.2.3 keeps track of the total number of instances of its inheriting classes. Thus if `stackclass` inherited from `countclass` instead of `baseobject`, and `i` were an instance of `stackclass` or `boundedstackclass`, then `$howmany(i)` would return the total number of instances of `stackclass` and `boundedstackclass`. For this example, we assume that every initialization method invokes `$initialize(super)`, so that the initialization method of the count class will be run whenever an instance of an inheriting class is created.

We obtain an interpreter for modeling inheritance by extending the interpreter of the last section. Each class record is extended with a field that records its parent.

```
(define-record class (parent c-vars c-vals i-vars m-env))
```

Instance records are unchanged.

Figure 7.2.4   Interpreter and initial environment for inheritance language

```
(define eval-exp
  (lambda (exp env class inst)
    (variant-case exp
      (new-class (parent-exp c-vars i-vars methdecls init-exp)
        (let ((parent-class (eval-exp parent-exp env class inst))
              (open-methods (map (lambda (decl)
                                   (eval-exp (decl->exp decl) env class inst))
                                 methdecls)))
          (let ((new-c-vars (append c-vars (class->c-vars parent-class)))
                (new-i-vars (append i-vars (class->i-vars parent-class))))
            (letrec ((new-class
                       (make-class parent-class new-c-vars (make-vals new-c-vars)
                         new-i-vars
                         (extend-env (map decl->var methdecls)
                           (map (lambda (open-method)
                                  (open-method (lambda () new-class)))
                                open-methods)
                           (class->m-env parent-class)))))
              (eval-exp init-exp env new-class inst)
              new-class))))
      (super-meth-app (name rands)
        (let ((args (map (lambda (x) (eval-exp x env class inst)) rands)))
          (meth-call name (class->parent class) (cons inst args))))
      ...)))

(define init-env
  (extend-env '(parentof classof baseobject)
    (map make-cell
         (list (make-prim-proc 'class->parent)
               (make-prim-proc 'instance->class)
               (make-class '* '() '#() '() init-meth-env)))
    base-env))
```

Evaluation of a `class` form begins by evaluating the subexpression that provides the identity of its parent. See figure 7.2.4. Lists of class and instance variables are then obtained by *appending* the variables introduced by the class to those of its parent. If the list of instance variables of the class overlap with those of its parent, the ones in the class shadow those of the parent. The reason we count backward from the end of the value vector while we search forward in the variable list is to facilitate static instance variable lookup (see exercise 7.1.8). The method environment of the new class is formed by extending the method environment of the parent class with the newly declared methods.

Super method application is similar to a standard method application, except that the class used for method lookup is the parent of the current class and the current instance is passed as the first argument of the method. Thus method lookup will be in the environment of the current class, and the current instance will be bound to `self` in the body of the method.

The rest of the interpreter is the same as in the first object interpreter except that the initial environment *init-env* now contains bindings for two class-related primitive procedures and a special object. The `parentof` procedure returns the parent of a class, and the old `classof` procedure returns the class of an instance. The variable `baseobject` is bound to an object that has no parent, no variables, and no methods. It is used as the parent of classes that do not inherit from other classes.

We now have at least four categories of variables: instance variables, class variables, method names, and ordinary lexical variables. Why do we need such complex mechanisms? The procedural model, for example, uses lexical variables to simulate instance and class variables. However, this may not suffice in general, especially when inheritance is used. We often want to create a class that inherits from another class whose instance and class variables are not in the current scope. See figure 7.2.5. Under lexical scoping, there would be no way for the methods of `bclass` to see the class or instance variables of `aclass`. Indeed, whenever we inherit from a class, the new methods get to see the instance variables of the parent class, which are not lexically apparent, as in the use of `&iv` in the `getiv` method in figure 7.2.5.

We ended chapter 5 knowing that variables could be scoped in two ways: statically (i.e., lexically) and dynamically. The same can be said about instance and class variables. (Keep in mind, though that in this context, static is not the same as lexical. It is called static because for each variable an address can be determined, but it is not the lexical address.) Consider the program in figure 7.2.6. Is c 6 or 7? Is i 8 or 9? References to class and instance variables within a method are resolved in the environment of the

Figure 7.2.5   Example showing lexical scope vs. instance variables

```
define aclass = class baseobject, (cv) (iv) () noop;

let x = 3; cv = 4
in let bclass = class aclass, () ()
                (initialize = method () +(x, &&cv);
                 getiv = method () &iv)
                noop
    in ...
```

Figure 7.2.6   Static vs. dynamic inheritance of class and instance variables

```
define aclass =
 class baseobject, (cv) (iv)
  (initialize = method () &iv := 8;
   getcv = method () &&cv;
   getiv = method () &iv)
  &&cv := 6;

define bclass =
 class aclass, (cv) (iv)
  (inititialize = method ()
                  begin
                    $initialize(super);
                    &iv := 9
                  end)
  &&cv := 7;

define x = simpleinstance bclass;
define c = $getcv(x);
define i = $getiv(x)
```

class to which the method belongs. (See the variable reference and assignment clauses of figure 7.1.3 and the method clause of figure 7.2.4.) Thus in this example &&cv and &iv refer to the bindings introduced by aclass, so that c is 6 and i is 8. In this case the relationship between class and instance variable references and their bindings is static, and the interpreted language is said to employ *static inheritance* of class and instance variables.

In the interpreter of figure 7.1.3, except for when `init-exp` was evaluated, the *current class* (bound to the *class* argument of *eval-exp*) was always the class of the current instance (bound to *inst*). As the example of figure 7.2.6 demonstrates, this is not always the case once inheritance has been introduced. When a method is called, its body is evaluated with *inst* bound to the current instance and *class* bound to the class containing the method. This class will not be the same as the current class if the method is found in an ancestor of the current class. Inheritance mechanisms in which the current instance supplies the environment, even for methods associated with ancestors of the current class, are said to be *dynamic*. With dynamic inheritance of class and instance variables, *c* will be 7 and *i* will be 9. It is possible for class and instance variables to inherit differently. For example, by replacing the `class` by (`instance->class inst`) in the subexpression (`class->i-vars class`) in both the `i-varref` and `i-varassign` clauses of figure 7.2.4, we would support dynamic inheritance of instance variables, but retain static inheritance of class variables. Among some of the widely used object-oriented languages are C++ and Smalltalk. C++ statically inherits, whereas Smalltalk dynamically inherits.

- *Exercise 7.2.1*

Modify the program in figure 7.1.2 to keep a count of the number of instances of `stackclass` and all other classes (such as `boundedstackclass`) that inherit directly or indirectly from `stackclass`. ☐

o *Exercise 7.2.2*

In Smalltalk, a reference to the variable `super` in a position other than the first argument of a method call is treated exactly like a reference to `self`. Modify the interpreter of figure 7.2.4 to provide this feature. ☐

o *Exercise 7.2.3*

Another representation of the method environment is to store all the closed methods accessible from a particular class in a single vector and use an index, instead of a symbol, to reference into the method environment. This may be the basis for further optimizations, such as hashing and caching. Modify the interpreter of figure 7.2.4 and its associated parser to preprocess method expressions so that the abstract syntax of method applications and super method applications includes an index that is used for method lookup. This exercise, along with that of exercise 7.1.8, gives a large part of the object mechanism of C++. ☐

- *Exercise 7.2.4*

  Modify the interpreter of figure 7.2.4 to support dynamic inheritance of class and instance variables. ☐

○ *Exercise 7.2.5*

  In our discussion of figure 7.2.3, we relied on the assumption that each `initialize` method called `$initialize(super)`. How might this be guaranteed? Design and implement a mechanism to do so. ☐

○ *Exercise 7.2.6*

  Modify the interpreter to support multiple inheritance, with the provision that no two ancestors of any class supply methods of the same name. ☐

7.3 Meta-Classes

Suppose we wanted to keep track of the total number of classes that inherit from a given class. This is similar in character to the problems of keeping a count of all the instances of a class (as in figure 7.2.3) and keeping a count of the number of pushes in all stacks (as in figure 7.1.2). We have seen these problems are solved naturally using class variables. Due to the inheritance of class variables and methods, the instance and class counts need be kept in only one class. It would be desirable if a count of the number of stack classes could be maintained with similar ease.

In the interpreted language this is not possible, since the only expression that is evaluated when a class is created is the initialization expression of the new class. We wish the class count to be incremented automatically when we create a class, without our having to program this in each class definition. To achieve this, we move class initialization code into a method body, so that we have class creation as well as class initialization methods. If classes may be created under varying circumstances, it might even be desirable to support multiple class-creation methods. To what class should class-creation methods belong? They cannot belong to a parent of the class, for it would not then be able to access the class variables of the new class (unless the system uses dynamic class variable inheritance).

Class-creation methods are stored in a new class, called a *meta-class*. Just as instances have an associated class, it is natural to associate a meta-class with each class. The class variables of a class are then the instance variables of its meta-class. Thus it is only necessary to declare instance variables. We still maintain the notion of class variable references and assignments, but they are understood to be operating on variables declared in the meta-class of the current class. The values of the instance variables of a class are, of course, still stored in the instances of the class. Similarly, a class contains the values of its class variables, which are declared as instance variables in its meta-class. For example, the stack class could declare instance variables named `stk` and `localpushed` (whose values would be contained in instances of the class), and contain values for the instance variables `pushed` and `instcount` declared by its meta-class.

Consider a class-creation method belonging to a meta-class. To count the number of classes created, it must increment a class variable. Since we declare only instance variables, this class variable must be declared as an instance variable of a meta-meta-class of which the meta-class is an instance.

We provide for an unlimited number of meta-levels by eliminating the distinction between instances and classes. All objects are then instances, and each instance has an associated parent and class. This is supported by the syntactic form `instance`, which replaces the `simpleinstance` and `class` forms. It is similar to the `class` form but has a subexpression for indicating a class as well as a parent.

⟨exp⟩ ::= instance ⟨exp⟩, ⟨exp⟩,   new-instance (class-exp parent-exp
          ⟨varlist⟩ ⟨methdecls⟩   i-vars methdecls)

Adding support for meta-classes would seem to complicate the defined language, but since we are eliminating the class/instance distinction, the interpreter is simplified. Instance records now have a parent field.

```
(define-record instance (class parent i-vars m-env i-vals))
```

Class records are now replaced by instance records, but for continuity we continue to use class record field selection procedures when an instance is being used as a class.

```
(define class->m-env instance->m-env)
(define class->i-vars instance->i-vars)
(define class->parent instance->parent)
```

The class variable reference and assignment clauses of *eval-exp* are modified to obtain the class variable lists from the meta-class of the current class. See figure 7.3.1. The `new-instance` clause is similar to the `new-class` clause of

Figure 7.3.1   Meta-class interpreter

```
(define eval-exp
  (lambda (exp env class inst)
    (variant-case exp
      (c-varref (var)
        (lookup var (instance->i-vars (instance->class class))
          (instance->i-vals (instance->class inst))))
      (c-varassign (var exp)
        (let ((value (eval-exp exp env class inst)))
          (assign var value (instance->i-vars (instance->class class))
            (instance->i-vals (instance->class inst)))))
      (new-instance (class-exp parent-exp i-vars methdecls)
        (let ((inst-class (eval-exp class-exp env class inst))
              (parent-class (eval-exp parent-exp env class inst))
              (open-methods
                (map (lambda (decl)
                       (eval-exp (decl->exp decl) env class inst))
                     methdecls)))
          (let ((new-i-vars (append i-vars (instance->i-vars parent-class))))
            (letrec ((new-inst
                       (make-instance inst-class parent-class
                         new-i-vars
                         (extend-env (map decl->var methdecls)
                           (map (lambda (open-method)
                                  (open-method (lambda () new-inst)))
                                open-methods)
                           (class->m-env parent-class))
                         (make-vals (class->i-vars inst-class)))))
              (meth-call 'initialize inst-class (list new-inst))
              new-inst))))
      ...)))

(define init-env
  (extend-env '(parentof classof baseobject)
    (map make-cell
         (list (make-prim-proc 'class->parent)
               (make-prim-proc 'instance->class)
               (make-instance '* '* '() init-meth-env '#())))
    base-env))
```

figure 7.2.4, but it now evaluates the class subexpression and stores its value in the record representing the new instance. The initial environment is the same except for the representation of the base object.

The program of figure 7.3.2 illustrates the use of meta-classes. The program creates eight instances. It first defines `metametacountclass`, which simply declares that any instance of `metametacountclass` will have a binding for the variable `classcount`. Then it defines `metacountclass` as an instance of `metametacountclass`. The initialization method of its class is invoked to set its binding of `classcount` to zero. This variable is incremented as a class variable by the initialization method of `metacountclass`. It also provides a `new` method for creating simple (methodless) instances of a given class and a `howmany` method for returning the current value of `classcount`. The class, `metacountclass`, is inherited by `metastackclass`, which declares the `pushed` variable used as a class variable by the stack class. Finally, `countclass`, `stackclass`, and `boundedstackclass` are defined based on the earlier examples, and instances of the stack and bounded stack classes are created using `new`.

Figure 7.3.3 illustrates the instance structure created by the program of figure 7.3.2. We have chosen short names to label each instance that correspond to the longer names used in the program below. For example, `BO` is `baseobject` and `MCC` is `metacountclass`. There are nine instances in figure 7.3.3. Each instance represents the five fields of an instance record as follows. A pointer emanating from the left of an instance is a class pointer and one emanating from its top is a parent pointer. The remaining three fields are its `i-vars`, which are stored in the top section; the first rib of its `m-env`, which is stored in the middle section; and the `i-vals`, which are stored in the bottom section. Blank sections denote the obvious default values: the empty list, the `init-meth-env`, or an empty vector. The ellipses indicate omitted methods. When looking at such figures, it is important to keep in mind that the `i-vars` and `i-vals` of the same instance are not related: The `i-vals` of any object correspond to the `i-vars` of its class. For example, in `BSI` there are three `i-vals` and zero `i-vars`. There are, however, three `i-vars` in its class `BSC`. Also this figure does not show all the details of the data structures used by our implementation. For example, the order of the `i-vals` is not reversed as they are in our implementation, nor is the presence of updatable cells shown.

Figure 7.3.4 is a trace, using the abbreviated names, of assignments to instance variables that occur when the program in figure 7.3.2 is run.

Figure 7.3.2 Meta-class example

```
define metametacountclass =
  instance baseobject, baseobject, (classcount)
    (initialize = method () &classcount := 0);

define metacountclass =
  instance metametacountclass, baseobject, (instcount)
    (initialize = method () begin
                          &instcount := 0;
                          &&classcount := +(&&classcount, 1)
                        end;
       new = method () instance self, baseobject, () ();
       howmany = method () &&classcount);

define countclass =
  instance metacountclass, baseobject, ()
    (initialize = method () &&instcount := +(&&instcount, 1);
       howmany = method () &&instcount);

define metastackclass =
  instance classof(metacountclass), metacountclass, (pushed)
    (initialize = method () begin &pushed := 0; $initialize(super) end);

define stackclass =
  instance metastackclass, countclass, (stk, localpushed)
    (initialize = method () begin
                          &localpushed := 0;
                          &stk := emptylist;
                          $initialize(super)
                        end;
     ...);

define boundedstackclass =
  instance classof(stackclass), stackclass, (bound)
    (initialize = method () begin
                          &bound := 10;
                          $initialize(super)
                        end;
     ...);

define stackinstance = $new(stackclass);

define boundedstackinstance = $new(boundedstackclass);
```

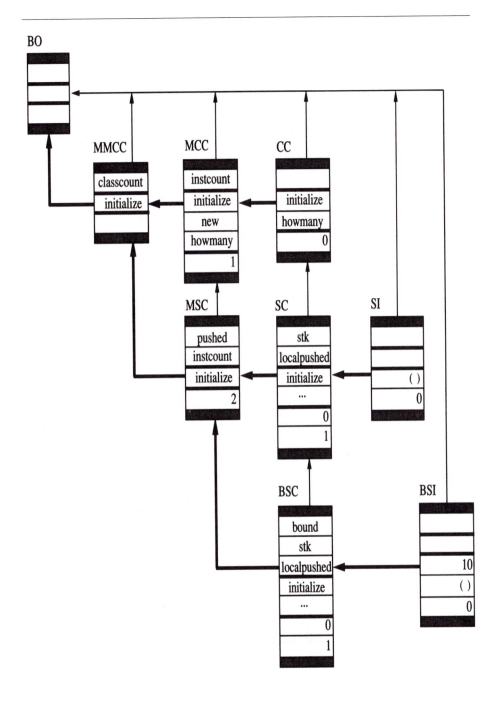

Figure 7.3.3   Structure of meta-class example

| Instance | Instance value assigned | | |
created	Value in	Name	Value
MMCC			
MCC	MCC	classcount	0
CC	CC	instcount	0
	MCC	classcount	1
MSC	MSC	classcount	0
SC	SC	pushed	0
	SC	instcount	0
	MSC	classcount	1
BSC	BSC	pushed	0
	BSC	instcount	0
	MSC	classcount	2
SI	SI	stk	()
	SI	localpushed	0
	SC	instcount	1
BSI	BSI	bound	10
	BSI	stk	()
	BSI	localpushed	0
	BSC	instcount	1

Figure 7.3.4   Trace of figure 7.3.2

- *Exercise 7.3.1*

  Extend figure 7.3.3 if the program continues as follows:

  ```
  define stackinstance2 = $new(stackclass);
  define boundedstackinstance2 = $new(boundedstackclass);
  define boundedstackinstance3 = $new(boundedstackclass);
  define boundedstackinstance4 = $new(boundedstackclass);
  $push(boundedstackinstance, 13);
  $push(boundedstackinstance2, 14);
  $push(boundedstackinstance2, 15)
  ```
  ⬚

In figure 7.3.2 the new method is provided by metacountclass. It may be desirable for the new method to be inherited by all classes in a system, while metacountclass is inherited by some, but not all, classes. To allow for this possibility, modify the program of figure 7.3.2 so that the new method is provided by a class named metabaseclass, rather than by metacountclass. □

○ *Exercise 7.3.3*

This system of meta-classes is extremely general. Take your favorite object system and formulate it in this scheme. What regularities or restrictions does your system obey? □

7.4 Summary

An object is a set of operations that share a state. Objects are a way for a language to enforce data abstraction. Objects may be modeled using lexical scoping and message passing. The self variable allows the operations of an object to send messages to each other recursively.

A class is a set of objects, called instances, that share the same operations, called methods. A class may have state through the mechanism of class variables, which are accessible to all its instances.

Classes may be defined incrementally by the use of inheritance. The super variable allows access to methods of the parent class that would otherwise be shadowed. Class and instance variables may be scoped statically or dynamically, but static scoping for these variables is distinct from ordinary lexical scoping.

A class can be considered to be an ordinary object, among whose methods is an operation for making an instance of the class. The operation for making a new class must therefore be a method of a meta-class. This leads to a design in which each class is an instance of its meta-class but inherits its operations from a parent class.

8 Continuation-Passing Style

We have seen how interpreters can be used to model and explain the behavior of programming languages. The explicit treatment of environments serves to explain scope and identifier-lookup rules, and the modeling of procedures as closures explains how procedures use lexical scope to make their behavior independent of the environment in which they are invoked. Our interpreters are written in Scheme but are suitable for implementation in many other languages because they use ordinary data structures and procedure calls.

The interpreters we have written so far require, however, that the implementation language supports recursive procedures. Thus recursion in the defined language has used recursion in the defining language. If we do not understand recursion, or we wish to use an implementation language that does not directly support recursion, this situation would be unsatisfactory.

The difficulty in implementing recursive procedures is that when a procedure call is made, it is necessary to record the operations that remain to be performed when the call returns. For example, when an interpreter is invoked recursively to evaluate the test part of a conditional expression, it must be noted that the result is to be used to determine whether the next subexpression to evaluate is the then part or the else part. This information, which is used to control the future course of the computation, is called *control* information. So far our interpreters have relied on Scheme to transparently keep track of control information for the defined language. We now wish to handle recursion by making the control information explicit.

We have already seen an example of how the future course of a computation may be represented explicitly. The *reduce-once-appl* procedure of section 4.3 is passed procedures that express how the computation is to be continued. The procedure is written so that it never returns values directly but instead passes them to one of these procedural arguments. These arguments are called *continuations*.

This technique is called *continuation-passing style,* or *CPS*. There are several reasons why CPS may be useful. In the `reduce-once-appl` procedure it is used because there are two possible continuations, one to be followed in the event of success and the other in the event of failure. It is more convenient to let the procedure choose between its continuations than to force its caller always to perform a test based on some returned result, particularly since the nature of the information that must be returned depends on how the computation is to continue. Another use of CPS is to return multiple results by passing them to a multiple-argument continuation. This is often better than returning some data structure out of which the caller of the procedure would have to extract the values. Examples of this style are found in the use of the procedure `find-all-argcont` in chapter 10 and in exercise 11.4.4 on recursive descent parsing in chapter 11. The concept of continuation passing has broad applicability, but the details of CPS are determined by the context of its use. For example, in chapter 12 we shall see how compilers may be viewed as translating expressions into a different form of CPS with a finer "granularity" than the CPS of this chapter.

In this chapter we explore the use of the simplest version of this style, in which procedures are passed a single continuation of one argument. We show how any expression may be translated into CPS. This is the first (and most challenging) step in a systematic process that may be used to transform any program into a form that may be translated directly into assembly language. Thus the CPS algorithm is a fundamental program development tool and can play a critical role in compiler generation.

In section 8.1 we illustrate the distinction between iterative and recursive control behavior and introduce an important implementation property called proper tail recursion. In section 8.2 we give some examples of how a procedure may be transformed into an equivalent procedure in continuation-passing style; the new procedure is guaranteed to have iterative control behavior. In section 8.3 we define a static property of programs called tail form, which is enjoyed by programs that have been transformed into CPS, and in section 8.4 we develop the CPS conversion algorithm itself. Section 8.5 presents examples of the transformation algorithm in action. In section 8.6 we present an implementation of our CPS algorithm. Last, in section 8.7 we refine the characterization of proper tail-recursive implementation.

The subject of conversion to continuation-passing style is deep and subtle. Most CPS algorithms are simpler than ours, but the results generated by those algorithms are primarily to be interpreted by a computer, not a programmer. Much of the complication in this chapter is caused by our desire to present a CPS transformation algorithm that incorporates knowledge about the special

forms and primitive operations of Scheme, and gives results as readable as
those done by hand.

A good introduction to the subject can be obtained by reading sections 8.1
and 8.2, and going through the examples in section 8.5. This knowledge will
generally be adequate for the rest of the material in the book and will also
lay the ground for a more fruitful reading of the rest of the chapter.

8.1 Iterative Control Behavior and Proper Tail Recursion

Consider the following definition of the factorial function.

```
(define fact
  (lambda (n)
    (if (zero? n) 1 (* n (fact (- n 1))))))
```

We can use a derivation to model a calculation with *fact*:

```
   (fact 4)
⇒ (* 4 (fact 3))
⇒ (* 4 (* 3 (fact 2)))
⇒ (* 4 (* 3 (* 2 (fact 1))))
⇒ (* 4 (* 3 (* 2 (* 1 (fact 0)))))
⇒ (* 4 (* 3 (* 2 (* 1 1))))
⇒ (* 4 (* 3 (* 2 1)))
⇒ (* 4 (* 3 2))
⇒ (* 4 6)
⇒ 24
```

This is the natural recursive definition of factorial. Each call of *fact* is
made with a promise that the value returned will be multiplied by the value
of n at the time of the call. Thus *fact* is invoked in larger and larger control
contexts as the calculation proceeds.

Compare this behavior with that of the following procedures.

```
(define fact-iter
  (lambda (n)
    (fact-iter-acc n 1)))

(define fact-iter-acc
  (lambda (n a)
    (if (zero? n) a (fact-iter-acc (- n 1) (* n a)))))
```

With these definitions, we calculate:

```
  (fact-iter 4)
⇒ (fact-iter-acc 4 1)
⇒ (fact-iter-acc 3 4)
⇒ (fact-iter-acc 2 12)
⇒ (fact-iter-acc 1 24)
⇒ (fact-iter-acc 0 24)
⇒ 24
```

Here, *fact-iter-acc* is always invoked in the same context (in this case, no context at all). When *fact-iter-acc* calls itself, it does so at the "tail end" of a call to *fact-iter-acc*. That is, no promise is made to do anything with the returned value other than return it as the result of the call to *fact-iter-acc*. Thus each step in the derivation above has the form (fact-iter-acc *n* *a*).

When a procedure such as *fact* executes, additional control information must be recorded with each recursive call, and this information must be retained until the call returns. This reflects growth of the control context in the first derivation above. Such a process is said to exhibit *recursive control behavior*. This control behavior places a potentially serious limit on the utility of such procedures, since in practice execution is limited to a finite amount of memory. For example, if *fact* is called with a sufficiently large value of n, an exception will be signalled indicating that the system ran out of memory.

By contrast, no additional control information need be recorded when *fact-iter-acc* calls itself. This is reflected in the derivation by recursive calls occurring at the same level within the expression (on the outside in the above derivation). In such cases the system does not need an ever-increasing amount of memory as the depth of recursion (the number of recursive calls without corresponding returns) increases. A process that uses a bounded amount of memory for control information is said to exhibit *iterative control behavior*.

The concept of *tail position* is used to determine whether additional control information need be recorded when a call is made. When certain subexpressions are evaluated, their value is immediately taken as the value of the enclosing expression. The primary example is the then and else subexpressions of an if expression. These subexpressions are said to be in tail positions of the enclosing expression. Thus when evaluating a subexpression in a tail position of the body of a procedure, no control information need be stored. This was the case, for example, in the recursive call of *fact-iter-acc*.

While evaluating an expression, if the value of a subexpression is returned, but some action must be performed after the subexpression's value is obtained,

Continuation-Passing Style

but before the expression's value is returned, the subexpression is not in a tail position of the expression. For example, even if a Scheme `set!` expression returned the value of its subexpression, the subexpression would not be in tail position because the assignment must be performed after it is evaluated, but before evaluation of the `set!` expression is complete.

The concept of tail position generalizes naturally to deeply nested subexpressions. A subexpression E' of E is said to be in a *tail position with respect to E* if every subexpression of E containing E' is in a tail position of the expression within which it is immediately contained. For example, the subexpressions `(if (positive? x) 1 (f x))`, `(f (g x))`, `1`, and `(f x)` are in tail position with respect to the expression

```
(if (zero? x)
    (f (g x))
    (if (positive? x)
        1
        (f x)))
```

but all other subexpressions are not in tail position with respect to the entire expression. We say that an expression is in *tail position* if it is in tail position with respect to the nearest lexically enclosing lambda expression. (Though we discuss lambda expressions in this chapter, the concepts apply to procedural expressions in general.)

Evaluation of an application is said to *initiate* a call of the procedure obtained by evaluation of its operator. For example, evaluation of `(f (g x))` initiates a call of f, but not g. The call of g is initiated by the subexpression `(g x)`. The term *tail call* refers to a call initiated by an application in tail position.

The significance of tail calls is that no additional control information need be recorded when a tail call occurs. An implementation in which tail calls result in no net growth of control space is said to be a *properly tail-recursive implementation*, or simply a *tail-recursive implementation*. (Though this definition suffices now, we refine it in section 8.7.) Scheme implementations are required to be properly tail recursive, but this is unusual. Most language specifications do not require that implementations be properly tail recursive, and most implementations are not.

In a tail-recursive implementation, procedures such as *fact-iter-acc* are guaranteed to exhibit iterative control behavior. There are many forms of iterative control behavior, each of which is subsumed by recursion in a language that is properly tail recursive. In the absence of proper tail recursion, language designers must provide other means of expressing iteration. Typically a variety of iteration mechanisms are provided, such as `while` loops, `until` loops, and `for` loops, and often mechanisms for breaking out of iterative loops at various points in their bodies. The life of programmers (and compilers) is complicated by the need to deal with this variety of iteration mechanisms, and yet, in practice, the need invariably arises for iteration mechanisms that the language designer did not anticipate—all for the lack of proper tail recursion.

This section introduces the concept of iterative control behavior by example but is deliberately vague about just when iterative control behavior is possible and how programs may be analyzed for this behavior. These issues are addressed more formally in section 8.3.

In chapter 10 we shall see that procedures such as `fact-iter-acc` may be systematically transformed into equivalent procedures in which no arguments are passed in calls to recursive procedures. As an example of a procedure in such a "flowchart" form, consider the following version of `fact-iter`.

```
(define fact-iter
  (lambda (n)
    (let ((a 1))
      (letrec ((loop (lambda ()
                       (if (zero? n)
                           a
                           (begin
                             (set! a (* n a))
                             (set! n (- n 1))
                             (loop))))))
        (loop))))))
```

Since a zero-argument tail call is equivalent to a "goto" statement, such a procedure may be expressed in a language that does not support recursion. In fact, such a transformation goes a long way toward compiling the procedure into assembly language.

In the case of `fact-iter`, the amount of memory required to store argument values does not increase either (as long as the result is less than the maximum value for the standard number representation). A process whose total memory requirements are bounded is said to exhibit *iterative behavior*. The following procedure is an example of one that executes (in Scheme) with iterative control behavior, but not iterative behavior, since the maximum size of its accumulator argument is a function of the length of its first argument (and hence is not bounded by a constant).

```
(define revappend
  (lambda (ls1 ls2)
    (if (null? ls1)
        ls2
        (revappend (cdr ls1) (cons (car ls1) ls2)))))
```

- *Exercise 8.1.1*

  Trace the behavior of the flowchart version of `fact-iter` when called with
  the argument 4. Compare this trace with a trace of `fact-iter-acc`. □

- *Exercise 8.1.2*

  Construct a derivation for the call (`revappend '(a b c d) '(1 2)`). Note that
  the size of `ls2` increases (and hence **revappend** does not exhibit iterative
  behavior), but recursive calls occur on the outside (and hence it exhibits
  iterative control behavior). □

- *Exercise 8.1.3*

  Use a derivation to compute the value of (`even-length? '(a b c)`) for each of
  the definitions below. Then write a version in flowchart form using the one
  that exhibits iterative control behavior.

```
(define even-length?
  (lambda (ls)
    (if (null? ls) #t (odd-length? (cdr ls)))))

(define odd-length?
  (lambda (ls)
    (if (null? ls) #f (even-length? (cdr ls)))))


(define even-length?
  (lambda (ls)
    (even? (length ls))))

(define length
  (lambda (ls)
    (if (null? ls) 0 (+ 1 (length (cdr ls)))))))
```
  □

In the last section we saw that the `fact` procedure

```
(define fact
  (lambda (n)
    (if (zero? n) 1 (* n (fact (- n 1))))))
```

does not have iterative control behavior, but it can be replaced by one, `fact-iter`, that does. This transformation introduces another procedure, `fact-iter-acc`, taking an extra argument, a, that serves as a register into which the answer is accumulated. This technique is useful, but not every procedure can be converted so simply. In this section, we demonstrate some techniques that will work on any procedure. Our presentation in this section is informal; in section 8.4 we formally specify a conversion algorithm.

The problem with `fact` is that the call (`* n (fact (- n 1))`) requires us to store information about what is to be done *after* the call to `fact`. Looking at the derivation, we see that a step in the calculation looks something like this:

$$(* 4 (* 3 (* 2 (\text{fact } 1))))$$

Here the procedure call is being computed in the *context*

$$(* 4 (* 3 (* 2 \ \Box)))$$

where $\Box$ represents (`fact 1`). We may represent a context—an expression with a hole in it—by a one-argument lambda expression that fills the hole. For example, the above context may be represented by the following:

```
(lambda (v) (* 4 (* 3 (* 2 v))))
```

If we named this lambda expression k, we would have this:

```
(k (fact 1))  ⇒  (* 4 (* 3 (* 2 (fact 1))))
```

In a derivation of a call of `fact`, each line will be of the form (k (fact n)) for some integer n and some lambda expression k.

This prompts us to write another version of `fact`, which we call `fact-cps`, such that (`fact-cps` n k) computes (k (fact n)).

```
(define fact-cps
  (lambda (n k)
    (if (zero? n)
        (k 1)
        (fact-cps (- n 1)
          (lambda (v) (k (* n v)))))))
```

We argue, by induction on n, that (k (fact n)) $\Rightarrow$ (fact-cps n k) for any
k. If $n = 0$, (k (fact 0)) $\Rightarrow$ (k 1) $\Rightarrow$ (fact-cps 0 k). If $n > 0$, we reason as
follows:

```
    (k (fact n))
⇒ (k (* n (fact (- n 1))))            by the definition of fact
⇒ ((lambda (v) (k (* n v)))           by β-conversion
    (fact (- n 1)))
⇒ (fact-cps (- n 1)                   by the induction hypothesis
    (lambda (v) (k (* n v))))
⇒ (fact-cps n k)                      by the definition of fact-cps
```

Another way to see what is happening here is to calculate the result of a
call to *fact-cps*.

```
    (fact-cps 4 k)
⇒ (fact-cps 3 (lambda (v) (k (* 4 v))))
⇒ (fact-cps 2 (lambda (v)
                ((lambda (v) (k (* 4 v)))      by definition of fact-cps
                  (* 3 v))))
⇒ (fact-cps 2 (lambda (v) (k (* 4 (* 3 v)))))  by β-reduction
⇒ (fact-cps 1 (lambda (v)
                ((lambda (v)
                   (k (* 4 (* 3 v))))           by definition of fact-cps
                  (* 2 v))))
⇒ (fact-cps 1 (lambda (v) (k (* 4 (* 3 (* 2 v))))))  by β-reduction
⇒ (fact-cps 0 (lambda (v)                      by definition of fact-cps
                (k (* 4 (* 3 (* 2 (* 1 v)))))))
⇒ ((lambda (v) (k (* 4 (* 3 (* 2 (* 1 v))))))
    1)                                         by definition of fact-cps
⇒ (k (* 4 (* 3 (* 2 (* 1 1)))))                by β-reduction
⇒ (k 24)
```

Here we have shown most of the intermediate steps in the calculation. The
pattern becomes clearer if we show only the result of each application of
fact-cps followed by a β-reduction.

```
      (fact-cps 4 k)
  ⇒ (fact-cps 3 (lambda (v) (k (* 4 v))))
  ⇒ (fact-cps 2 (lambda (v) (k (* 4 (* 3 v)))))
  ⇒ (fact-cps 1 (lambda (v) (k (* 4 (* 3 (* 2 v))))))
  ⇒ (fact-cps 0 (lambda (v) (k (* 4 (* 3 (* 2 (* 1 v)))))))
  ⇒ (k (* 4 (* 3 (* 2 (* 1 1)))))
  ⇒ (k 24)
```

These derivations show that *fact-cps* has iterative control behavior, since the calls of *fact-cps* always occur in the same context, though its arguments may grow. The procedure uses its second argument *k* to represent the context in which the calculation of *fact* was to take place. We can think of *k* as representing a *promise* of the calculation to be done after computing the factorial of *n*. We recognize that *k*, which fulfills such a promise and represents a context such as (* n □), is being used as a *continuation*. Hence we say that *fact-cps* is written in *continuation-passing style*.

For a second example, consider *length*:

```
(define length
  (lambda (ls)
    (if (null? ls)
        0
        (+ (length (cdr ls)) 1))))
```

This can be expressed in continuation-passing style as

```
(define length-cps
  (lambda (ls k)
    (if (null? ls)
        (k 0)
        (length-cps (cdr ls)
          (lambda (v) (k (+ v 1)))))))
```

By convention, we use the variable *k* for continuations and pass the continuation as the last argument. The application (length-cps ls k) simulates the calculation of (length ls) in the context *k*. When *ls* is empty, it returns 0 to the context *k*. If *ls* is nonempty, then we need to determine the value of (+ (length (cdr ls)) 1) in the context *k*. This is the same as calculating (length (cdr ls)) in the context (k (+ □ 1)), which may be represented as (lambda (v) (k (+ v 1))).

- *Exercise 8.2.1*

Prove that (length-cps ls k) = (k (length ls)). □

8.3 Tail Form

We would like to develop a systematic method for transforming any procedure into an equivalent procedure that has iterative control behavior. (When we say a procedure has iterative control behavior, we mean that a call to the procedure executes with iterative control behavior in a properly tail-recursive implementation.)

There is no completely general way of determining whether the control behavior of a procedure is iterative or not. Consider

```
(lambda (n)
  (if (strange-predicate? n)
      (fact n)
      (fact-iter n)))
```

This procedure is iterative only if *strange-predicate?* always returns false. However, it may not always be possible to determine the truth or falsity of this condition, even if it were possible to examine the code of *strange-predicate?*.

Therefore the best we can hope for is to define a static criterion that guarantees iterative control behavior. Because it is impossible to tell whether an arbitrary program has iterative control behavior, our criterion will reject some programs that actually have iterative control behavior, but that is unavoidable.

The static criterion is called *tail form*. Our intention is that in a tail-form expression, procedure calls always occur at the outermost level of a derivation of the result of a call. Thus the result of any procedure call is the result of the whole expression. For example, in *fact-iter-acc*, the result of the procedure call is the result of the whole call. In calculating (fact-iter 4), this means that when we do a procedure call, we do not build any context. This is in contrast to *fact*, in which the procedure call is "wrapped" in the code (* n □), where □ represents the procedure call. A promise must be made to execute this code when the procedure call returns.

Before we can define tail form, we need to describe the sort of language that we shall be analyzing. We assume we are using a language in which programs consist of expressions of the following five types.

- Variables and literals, as usual.

- Procedural expressions.

- Primitive applications. We assume that we have identified a class of *primitive operations* that have the following properties:

  a. they are not implemented using procedure calls,

  b. they never invoke any procedures that may be passed to them as arguments, and

  c. they are not first class (they may not be passed as arguments to other procedures).

Our intention is that primitive operations can be implemented in a few lines of machine code, without involving procedure calls.

In our previous interpreters, we put such primitive operations in the initial environment. In this chapter, however, we treat invocations of primitive operations as special forms, recognizable by the parser, that are distinct from ordinary applications. We call such invocations *primitive applications* and provide them with their own type of abstract syntax record.

```
(define-record prim-app (primitive rands))
```

This organization is used in most programming languages, in which applications of primitive operations often have syntactic forms that are distinct from procedure calls: compare x+y to p(x,y).

The assumption that primitive procedures are not first class is only a minor restriction. For example, if we want to pass the primitive + as an argument, we could pass (lambda (x y) (+ x y)) instead. In the examples of this chapter, we assume all the Scheme procedures introduced prior to section 1.3 are primitive. This precludes, among others, apply and map.

- Special forms in which all subexpressions are evaluated in an arbitrary order. In all cases some operation (e.g., an application or assignment) is performed after the subexpressions are evaluated, and this operation determines the value of the whole expression. In this chapter we treat application as the prototype for special forms of this type. Other forms of this type, such as assignment (set!) forms, are treated similarly.

For the purposes of this chapter, we distinguish primitive applications and (general) applications. For example,

$$(+ (p\ 3)\ ((lambda\ (x)\ (+\ x\ 1))\ 4))$$

is a primitive application whose operands are both applications.

- Special forms that are evaluated as follows:

    a. First those subexpressions in certain positions are evaluated, in arbitrary order.

    b. Then exactly one of the remaining subexpressions is evaluated, and its value is immediately returned. (Hence these subexpressions are in tail position.)

There are two common forms in Scheme that do not fit any of the five types above: `begin` and `cond`. Fortunately, these forms may be expanded into equivalent forms that are of the required types. Although we develop the concepts of this chapter using Scheme, it must be emphasized that these concepts apply to a broad class of languages—not just Scheme.

Those subexpressions that may be evaluated first are said to be in *head* position. Expressions in tail position may be evaluated within the scope of certain variables, called the *binding positions* of the form. With one exception, all subexpressions of forms belonging to one of the five types must be in either head or tail position. The exception is the body of a lambda expression. The body is not evaluated at the time the lambda expression is evaluated; it is evaluated only when the resulting closure is applied.

In the Scheme forms of figure 8.3.1, the head positions are indicated by H, the tail positions by T, the binding positions by b, and those in neither head nor tail position by E. Note that in a primitive application (with primitive operation *prim-op*), the operand positions are all head positions, since they all are evaluated prior to invocation of the primitive operation. Similarly, the operator and operand positions of an application are all head positions. The formal parameters of a lambda are not considered binding positions, since their scope does not include any tail positions.

○ *Exercise 8.3.1*
Write an interpreter for the language of figure 8.3.1, plus variables and literals. For each production in the language, consider the action specified for that type of expression. Observe that the head positions are those for which evaluation of the subexpression is in head position in the action, and that the tail positions are those for which evaluation of the corresponding subexpression is in tail position in the action. □

We wish to identify those procedures in a program that may be responsible for recursive (noniterative) control behavior. To do so, we assign "responsibility" for the use of control space to procedures and to subexpressions of procedure bodies. We hold a given procedure responsible for control space

```
(lambda (v ... v) E)
(prim-op H ... H)
(H H ... H)
(set! v H)
(if H T T)
(let ((b H) ... (b H)) T)
(letrec ((b H) ... (b H)) T)
(begin H E ... E T)
(case H ((x ... x) T) ... ((x ... x) T))
```

Figure 8.3.1   Some forms, with their head, tail, and binding positions

that is required by calls initiated directly by it, but not for calls initiated by
other procedures, including other procedures defined within its body.

To identify those subexpressions of a procedure's body for which it is responsible, we require a new term: we say a subexpression E' of E is *available*
in E if it is not contained within a lambda subexpression of E. For example,
in the expression

```
(if (f a) (lambda () (g 2)) (h x y))
```

the applications (f a) and (h x y) are available, while the application (g 2)
is not. Thus a procedure is responsible only for the control space required for
calls initiated by applications that are available in its body.

Next we define a class of expressions whose evaluation cannot possibly be
responsible for recursive control behavior. We call these *simple* expressions.
The easiest way to identify simple expressions is to assume that any procedure
call may result in recursive control behavior. Thus we say an expression is
simple if it does not contain an available application. (Though this characterization of simple expressions suffices for our present purpose, less restrictive
characterizations are possible. This is discussed in section 8.7.)

Thus (car x) and (if p x (car (cdr x))) are simple, but (f (car x)) and
(car (f x)) are not. On the other hand, (lambda (x) (car (f x))) is simple,
since the procedure application (f x) is not available. Simple expressions
may be evaluated without executing procedure calls (without the interpreter
calling *apply-proc*).

The program of figure 8.3.2 determines whether an expression is simple. If
the expression is an application, it is not simple. Otherwise, *simple?* checks

the subexpressions in head and tail position to see if they are simple. This recursion terminates when the expression has no head or tail expressions, that is, when it is a variable, a literal, or a lambda expression. This program depends on the fact that all subexpressions in figure 8.3.1 (except for the body of a lambda expression) are either in head or tail position. Note that *head-exps*, *tail-exps*, and *binding-vars* of figure 8.3.2 are *not* recursive. In addition, letrec variables can be bound to arbitrary values, not just procedures. This necessitates using a syntax more like let, which we assume for the remainder of this chapter; see exercise 5.6.2.

We are now prepared to define our static criterion. A *tail-form expression* is one in which every subexpression in nontail position is simple.

Expressions may be in tail form but not simple, or simple but not in tail form. For example,

`(car x)`	simple	tail-form
`(if p x (car (cdr x)))`	simple	tail form
`(f (car x))`	not simple	tail form
`(car (f x))`	not simple	not tail form
`(if p x (f (cdr x)))`	not simple	tail form
`(if (f x) x (f (cdr x)))`	not simple	not tail form
`(lambda (x) (f x))`	simple	tail form
`(lambda (x) (car (f x)))`	simple	not tail form

Because we know that when an application in tail position is evaluated, no control information need be stored, and because in a tail-form expression all procedure applications are in tail position, we conclude:

> If an expression is in tail form, and any procedures accessible through variable bindings are also in tail form, then the expression will execute with iterative control behavior in a properly tail-recursive implementation.

Thus our criterion guarantees iterative control behavior, as desired.

One more definition will be useful. We say a procedure is in *first-order form* if it contains no lambda subexpressions and if all operator expressions are variables referring to top-level bindings. For example, fact, fact-iter and fact-iter-acc are all in first-order form, but the following procedures are not:

```
(lambda (x) (x 3))
(lambda () (lambda (x) x))
```

Figure 8.3.2 *simple? head-exps tail-exps binding-vars*

```
(define simple?
  (lambda (exp)
    (and (not (app? exp))
         (andmap simple? (head-exps exp))
         (andmap simple? (tail-exps exp)))))

(define head-exps
  (lambda (exp)
    (variant-case exp
      (lit (datum) '())
      (varref (var) '())
      (if (test-exp then-exp else-exp) (list test-exp))
      (proc (formals body) '())
      (let (decls body) (map decl->exp decls))
      (letrec (decls body) (map decl->exp decls))
      (prim-app (primitive rands) rands)
      (app (rator rands) (cons rator rands)))))

(define tail-exps
  (lambda (exp)
    (variant-case exp
      (lit (datum) '())
      (varref (var) '())
      (if (test-exp then-exp else-exp) (list then-exp else-exp))
      (proc (formals body) '())
      (let (decls body) (list body))
      (letrec (decls body) (list body))
      (prim-app (primitive rands) '())
      (app (rator rands) '()))))

(define binding-vars
  (lambda (exp)
    (variant-case exp
      (let (decls body) (map decl->var decls))
      (letrec (decls body) (map decl->var decls))
      (else '()))))
```

A set of procedure definitions whose bodies are in first-order tail form can be translated to flowchart form as we did for *fact-iter*.

Our goal is to develop a systematic process by which any program may be translated into a set of first-order tail-form procedures. In this chapter we see how to perform the first step in this process: the transformation of a procedure into an equivalent tail-form procedure in continuation-passing style. We shall consider the conversion to first-order form in chapter 9.

● *Exercise 8.3.2*

Write a program that takes an abstract syntax tree for a language that includes literals, variables, if, lambda, let, letrec, and application expressions and translates it to a syntax tree in which applications whose operators are known to be primitives (that is, found in the initial environment) are represented using prim-app nodes (defined above). Write an unparser to convert your abstract syntax trees back into Scheme syntax. Be careful to consider procedures like

```
proc (+) +(x, y)
```

You will need this program in order to use the Scheme-based CPS algorithm presented in this chapter. ☐

● *Exercise 8.3.3*

Determine whether each of the following expressions is simple and whether it is in tail form. Assume car, cdr, cons, and zero? are primitive.

a. (car (f (cdr x)))

b. (f (car (cdr x)))

c. (if (zero? x) (car y) (car (cdr y)))

d. (letrec ((x (lambda (y) (y x)))) (cons x '()))

e. (let ((f (lambda (x) x))) (f 3))

f. (case (f x) ((a) (g x)) (else y)) ☐

○ *Exercise 8.3.4*

Using BNF grammar, define two mutually recursive syntactic categories, one of tail-form expressions and one of simple expressions, for a subset of Scheme consisting of the following forms: variable, literal, primitive application, application, if, cond, lambda, let, and letrec. ☐

Define a predicate `tail-form?` for the language of exercise 8.3.2 that takes an expression and returns a boolean value indicating whether the expression is in tail form. ☐

8.4 Converting to Continuation-Passing Style

In this section we develop a set of rules for transforming any procedure into an equivalent procedure in tail form. We do this by transforming the procedure into continuation-passing style, as we did for `fact-cps` and `length-cps`; CPS procedures are always in tail form.

Automation of the CPS transformation may be useful, for example in the early phase of compilation, but it is also a valuable technique for transforming code "by hand." Though our algorithm for CPS transformation may be automated, as in section 8.6, it is also designed to reflect the way an experienced programmer would transform code into CPS and clearly expose the code's control component.

The `fact` and `length` examples suggest how a CPS transformation might be accomplished. The CPS transformation changes the procedure-calling convention so that every procedure takes an extra argument: the continuation to which the answer should be passed. It is then possible to transform every expression so that only simple expressions occur in nontail positions.

We do this in two stages. In the first stage, we rewrite *every* lambda expression so that it takes an extra argument (the continuation) to which the procedure returns its answer. By convention, we append the variable k to the end of each formal parameter list. (We assume the variable k is not used for other purposes. A new name could always be used to avoid a name conflict.)

The new body of each procedure is an application of k to the value of the old body. This transformation may be expressed as follows.

$$\text{(lambda } (x_1 \ \ldots \ x_n) \ E)$$
$$\Rightarrow \text{(lambda } (x_1 \ \ldots \ x_n \ \text{k}) \ (\text{k } E))$$

For example,

```
   (lambda (x) (f x 1))
⇒ (lambda (x k) (k (f x 1)))
```

The subexpression (k (f x 1)) is underscored to indicate that it must be transformed further. Since all procedures are transformed at once, the procedure f must now be passed a continuation. Thus after this first step we shall not have a working program until the CPS transformation has been completed.

The second stage of our CPS algorithm involves repeatedly finding an unprocessed (underscored) application of the form (k E) and applying one of four rules given below. These rules either "drive the k inward" (this phrase will mean something shortly) or determine that it has been driven inward as far as it can be. In general, we may have several k's to work on, but it makes no difference which one we choose at any step. (Of course, any implementation of this algorithm must include a strategy for making this choice.) We use a darker underscore to distinguish an unprocessed subexpression of an already underscored expression. Furthermore, we never underscore a lambda (and its formal parameters) that is generated by the first step of the algorithm.

The four transformation rules for unprocessed expressions of the form (k E), handle four cases, depending on the structure of E. The first two are relatively straightforward:

C_{simple}: If E is simple, k cannot be driven further through E, so we are done processing this k.

For example, both (k (cons v w)) and (k 0) are already in tail form. After applying this rule, there may still be lambda expressions inside E that need to be processed. Thus in (k (lambda (x y k) (k (g (- n 1))))), we cannot do anything more with the outside k, but we must still transform the inner one.

C_η: If E is a procedure application of the form $(E_1 \ldots E_n)$, where $E_1, \ldots,$ E_n are simple, the procedure call is converted to the new protocol by replacing (k E) by $(E_1 \ldots E_n$ k).

For example, (k (g (- n 1))) becomes (g (- n 1) k). As before, there may still be lambda expressions inside $E_1, \ldots, E_n$ that need to be processed.

The remaining two cases are more complicated. In each case, we must find an "innermost" expression to be evaluated first. This is usually an application, in which case we create a call with a new continuation that abstracts the context in which the innermost application appears. For example, if we had

```
(k (* n (fact (- n 1))))
```

then the innermost call is (fact (- n 1)), so we perform the following transformation.

```
    (k (* n (fact (- n 1))))
⇒ (fact (- n 1) (lambda (v) (k (* n v))))
```

Observe that k has been "driven inward," and the application needs no further processing except for the body of the new continuation.

In this example, the body of the continuation is already in tail form, so there is nothing else to do. If it were not, then we would continue processing the expression. For example, in (k (+ (f x) (g y))), there are two innermost applications: (f x) and (g y). Choosing to evaluate (f x) first, we obtain

```
    (k (+ (f x) (g y)))
⇒ (f̃ x (lambda (v) (k (+ v (g y)))))
⇒ (f̃ x (lambda (v) (g̃ y (lambda (w) (k (+ v w))))))
⇒ (f̃ x (lambda (v) (g̃ y (lambda (w) (k (+ v w))))))
```

We use a tilde above the name to denote the transformed procedure, which takes an additional argument. More precisely, we need to locate an *innermost nonsimple subexpression that can be evaluated first*. We call this an *initial expression* of E. By an *innermost subexpression* we mean one whose immediate subexpressions in head position are all simple. Thus the following are all innermost expressions:

```
(f x y)
(f (+ x y) z)
(if (> x y) (f (g x)) (h (j x)))
```

The last expression is innermost because it has only one immediate subexpression in head position, (> x y), and it is simple.

Of all the subexpressions, how do we determine which ones may be evaluated first? To do this, we look once again at the forms of figure 8.3.1. Recall that the first step in evaluating each of these forms is to evaluate (in any order) the subexpressions in head position, indicated by H. Thus, if E is not itself innermost, then the candidates for the initial expression must be found in the head-position subexpressions of E.

Therefore, we search for an initial expression as follows. If the expression E is nonsimple, but all its immediate subexpressions in head position are simple, then the expression is its own initial expression. Otherwise, we move our search to any one of the nonsimple immediate subexpressions of E that are in head position. Figure 8.4.1 gives a program for finding the leftmost initial expression.

For example, the initial expression of (p x y) is the application itself, since all of its subexpressions are simple. The initial expression of

Figure 8.4.1   Finding an initial expression

```
(define initial-exp
  (lambda (exp)
    (letrec
      ((loop (lambda (ls)
               (cond
                 ((null? ls) exp)
                 ((simple? (car ls)) (loop (cdr ls)))
                 (else (initial-exp (car ls)))))))
      (loop (head-exps exp)))))
```

```
(if (null? x) (f x y) z)
```

is also the entire expression, since (null? x), the only expression in head position, is a simple primitive application. The expression

```
(g (f a b)
   (h (p x y))
   (if (null? x) (f x y) z))
```

has three initial expressions. The first, (f a b), is in head position and all of its immediate subexpressions are simple, so it is an initial expression. The subexpression (h (p x y)) is also in head position, but it contains a nonsimple subexpression (p x y) in head position, so (h (p x y)) is not an innermost nonsimple expression that can be evaluated first. Moving the search for an initial expression inward, we find (p x y), which is nonsimple *and* contains no nonsimple subexpressions, so it is an initial expression. Finally, the expression (if (null? x) (f x y) z) is an initial expression, since it is nonsimple, it is in head position with respect to the entire expression, and it contains only the simple subexpression (null? x) in immediate head position.

As further examples, in the expressions that follow, the initial expressions are enclosed within a rectangle. (Verify!)

```
(f (* a b) 3)
```

```
(+ (fact 3) (* (fact (fib 2)) 5))
```

```
(if (f 3) (g 4) (g 5))
```

```
(let ((y 4)) (f 4))
```

```
(let ((x ⌈(let ((y 4)) (f 3))⌉)
      (y (+ a b))
      (z ⌈(f 3)⌉))
  (g 5))
```

• *Exercise 8.4.1*

Place a rectangle around the initial expressions of each of the following expressions. Remember that a single expression may have more than one initial expression.

a. (k (a (+ 1 b)))

b. (k (+ (f (g (h 3))) (a (+ 1 b))))

c. (k (f (if (zero? x) (g 3) (g 4)) (g 5)))

d. (k (f (if (zero? x) 3 4) (if (p x) 3 4)))

e. (k (let ((x 3) (y (fact 4))) (p x b))) □

○ *Exercise 8.4.2*

Modify `initial-exp` in figure 8.4.1 to produce a list of all the initial expressions in its argument. □

Once we find an initial expression, the next step in the algorithm depends on whether or not the initial expression is an application. If it is, the CPS version must perform that application first, using a suitable continuation. Therefore we make the application the outermost form of the CPS transformation. Thus if an application $(E_1 \ldots E_n)$ is an initial expression of (k E), then the transformed expression will be of the form

$$(E_1 \ldots E_n \ K)$$

for some suitable continuation K.

This continuation K must take a value v and complete the computation of (k E) using v as the result of the initial expression. Such a continuation may be created by constructing a lambda expression whose body is formed by replacing the initial expression with the formal parameter of the lambda expression. To avoid name clashes, we choose as the formal parameter a variable that does not occur free in the expression.

This is not as complicated as it sounds. Let us look at some examples. Consider first (k (h (p x y))). The only initial expression is (p x y), so we transform:

$$\frac{\text{(k (h (p x y)))}}{\Rightarrow \text{(p̃ x y (lambda (v) \underline{(k (h v))}))}}$$

Since (h v) is its own initial expression, we continue the transformation using the rule C_η.

$$\Rightarrow \text{(p̃ x y (lambda (v) (h̃ v k)))}$$

Next consider the expression (k (+ (f x) (g y))), which has two initial expressions, (f x) and (g y). If we choose to evaluate (f x) first, we obtain the following derivation:

$$\frac{\text{(k (+ (f x) (g y)))}}{\Rightarrow \text{(f̃ x (lambda (v) \underline{(k (+ v (g y)))}))}}$$
$$\Rightarrow \text{(f̃ x (lambda (v) (g̃ y (lambda (w) \underline{(k (+ v w))}))))}$$

Since (k (+ v w)) is in tail form, the whole expression is in tail form, and we are done. We could just as correctly and easily have chosen to evaluate (g y) first.

A somewhat more complicated expression is

(k (+ ⌈(f a b)⌉
       ⌈(g (lambda (a k) (k (f a b))))⌉))

Here we have already performed the algorithm's first stage, adding an extra continuation argument k to every lambda expression and passing its body to k. There are two occurrences of (f a b) in this expression: the first is an initial expression, and the second is not. We choose the first occurrence of the expression (f a b) as the initial expression and obtain

```
  (k (+ (f a b)
        (g (lambda (a k)
             (k (f a b))))))
⇒ (f̃ a b
     (lambda (v)
       (k (+ v
             (g (lambda (a k)
                  (k (f a b))))))))
```

Here we performed the substitution of v for the chosen occurrence of (f a b), *not for all* occurrences: the second, noninitial occurrence should not be changed. Continuing the derivation, we see that the application of g is an initial expression of the body of the first procedural expression. This gives us

```
⇒ (f̃ a b
    (lambda (v)
      (g̃ (lambda (a k) (k (f a b)))
         (lambda (w) (k (+ v w)))))))
```

We still have two occurrences of `k` to deal with. The second is already in tail
form, but the first can still be pushed farther inward. The result of one more
push is

```
⇒ (f̃ a b
    (lambda (v)
      (g̃ (lambda (a k) (f̃ a b k))
         (lambda (w) (k (+ v w)))))))
```

and we are done. (At this point we drop the tilde notation. Although, confusion can arise between the original procedure and its transformed counterpart,
the transformed program only contains transformed procedures. Furthermore,
it is simpler to think about the original and transformed procedures having
the same name, since they accomplish equivalent tasks.)

To formalize these operations, we introduce the notion of *positional substitution*. We write $E\{M/X\}$ to denote the positional substitution of M at the
position of X in E. This means we substitute M for a particular occurrence
of the subexpression X, not for *every* occurrence. Positional substitution
is rather different from the notion of substitution considered in section 4.2.
There, when we wrote $E[M/x]$, x had to be a variable, whereas here the
analogous quantity refers to an expression. Furthermore, the substitution renamed formal parameters to avoid capture of bound variables. Here capture
of bound variables does not occur, due to the nature of our algorithm. We
are now ready to state formally our third CPS transformation rule, which is
illustrated in figure 8.4.2.

C_{app}: If (k E) has an initial expression I that is an application (E_1 ...
E_n), replace (k E) by

$$(E_1 \ \ldots \ E_n \ (\texttt{lambda} \ (v) \ (\texttt{k} \ E\{v/I\})))$$

where v is a previously unused variable.

See figure 8.4.3 for a program to compute a *simultaneous* positional substitution. In this program the use of the procedure `eq?` (by `assq`) is essential,
since we are substituting at specific positions regardless of their content.

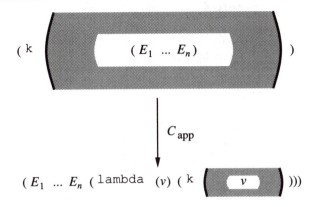

Figure 8.4.2   The CPS rule for application in a context: C_{app}

- *Exercise 8.4.3*
  Our transformation of (k (+ (f x) (g y))) evaluated the immediate subexpressions left-to-right by evaluating the left initial expression first. CPS-transform (k (+ (f x) (g (h y)))) to correspond to right-to-left evaluation. ☐

- *Exercise 8.4.4*
  CPS-transform (k (p (+ 8 x) (q y))). ☐

○ *Exercise 8.4.5*
  Find the CPS transformation for

```
(k (+ (f a b)
      (g (lambda (a k)
           (k (f a b))))))
```

in which the application of *g* is chosen as the initial expression. ☐

○ *Exercise 8.4.6*
  C_η corresponds to the case of C_{app} in which the initial expression of (k *E*) is *E* itself. Compare the result of applying C_{app} and C_η to (k (f x y)). ☐

Figure 8.4.3   Simultaneous positional substitution

```
(define positional-substitution
  (lambda (exp pairs)
    (letrec
      ((loop
         (lambda (exp)
           (let ((found-pair (assq exp pairs)))
             (if (pair? found-pair)
                 (cdr found-pair)
                 (variant-case exp
                   (lit (datum) exp)
                   (varref (var) exp)
                   (if (test-exp then-exp else-exp)
                     (make-if
                       (loop test-exp)
                       (loop then-exp)
                       (loop else-exp)))
                   (proc (formals body)
                     (make-proc formals (loop body)))
                   (let (decls body)
                     (make-let
                       (map (lambda (decl)
                              (make-decl
                                (decl->var decl)
                                (loop (decl->exp decl))))
                            decls)
                       (loop body)))
                   (letrec (decls body)
                     (make-letrec
                       (map (lambda (decl)
                              (make-decl
                                (decl->var decl)
                                (loop (decl->exp decl))))
                            decls)
                       (loop body)))
                   (prim-app (primitive rands)
                     (make-prim-app primitive (map loop rands)))
                   (app (rator rands)
                     (make-app (loop rator) (map loop rands)))))))))
      (loop exp))))
```

If all we had to deal with were applications (as in the lambda calculus), we could have escaped with a much simpler description of the conversion process. Transforming special forms, however, requires more care. Thus we have one more case, in which the initial expression is not an application but is instead a special form.

If a special form is initial, then its head subexpressions are all simple. Furthermore, its value is the value of *one* of its tail subexpressions. For example, consider

```
(k (if (null? ls) 0 (+ (length (cdr ls)) 1)))
```

The conditional expression is initial, because its only head subexpression, `(null? ls)`, is simple. The value of the conditional is either `0` or `(+ (length (cdr ls)) 1)`, so the value of the whole expression is the same as

```
(if (null? ls)
    (k 0)
    (k (+ (length (cdr ls)) 1)))
```

Once more `k` is pushed inward, and in this example it splits into two. From here, the other rules can be used.

Let us consider a slightly more complicated case.

```
(k (* (if (null? ls) x (+ (length (cdr ls)) 1))
      3))
```
⇒
```
(if (null? ls)
    (k (* x 3))
    (k (* (+ (length (cdr ls)) 1) 3)))
```

From such examples we surmise that *each* tail expression of the special form must be wrapped in the entire context in which the special form appears within the application of `k`.

There is one further complication. Because special forms, such as `let` and `letrec`, may bind variables, we must be careful to avoid variable capture. For example, consider

```
(k (g (let ((g 3))
        (f g x))))
```

Here the `let` expression is initial, and its body is its only tail expression. If we wrap the body in the context `(k (g □))`, then the context's outer `g` will be brought inside the scope of the inner `g` and be captured:

```
(let ((g 3))
  (k (g (f g x))))
```

This is clearly wrong, since the outer `g` is a procedure and the inner one is a number.

This problem may be avoided by α-converting the offending binding variables. Substituting `g:` for the inner `g` in our example, the transformation proceeds as follows.

$$
\begin{array}{ll}
& \underline{\text{(k (g (let ((g 3))}} \\
& \qquad \underline{\text{(f g x))))}} \\[4pt]
\Rightarrow & \underline{\text{(k (g (let ((g: 3))}} \\
& \qquad \underline{\text{(f g: x))))}} \qquad \text{by } \alpha\text{-conversion} \\[4pt]
\Rightarrow & \text{(let ((g: 3))} \\
& \qquad \underline{\text{(k (g (f g: x))))}} \\[8pt]
& \cdots \\[8pt]
\Rightarrow & \text{(let ((g: 3))} \\
& \qquad \text{(f g: x (lambda (v) (g v k))))}
\end{array}
$$

Figure 8.3.1 shows the positions of the variables bound by each special form. To formalize the notion of α-conversion here, we need some notation. We write $E\langle x_1, \ldots, x_p \rangle$ for the expression obtained by α-converting E to rename the bound variables $x_1, \ldots, x_p$ (see figure 8.4.5). To maintain readable programs, it is helpful when renaming a variable if the new name is obtained in a systematic fashion from the old name. Our convention is to add a colon to the end of the old name. (We presume that user variable names do not end with a colon.)

Combining these observations, we obtain the final CPS transformation rule (illustrated with `if` in figure 8.4.4).

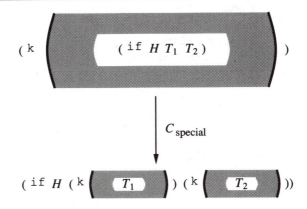

Figure 8.4.4 Typical CPS rule for special form in a context: C_{special}

C_{special}: If (k E) has an initial expression I with $n > 0$ expressions in tail
position, and $b_1, \ldots, b_p$ are the binding variables of I that occur free in
E, transform E as follows:

1. First let $I' = I\langle b_1, \ldots, b_p\rangle$,
2. Then replace (k E) by I' with each tail position expression T_i of I'
replaced by (k $E\{T_i/I\}$). That is, replace (k E) by

$$I'\{(\text{k } E\{T_1/I\})/T_1, \ldots, (\text{k } E\{T_n/I\})/T_n\}$$

We would like to treat **variant-case** expressions as if they had the form

$$(\text{variant-case } H \ (x \ (b \ \ldots \ b) \ T) \ \ldots \ (x \ (b \ \ldots \ b) \ T))$$

It would be improper, however, to α-convert the binding variables $b \ldots b$, since
they must also be record field names. α-conversion must instead occur on the
code surrounding the **variant-case** expression.

- *Exercise 8.4.7*
Apply rule C_{special} to the following expressions.

a. (k (zero? (if a (p x) (p y))))
b. (k (let ((x (let ((y 8)) (p y)))) x))
c. (k (let ((x (if a (p x) (p y)))) x))
d. (k (let ((x (f))) (x (variant-case e (a (x) (+ x 1)))))) ☐

Figure 8.4.5   An alpha converter

```
(define alpha-convert
  (lambda (exp bvs)
    (let ((table
            (let ((pairs (map (lambda (bv)
                                 (cons bv (next-symbol-right bv)))
                              bvs)))
              (lambda (sym)
                (let ((found-pair (assq sym pairs)))
                  (if (pair? found-pair)
                      (cdr found-pair)
                      sym))))))
      (variant-case exp
        (let (decls body)
          (make-let
            (map (lambda (decl)
                   (make-decl
                     (table (decl->var decl))
                     (decl->exp decl)))
                 decls)
            (beta body table)))
        (letrec (decls body)
          (make-letrec
            (map
              (lambda (decl)
                (make-decl
                  (table (decl->var decl))
                  (beta (decl->exp decl) table)))
              decls)
            (beta body table)))
        (else exp)))))
```

Figure 8.4.5   An alpha converter (continued)

```
(define beta
  (lambda (exp table)
    (variant-case exp
      (lit (datum) exp)
      (varref (var) (make-varref (table var)))
      (if (test-exp then-exp else-exp)
        (make-if
          (beta test-exp table)
          (beta then-exp table)
          (beta else-exp table)))
      (proc (formals body)
        (make-proc formals
          (beta body (lambda (var)
                       (if (memq var formals) var (table var))))))
      (let (decls body)
        (make-let
          (map (lambda (decl)
                 (make-decl (decl->var decl)
                   (beta (decl->exp decl) table)))
               decls)
          (beta body (let ((vars (map decl->var decls)))
                       (lambda (var)
                         (if (memq var vars) var (table var)))))))
      (letrec (decls body)
        (let ((new-table
                (let ((vars (map decl->var decls)))
                  (lambda (var)
                    (if (memq var vars) var (table var))))))
          (make-letrec
            (map (lambda (decl)
                   (make-decl (decl->var decl)
                     (beta (decl->exp decl) new-table)))
                 decls)
            (beta body new-table))))
      (prim-app (primitive rands)
        (make-prim-app primitive
          (map (lambda (rand) (beta rand table)) rands)))
      (app (rator rands)
        (make-app (beta rator table)
          (map (lambda (rand) (beta rand table)) rands))))))
```

If an `if` expression such as

```
(if (null? ls) 0 (+ (length (cdr ls)) 1))
```

appears as an initial subexpression of a large expression, then the CPS transform will look like

```
(if (null? ls) (K 0) (length (cdr ls) (lambda (v) (K (+ v 1)))))
```

where K represents the continuation that abstracts the context of the large expression. This reveals a shortcoming of the CPS transformation, since the program text of K appears in two places. If we wrap a `let` expression binding `k` to K around the entire expression, we would obtain

```
(let ((k K))
  (if (null? ls) (k 0) (length (cdr ls) (lambda (v) (k (+ v 1))))))
```

This technique keeps the expression from growing exponentially. Discuss the advantages and disadvantages of such an approach. This shortcoming is addressed more completely in chapter 12, where the output of a CPS transformation corresponds to the output of a compiler. □

● *Exercise 8.4.9*

Modify rule C_{app} to obtain a transformation rule for `set!`. □

8.5 Examples of the CPS Transformation

To obtain a feel for the CPS transformation rules, it is necessary to work through a number of examples. Let us try *remove* from section 2.2.2 first.

```
(define remove
  (lambda (s los)
    (if (null? los)
        '()
        (if (eq? s (car los))
            (remove s (cdr los))
            (cons (car los) (remove s (cdr los)))))))
```

Our first step is to add the extra continuation argument to each procedural expression; in this case there is only one:

```
(lambda (s los k)
  (k (if (null? los)
         '()
         (if (eq? s (car los))
             (remove s (cdr los))
             (cons (car los) (remove s (cdr los))))))))
```

We now begin pushing the k through the expression. In this example the only subexpression in head position is (null? los), and it is simple. Thus we apply C_{special} and obtain

```
(lambda (s los k)
  (if (null? los)
      (k '())
      (k (if (eq? s (car los))
             (remove s (cdr los))
             (cons (car los) (remove s (cdr los))))))))
```

The first application of k is in tail form, so after observing this we remove the underscoring. (We do this without comment from now on.) The if subexpression of the second application of k is its initial expression, since (eq? s (car los)) (its only head expression) is simple. Hence we apply rule C_{special} and obtain

```
(lambda (s los k)
  (if (null? los)
      (k '())
      (if (eq? s (car los))
          (k (remove s (cdr los)))
          (k (cons (car los) (remove s (cdr los)))))))
```

Now we can apply the simple-application rule C_η to the first unprocessed k to obtain

```
(lambda (s los k)
  (if (null? los)
      (k '())
      (if (eq? s (car los))
          (remove s (cdr los) k)
          (k (cons (car los) (remove s (cdr los)))))))
```

The subexpression (remove s (cdr los)) is an initial expression of the last application of k, so by C_{app} we obtain

```
(lambda (s los k)
  (if (null? los)
      (k '())
      (if (eq? s (car los))
          (remove s (cdr los) k)
          (remove s (cdr los)
            (lambda (v)
              (k (cons (car los) v)))))))
```

and we are done.

To create a tail-form version of the original *remove* procedure, we rename the CPS version of remove to remove-cps throughout the program and redefine *remove* as follows:

```
(define remove
  (lambda (s los)
    (remove-cps s los (lambda (v) v))))
```

For another example, consider *subst* from section 2.2.2.

```
(define subst
  (lambda (new old slst)
    (if (null? slst)
        '()
        (if (symbol? (car slst))
            (if (eq? (car slst) old)
                (cons new (subst new old (cdr slst)))
                (cons (car slst) (subst new old (cdr slst))))
            (cons (subst new old (car slst))
                  (subst new old (cdr slst)))))))
```

This is an interesting example, since it contains four applications, two of which are initial expressions of the same primitive application. Also, here we see the importance of positional substitution since there are three different instances of (subst new old (cdr slst)).

Again, we start by transforming the lambda expression.

```
(lambda (new old slst k)
  (k (if (null? slst)
         '()
         (if (symbol? (car slst))
             (if (eq? (car slst) old)
                 (cons new (subst new old (cdr slst)))
                 (cons (car slst) (subst new old (cdr slst))))
             (cons (subst new old (car slst))
                   (subst new old (cdr slst)))))))

⇒ (lambda (new old slst k)
     (if (null? slst)
         (k '())
         (k (if (symbol? (car slst))
                (if (eq? (car slst) old)
                    (cons new (subst new old (cdr slst)))
                    (cons (car slst) (subst new old (cdr slst))))
                (cons (subst new old (car slst))
                      (subst new old (cdr slst)))))))

⇒ (lambda (new old slst k)
     (if (null? slst)
         (k '())
         (if (symbol? (car slst))
             (k (if (eq? (car slst) old)
                    (cons new (subst new old (cdr slst)))
                    (cons (car slst) (subst new old (cdr slst)))))
             (k (cons (subst new old (car slst))
                      (subst new old (cdr slst)))))))

⇒ (lambda (new old slst k)
     (if (null? slst)
         (k '())
         (if (symbol? (car slst))
             (if (eq? (car slst) old)
                 (k (cons new (subst new old (cdr slst))))
                 (k (cons (car slst) (subst new old (cdr slst)))))
             (subst new old (car slst)
               (lambda (v)
                 (k (cons v (subst new old (cdr slst)))))))))
```

In the last step, we chose the first application in the last *cons* primitive application as the initial expression to evaluate, effectively guaranteeing a left-to-right evaluation order of the cons operands. The second application could just as well have been chosen, since the order of operand evaluation is unspecified in Scheme. In continuing our trace, we use v as the parameter for newly created continuations when it does not shadow another binding of v.

```
⇒ (lambda (new old slst k)
    (if (null? slst)
        (k '())
        (if (symbol? (car slst))
            (if (eq? (car slst) old)
                (subst new old (cdr slst)
                  (lambda (v) (k (cons new v))))
                (subst new old (cdr slst)
                  (lambda (v) (k (cons (car slst) v)))))
            (subst new old (car slst)
              (lambda (v)
                (k (cons v (subst new old (cdr slst)))))))))

⇒ (lambda (new old slst k)
    (if (null? slst)
        (k '())
        (if (symbol? (car slst))
            (if (eq? (car slst) old)
                (subst new old (cdr slst)
                  (lambda (v) (k (cons new v))))
                (subst new old (cdr slst)
                  (lambda (v) (k (cons (car slst) v)))))
            (subst new old (car slst)
              (lambda (v)
                (subst new old (cdr slst)
                  (lambda (v1) (k (cons v v1)))))))))
```

Following our convention of using names ending in -cps for procedures in CPS, we would define *subst-cps* using the expression above with each occurrence of subst replaced by subst-cps.

Our rules are designed to work on expressions with embedded lambda expressions. Let us consider another version of *remove* that uses letrec:

```
(define remove
  (lambda (s los)
    (letrec
      ((loop
         (lambda (los)
           (if (null? los)
               '()
               (if (eq? s (car los))
                   (loop (cdr los))
                   (cons (car los) (loop (cdr los)))))))))
      (loop los))))
```

Our first step is to add a continuation argument to each lambda expression. Here, there are two such expressions. We obtain

```
(lambda (s los k)
  (k (letrec
       ((loop
          (lambda (los k)
            (k (if (null? los)
                   '()
                   (if (eq? s (car los))
                       (loop (cdr los))
                       (cons (car los) (loop (cdr los)))))))))
       (loop los))))
```

Consulting figure 8.3.1, we see that the only head expression of the letrec is the declaration of loop, which is a lambda expression and therefore simple. Hence the letrec is the initial expression, and we can apply C_{special} to get

```
(lambda (s los k)
  (letrec
    ((loop
       (lambda (los k)
         (k (if (null? los)
                '()
                (if (eq? s (car los))
                    (loop (cdr los))
                    (cons (car los) (loop (cdr los)))))))))
    (k (loop los))))
```

Applying the rule C_η for simple applications, we obtain

```
(lambda (s los k)
  (letrec
    ((loop
       (lambda (los k)
         (k (if (null? los)
                '()
                (if (eq? s (car los))
                    (loop (cdr los))
                    (cons (car los) (loop (cdr los)))))))))
    (loop los k))))
```

Now we can continue transforming the body of the inner lambda expression.

○ *Exercise 8.5.1*
Finish this transformation. □

To transform a cond expression, we can always convert it into an if expression and transform that. But, often the test expressions of a cond form are all simple. When such cond forms are expanded into if expressions, the nesting structure of the if expressions is retained after CPS transformation. This allows the transformed if expressions in the resulting CPS code to be converted back into a cond expression. From these observations we conclude that when all of the test expressions of a cond expression are simple, rule C_{special} may be applied directly to the expression, treating each test expression as if it were in head position. For example, if *remove* were expressed using cond, its CPS transformation would include the following step:

```
(k (cond
     ((null? los) '())
     ((eq? s (car los)) (remove s (cdr los)))
     (else (cons (car los) (remove s (cdr los))))))
⇒ (cond
    ((null? los) (k '()))
    ((eq? s (car los)) (k (remove s (cdr los))))
    (else (k (cons (car los) (remove s (cdr los))))))
```

and so on. If one of the tests is nonsimple, the best we can do is to convert that part of the cond expression into an if expression and transform that into CPS.

Verify the statements made in the last paragraph. □

Consider the definition and use of *final-valcont* below.

```
> (define final-valcont
    (lambda (v)
      (display "The answer is: ")
      (write v)
      (newline)))
> (remove-cps 'b '(a b c b a) final-valcont)
The answer is: (a c a)
```

Here we have used something other than (lambda (v) v) as the continuation that receives the final value. When testing CPS procedures, it is better to use this *final-valcont* rather than the identity procedure. since correct solutions will print The answer is: just one time for each test of a CPS procedure. This avoids confusion between values received by the final value continuation and those printed by the read-eval-print loop.

● *Exercise 8.5.3*
Transform these procedures to CPS and then test them using *final-valcont*.

a. remove*

```
(define remove*
  (lambda (a alst)
    (cond
      ((null? alst) '())
      ((pair? (car alst))
       (cons (remove* a (car alst)) (remove* a (cdr alst))))
      ((eq? (car alst) a) (remove* a (cdr alst)))
      (else (cons (car alst) (remove* a (cdr alst)))))))
```

b. member*

```
(define member*
  (lambda (a alst)
    (cond
      ((null? alst) #f)
      ((pair? (car alst))
       (or (member* a (car alst)) (member* a (cdr alst))))
      ((eq? (car alst) a) alst)
      (else (member* a (cdr alst))))))
```

c. remfirst*

```
(define remfirst*
  (lambda (a alst)
    (letrec
      ((loop (lambda (alst)
               (cond
                 ((null? alst) '())
                 ((not (pair? (car alst)))
                  (if (eq? (car alst) a)
                      (cdr alst)
                      (cons (car alst) (loop (cdr alst)))))
                 ((equal? (loop (car alst)) (car alst))
                  (cons (car alst) (loop (cdr alst))))
                 (else (cons (loop (car alst)) (cdr alst)))))))
      (loop alst))))
```

d. depth

```
(define depth
  (lambda (alst)
    (cond
      ((null? alst) 1)
      ((not (pair? (car alst))) (depth (cdr alst)))
      ((< (+ (depth (car alst)) 1) (depth (cdr alst)))
       (depth (cdr alst)))
      (else (+ (depth (car alst)) 1)))))
```

e. depth-with-let

```
(define depth-with-let
  (lambda (alst)
    (if (null? alst)
        1
        (let ((drest (depth-with-let (cdr alst))))
          (if (pair? (car alst))
              (let ((dfirst (+ (depth-with-let (car alst)) 1)))
                (if (< dfirst drest) drest dfirst))
              drest)))))
```

□

- *Exercise 8.5.4*

  Transform the following procedures into CPS.

  a. *map-cps*—the procedure *map* in continuation-passing style. Its first argument must also be a procedure that is written in continuation-passing style. For example, we could map *car* over a list as follows:

  ```
  > (map-cps
      (lambda (v k) (k (car v)))
      '((1 2 3) (a b c) (x y z))
      final-valcont)
  The answer is: (1 a x)
  ```

  b. *fnlr>n*—takes any list of numbers and a number *n* and returns the first number in the list (in left-to-right order) that is greater than *n*. Once the result is found, no further elements in the list are examined. For example

  ```
  > (fnlr>n '(1 (3 (2) 7 (9))) 6 final-valcont)
  The answer is: 7
  ```

  c. *add>n*—takes any list of numbers and a number *n* as arguments. It returns the sum of all numbers in the list that are greater than *n*.

  d. *andmap-cps*—takes a predicate and a list and returns true if the predicate returns true for each list element. Use this definition:

  ```
  (define andmap
    (lambda (f ls)
      (if (null? ls)
          #t
          (and (f (car ls)) (andmap f (cdr ls))))))
  ```

  □

8.6 Implementing the CPS Transformation

The CPS transformation in section 8.4 changes the procedure-calling protocol to a continuation-passing style in which every procedure takes an additional continuation argument and every call supplies that argument. We described the transformation in terms of two passes: one to change all the lambda expressions and one to change all the applications. The second pass was described in terms of pushing a continuation argument k through the expression until its argument was simple.

Figure 8.6.1 `cps-simple`

```
(define cps-simple
  (lambda (exp)
    (if (proc? exp)
        (make-proc (append (proc->formals exp) '(k))
          (cps-exp (proc->body exp)))
        (positional-substitution exp
          (map (lambda (head-or-tail-exp)
                 (cons head-or-tail-exp
                   (cps-simple head-or-tail-exp)))
            (append (head-exps exp) (tail-exps exp)))))))))
```

Our description specified the individual transformation rules, but it was vague about the control structure of the algorithm. To implement this algorithm, we must be more specific about the control structure. Observe that no expression ever gets transformed twice: once we have pushed k through a piece of code, we are through transforming that code. This allows us to combine the two stages of the transformation into a single traversal of an expression's parse tree. We use two procedures, *cps-simple* and *cps-exp*, one for each stage of the transformation, which call each other recursively.

The procedure `cps-simple` is shown in figure 8.6.1. Rather than code the algorithm directly in terms of the abstract syntax tree, we use a set of auxiliary procedures, such as *head-exps* and *positional-substitution*, which deal with the syntax tree. Therefore, to modify the language being transformed, we need only modify these auxiliary procedures, not the main procedures of the algorithm.

If *exp* is a lambda expression, *cps-simple* adds an additional argument to its formal parameter list and then initiates the second phase on the body of the procedure. Otherwise, it continues to search through the parse tree, using *positional-substitution* to rebuild the transformed tree.

The procedure *cps-exp* is shown in figure 8.6.2. It simulates pushing the continuation variable k through its argument by calling an auxiliary procedure to perform the appropriate rule. If its argument is simple, it calls the procedure *c-simple* to perform rule C_{simple}. Otherwise, it finds an initial expression. If the initial expression is an application, it performs rule C_η if the initial expression is E and rule C_{app} otherwise. If the initial expression is not an application, then it performs rule C_{special}.

Figure 8.6.2　*cps-exp*

```
(define cps-exp
  (lambda (exp)
    (if (simple? exp)
        (c-simple exp)
        (let ((init-exp (initial-exp exp)))
          (if (app? init-exp)
              (if (eq? init-exp exp)
                  (c-eta init-exp)
                  (c-app init-exp exp))
              (c-special init-exp exp)))))))
```

Figure 8.6.3　Procedures for generating new symbols

```
(define next-symbol-right
  (lambda (sym)
    (string->symbol
      (string-append (symbol->string sym) ":"))))

(define next-symbol-left
  (let ((c 0))
    (lambda (rator)
      (set! c (+ c 1))
      (string->symbol
        (string-append ":"
          (if (varref? rator)
              (symbol->string (varref->var rator))
              "g")
          (number->string c))))))
```

The procedures for applying the rules are shown in figure 8.6.4. Most of this code is just what is in the rules, using *positional-substitution* to reassemble the parse trees. In *c-simple*, note that we apply *cps-simple* to *exp* in order to continue the first-stage search for embedded procedural expressions. Similarly, *cps-simple* is applied to the operator and operands in each procedure application and to the head positions of each special form. In *c-special*, we perform alpha conversion on some of the binding variables of let and letrec expressions; see figure 8.6.3. When we need a new variable in *c-app*, we use *next-symbol-left*; see exercise 4.6.3.

Figure 8.6.4 Procedures for the C-rules

```
(define c-simple
  (lambda (exp)
    (make-app (make-varref 'k) (list (cps-simple exp)))))

(define c-app
  (lambda (init-exp exp)
    (make-app (cps-simple (app->rator init-exp))
      (append (map cps-simple (app->rands init-exp))
        (list (let ((g (next-symbol-left (cps-simple (app->rator init-exp)))))
                (make-proc (list g)
                  (cps-exp
                    (positional-substitution exp
                      (list (cons init-exp (make-varref g)))))))))))

(define c-eta
  (lambda (init-exp)
    (make-app (cps-simple (app->rator init-exp))
      (append
        (map cps-simple (app->rands init-exp))
        (list (make-varref 'k))))))

(define c-special
  (lambda (init-exp exp)
    (let ((new-init-exp (alpha-convert init-exp
                          (intersect
                            (binding-vars init-exp)
                            (free-vars exp)))))
      (positional-substitution new-init-exp
        (append
          (map (lambda (h)
                 (cons h (cps-simple h)))
               (head-exps new-init-exp))
          (map (lambda (t)
                 (cons t (cps-exp
                           (positional-substitution exp
                             (list (cons init-exp t))))))
               (tail-exps new-init-exp)))))))
```

- *Exercise 8.6.1*

  Since the parser expands `begin` expressions into two subexpressions, modifying the CPS algorithm to include `begin` expressions is now quite easy. Add `begin` expressions to the implementation of the CPS algorithm. □

- *Exercise 8.6.2*

  Modify the implementation of the CPS algorithm to include `set!`. □

○ *Exercise 8.6.3*

  Rewrite the algorithm to work directly in terms of the parse tree, rather than working through the various intermediary procedures. The resulting code should have only two occurrences of *positional-substitution*, one in *c-app* and the other in *c-special*. □

○ *Exercise 8.6.4*

  The algorithm as stated does not work if the symbol k is used as a parameter in the input code. Modify the algorithm to work correctly in this case. □

○ *Exercise 8.6.5*

  Extend the implementation to handle `cond` expressions, by expanding them into `if` expressions. Then modify the unparser to replace nested `if` expressions by `cond` expressions. □

○ *Exercise 8.6.6*

  While our algorithm is organized to take only a single pass over the syntax tree, it actually makes several subpasses as it works, because each call to *initial-exp* or *positional-substitution* initiates a traversal of at least part of the tree. Rewrite the algorithm so that initial expressions and continuation arguments are computed "on-the-fly." Your final code should not use *positional-substitution* at all. Hint: Give *cps-exp* a second argument representing the continuation context. □

8.7 Call Chains

In this section we define the concept of a "call chain" in a manner appropriate for analysis of iterative control behavior. This allows us to formulate a more general definition of proper tail recursion, to clarify the connection between proper tail recursion and iterative control behavior, and to develop a less restrictive characterization of simple expressions. This in turn makes the definition of tail form less restrictive and improves the CPS algorithm.

Consider (+ (fact-iter n) m). When *fact-iter* is called, the context of the outer primitive application must be recorded, so some control space is required. This space is certainly bounded, and since *fact-iter* just calls the tail-form procedure *fact-iter-acc*, the entire expression evaluates with iterative control behavior. Thus *fact-iter* need not be expressed in CPS.

According to the characterization of simple expressions in section 8.3, however, the expression (+ (fact-iter n) m) is not simple, and hence the CPS algorithm will transform it into

```
(fact-iter n (lambda (v) (k (+ v m))))
```

If *fact-iter* is not in CPS, the appropriate result is

```
(k (+ (fact-iter n) m))
```

which can be obtained only if (+ (fact-iter n) m) is simple.

The solution is to introduce a less restrictive characterization of simple expressions. Recall that simple expressions were introduced as a way of identifying a class of expressions whose evaluation would not be responsible for recursive control behavior. Our characterization of simple expressions as those expressions that contained no available applications certainly has this property. Many other expressions, however, such as (+ (fact-iter n) m), also enjoy this property. No static analysis will be able to identify precisely those expressions that are responsible for recursive control behavior, but by using call chains, we can obtain a less restrictive characterization of simple expressions.

A *call chain* is associated with every call to a procedure. When a procedure initiates a call to another, the call chain of the current call to the first procedure is extended to include the initiating application. For example, consider the following definitions.

```
(define f (lambda (x) (g x)))
(define g (lambda (y) (f (h y))))
(define h (lambda (z) z))
```

The application (f 3) creates an infinite call chain that alternatively contains the applications (f (h y)) and (g x). Though call chains including (h y) are created, these applications are not in the call chain created by (f 3), since *h* returns to *g* before *g* calls *f*.

It is tempting to think of a call chain as a stack onto which an application is pushed when a procedure is called and from which an application is popped when a procedure "returns." The problem with this view is that procedures with iterative control behavior do not perform a return for every time they are called—they return just once when they are done. The call (`fact-iter-acc 100 0`) results in *fact-iter-acc* being called 100 times, but it is misleading to think that it then "returns" 100 times; in a properly tail-recursive implementation the answer is returned in a single operation.

In section 8.1 we said a properly tail-recursive implementation was one in which tail calls resulted in no net growth of control space. Using call chains, we can give it a more precise and general definition.

> A properly tail-recursive implementation, or simply a tail-recursive implementation, is one in which any chain of tail calls results in bounded growth of control space.

Thus a properly tail-recursive implementation might use additional control space for some tail calls, as long as it is guaranteed that *any* chain (even an infinite one) composed entirely of tail calls will not require an unbounded amount of control space. In the discussion that follows, a tail-recursive implementation is assumed.

We are ultimately concerned with call chains that are unbounded. A call chain is unbounded if it is infinite (no limit can be placed on its length) or if a bound on its length can only be obtained with knowledge of run-time data. It is these call chains that may require unbounded control storage space (if they contain nontail calls) and hence result in recursive control behavior.

There are only a finite number of applications in the text of a given program. Thus in an unbounded call chain there must be an unbounded number of occurrences of at least one application. We say an application is *repeating* if it *may* occur an unbounded number of times in a call chain. Thus, the only time that a procedure can exhibit recursive control behavior is when it contains a repeating application in nontail position.

Now we can present a more general characterization of simple expressions.

> An expression is simple if it is known that none of its available applications are repeating.

For example, it is easy to verify that (`+ (fact-iter n) m`) is simple, because although (`fact-iter n`) is not in tail position, it appears only once (hence a bounded number of times) in its call chain.

By introducing a less restrictive characterization of simple expressions, we have also made the definition of tail form considerably less restrictive. For example, (+ (fact-iter n) m) is now in tail form, provided we know that the application (fact-iter n) is not repeating. It is still the case that if an expression is in tail form, and any procedures accessible through variable bindings are also in tail form, the expression executes with iterative control behavior (in a properly tail-recursive implementation). This is the property that any characterization of simple expressions must preserve.

Though we cannot always know if an application is repeating, it is often possible to determine that applications are not repeating by using a *call graph*. A call graph contains a node for every procedure in a program. A link from one node to another in the graph indicates that the procedure at the tail of the link *may* call the procedure at the head of the link. For example, the graph for the *fact-iter* program will have a link from *fact-iter* to *fact-iter-acc* and another link from *fact-iter-acc* to itself.

If an available application in a procedure A initiates a call to a procedure B, the application can be repeating only if there is a cycle in the call graph that includes the link from A to B. The presence of a call graph cycle including this link does not mean that the application will necessarily occur an unbounded number of times in a call chain, but there is at least that possibility. If there is no call graph cycle including the link from A to B, however, then the application cannot occur an unbounded number of times in a call chain, so the application cannot be repeating.

• *Exercise 8.7.1*
Write a CPS version of the following program, using call graph analysis to avoid unnecessary CPS conversion. The resulting program should exhibit iterative-control behavior using a minimum number of continuations.

```
(letrec ((p1 (lambda (n)
               (list (p3 n))))
         (p2 (lambda (n)
               (- n 1)))
         (p3 (lambda (n)
               (if (p4 n) 1 (* n (p5 n)))))
         (p4 (lambda (n)
               (zero? n)))
         (p5 (lambda (n)
               (p3 (p2 n)))))
  (p1 5))
```
⬚

∘ *Exercise 8.7.2*

In a language with first-class procedures, such as Scheme, it is not always possible to construct call graphs by static analysis of a program. In the most common situation, however, in which procedures are bound directly to variables and these variables appear only in operator positions, it is possible to construct a call graph by program analysis.

Assume that `lambda` expressions can occur only on the right-hand side of `letrec` bindings and that `letrec`-bound variables may appear only in operator position. Write a procedure that takes a program represented as a `letrec` expression and constructs a list of pairs representing its call graph. Redefine *simple?* to make use of this list. Use *cps-exp* to test *simple?* on examples that demonstrate the advantages of this approach. □

8.8 Summary

Continuations make the control behavior of a program explicit by representing the portion of the computation to which the result of a subcomputation should be sent.

A subexpression of an expression is in tail position if the value of the subexpression is guaranteed to be returned immediately as the value of the expression. Procedure calls in tail position require no additional control information to be stored. Programs in which every non-trivial procedure call is in tail position are said to be in tail form, and a proper implementation will execute them like a flowchart, without requiring extra space for control information.

Any program can be transformed to an equivalent program in tail form by translating it into continuation-passing style. In continuation-passing style, every procedure takes an extra argument which is the continuation to which the result of the procedure should be sent. Procedure calls that are not in tail position are transformed into tail calls with a continuation argument that represents the context of the original call.

The exact definitions of tail form and of the CPS transformation algorithm are complicated by the need to account for the special forms and primitive operations of Scheme. The key step in the algorithm is the identification of an innermost non-simple subexpression that can be evaluated first, called an initial subexpression.

9 Continuation-Passing Interpreters

In the previous chapter we showed how to convert an arbitrary program in a Scheme-like language into tail form. In this chapter, we continue this transformation. First, in section 9.1 we show how to convert procedural continuations into data structures. The result is a program in first-order tail form that can be directly transformed into flowchart form. We shall consider the details of the transformation to flowcharts in chapter 10. Then, in section 9.2, we apply this transformation to an interpreter. The resulting interpreter achieves our goal of explaining recursive procedures without using recursion. Next, in section 9.3 we turn to the use of continuations as values in programming languages, and show how continuations as denoted values can be used to escape from procedures. In section 9.4, we show how continuations as expressed values can be used to build complex control structures such as coroutines. Last, in sections 9.5 and 9.6, we consider some of the complexities that first-class continuations add to a language.

9.1 Data Structure Representations of Continuations

We now have a method for transforming any program into tail form. However, this method introduces new procedures in the form of continuations. In this section we show how these continuations can be represented as data structures, rather than as procedures. This allows us, among other things, to take a procedure that was in first-order form before CPS transformation and return it to first-order form.

We want the ability to use alternative representations for continuations. The first step is to make continuations *abstract* by constructing an abstract data type (ADT) for them, as we did for finite functions in section 3.6. For an example, consider a version of *remove* using cond.

```
(define remove
  (lambda (s los)
    (remove-cps s los (lambda (v) v))))

(define remove-cps
  (lambda (s los k)
    (cond
      ((null? los) (k '()))
      ((eq? s (car los)) (remove-cps s (cdr los) k))
      (else (remove-cps s (cdr los)
              (lambda (v)
                (k (cons (car los) v))))))))
```

There are only four points in this program at which continuations are created or invoked. The expressions `(lambda (v) (k (cons (car los) v)))` and `(lambda (v) v)` indicate points at which continuations are created. The two points at which a continuation is invoked are the `(k (cons (car los) v))` and `(k '())`.

By defining a procedure for invoking continuations and a set of procedures for creating continuations, one for each kind of continuation, we obtain an ADT for continuations. By using such an ADT, a CPS procedure can be factored into two parts: the implementation of the ADT, which is of course dependent on the representation of continuations, and the remainder of the procedure, which is independent of this representation.

When a lambda expression representing a continuation is evaluated, a closure is formed that captures the current bindings of variables that occur free in the lambda expression. These bindings contain information that must be passed to procedures that create continuations. (For the purposes of this analysis, variables such as `cons` and `car` that refer to top-level bindings are not considered free, since their bindings always contain the same information and this information is available anywhere in the program.) These considerations lead us to the following code for the representation-independent portion of *remove*, where *apply-continuation*, *make-final-valcont*, and *make-rem1* are the procedures of the continuation ADT.

```
(define remove
  (lambda (s los)
    (remove-cps s los (make-final-valcont))))
```

```
(define remove-cps
  (lambda (s los k)
    (cond
      ((null? los) (apply-continuation k '()))
      ((eq? s (car los)) (remove-cps s (cdr los) k))
      (else (remove-cps s (cdr los) (make-rem1 los k))))))
```

To implement the continuation ADT, we must choose a representation for continuations. Initially, we represent them as procedures, using lambda expressions that are identical to those used in our initial version of *remove-cps*. For each expression (lambda (v) M) that builds a continuation, the corresponding constructor is (lambda $(x_1$ ... $x_n)$ (lambda (v) M')), where $x_1, \ldots, x_n$ are the free variables of M, and M' is M with suitable instances of apply-continuation inserted.

```
(define make-final-valcont
  (lambda ()
    (lambda (v) v)))

(define make-rem1
  (lambda (los k)
    (lambda (v)
      (apply-continuation k (cons (car los) v)))))

(define apply-continuation
  (lambda (k v)
    (k v)))
```

It is now straightforward to replace the procedural representation of continuations by data structure representations, as we did for finite functions in section 3.6.2. We define a different type of record for each type of continuation and a procedure apply-continuation that determines what type of continuation it has been passed and simulates an application of the appropriate procedure.

```
(define-record final-valcont ())
(define-record rem1 (los k))

(define apply-continuation
  (lambda (k v)
    (variant-case k
      (final-valcont () v)
      (rem1 (los k) (apply-continuation k (cons (car los) v))))))
```

These three definitions complete a new implementation of the continuation ADT. The code for `remove` and `remove-cps` remains unchanged.

Next consider a more complex example.

```
(define subst
  (lambda (new old slst)
    (subst-cps new old slst (lambda (v) v))))

(define subst-cps
  (lambda (new old slst k)
    (if (null? slst)
        (k '())
        (if (not (pair? (car slst)))
            (if (eq? (car slst) old)
                (subst-cps new old (cdr slst)
                  (lambda (v) (k (cons new v))))
                (subst-cps new old (cdr slst)
                  (lambda (v) (k (cons (car slst) v)))))
            (subst-cps new old (car slst)
              (lambda (v)
                (subst-cps new old (cdr slst)
                  (lambda (v1) (k (cons v v1)))))))))))
```

Here we have five different continuations, corresponding to the four procedure calls to *subst-cps* and the final value continuation. We note, however, that the continuations

```
(lambda (v) (k (cons new v)))
```

and

```
(lambda (v1) (k (cons v v1)))
```

are the same except for variable names. Thus we need only make four different types of continuations. As before, the procedures of the ADT for continuations take as arguments those free variables of the corresponding `lambda` expressions that contain variable information. This gives us the following ADT for *subst-cps* continuations.

```
(define make-final-valcont
  (lambda ()
    (lambda (v) v)))

(define make-subst1
  (lambda (new k)
    (lambda (v)
      (apply-continuation k (cons new v)))))

(define make-subst2
  (lambda (slst k)
    (lambda (v)
      (apply-continuation k (cons (car slst) v)))))

(define make-subst3
  (lambda (new old slst k)
    (lambda (v)
      (subst-cps new old (cdr slst)
        (make-subst1 v k)))))

(define apply-continuation
  (lambda (k v)
    (k v)))
```

Using this ADT, the definition of *subst* becomes

```
(define subst
  (lambda (new old s)
    (subst-cps new old s (make-final-valcont))))

(define subst-cps
  (lambda (new old slst k)
    (if (null? slst)
        (apply-continuation k '())
        (if (not (pair? (car slst)))
            (if (eq? (car slst) old)
                (subst-cps new old (cdr slst)
                  (make-subst1 new k))
                (subst-cps new old (cdr slst)
                  (make-subst2 slst k)))
            (subst-cps new old (car slst)
              (make-subst3 new old slst k))))))
```

To represent continuations as data structures rather than as procedures, the following record types are used.

```
(define-record final-valcont ())
(define-record subst1 (new k))
(define-record subst2 (slst k))
(define-record subst3 (new old slst k))
```

The fields of these records correspond exactly to the formal parameters of the *make-* procedures in the continuation ADT. The knowledge of what actions to perform for each type of continuation must now be contained in apply-continuation, which dispatches on the record type. How do we find the action performed for each record type? That action is exactly the action performed by the body of the lambda expression associated with the corresponding continuation (when continuations were represented as procedures).

```
(define apply-continuation
  (lambda (k v)
    (variant-case k
      (final-valcont () v)
      (subst1 (new k)
        (apply-continuation k (cons new v)))
      (subst2 (slst k)
        (apply-continuation k (cons (car slst) v)))
      (subst3 (new old slst)
        (subst-cps new old (cdr slst)
          (make-subst1 v k)))
      (else (error "Invalid continuation:" k)))))
```

In this case, the expression on the right-hand side of each variant-case clause is exactly the same as the body of the corresponding lambda expression. This is possible whenever the formal parameters of each procedural continuation are the same (in this case v). When this is not the case, α-conversion can be used to make the formal parameters of all the continuation procedures the same as the second argument of *apply-continuation*.

These examples complete the second step in our transformation: from continuation-passing style to first-order tail form. Therefore we can now take an arbitrary recursive procedure and convert it into such a form. We show in chapter 10 how we can transcribe the resulting program into virtually any programming language.

So far, we have used a very simple representation of continuations as record structures. In chapter 10 we also explore several other representations for continuations, and in chapter 12 we demonstrate how a suitable choice of representation leads to the development of a simple compiler.

- *Exercise 9.1.1*
  First write recursive definitions for the procedures listed below. Then transform these definitions to continuation-passing style. Next, transform them into a form using a continuation ADT in which continuations are represented as procedures. Finally, modify the ADT implementation so that continuations are represented as records.

  a. reverse

  b. append

  c. fact
  □

- *Exercise 9.1.2*
  Transform the CPS procedures developed in the solution of exercise 8.5.3 into a form that uses a record-based representation of continuations. □

9.2 The Continuation Interpreter

We have now learned how to take a recursive program and transform it into first-order tail form. This allows us to implement a recursive program in a language that does not support recursion. In this section we perform this transformation on an interpreter. The resulting interpreter defines the semantics of recursion in the defined language in a way that is independent of recursion in the defining language.

The interpreter that we shall transform is given in figure 9.2.1. This is the same as the interpreter of figure 5.4.1, except that the abstract syntax of expressions does not include let expressions, which can be handled by the parser, and we have expanded the definition of *eval-rands* so that it does not use *map*, thus avoiding the use of *map-cps*.

As with our previous examples, we first translate the interpreter into CPS form using procedural continuations. Since *eval-exp*, *eval-rands*, and *apply-proc* are mutually recursive procedures, they must be transformed into CPS simultaneously. The result is shown in figure 9.2.2. The transformation

Figure 9.2.1   Interpreter for transformation to CPS

```
(define eval-exp
  (lambda (exp env)
    (variant-case exp
      (lit (datum) datum)
      (varref (var) (apply-env env var))
      (app (rator rands)
        (let ((proc (eval-exp rator env))
              (args (eval-rands rands env)))
          (apply-proc proc args)))
      (if (test-exp then-exp else-exp)
        (if (true-value? (eval-exp test-exp env))
            (eval-exp then-exp env)
            (eval-exp else-exp env)))
      (proc (formals body) (make-closure formals body env))
      (else (error "Invalid abstract syntax:" exp)))))

(define eval-rands
  (lambda (rands env)
    (if (null? rands)
        '()
        (cons (eval-exp (car rands) env)
              (eval-rands (cdr rands) env)))))

(define apply-proc
  (lambda (proc args)
    (variant-case proc
      (prim-proc (prim-op) (apply-prim-op prim-op args))
      (closure (formals body env)
        (eval-exp body (extend-env formals args env)))
      (else (error "Invalid procedure:" proc)))))
```

treats `apply-env` and `apply-prim-op` as primitive operations, because they are guaranteed to return a value in a few steps; a more detailed transformation might regard these as nonprimitive as well. Of course when invoking the new `eval-exp`, it is necessary to pass a suitable continuation to receive the final value.

This code could have been obtained using the CPS transformation exactly as presented in chapter 8, except that we have chosen meaningful names for the continuation arguments and have not passed a continuation to the procedure *error*, since, for simplicity, we have chosen not to continue the computation after an error is reported. Passing the continuation to *error* procedure would allow the building of sophisticated exception handlers; see section 9.5 for some ideas on how this might be done.

Our CPS interpreter evaluates the operator of an application first, then evaluates the operands in left-to-right order. This contrasts with the interpreter of figure 9.2.1, in which the order of operator and operand evaluation in the defined language is determined by the order of evaluation in the defining language.

Because CPS makes control behavior explicit, a CPS interpreter will always specify the order of subexpression evaluation. The order in which the operator and operands of an application are evaluated is left unspecified in many languages (including Scheme), leaving implementors to chose an order that is most convenient or efficient. In such languages, programs that rely on a fixed order of evaluation are incorrect. If an interpreter is used to specify the semantics of such a language, the use of CPS in the interpreter will *overspecify* the order of operator and operand evaluation. If CPS is not used, however, the control semantics will usually be *underspecified*. For example, if the interpreter of figure 9.2.1 were evaluated by a defining language in which all procedures, including *cons*, were call-by-name, the defined language would also have call-by-name semantics, which might not have been intended.

• *Exercise 9.2.1*
If a Scheme implementation in which the subexpressions of an application are evaluated from right to left were used to execute the interpreter of figure 9.2.1, in what order will subexpressions of an application be evaluated in the defined language? ☐

• *Exercise 9.2.2*
Modify the CPS interpreter of figure 9.2.2 to evaluate the subexpressions of an application in right-to-left order. The order in which subexpressions are evaluated can be detected by using operations with side effects, as in `+(write(1), write(2))`. ☐

o *Exercise 9.2.3*
Modify the CPS interpreter of figure 9.2.2 to evaluate the operator of an application first, and then evaluate its operands in right-to-left order. ☐

o *Exercise 9.2.4*
Add `begin` to the interpreter of figure 9.2.2; see exercise 5.5.4. ☐

Figure 9.2.2   CPS interpreter

```
(define eval-exp
  (lambda (exp env k)
    (variant-case exp
      (lit (datum) (k datum))
      (varref (var) (k (apply-env env var)))
      (app (rator rands)
        (eval-exp rator env
          (lambda (proc)
            (eval-rands rands env
              (lambda (all)
                (apply-proc proc all k))))))
      (if (test-exp then-exp else-exp)
        (eval-exp test-exp env
          (lambda (test)
            (if (true-value? test)
                (eval-exp then-exp env k)
                (eval-exp else-exp env k)))))
      (proc (formals body) (k (make-closure formals body env)))
      (else (error "Invalid abstract syntax:" exp)))))

(define eval-rands
  (lambda (rands env k)
    (if (null? rands)
        (k '())
        (eval-exp (car rands) env
          (lambda (first)
            (eval-rands (cdr rands) env
              (lambda (rest)
                (k (cons first rest)))))))))

(define apply-proc
  (lambda (proc args k)
    (variant-case proc
      (prim-proc (prim-op) (k (apply-prim-op prim-op args)))
      (closure (formals body env)
        (eval-exp body (extend-env formals args env) k))
      (else (error "Invalid procedure:" proc)))))
```

Figure 9.2.3   A representation-independent CPS interpreter

```
(define eval-exp
  (lambda (exp env k)
    (variant-case exp
      (lit (datum)
        (apply-continuation k datum))
      (varref (var)
        (apply-continuation k (apply-env env var)))
      (app (rator rands)
        (eval-exp rator env
          (make-proc-valcont rands env k)))
      (if (test-exp then-exp else-exp)
        (eval-exp test-exp env
          (make-test-valcont then-exp else-exp env k)))
      (proc (formals body)
        (apply-continuation k
          (make-closure formals body env)))
      (else (error "Invalid abstract syntax:" exp)))))

(define eval-rands
  (lambda (rands env k)
    (if (null? rands)
        (apply-continuation k '())
        (eval-exp (car rands) env
          (make-first-valcont rands env k)))))

(define apply-proc
  (lambda (proc args k)
    (variant-case proc
      (prim-proc (prim-op)
        (apply-continuation k
          (apply-prim-op prim-op args)))
      (closure (formals body env)
        (eval-exp body (extend-env formals args env) k))
      (else (error "Invalid procedure:" proc)))))
```

The next step is to transform our interpreter into a form that is independent of the representation chosen for continuations. As before, we replace each invocation of a continuation with an invocation of the procedure `apply-continuation`, and we replace each lambda expression that constructs a continuation by a call to a procedure. These procedures are passed the information contained in the free variables of the corresponding lambda expressions. The result is shown in figure 9.2.3.

To complete the representation-independent CPS interpreter, we implement the continuation ADT. We name the constructors after the values their continuations are intended to receive. For example, `make-final-valcont` builds the continuation that will receive the final value of the computation, and `make-test-valcont` builds a continuation that will receive the value of the test in a conditional expression. Initially, we represent continuations as procedures, as in figure 9.2.4. The procedure `make-final-valcont` is invoked when `eval-exp` is first called. In the continuations created by `make-proc-valcont` and `make-first-valcont` other types of continuations are formed. This requires that we introduce two additional procedures, `make-all-argcont` and `make-rest-argcont`.

Finally, we convert the continuation ADT implementation to use a record-based data structure representation. See figure 9.2.5. As before, the right-hand sides of the `variant-case` clauses in `apply-continuation` are obtained directly from the bodies of the corresponding lambda expressions in figure 9.2.4, however, this time instead of using α-conversion and arbitrarily renaming the variable, we use a `let` expression to bind `val`.

Figure 9.2.3 and figure 9.2.5 define an interpreter in first-order tail form. This was our goal: an interpreter for recursive procedures that does not rely on recursion to explain its behavior. All the control information in the interpreter has been made explicit in the continuation records. All procedure calls in the interpreter are in tail position, so no other control information need be stored; this intuition will be made precise by a translation to imperative form in the following chapter. Furthermore, since the interpreter does not use the power of recursion or first-class procedures in the defining language, it can be translated into a variety of other languages. All that remains is to implement the parser and the data structures in the desired implementation language.

● *Exercise 9.2.5*

Add variable assignment, `let`, `letrecproc`, `begin`, and dynamic assignment to the interpreter of figure 9.2.1 and repeat the series of transformations to first-order tail form for this extended interpreter. ☐

Figure 9.2.4 Operations in procedural representation of continuations

```
(define make-final-valcont
  (lambda ()
    (lambda (final) final)))

(define make-proc-valcont
  (lambda (rands env k)
    (lambda (proc)
      (eval-rands rands env (make-all-argcont proc k)))))

(define make-all-argcont
  (lambda (proc k)
    (lambda (all)
      (apply-proc proc all k))))

(define make-test-valcont
  (lambda (then-exp else-exp env k)
    (lambda (test)
      (if (true-value? test)
          (eval-exp then-exp env k)
          (eval-exp else-exp env k)))))

(define make-first-valcont
  (lambda (rands k)
    (lambda (first)
      (eval-rands (cdr rands) env
        (make-rest-argcont first k)))))

(define make-rest-argcont
  (lambda (first k)
    (lambda (rest)
      (apply-continuation k (cons first rest)))))

(define apply-continuation
  (lambda (k val)
    (k val)))
```

Figure 9.2.5   Data structure representation of continuations

```
(define-record final-valcont ())
(define-record proc-valcont (rands env k))
(define-record all-argcont (proc k))
(define-record test-valcont (then-exp else-exp env k))
(define-record first-valcont (rands env k))
(define-record rest-argcont (first k))

(define apply-continuation
  (lambda (k val)
    (variant-case k
      (final-valcont ()
        (let ((final val))
          final))
      (proc-valcont (rands env k)
        (let ((proc val))
          (eval-rands rands env
            (make-all-argcont proc k))))
      (all-argcont (proc k)
        (let ((all val))
          (apply-proc proc all k)))
      (test-valcont (then-exp else-exp env k)
        (let ((test val))
          (if (true-value? test)
              (eval-exp then-exp env k)
              (eval-exp else-exp env k))))
      (first-valcont (rands env k)
        (let ((first val))
          (eval-rands (cdr rands) env
            (make-rest-argcont first k))))
      (rest-argcont (first k)
        (let ((rest val))
          (apply-continuation k (cons first rest)))))))
```

We have implemented a recursive language using an interpreter that exhibits iterative control behavior. We have done this by applying the CPS transformation to the interpreter itself. Another strategy is to apply the CPS transformation to the source program and then use the original interpreter. Do this for the interpreter of figure 9.2.1. The process involves two steps. First, write a CPS transformation program that takes as input programs in the language of the interpreter in figure 9.2.1 and produces abstract syntax trees of programs in the same language but in continuation-passing style. Next, confirm that the interpreter of figure 9.2.1 actually has iterative control behavior when it is given a tail-form program to interpret. □

9.3 Making Continuations Available to the Programmer

We have seen that "standard" control operations, such as procedure call and the sequencing of argument evaluation, can be made explicit in an interpreter through the use of continuations. In this section we shall first see how continuations can express nonstandard control operations in an interpreter. Then we shall see how continuations can be made available to the programmer as objects of computation, thereby allowing the programmer to obtain a variety of nonstandard control behaviors.

Every continuation of our CPS interpreter, except for the one that receives a final value, concludes its business by invoking the immediately prior continuation—the one that was current at its creation. This is characteristic of standard control operations but need not always be the case. Consider, for example, adding an "abort" procedure to our defined language. When invoked, the procedure `abort` should terminate the computation immediately, returning the value of its argument as the value of the entire computation. Thus the value of

```
+(1, *(abort(2), +(3, 5)))
```

should be 2.

The procedure `abort` can be implemented as a new kind of procedure object, represented by the record type `abort`, that is interpreted by extending `apply-proc`.

```
(define final-valcont (make-final-valcont))

(define apply-proc
  (lambda (proc args k)
    (variant-case proc
      (prim-proc (prim-op)
        (apply-continuation k (apply-prim-op prim-op args)))
      (closure (formals body env)
        (eval-exp body (extend-env formals args env) k))
      (abort () (apply-continuation final-valcont (car args)))
      (else (error "Invalid procedure:" proc)))))
```

When applied to the list `args` of arguments, `abort` returns the first argument to the final value continuation. The continuation `k`, to which the result would normally be passed, is ignored. In this way the first argument is effectively returned as the value of the entire computation.

- *Exercise 9.3.1*
  Modify the CPS interpreter of figure 9.2.2 so that `apply-prim-op` is passed the current continuation, `k`. Then implement `abort` as a primitive operation, rather than as a new type of procedure. □

- *Exercise 9.3.2*
  Modify the CPS interpreter of figure 9.2.2 so that `apply-env` is written in CPS. Then modify `apply-env` so that when reference is made to an unbound variable, the procedure `error` is not invoked. Instead, a message is printed (using `display` and `newline`) and then the final value continuation is invoked with the symbol *error*. □

- *Exercise 9.3.3*
  The capability to abort a computation can be added to a language with the concrete and abstract syntax

  ---

  ⟨exp⟩ ::= abort ⟨exp⟩   abort (exp)

  ---

  instead of as a procedure. Modify the CPS interpreter of figure 9.2.2 so that it handles this form by evaluating the argument to abort in the context of the final value continuation. □

So far we have seen that values can be returned by passing them to the current continuation or to a continuation that receives a final value. We can allow control to be passed to an arbitrary continuation by creating a new kind of procedure. We represent one of these procedures with a record of type continuation that contains a continuation, *cont*. When this procedure is invoked with one argument, the argument is simply passed to *cont*, ignoring the continuation that is current at the time.

```
(define-record continuation (cont))

(define apply-proc
  (lambda (proc args k)
    (variant-case proc
      (prim-proc (prim-op)
        (apply-continuation k (apply-prim-op prim-op args)))
      (closure (formals body env)
        (eval-exp body (extend-env formals args env) k))
      (abort ()
        (apply-continuation final-valcont (car args)))
      (continuation (cont)
        (apply-continuation cont (car args)))
      (else (error "Invalid procedure:" proc)))))
```

How might continuation procedures be created, and how might they be used? Suppose we have added some list-processing primitives to our defined language. We wish to write the procedure *listindex*, which takes a symbol and a list, and returns the zero-based index of the symbol in the list, or −1, denoted by the variable minus1 in the initial environment, if the symbol does not occur in the list. We might try to implement *listindex* as follows:

```
define listindex =
  proc (a, alst)
    letrecproc
      loop(alst) =
        if null(alst)
        then minus1
        else if equal(a, car(alst))
             then 0
             else add1(loop(cdr(alst)))
      in loop(alst)
```

Unfortunately, this does not work. Let us assume that k is the length of the list. If a is not in alst, then the value returned is $k - 1$, not -1, because the -1 is sent to a continuation that invokes *add1* k times. What we want is to return -1 immediately to the caller of *listindex*. If it were possible to obtain the continuation of the call to *listindex* as a procedural object and bind it to some variable, say f, then -1 could be returned by evaluating f(minus1). We can express this by introducing a new expression type, letcont.

```
define listindex =
  proc (a, alst)
    letcont f
    in letrecproc
         loop(alst) =
           if null(alst)
           then f(minus1)
           else if equal(a, car(alst))
                   then 0
                   else add1(loop(cdr(alst)))
       in loop(alst)
```

When f is invoked with -1, the current continuation is ignored and -1 is returned to the continuation that was current at the time the letcont expression was entered, which is the continuation of the call to *listindex*. The procedure f is like abort in that it never returns to its caller but rather transfers control to another point in the program.

We use the following concrete and abstract syntax of letcont:

⟨exp⟩ ::= letcont ⟨var⟩ in ⟨exp⟩   letcont (var body)

Given this abstract syntax we define the record type that contains the symbol and the expression, and then modify eval-exp.

```
(define-record letcont (var body))

(define eval-exp
  (lambda (exp env k)
    (variant-case exp
      (letcont (var body)
        (eval-exp body
          (extend-env (list var) (list (make-continuation k)) env)
          k))
      ...)))
```

Thus body will be evaluated in an environment in which the given variable is bound to a continuation procedure. This makes continuations denoted values.

- *Exercise 9.3.4*
Another approach to implementing listindex is to write it in continuation-passing style. Compare this to the solution using letcont. □

This is not the only way to make continuations available to the programmer. In Scheme, continuation procedures are obtained via the procedure *call-with-current-continuation*, which we abbreviate as *call/cc*. The single argument to *call/cc* must be a procedure of one argument. This procedure is called with the current continuation (the continuation of the call to *call/cc*), represented as a one-argument continuation procedure, k. Informally, k represents the remainder of the computation from the *call/cc* application point. At any time, k can be invoked with any value, with the effect that this value is taken as the value of the *call/cc* application.

If our defined language had a similar procedure *callcc*, we could replace expressions of the form letcont *var* in *body* by callcc(proc (*var*) *body*). (We use the variable callcc rather than call/cc because of the lexical structure of our language; see chapter 11.) Our *listindex* example would then be

```
define listindex =
  proc (a, alst)
    callcc(proc (f)
            letrecproc
              loop(alst) =
                if null(alst)
                then f(minus1)
                else if equal(a, car(alst))
                        then 0
                        else add1(loop(cdr(alst)))
            in loop(alst))
```

This approach has two advantages. First, it separates the creation and use of continuation procedures from variable binding. Second, it does not require adding new syntax, such as letcont, to the language. All that is required is to add callcc to the initial environment and bind to it a new type of procedure that must be recognized by *apply-proc*.

```
(define-record callcc-proc ())

(define apply-proc
  (lambda (proc args k)
    (variant-case proc
      (prim-proc (prim-op)
        (apply-continuation k (apply-prim-op prim-op args)))
      (closure (formals body env)
        (eval-exp body (extend-env formals args env) k))
      (continuation (cont)
        (apply-continuation cont (car args)))
      (callcc-proc ()
        (apply-proc
          (car args)
          (list (make-continuation k))
          k))
      (else (error "Invalid Procedure:" proc)))))
```

The new line in *apply-proc* does just what the description of *call/cc* said:
the first (and only) argument to *callcc* is applied as a procedure to the current continuation. More precisely, it is applied to a continuation procedure containing the current continuation. Furthermore (and this was not specified in the description!), this is done using the current continuation as the continuation of the call that passes the current continuation. Thus

$$\text{callcc(proc (k) } body)$$

is equivalent to

$$\text{callcc(proc (k) } k(body))$$

Though *callcc* is a procedure, it is unlike all other procedures. Many primitive operations can be added to or deleted from a language with little effect on the language's expressive power or on the techniques that can be used to implement it. But *callcc* provides an expressive power that is difficult or impossible to achieve without an equivalent facility, and its presence has a profound impact on the way in which control information must be maintained by an implementation.

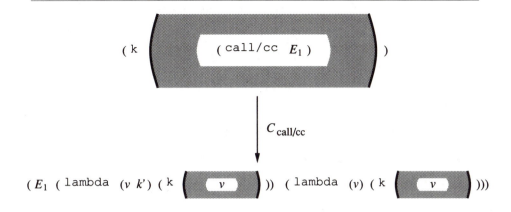

Figure 9.3.1 The CPS rule for `call/cc` expression in a context: $C_{\text{call/cc}}$

- *Exercise 9.3.5*

  Using `letcont`, define `callcc` as a procedure in the defined language. □

○ *Exercise 9.3.6*

  Add `callcc` to the defined language with syntax

$\langle exp \rangle ::= $ `callcc` $\langle exp \rangle$ `callcc (exp)`

---

  instead of as a procedure. □

○ *Exercise 9.3.7*

  The interpreter we have sketched in this section actually treats continuations as expressed values. Modify it to enforce the restriction that continuations be denoted but not expressed. □

○ *Exercise 9.3.8*

  Add *call/cc* to a CPS interpreter in which procedures and continuations are represented as procedures, as in exercise 5.4.3. □

○ *Exercise 9.3.9*

  If expressions in the defining language are transformed to CPS before being interpreted or compiled and `call/cc` is treated as a special form, rather than as a procedure, it can be implemented with the addition (see figure 9.3.1) of the following CPS transformation rule.

$C_{\text{call/cc}}$: If (k E) has an initial expression I of the form (call/cc E_1), then replace (k E) by

$$(E_1 \text{ (lambda } (v \; k') \text{ (k } E\{v/I\})) \text{ (lambda } (v) \text{ (k } E\{v/I\})))$$

where v and k' do not occur free in E_1.

This rule makes call/cc disappear. The two procedures constructed by this rule have identical bodies. The first procedure is the continuation procedure passed to E_1 (which never refers to k'), and the second procedure is the continuation required by the CPS transformation. Add this case to the interpreter of exercise 9.2.6. □

9.4 Upward Continuations and Coroutines

In the last section we introduced continuations as denoted values and saw that they could be used to exit prematurely from a computation. Since they are denoted, continuations can be passed "down" as arguments to procedures or otherwise bound to lexical variables. Such continuations are sometimes called *escape procedures,* since they are used to escape from computations.

If continuations are allowed as expressed values, they become first-class values, and can also be returned "upward" from procedures, assigned to variables, and stored in data structures. These operations allow continuations to be invoked after control has left the dynamic context in which the continuation was created. Some languages provide escape procedures, or equivalent control mechanisms, but do not provide first-class continuations.

In this section we illustrate the use of upward continuations. In the remaining two sections, we consider the problem of maintaining the proper notion of dynamic context in the presence of continuations.

Perhaps the simplest use of upward continuations is to provide a breakpoint facility. When a breakpoint is reached, control is transferred to a designated point in a program or programming system, usually for programmer interaction, with the possibility of continuing the computation as if the breakpoint had not occurred. To allow a breakpoint to return control to the read-eval-print loop of the computation, we first obtain the top-level read-eval-print loop continuation and save it in a global variable.

```
--> define toplevel = ignored;
--> letcont cont
    in toplevel := cont;
```

Continuation-Passing Interpreters

We next define a procedure `break` that captures the continuation of its call, stores it in the variable `resume`, and then invokes the top-level continuation. Initially `resume` is bound to a procedure that raises an error, since no computation can be resumed unless a break has occurred. This break procedure passes on its argument, which can be used to identify the breakpoint, to the top-level continuation.

```
--> define resume = proc (x) error();
--> define break =
      proc (x)
        letcont cont
        in begin
            resume := cont;
            write(breakmsg);
            toplevel(x)
          end;
```

(Here we assume that we have a primitive *write*, and that *breakmsg* is some suitable string) To return from a breakpoint, the *resume* continuation is invoked. Whatever value is passed to the resume continuation is the value with which the most recent application of a break procedure will continue.

```
--> +(break(1), break(2));
break:
1
--> resume(5);
break:
2
--> resume(3);
8
```

○ *Exercise 9.4.1*
Consider the following transcript:

```
--> +(10000, break(2));
break:
2
--> *(100, break(4));
break:
4
--> resume(10);
1000
```

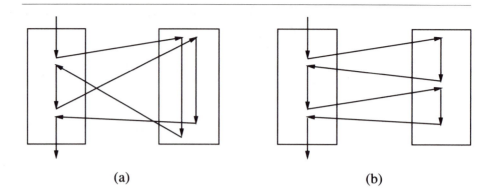

Figure 9.4.1   Procedures and coroutines

```
--> resume(20);
2000
```

What happened to the waiting addition? Redefine **break** using a stack of **resume** continuations so that we don't lose the addition operation. ☐

First-class continuations can also be used to implement a *coroutine* mechanism. Coroutines contain code, like procedures, but their control behavior is different. The control relationship between a procedure and its caller is asymmetric: a procedure can call another from any expression in its body, with the result that control transfers to the beginning of the called procedure's body. Control always leaves a procedure when it reaches the end of the body (assuming that no first-class continuation is invoked) and returns to the point at which the procedure was called. See figure 9.4.1 (a).

The control relationship between coroutines is symmetric. When control first enters a coroutine, it starts at the beginning of its body. Control can leave a coroutine at any point and when it returns, the computation continues from the point where it last left the coroutine. This behavior is illustrated in figure 9.4.1 (b). Coroutines are said to *resume*, rather than call, each other. Although in some systems it is meaningful for coroutines to return, a coroutine does not normally "fall off the end" of its body.

Whereas the interpreter must maintain control information for procedure calls, no record need be kept of coroutine resumptions. The essence of any coroutine mechanism is that each coroutine maintains its own *local control state:* the point from which it will continue its computation when it is next resumed. Thus a coroutine is like an object: it encapsulates some local state, except that its local state is a control state rather than a data stack. Indeed, we shall implement coroutines as procedures with local state, like the simple objects in section 4.6, except that the local state will contain a continuation.

We invoke our coroutines using a global procedure *resume*, which takes a procedure representing a coroutine and a value to be passed to the coroutine. The procedure *makecoroutine* takes a procedure of one argument and returns a coroutine that invokes the procedure with an argument, which is the first value passed to the new coroutine. When *resume* is called inside a coroutine, the coroutine suspends its activities. When the coroutine is resumed, the value passed to it appears as the value of the call to *resume* that suspended the coroutine. It is an error if a coroutine procedure ever returns, but it can exit by invoking another continuation.

Let us consider the simple example shown in figure 9.4.2. Here we create two coroutines, *co1* and *co2*, and start *co1* with the value 33 as initval1. The first coroutine prints 1 33 and then resumes *co2* with the value 34, which becomes *initval2*. The second coroutine prints 2 34 and then restarts *co1* with 35, which appears as the value of the *resume* in *co1*. Then *initval1* is assigned 35, and *co1* prints 1 35. It then resumes *co2* with 36, so *co2* prints 2 36 and resumes *co1* with 37. Finally, *co1* exits by escaping to *returncont* with 37. So the entire program prints 1 33 2 34 1 35 2 36 37. Note that the two coroutines refer to each other through a shared binding, as in the implementation of recursion through side effects in section 5.6. We cannot use letrecproc because the right-hand side of a letrecproc declaration must be a procedure expression and not an application.

A classic illustration of coroutine behavior is provided by the *samefringe* problem. The "fringe" of a tree can be represented by a list containing the tree's leaf node values in the order in which they are encountered by a depth-first traversal of the tree. (The *flatten* procedure of exercise 2.2.7 returns the fringe of a tree that is represented as a nested list structure.) Two trees may have very different shapes but still have the same fringe. The easy way to determine if two trees have the same fringe is to construct the fringe of each one as a list and then test the lists for equality. This solution requires that storage be allocated to construct the fringe lists. The samefringe problem is to determine if two tree have the same fringe *without* constructing fringe lists.

The solution is to create two coroutines, one for traversing each tree. Each time one of these traversal coroutines is resumed, it finds the next leaf, if there is one. It then resumes a third coroutine that drives the computation, passing it the leaf value, or zero (representing false) if there are no more leaves. See figure 9.4.3 for the definition of the *makesfcoroutine* procedure, which

Figure 9.4.2   Two interacting coroutines

```
define example =
  proc ()
    letcont returncont
    in let co1 = ignored;
           co2 = ignored
       in begin
            co1 := makecoroutine(proc (initval1)
                                   begin
                                     write(1);
                                     write(initval1);
                                     initval1 := resume(co2, add1(initval1));
                                     write(1);
                                     write(initval1);
                                     initval1 := resume(co2, add1(initval1));
                                     returncont(initval1)
                                   end);
            co2 := makecoroutine(proc (initval2)
                                   begin
                                     write(2);
                                     write(initval2);
                                     initval2 := resume(co1, add1(initval2));
                                     write(2);
                                     write(initval2);
                                     resume(co1, add1(initval2))
                                   end);
            co1(33)
          end
```

returns a traversal coroutine for a given tree and driver.

The procedure *samefringe* of figure 9.4.3 introduces let bindings for the three coroutines and then installs the coroutines using assignment. After the coroutines have been installed so they can refer to each other, the driver is invoked with an initial value that is ignored. The driver resumes each of the traversal coroutines and checks that they have passed back the same value. This is repeated until both traversal coroutines indicate simultaneously that they have no more leaves, at which point the driver exits by sending a 1 to the escape continuation *returncont*, indicating that the fringes are the same. If one of the traversal coroutines runs out of leaves before the

Figure 9.4.3   Samefringe coroutine program

```
define makesfcoroutine =
  proc (driver, tree)
    makecoroutine(proc (initvalue)
                    letrecproc
                      traverse(tree) =
                        if pair(tree)
                        then begin
                               traverse(car(tree));
                               if pair(cdr(tree))
                               then traverse(cdr(tree))
                               else noop
                             end
                        else resume(driver, tree)
                    in begin
                         traverse(tree);
                         resume(driver, 0)
                       end);

define samefringe =
  proc (tree1, tree2)
    letcont returncont
    in let co1 = ignored;
           co2 = ignored;
           driver = ignored
       in begin
            driver :=
              makecoroutine(proc (initvalue)
                              letrecproc
                                loop() =
                                  let leaf1 = resume(co1, ignored);
                                      leaf2 = resume(co2, ignored)
                                  in if equal(leaf1, leaf2)
                                     then if zero(leaf1)
                                          then returncont(1)
                                          else loop()
                                     else returncont(0)
                              in loop());
            co1 := makesfcoroutine(driver, tree1);
            co2 := makesfcoroutine(driver, tree2);
            driver(ignored)
          end
```

other, or they do not find the same leaves, the driver exits by sending a 0 to *returncont*, indicating that the fringes differ. No extra storage is used, and the program returns as soon as it finds that fringes are different. Unlike our first example, where data was passed back and forth between the coroutines, the only place where data flows from one coroutine to another is from *co1* and *co2* to *driver*, so this example does not use the full power of bidirectional data transmission in *resume*.

Now we can show the implementation of coroutines; see figure 9.4.4. The key to this bit of code is the procedure *localresume*. Assume that *localresume* is called from within the coroutine with a continuation argument *cont* and a value *value*. The procedure *localresume* gets a continuation *localcont* and stores it in *lcs*. This saves the control state of the coroutine at the time *localresume* was called. It then jumps to the continuation argument *cont* (passing it *value*) and continues from there.

What happens when the continuation stored in `lcs` is invoked? This is the continuation waiting for the result of the `letcont` expression, so when it is invoked, the value that it is passed is bound to the variable `value` in the `let`, the expression `resume := localresume` is evaluated, and the value is returned. So when this continuation is invoked it is (except for the assignment statement) as if the call to *localresume* had just returned with this new value. This is just the behavior we expect from a *resume* procedure.

Now we have two more mysteries to solve. How do we call *localresume* from the body of the coroutine even though it is not lexically visible there? And how do we get the coroutine initialized?

To answer the first question, assume that a coroutine will always be resumed by invoking its `lcs` continuation. The first thing the `lcs` continuation does is to copy the *localresume* of its coroutine into the global variable *resume*. So when *body* calls *resume*, it will always get the right version, which refers to this coroutine.

How is the coroutine initialized? When the procedure *makecoroutine* is called, a binding for the local control state `lcs` of the new coroutine is created, along with the procedures that will represent the new coroutine and the new coroutine's local resume procedure. The `letcont exit` expression is then evaluated. What does the call `localresume(exit, newcoroutine)` do? It doesn't return immediately. It stores its continuation (extended by the `resume := localresume` statement) in `lcs` and applies *exit* to *newcoroutine*. If this continuation is ever applied to a value, the assignment statement will be executed, and the value will be passed to *body*. Therefore the first time this continuation is invoked, the coroutine body will be started, with *resume* set to the right value. This is enough to get the coroutine started.

Figure 9.4.4 Coroutines via first-class continuations

```
define makecoroutine =
  proc (body)
    let lcs = ignored
    in letrecproc
        newcoroutine(value) = lcs(value);
        localresume(cont, value) =
          let value = letcont localcont
                      in begin
                             lcs := localcont;
                             cont(value)
                         end
          in begin
               resume := localresume;
               value
             end
      in letcont exit
         in begin
              body(localresume(exit, newcoroutine));
              error()
            end
```

But `localresume(exit, newcoroutine)` invokes *exit* on *newcoroutine*. Since *exit* is an escape continuation, this means that the value of the call to *makecoroutine* is the procedure *newcoroutine*. So executing

$$co1 := makecoroutine(body)$$

assigns *newcoroutine* to *co1*. What does *newcoroutine* do? When *newcoroutine* is called, it dereferences *lcs* to find the saved control state of the coroutine and invokes it, resetting *resume* and continuing from the last point at which the coroutine called *resume*. So if any other coroutine calls `resume(co1, value)`, that coroutine's state will be saved and this coroutine's control state will be restarted. Thus the value in *co1*, a procedure that is closed over the coroutine's control state, represents the coroutine.

○ *Exercise 9.4.2*
In our implementation of coroutines, what happens if *body* ever returns? ☐

○ *Exercise 9.4.3*
Draw a diagram that explains the behavior of *makecoroutine*. ☐

- *Exercise 9.4.4*

A common programming need is to copy characters between buffers of different lengths. There are two operations called get and put that use the buffer. Initially, get attempts to take items from the buffer, but if none are available, it resumes put. The put operation processes until it can install a value in the buffer at which time it resumes the get operation. This is a cumbersome program using traditional techniques, but it has a natural solution using coroutines. This problem can be simulated in our defined language as the problem of converting a list of lists of length n to a list of lists of length m, such that the result of flattening the two lists is the same. Write a procedure using coroutines to solve this problem. □

- *Exercise 9.4.5*

Translate the procedure makecoroutine into Scheme. □

- *Exercise 9.4.6*

Add a coroutine facility to the defined language by adding a new special form coroutine to the CPS interpreter of section 9.2, with grammar given by

---

$\langle exp \rangle ::=$ coroutine $\langle exp \rangle$	coroutine (exp)

This should behave like *makecoroutine*. □

9.5 Leaving and Entering Control Contexts

Previously, we understood the concept of the dynamic extent: it was the period from the time a procedure was called until it exited. But in the presence of first-class continuations, this concept is no longer so clear. What happens if the procedure invokes a continuation instead of returning normally? What happens if a continuation jumps back into the middle of the procedure? This is not merely an academic question. Certain operations must sometimes be performed whenever control enters or leaves a dynamic context. We must assure that these operations are performed whether control enters or leaves normally, or "flies" in or out via invocation of a continuation. For example, a file might need to be closed on exit from a procedure, whether the exit is normal or via an escape procedure or exception.

The simplest example is the dynamic assignment, which has the form *var := exp* during *body*. In the context of the assignment—the evaluation of *body*—the value of *var* is to be the value of *exp* (unless reassigned). When control leaves the context, the value of *var* must be restored to the value it had on entry to the context. The implementation of dynamic assignment that was presented in section 5.7.2 (or exercise 9.2.5) is incorrect in the presence of first-class continuations, because the original value of *var* is restored only if control leaves the procedure via its original continuation. If control leaves the procedure via some other continuation, then the original value will not be restored.

A simpler but related problem arises in many programming languages, whether they support first-class continuations or not. When an exception occurs, such as a divide by zero or a problem with file I/O, some exception handling mechanism is usually invoked. In most cases, exception handlers are effectively escape procedures. Many errors in large computer systems are the result of failure to recover properly from exceptions, because it is difficult to write a program in such a way that sufficient information about the state of the computation is available to the exception handler. A common example is failure to close a file when an exception forces the computation to exit prematurely from the dynamic context in which the file is used.

These problems can all be solved with a mechanism that explicitly manages dynamic contexts. This mechanism is called *dynamic wind* because it winds and unwinds a computation when control enters and leaves a dynamic context. (The term *unwind protect* is used instead in systems that support only downward escape procedures.) We use the following syntax.

⟨exp⟩ ::= `wind` ⟨exp⟩ `within` ⟨exp⟩ `unwind` ⟨exp⟩   `wind (pre body post)`

A `wind` expression consists of a body surrounded by prelude and postlude expressions, which are to be evaluated before and after `body`, respectively. This causes the dynamic context within which the body is evaluated to ensure that the prelude (respectively, postlude) expression is evaluated whenever control enters (respectively, leaves) it. It is assumed that the prelude and postlude are executed for effect only; their values are ignored, and the value of the `wind` expression is the value of the body.

Our coroutine implementation suffers from the same problem; if control leaves a coroutine via a continuation and then re-enters it, there is no guarantee that the `resume` variable will be reset to the proper value. We want to guarantee that *resume* is set to *localresume* on each entry into the dynamic context of the coroutine's body. This can be accomplished by wrapping the body of the coroutine in a `wind` expression whose prelude expression assigns the coroutine's local resume procedure to the global `resume` variable every time

Figure 9.5.1   Coroutines using `wind`

```
define makecoroutine =
  proc (body)
    let lcs = ignored
    in let newcoroutine = proc (value) lcs(value);
           localresume = proc (cont, value)
                               letcont localcont
                               in begin
                                       lcs := localcont;
                                       cont(value)
                                   end
       in letcont exit
          in wind resume := localresume
             within begin
                         body(resume(exit, newcoroutine));
                         error()
                     end
             unwind noop
```

control enters the dynamic context within which the coroutine body executes; see figure 9.5.1. In this example the postlude does not need to do anything, provided only coroutines use the global `resume` variable.

In other cases there may be a need for a postlude expression but no prelude. For example, it may be required that a file be closed when control leaves a dynamic context, even in the event of an exception that causes control to leave the context prematurely. Dynamic assignment is a simple example requiring both a prelude and a postlude.

• *Exercise 9.5.1*

Using `wind`, but not dynamic assignment, write an expression in our defined language that achieves the effect of an expression of the form $x := exp$ during *body*. ▯

We now extend our previous CPS interpreter (extended with assignment as in exercise 9.2.5) to support dynamic wind and first-class continuations. Dynamic wind is implemented by building a graph representing the active dynamic contexts. A node is created each time a `wind` expression is executed. Each node contains the prelude and postlude expressions of the associated `wind` expression, plus *creator* and *context* links that refer to other nodes. Since the

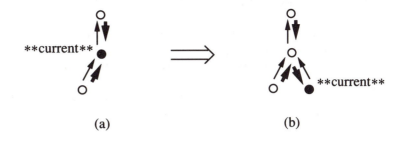

(a)   (b)

Figure 9.5.2   Adding a node to the context graph

context-link is modified during the course of a computation, it is stored in a cell.

```
(define-record context-node (prelude postlude creator context-cell))
```

When a context node is created, its creator field points to the node representing the existing dynamic context. When the computation exits from the new context, the node becomes inaccessible and can be reclaimed. In the absence of first-class continuations, this gives us a stack of contexts. If we have first-class continuations, however, a computation might exit from a context but save a continuation that allows the context to be re-entered, as in the breakpoint example of section 9.4. That is, we might exit from a context and yet have it still accessible. If we then enter a new context, this creates a tree of contexts.

At any given time, a single node represents the current dynamic context. The global variable **current** is always bound to this node. In order to help the interpreter navigate through the tree, the context link of every node points along the unique path from that node to the current node. The context link of **current** is always the empty list. See figure 9.5.2. There the thin arrows represent the creator links and the thick arrows the context-links. Initially the context graph consists of a single node with prelude and postlude fields that are ignored, a context cell that contains the empty list, and a creator link that is anything *but* the empty list. See figure 9.5.3.

A new context node is created each time a wind expression is evaluated. The wind clause of *eval-exp* creates prelude, postlude, and body thunks and passes them to the auxiliary procedure *create-context*, which adds a new context node to the graph, sets the context cell of the current node to point to the new node, and makes the new node the current node. Fig-

Figure 9.5.3   Context graph manipulation procedures

```
(define make-initial-context-graph
  (lambda ()
    (make-context-node '* '* #t (make-cell '()))))

(define **current** (make-initial-context-graph))
```

ure 9.5.2 (a) and (b) shows the context graph before and after the addition of the new node. It then executes the prelude and body thunks. The postlude thunk will be executed when control leaves the body.

The prelude, body, and postlude of a context node are represented as thunks. Since we are using a CPS interpreter, these procedures take one argument—a continuation. See figure 9.5.5 for an implementation of a thunk ADT that represents thunks as procedures. The *make-thunk* procedure creates a new thunk given an expression and an environment, and the procedure *apply-thunk* executes the thunk by supplying it with a continuation. The procedure *wrap-thunk* will be discussed below.

The central operation on a context graph is changing **current** when a continuation is invoked. First-class continuations created by letcont retain the node that represents the dynamic context at the time the continuation was created. See the letcont line of *eval-exp* in figure 9.5.4. When the continuation is invoked, this saved dynamic context must be restored. This job is performed by the procedure *throw* (figure 9.5.7).

When a previously saved node is to be restored as the current context, all the links in the context-link chain from the saved node to the current node must be reversed, since all the context-links must point toward the current node. Furthermore, these are the only links that need to be reversed. For example, Figure 9.5.6 (a) shows a context graph. Figure 9.5.6 (b) shows the same graph, but with the **current** moved to another node. The only difference between (a) and (b) is that the direction of the context-link on the path between the two nodes has been reversed to maintain the property that every context-link points in the direction of **current**.

The *throw* procedure first calls *reverse-context-links!*, which performs this link reversal and returns the last node in the chain. If this node is not the current node, an error is signalled; we shall see later how this might occur. After the links have been reversed, the current node is the head of a context-link chain that ends with the saved node.

Figure 9.5.4   CPS interpreter with context graph

```
(define eval-exp
  (lambda (exp env k)
    (variant-case exp
      (wind (pre body post)
        (create-context
          (wrap-thunk (make-thunk pre env))
          (make-thunk body env)
          (wrap-thunk (make-thunk post env))
          k))
      (letcont (var body)
        (eval-exp body
          (extend-env
            (list var)
            (list (make-cell
                    (make-continuation k **current**)))
            env)
          k))
      ...)))

(define create-context
  (lambda (prelude body postlude k)
    (let ((saved-context **current**))
      (set! **current**
        (make-context-node prelude postlude saved-context (make-cell'())))
      (cell-set! (context-node->context-cell saved-context) **current**)
      (apply-thunk prelude
        (lambda (ignored)
          (apply-thunk body
            (lambda (val) (throw k val saved-context)))))))))

(define apply-proc
  (lambda (proc args k)
    (variant-case proc
      (prim-proc (prim-op) ...)
      (closure (formals body env) ...)
      (continuation (cont saved-context-node)
        (throw cont (car args) saved-context-node)))))

(define-record continuation (cont saved-context-node))
```

Figure 9.5.5   A CPS thunk ADT

```
(define make-thunk
  (lambda (exp env)
    (lambda (k)
      (eval-exp exp env k))))

(define apply-thunk
  (lambda (thunk k)
    (thunk k)))

(define wrap-thunk
  (lambda (thunk)
    (lambda (k)
      (let ((saved-context **current**))
        (set! **current** (make-initial-context-graph))
        (apply-thunk thunk
          (lambda (ignored)
            (set! **current** saved-context)
            (k '*)))))))
```

The next step is to walk along this chain, unwinding and then winding its contexts. This walk has two stages, the *postlude walk* and the *prelude walk*. The postlude walk visits nodes associated with dynamic contexts being exited. The postlude thunks of these nodes are invoked as they are visited. This part of the walk travels "upward" in the creator tree. Then the prelude walk visits nodes associated with dynamic contexts being entered. The prelude thunks of these nodes are invoked as they are visited. This part of the walk travels "downward" toward the saved node (soon to be restored as the current node) in the creator tree. The postlude walk occurs before the prelude walk because we must leave all the contexts that we are in before re-entering the contexts associated with the continuation.

How do we know where the postlude walk ends and the prelude walk begins? We can get an answer by examining figure 9.5.6. So long as the creator- and context-links are the same, we are traveling upward, on the postlude walk. The first node on the walk for which the creator- and context-links differ will be the node at the "top" of the walk. Since control is neither leaving nor entering this context, it is passed by without invoking a postlude or prelude. The remaining nodes of the chain are those of the prelude walk. See the

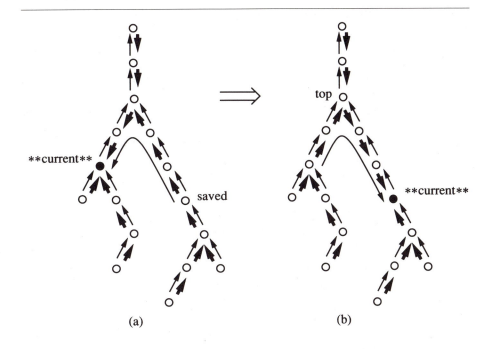

Figure 9.5.6   Changing the current node in the context graph

procedures *postlude-walk* and *prelude-walk* of figure 9.5.7. The continuation of the prelude walk is to assign the new root to the global **current** variable and, finally, invoke the continuation to which control is actually being thrown.

Either the postlude walk or the prelude walk may be trivial (involve no nodes). Commonly continuations are created and invoked within the same dynamic context, with no *wind* operations performed while evaluating this body. In this case both the postlude walk and prelude walk will be trivial.

To maintain the integrity of the context graph, we do not allow control to enter or leave a prelude or postlude via invocation of a first-class continuation. This constraint is enforced by "wrapping" prelude and postlude thunks in their own context graphs. The procedure *wrap-thunk* saves **current**, creates an entirely new context graph for the evaluation of the thunk, and then restores the old one when the thunk returns. An attempt to invoke a continuation that does not belong to the current context graph can now be detected by *throw*, because the context-link chain terminates in the "current" node of the wrong graph, and an error is signalled.

Figure 9.5.7   Procedures for switching the current context

```
(define throw
  (lambda (k value saved-context)
    (if (not (eq? (reverse-context-links! saved-context) **current**))
        (error "Context violation")
        (postlude-walk **current**
          (lambda (top-node)
            (prelude-walk (cell-ref (context-node->context-cell top-node))
              (lambda (ignored)
                (set! **current** saved-context)
                (apply-continuation k value)))))))))

(define reverse-context-links!
  (letrec
    ((loop
      (lambda (node last)
        (let ((cell (context-node->context-cell node)))
          (let ((next (cell-ref cell)))
            (cell-set! cell last)
            (if (null? next) node (loop next node)))))))
    (lambda (node)
      (if (null? node) node (loop node '())))))

(define postlude-walk
  (lambda (node k)
    (if (top-node? node)
        (k node)
        (apply-thunk (context-node->postlude node)
          (lambda (ignored)
            (postlude-walk (cell-ref (context-node->context-cell node)) k))))))

(define prelude-walk
  (lambda (node k)
    (if (null? node)
        (k '*)
        (let ((next (cell-ref (context-node->context-cell node))))
          (apply-thunk (context-node->prelude node)
            (lambda (ignored) (prelude-walk next k)))))))

(define top-node?
  (lambda (node)
    (not (eq? (cell-ref (context-node->context-cell node))
              (context-node->creator node)))))
```

- *Exercise 9.5.2*

Write a Scheme procedure `dynamic-wind` that takes prelude, body, and postlude thunks (procedures of no arguments), and performs the same context graph operations used in our interpreter. This procedure may be of great value when programming with continuations in Scheme. For example, the code of figure 9.5.1 where `wind` is used would become

```
(dynamic-wind
  (lambda () (set! resume localresume))
  (lambda () (begin
              (body (resume exit newcoroutine))
              (error)))
  (lambda () noop))
```
☐

o *Exercise 9.5.3*

If a prelude is executing for the first time, or a postlude is executing after the body has returned normally, it would be acceptable for control to enter or leave the prelude or postlude via invocation of a continuation. The effect in these cases would be that obtained if the dynamic wind expression were replaced by

```
begin
  prelude
  let ans = body
  in begin
        postlude
        ans
      end
end
```

where `ans` does not occur free in *postlude*. Modify the wrapping operation of the context-graph algorithm to allow this behavior. ☐

o *Exercise 9.5.4*

There are two places in the programs of figure 9.5.4 that do a `throw`. In one of them, the distance from `**current**` to the node to be restored as the current node is one. Determine which of the throws is simpler, and rename it `little-throw`. Then implement `little-throw` to take advantage of this observation. ☐

- *Exercise 9.5.5*

What is written in the evaluation of the following expression?

```
letcont return
in wind write(0)
   within wind write(1)
         within wind write(2)
                within cons(return(3), 4)
                unwind write(200)
         unwind write(300)
   unwind write(400)
```

□

9.6 Dynamic Assignment Revisited

In the previous section we claimed that our implementation of dynamic assignment was flawed when used with first-class continuations. We now have the tools to fix dynamic assignment. Each time control moves out of the body of a dynamic assignment, the original value of the variable must be reset. Furthermore, the current value of the variable must be saved for a subsequent re-entrance, in the event that a continuation was captured within the body. The top portion of figure 9.6.1 is a program that shows how that might happen. The result of executing this program should be 114, not 100.

The lower portion of Figure 9.6.1 shows a program that uses wind to model the behavior of dynamic assignment. The difference is that this program has a prelude and a postlude that manage the resetting of the variable x, using two additional variables, fluidx and lexicalx. The lexicalx variable always contains the lexical value of x while control is *in* the body of the dynamic assignment and the fluidx variable always contains the fluid value of x while control is *out* of the body of the dynamic assignment. When control re-enters the body of the dynamic assignment, the lexical value is saved again (because assignments to it may have occurred).

- *Exercise 9.6.1*

The program in figure 9.6.1 uses two additional variables, fluidx and lexicalx. Rewrite it with just one additional variable tempx. □

The solution to adding dynamic assignment to the defined language in the presence of first-class continuations is now straightforward. First, we add a new make- procedure, *make-swap-thunk*, to the thunk ADT.

Figure 9.6.1   Two programs that do dynamic assignment

```
let x = 3;
    a = 12
in let ans = letcont out
             in let ret = letcont k
                          in x := +(a, 20) during begin
                                                    x := +(x, x);
                                                    letcont k1 in k(k1);
                                                    out(x)
                                                  end
                in begin
                     x := 50;
                     a := 100;
                     ret(5)
                   end
   in +(ans, x)

let x = 3;
    a = 12
in let ans = letcont out
             in let ret = letcont k
                          in let fluidx = +(a, 20);
                                 lexicalx = ignored
                             in wind begin
                                       lexicalx := x;
                                       x := fluidx
                                     end
                                within begin
                                         x := +(x, x);
                                         letcont k1 in k(k1);
                                         out(x)
                                       end
                                unwind begin
                                         fluidx := x;
                                         x := lexicalx
                                       end
                in begin
                     x := 50;
                     a := 100;
                     ret(5)
                   end
   in +(ans, x)
```

```
(define make-swap-thunk
  (lambda (cell-1 cell-2)
    (lambda (k)
      (cell-swap! cell-1 cell-2)
      (k '*))))
```

This procedure returns a thunk that simply swaps the contents of two cells;
see figure 4.5.1. One of the cells corresponds to the binding of the dynamic
assignment variable, and the other acts like a temporary (see exercise 9.6.1).
Here is the dynassign clause to be added to the interpreter of figure 9.5.4.

```
(dynassign (var exp body)
  (eval-exp exp env
    (lambda (value)
      (let ((swap (wrap-thunk
                    (make-swap-thunk
                      (apply-env env var)
                      (make-cell value)))))
        (create-context swap (make-thunk body env) swap k)))))
```

The first step in this clause is to evaluate *exp*. Then a wrapped thunk is
created that swaps the contents of the cell of the environment representing
the L-value of var and its associated temporary cell; see exercise 9.6.1 to see
why we need only one swapping routine. Finally, as in the execution of the
program in the lower portion of figure 9.6.1, *create-context* is invoked.

- *Exercise 9.6.2*
  In the top portion of figure 9.6.1 the program uses dynamic assignment. In
  chapter 5 we showed that the operation of dynamic assignment was just manipulating the values stored in lexical variables. Rewrite that program without
  using dynamic assignment, but with using fluidx and lexicalx to behave as
  the dynamic assignment did in the earlier chapter. The result should be 114,
  the wrong answer. □

9.7 Summary

The CPS transformation converts programs to tail form, but at the expense of
relying on the existence of first-class procedures in the defining language. This
reliance can be eliminated by representing continuations as data structures.

Applying these transformations to an interpreter yields an interpreter in first-order tail form. This provides an interpreter that does not rely on first-class procedures or recursion in the defining language.

If the interpreter for the defined language is in continuation-passing style, these continuations can be made available in the defined language. Such continuations can be used to escape from inside nested procedures. If the defined language includes continuations as expressed values, then complex control structures such as coroutines can be defined without further extending the defined language.

First-class continuations complicate the definition of dynamic extent. Sometimes it is necessary to guarantee that certain actions, such as opening or closing a file, are taken on entrance to or exit from a dynamic extent, whether by normal control flow or invocation of a continuation. This can be accomplished by a mechanism, called dynamic wind, that manipulates a graph of managed contexts.

10 Imperative Form and Stack Architecture

In chapter 8 we saw that by using continuation-passing style, any procedure can be transformed into an equivalent tail-form procedure, in which all recursive procedures are called in tail position. In this chapter we show that any tail-form procedure may be transformed into an equivalent set of procedures in *imperative form*, in which all procedures have no arguments. Procedures in imperative form receive information from their callers in variable bindings that are assigned by the caller prior to procedure invocation, rather than via arguments.

A tail call of no arguments simply transfers control to the beginning of the called procedure's body: it is equivalent to a *go to* (unconditional jump) statement. Thus, through continuation-passing and imperative form transformations it is possible to reduce procedure calls to the most rudimentary form of control transfer.

In section 10.1 we introduce the imperative form transformation with simple examples and show how it may be applied to procedures to which the CPS transformation of chapter 8 and the first-order transformation of chapter 9 have first been applied. In section 10.2 we then show how these procedures may be further transformed so that control information is recorded on a stack, rather than in heap-allocated continuations. In section 10.3 we apply these transformations to an interpreter that heap-allocates its argument lists, closures, continuations and environments. In this section, we successfully move all but the environments to the control stack. Finally, in section 10.4 we show how the interpreter's environment bindings may also be recorded on the control stack if restrictions on the extent of procedures are imposed. The resulting stack architecture is typical of those used to implement block structured imperative-style programming languages. Then a heap is required only if heap-allocated run-time structures are supported.

10.1 Imperative Form

We have seen that, in general, execution of a procedure call requires the following steps:

1. saving the current control context,

2. extending the environment with new variable bindings for the arguments of the call, and

3. transferring control to the beginning of the called procedure's body.

In chapter 8 we saw that a tail call requires no additional control information be recorded, so in such cases step 1 may be omitted. If step 1 is omitted whenever possible, tail-form procedures exhibit iterative control behavior. Such an implementation is properly tail recursive. Next we introduce a technique by which any tail-form procedure may be transformed into one in which all tail calls have no operands. This eliminates step 2, leaving only step 3, which is equivalent to a *go to* statement.

When a procedure calls itself from a tail position, the bindings of its formal parameters will never be used again, since control does not return to the procedure following the call. Therefore, the new values required by the call could be assigned to the bindings prior to the call. For example, consider *member?*.

```
(define member?
  (lambda (s los)
    (cond
      ((null? los) #f)
      ((equal? (car los) s) #t)
      (else (member? s (cdr los))))))
```

This is equivalent to

```
(define member?
  (lambda (s los)
    (cond
      ((null? los) #f)
      ((equal? (car los) s) #t)
      (else (set! los (cdr los))
            (member? s los)))))
```

Since *s* and *los* are not changed by the tail call, they could both be global variables, provided they were properly initialized by assignments. We use the term *register* when referring to variables that are assigned in this manner and name these variables with the suffix -reg. An *imperative,* or register, version of *member?* is obtained as follows using global registers.

```
(define s-reg '*)
(define los-reg '*)

(define member?
  (lambda (s los)
    (set! s-reg s)
    (set! los-reg los)
    (member?/reg)))

(define member?/reg
  (lambda ()
    (cond
      ((null? los-reg) #f)
      ((equal? (car los-reg) s-reg) #t)
      (else (set! los-reg (cdr los-reg))
            (member?/reg)))))
```

Such a program, in which all first-order tail-form procedures have no arguments, is said to be in *imperative form.* We use the suffix /reg (read "with registers") in naming imperative form procedures.

As a second example, here is a version of the *fact-iter* example of chapter 8, in which we have converted the inner loop *fact-iter-acc* to imperative form:

```
(define n-reg '*)
(define a-reg '*)

(define fact-iter
  (lambda (n)
    (set! n-reg n)
    (set! a-reg 1)
    (fact-iter-acc/reg)))
```

```
(define fact-iter-acc/reg
  (lambda ()
    (if (zero? n-reg)
        a-reg
        (begin
          (set! a-reg (* n-reg a-reg))
          (set! n-reg (- n-reg 1))
          (fact-iter-acc/reg)))))
```

Since the subexpression of the first set! expression refers to *n-reg*, the transformation would be incorrect if the order of the set! statements were reversed. Since it is essential that there be no references to a variable from the point at which it is assigned to the point of the tail call, the order of assignments may be critical. In some cases, no order is correct unless one or more of the old variable bindings is temporarily recorded using a let expression or some other means. For example, in the following version of fact the order of the set! statements has been reversed.

```
(define fact-iter-acc/reg
  (lambda ()
    (if (zero? n-reg)
        a-reg
        (let ((temp-n-reg n-reg))
          (set! n-reg (- n-reg 1))
          (set! a-reg (* temp-n-reg a-reg))
          (fact-iter-acc/reg)))))
```

• *Exercise 10.1.1*

Transform the following tail-form procedures *reverse-acc* and *fib-acc* to imperative form and make the appropriate changes to *reverse* and *fib*.

```
(define reverse
  (lambda (ls)
    (reverse-acc ls '())))

(define reverse-acc
  (lambda (ls a)
    (if (null? ls)
        a
        (reverse-acc (cdr ls) (cons (car ls) a)))))
```

```
(define fib
  (lambda (n)
    (fib-acc n 0 1)))

(define fib-acc
  (lambda (n a1 a2)
    (if (= n 0)
        a2
        (fib-acc (- n 1) a2 (+ a1 a2)))))
```

☐

In general, the imperative-form transformation only works on programs that are first-order tail form. In some cases accumulators will suffice for translation into tail form, but the CPS transformation always does the job.

We next demonstrate the imperative-form transformation on a procedure that is similar to the one we derived in chapter 8.

```
(define subst
  (lambda (new old s)
    (subst-cps new old s (lambda (x) x))))

(define subst-cps
  (lambda (new old s k)
    (if (pair? s)
        (subst-cps new old (car s)
          (lambda (v)
            (subst-cps new old (cdr s)
              (lambda (w)
                (k (cons v w))))))
        (if (eq? s old) (k new) (k s)))))
```

Before we can apply the imperative-form transformation, we must first convert *subst-cps* to first-order form. Applying our imperative-form transformation to the first-order form, we obtain the program of figure 10.1.1. It is not necessary for the continuation data structures to close over *new-reg* and *old-reg*, because these values remain the same throughout a call to *subst-cps*.

One final note: if the continuation was created by the CPS transformation, it is always safe to perform the continuation assignment before other assignments. (The other operands never refer to the continuation because they existed before the CPS transformation created the continuation.) Often the continuation *must* be first, because it contains the values of other variables.

Figure 10.1.1 First-order imperative-form transformation example

```
(define-record final-valcont ())
(define-record subst1-cont (s k))
(define-record subst2-cont (v k))

(define new-reg '*)     (define s-reg '*)
(define old-reg '*)     (define k-reg '*)
(define v-reg '*)

(define subst
  (lambda (new old s)
    (set! k-reg (make-final-valcont))
    (set! new-reg new)
    (set! old-reg old)
    (set! s-reg s)
    (subst-cps/reg)))

(define subst-cps/reg
  (lambda ()
    (if (pair? s-reg)
        (begin (set! k-reg (make-subst1-cont s-reg k-reg))
               (set! s-reg (car s-reg))
               (subst-cps/reg))
        (if (eq? s-reg old-reg)
            (begin (set! v-reg new-reg)
                   (apply-continuation/reg))
            (begin (set! v-reg s-reg)
                   (apply-continuation/reg))))))

(define apply-continuation/reg
  (lambda ()
    (variant-case k-reg
      (final-valcont () v-reg)
      (subst1-cont (s k)
        (set! k-reg (make-subst2-cont v-reg k))
        (set! s-reg (cdr s))
        (subst-cps/reg))
      (subst2-cont (v k)
        (set! k-reg k)
        (set! v-reg (cons v v-reg))
        (apply-continuation/reg)))))
```

- *Exercise 10.1.2*

  Apply the imperative form transformation to the procedures developed in exercise 8.5.4. ☐

- *Exercise 10.1.3*

  Apply the imperative form transformation to the interpreter of figure 9.2.3 and figure 9.2.5. ☐

o *Exercise 10.1.4*

  The imperative-form transformation does not work correctly if the program is not in first-order form. Demonstrate this by converting the CPS version of `subst`. What goes wrong? ☐

10.2 Control Stacks

In the *subst-cps/reg* program, the `subst1-cont` and `subst2-cont` continuations both contain a single continuation, in addition to other information, and the final value continuation contains no continuations. A similar pattern arises in all CPS programs. Thus every continuation may be thought of as being the head of a chain of continuations, the tail of which is the continuation that it contains and the end of which is the final value continuation. See figure 10.2.1 (a). For uniformity, we consider the final value continuation to contain an empty chain.

This observation prompts us to transform the representation of continuations so that they are not structures containing other continuations but lists of structures, called *frames*, which contain the information other than the continuation that was recorded in the corresponding continuation structures. We refer to this as a *list of frames* representation. See figure 10.2.1 (b).

To transform the *subst-cps/reg* program to use a list of frames representation, we first define the frame structures.

```
(define-record final-valframe ())
(define-record subst1-frame (s))
(define-record subst2-frame (v))
```

Since the *subst-cps/reg* procedure is independent of the representation of continuations, it does not need to be redefined. We need only redefine the procedures in its continuation ADT. Each of the procedures that create a continuation now returns a list, rather than a record.

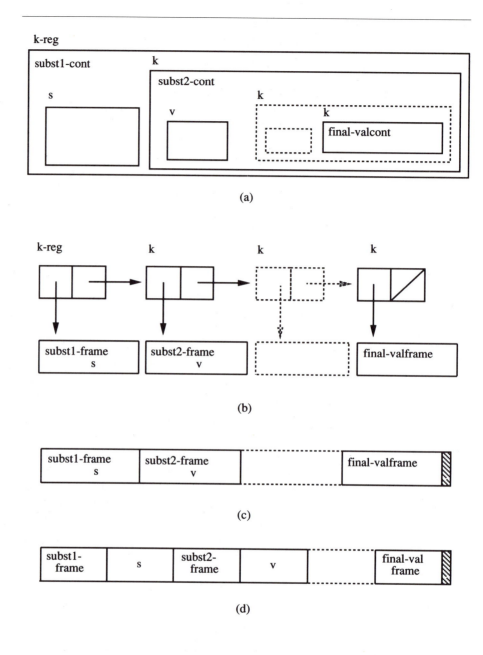

Figure 10.2.1 Representations of continuations

```
(define make-final-valcont
  (lambda ()
    (cons (make-final-valframe) '())))

(define make-subst1-cont
  (lambda (s k)
    (cons (make-subst1-frame s) k)))

(define make-subst2-cont
  (lambda (v k)
    (cons (make-subst2-frame v) k)))

(define apply-continuation/reg
  (lambda ()
    (let ((frame (car k-reg)) (k (cdr k-reg)))
      (variant-case frame
        (final-valframe () v-reg)
        (subst1-frame (s)
          (set! k-reg (make-subst2-cont v-reg k))
          (set! s-reg (cdr s))
          (subst-cps/reg))
        (subst2-frame (v)
          (set! k-reg k)
          (set! v-reg (cons v v-reg))
          (apply-continuation/reg))))))
```

Examining the assignments to k-reg, we next observe that in every case the new continuation is obtained either by consing a new frame onto the current continuation or by taking the cdr of the current continuation. Thus frames are accessed in a last-in-first-out order; in other words, the continuation data structure (in this case a list) is being used as a stack. To express this, we modify our list of frames program to use a stack ADT with the procedure *push!*, which pushes its argument onto a stack, and two procedures of no arguments, *top* and *pop!*, which return the top value on the stack and pop the stack, respectively. See figure 10.2.2.

In implementing the stack ADT, we can store all continuation frames in a single vector, rather than requiring a cons cell for each new continuation. Of course we must assume that it is possible to place a reasonable limit, say *stack-size*, on the maximum number of stack elements.

● *Exercise 10.2.1*
Implement the stack ADT, representing the stack as a vector, and use it to test the code of figure 10.2.2. ☐

Figure 10.2.2   Using stack of frames representation of continuations

```
(define subst
  (lambda (new old s)
    (push! (make-final-valframe))
    (set! new-reg new)
    (set! old-reg old)
    (set! s-reg s)
    (subst-cps/reg)))

(define subst-cps/reg
  (lambda ()
    (if (pair? s-reg)
        (begin
          (push! (make-subst1-frame s-reg))
          (set! s-reg (car s-reg))
          (subst-cps/reg))
        (if (eq? s-reg old-reg)
            (begin
              (set! v-reg new-reg)
              (apply-continuation/reg))
            (begin
              (set! v-reg s-reg)
              (apply-continuation/reg))))))

(define apply-continuation/reg
  (lambda ()
    (let ((frame (top)))
      (pop!)
      (variant-case frame
        (final-valframe () v-reg)
        (subst1-frame (s)
          (push! (make-subst2-frame v-reg))
          (set! s-reg (cdr s))
          (subst-cps/reg))
        (subst2-frame (v)
          (set! v-reg (cons v v-reg))
          (apply-continuation/reg))))))
```

Figure 10.2.3   An example using an unframed-stack representation

```
(define subst
  (lambda (new old s)
    (push! 'final-valframe)
    (set! new-reg new)
    (set! old-reg old)
    (set! s-reg s)
    (subst-cps/reg)))

(define subst-cps/reg
  (lambda ()
    (if (pair? s-reg)
        (begin (push! s-reg)
               (push! 'subst1-frame)
               (set! s-reg (car s-reg))
               (subst-cps/reg))
        (if (eq? s-reg old-reg)
            (begin (set! v-reg new-reg)
                   (apply-continuation/reg))
            (begin (set! v-reg s-reg)
                   (apply-continuation/reg))))))

(define apply-continuation/reg
  (lambda ()
    (let ((frame-tag (top)))
      (pop!)
      (case frame-tag
        ((final-valframe) v-reg)
        ((subst1-frame)
         (let ((s (top)))
           (pop!)
           (push! v-reg)
           (push! 'subst2-frame)
           (set! s-reg (cdr s))
           (subst-cps/reg)))
        ((subst2-frame)
         (let ((v (top)))
           (pop!)
           (set! v-reg (cons v v-reg))
           (apply-continuation/reg)))))))
```

To complete our derivation of a stack architecture for *subst*, we eliminate the frame records. Instead of pushing a frame onto the stack, we push onto the stack any values that were contained in the stack frame and then we push a tag (a symbol) representing the type of frame. The `variant-case` expression in `apply-continuation/reg` must then be replaced with a `case` expression that dispatches on the tag that was on the top of the stack, and the `case` expression consequent clauses must remove any associated values from the stack. We refer to this as an *unframed-stack* representation. See figure 10.2.1 (b), (c), and (d) for a graphic comparison of the list of frames, stack of frames, and unframed-stack control representations, and see figure 10.2.3 for an implementation of *subst* using an unframed stack.

This completes our series of transformations of *subst*. We started by transforming a procedure into CPS. This introduced new procedures: the continuations. The next transformation made the program independent of the representation of continuations, which allowed us to then change the representation of continuations from procedures to records. The resulting program is said to be in first-order tail form. This enabled us to transform our program to an imperative form. By observing a pattern in the structure of continuations, we next transformed the continuations into a list of frames representation. Then we noticed that the frames were being added to and taken from the list in a last-in-first-out manner, like a stack, resulting in a stack of frames representation. In our final transformation we eliminated the frame records by placing their contents directly on the stack, resulting in an unframed-stack representation.

These transformations are of great value because they reduce the mechanics of procedures to the level of assembly language: register assignments, jumps, and stack operations. Furthermore, the transformations may be applied to *any* program, and each transformation is well defined and preserves the correctness of the program.

- *Exercise 10.2.2*
  Transform the programs of exercise 9.1.2 so that the continuations are represented successively as a list of frames, a stack of frames, and an unframed stack. ☐

- *Exercise 10.2.3*
  Transform the interpreter of exercise 9.2.5 so that the continuations are represented successively as a list of frames, a stack of frames, and an unframed stack. ☐

10.3 Interpreter Stack Architecture

Though programs may use heap-allocated objects (such as Scheme's pairs, records, and closures) for a variety of purposes, it is sometimes possible to transform programs so that no dynamic heap allocation is required. In such cases the run-time system necessary to support the program may be greatly simplified, since dynamic heap management (such as garbage collection) is no longer required. This typically results in implementations that are simpler and more efficient.

For example in *subst-cps/reg*, dynamic heap allocation was required when new continuation closures or records were created. In section 10.1 we saw that the continuations could be recorded on a stack, rather than in a heap. Our interpreters have used heap allocation for continuations, argument lists, environments, and closures. In this and the next section we derive an interpreter that records all this information using a single stack.

We know that the transformations in the previous sections allow us to represent continuations using an unframed stack. Our goal, therefore, is to transform the interpreter of figure 9.2.2 to avoid heap allocation of argument lists, environments, and closures. We instead incorporate this information in the continuation. Since the continuation is a stack, the entire interpreter will then obey stack discipline.

The stack architecture of our final interpreter is of special interest because it is typical of stack architectures used by implementations of most block-structured programming languages. This architecture is familiar and efficient, but it comes at two costs. First, it will not allow procedures or continuations to be returned as values from other procedures or to be stored in heap-allocated data structures. Second, it does not implement proper tail recursion (though, using other techniques, a properly tail-recursive implementation may employ a control stack). We shall discuss these limitations at the end of section 10.4.

10.3.1 Value and Argument Continuations

We assume the interpreted language has only literals, variables, procedures, and applications. Adding other forms is straightforward. We assume that all primitive procedures are unary or binary. We distinguish these based on their arity and represent them by Scheme procedures of one and two arguments, respectively. The interpreter is easily extended to accommodate primitive operators of other arities. Also, we change the functionality of `apply-env` to take a continuation argument, as in exercise 9.3.2. See figure 10.3.1.

Figure 10.3.1   Interpreter with abstract data representations

```
(define eval-exp
  (lambda (exp env k)
    (variant-case exp
      (lit (datum) (k datum))
      (varref (var) (apply-env env var k))
      (proc (formals body) (k (make-closure formals body env)))
      (app (rator rands)
        (eval-exp rator env
          (lambda (proc)
            (eval-rands rands env
              (lambda (all)
                (apply-proc proc all k)))))))
      (else (error "Invalid abstract syntax:" exp)))))

(define eval-rands
  (lambda (rands env k)
    (if (null? rands)
        (k '())
        (eval-exp (car rands) env
          (lambda (first)
            (eval-rands (cdr rands) env
              (lambda (rest)
                (k (cons first rest)))))))))

(define apply-proc
  (lambda (proc args k)
    (variant-case proc
      (prim-1 (unary-op)
        (k (unary-op (unary-arg args))))
      (prim-2 (binary-op)
        (k (binary-op (binary-arg-1 args) (binary-arg-2 args))))
      (closure (formals body env)
        (eval-exp body (extend-env formals args env) k))
      (else (error "Invalid primitive operation:" proc)))))
```

Our first step is to introduce abstract data types for the continuations. We provide separate abstractions (ADTs) for *argument continuations*, which expect to receive argument lists, and for *value continuations*, which expect values. The argument continuations are exactly the continuations that are passed to `eval-rands`; all the remaining continuations are value continuations.

This is a good opportunity to eliminate one instance of heap allocation: the one in `make-closure`. We can do this by adding an additional argument to value continuations. Let us explore this idea in more detail.

The formals list and body components of a closure are static, but the environment is dynamic. Our approach is to represent the static and dynamic components of a closure separately, but in such a manner that they are available together when they are both needed (that is, when a procedure is invoked). We represent the static component of a nonprimitive procedure as the abstract syntax tree for the expression that defines it; this contains the formals list and the body, as desired. One way of associating the static and dynamic components would be to join them using a pair in the heap.

We can avoid this heap allocation by having value continuations take two arguments: one for the ordinary values, including the static parts of closures, and one for closure environments. Closures no longer exist as physical data values, but we shall still use this term to refer to a procedure expression and an environment that are linked in this way. If the value being passed is not a closure, the second argument will be a dummy value.

For now, we still represent continuations of both kinds as procedures. See figure 10.3.2 for the basic interpretation procedures, along with new versions of the procedures that interpret environments and primitive procedures. We assume that the primitive procedures take and return only ordinary (nonclosure) values; we leave it as an exercise to rewrite `unary-arg`, etc., to extract only the ordinary value.

See figure 10.3.3 and figure 10.3.4 for the value and argument continuation ADTs, respectively. The extra argument to value continuations propagates through these procedures, resulting in extra arguments in all of the continuation builders. The extra argument is finally used in `apply-proc`. For the final value continuation, we add a test to see whether the value being returned is a closure or not; if it is a closure, we return a distinguished symbol `<Procedure>`, since we presume it should be impossible for the user of the language to see the internals of a closure.

The environment ADT, using a procedural representation, is shown in figure 10.3.5. The procedure `extend-env` takes a list of value-environment pairs, as built by the `rest` continuation of figure 10.3.4; when the right pair is found, its pieces are reported as the two arguments of the continuation `vk`.

Figure 10.3.2   Interpreter with abstract continuations

```
(define eval-exp
  (lambda (exp env vk)
    (variant-case exp
      (lit (datum) (apply-valcont vk datum dummy))
      (varref (var) (apply-env env var vk))
      (proc (formals body) (apply-valcont vk exp env))
      (app (rator rands)
        (eval-exp rator env (make-proc-valcont rands env vk)))
      (else (error "Invalid abstract syntax:" exp)))))

(define eval-rands
  (lambda (rands env ak)
    (if (null? rands)
        (apply-argcont ak '())
        (eval-exp (car rands) env
          (make-first-valcont rands env ak)))))

(define apply-proc
  (lambda (proc proc-env args vk)
    (variant-case proc
      (prim-1 (unary-op)
        (apply-valcont vk
          (unary-op (unary-arg args))
          dummy))
      (prim-2 (binary-op)
        (apply-valcont vk
          (binary-op (binary-arg-1 args) (binary-arg-2 args))
          dummy))
      (proc (formals body)
        (eval-exp body (extend-env formals args proc-env) vk))
      (else (error "Invalid primitive operation:" proc)))))

(define dummy '*)
```

Figure 10.3.3   Value continuation ADT

```
(define make-final-valcont
  (lambda ()
    (lambda (final final-env)
      (if (eq? final-env dummy)
          final
          '<Procedure>))))

(define make-first-valcont
  (lambda (rands env ak)
    (lambda (first first-env)
      (eval-rands (cdr rands) env
        (make-rest-argcont first first-env ak)))))

(define make-proc-valcont
  (lambda (rands env vk)
    (lambda (proc proc-env)
      (eval-rands rands env
        (make-all-argcont proc proc-env vk)))))

(define apply-valcont
  (lambda (vk val val-env)
    (vk val val-env)))
```

10.3.2 Transforming Continuations

Our next step is to convert the value and argument continuations to a data structure representation. We shall then be able to convert the resulting first-order program to imperative form.

First we introduce two record types for argument continuations:

```
(define-record rest-argcont (val env-or-dummy ak))
(define-record all-argcont (proc proc-env vk))
```

and three record types for value continuations:

```
(define-record final-valcont ())
(define-record first-valcont (rands env ak))
(define-record proc-valcont (rands env vk))
```

To go with this record representation of argument continuations, we define `apply-argcont` as in figure 10.3.6.

Figure 10.3.4   Argument continuation ADT

```
(define make-rest-argcont
  (lambda (val env-or-dummy ak)
    (lambda (rest)
      (apply-argcont ak
        (cons (cons val env-or-dummy) rest)))))

(define make-all-argcont
  (lambda (proc proc-env vk)
    (lambda (all)
      (apply-proc proc proc-env all vk))))

(define apply-argcont
  (lambda (ak args)
    (ak args)))
```

Figure 10.3.5   Environment ADT

```
(define apply-env
  (lambda (env var vk)
    (env var vk)))

(define extend-env
  (lambda (formals args env)
    (lambda (var vk)
      (if (memq var formals)
          (letrec
            ((loop (lambda (formals rib)
                     (if (eq? var (car formals))
                         (apply-valcont vk
                           (car (car rib))
                           (cdr (car rib)))
                         (loop (cdr formals) (cdr rib)))))))
            (loop formals args))
          (apply-env env var vk)))))
```

• *Exercise 10.3.1*

Define `apply-valcont` to interpret the value continuations constructed from the `final-valcont`, `first-valcont`, and `proc-valcont` record types. ☐

Figure 10.3.6   `apply-argcont` using record representation

```
(define apply-argcont
  (lambda (ak args)
    (variant-case ak
      (rest-argcont (val env-or-dummy ak)
        (let ((rest args))
          (apply-argcont ak
            (cons (cons val env-or-dummy) rest))))
      (all-argcont (proc proc-env vk)
        (let ((all args))
          (apply-proc proc proc-env all vk))))))
```

The argument continuation record type declarations reveal that every argument continuation has the form

```
#(rest-argcont  val-n  env-or-dummy-n
   ...
     #(rest-argcont  val-1  env-or-dummy-1
        #(all-argcont  proc  proc-env  vk)))
```

where the values of the operand expressions, *val-1*, *val-2*, ... with their associated environment slots, *env-or-dummy-1*, *env-or-dummy-2*, ... appear in reverse order. The value of the first operand is innermost, just outside the `all-argcont`, and the most recently evaluated operand (*val-n*) is outermost.

When `apply-argcont` is invoked by *eval-rands*, each of the `rest-argcont` continuations causes its argument to be added to the argument list. When the `all-argcont` continuation is reached, `apply-proc` is invoked to apply a primitive procedure or closure with the newly constructed argument list and the continuation `vk`. This effectively pops the control stack to the point representing `vk`.

Thus the only purpose of `apply-argcont` is to collect information for the benefit of `apply-proc`. By making `apply-proc` smarter, we can avoid `apply-argcont` altogether and simply pass the argument continuation to `apply-proc`, since it has all the information needed.

What information does *apply-proc* need to extract from the argument continuation? It needs to find the procedure value and environment to be applied, which are located inside `all-argcont`. The value continuation to be used is in the same continuation. We use a procedure, *find-all-argcont*, with a 3-argument receiver continuation to avoid doing the same search three

Figure 10.3.7   Procedures that avoid the creation of argument lists

```
(define eval-rands
  (lambda (rands env ak)
    (if (null? rands)
        (apply-proc ak)
        (eval-exp (car rands) env
          (make-first-valcont rands env ak)))))

(define apply-proc
  (lambda (ak)
    (find-all-argcont ak
      (lambda (proc proc-env vk)
        (variant-case proc
          (prim-1 (unary-op)
            (apply-valcont vk
              (unary-op (unary-arg ak))
              dummy))
          (prim-2 (binary-op)
            (apply-valcont vk
              (binary-op (binary-arg-1 ak) (binary-arg-2 ak))
              dummy))
          (proc (formals body)
            (eval-exp body
              (extend-env formals ak proc-env)
              vk))
          (else (error "Invalid primitive operation:" proc)))))))

(define find-all-argcont
  (lambda (ak receiver)
    (variant-case ak
      (all-argcont (proc proc-env vk)
        (receiver proc proc-env vk))
      (rest-argcont (val env-or-dummy ak)
        (find-all-argcont ak receiver)))))
```

Figure 10.3.8   Environments using argument continuations

```
(define extend-env make-extended-env)

(define apply-env
  (lambda (env var vk)
    (variant-case env
      (initial-env () (init-env var vk))
      (extended-env (formals ak env)
        (if (memq var formals)
            (letrec
              ((loop (lambda (formals ak)
                       (variant-case ak
                         (rest-argcont (val env-or-dummy ak)
                           (if (eq? var (car formals))
                               (apply-valcont vk val env-or-dummy)
                               (loop (cdr formals) ak)))
                         (else (error "Invalid environment"))))))
              (loop (reverse formals) ak))
            (apply-env env var vk))))))
```

times. We also need to recode the procedures that extract the arguments for
primitive operations. See figure 10.3.7.

The representation of environments must also be changed to account for the
location of values in the argument continuation, rather than in heap-allocated
lists. To do this, we change the record types for environments to

```
(define-record initial-env ())
(define-record extended-env (formals ak env))
```

The procedure *apply-env* must search for values in the argument continuation. Since the arguments appear in reverse order in the continuation,
the search loop in *apply-env* begins with a reversed formals list. See figure 10.3.8.

We now have an interpreter in which storage is allocated only for continuations and environments, and this allocation is in the form of records.

○ *Exercise 10.3.2*
The preceding statement is not quite accurate: there is still heap allocation
taking place in the expression (reverse formals) in *apply-env*. This reversal
could have been done at a number of points. Modify your parser so that it

reverses the formals lists in `proc` records, thus avoiding the need to perform this operation at run time. □

- *Exercise 10.3.3*
  Implement the interpreter described in this section. □

10.4 Stack Allocation of Continuations and Environments

We have now laid the groundwork for putting continuations and environments on a stack. This is done in two steps. First, we put continuations on a stack, leaving environments alone. Then we finish the job by putting environments on the stack as well.

First we define a suitable stack ADT. This ADT provides access to a single stack that is initialized by calling *init-stack!*. The procedure *push!* puts its argument on the top of the stack. Though of course values may only be added to or removed from this stack at its top, this stack ADT allows pointers to be maintained that refer to locations within the stack. The contents of the stack location referred to by a stack pointer may be obtained by passing the pointer to the procedure *stack-ref*. The variable *top-ptr* is always a pointer to the top of the stack. The procedure *pop-to-ptr!* takes a stack pointer and pops the stack until the pointer refers to the top of the stack, and *decrement-ptr* takes a stack pointer p and a number n and returns a pointer to the location n elements below the location referred to by p. Our implementation of this ADT represents the stack as a vector (allowing random access to its elements), with stack pointers represented as vector indices. See figure 10.4.1.

We now rewrite our interpreter in imperative style. The current continuation is represented by the global stack, as in section 10.2, rather than by a `k-reg` variable. The environment is communicated through a global register, `env-reg`. All other variables remain as they originally appeared in figure 10.3.2. It is left as an exercise to pass these in registers. We begin by defining *eval-exp* and *eval-rands*, which we rename *eval-exp/stack* and *eval-rands/stack*.

Continuations are represented as stack pointers into an unframed stack. The current continuation is obtained using `top-ptr`. Other continuations are also represented as stack pointers. Each procedure that constructs continuations simply pushes data on the stack, along with an appropriate tag, as in figure 10.2.3. See figure 10.4.3.

Figure 10.4.1　Control stack ADT

```
(define top-ptr '*)
(define the-stack '*)
(define stack-ptr-limit 100)

(define init-stack!
  (lambda ()
    (set! top-ptr -1)
    (set! the-stack (make-vector (+ stack-ptr-limit 1)))))

(define push!
  (lambda (val)
    (if (= top-ptr stack-ptr-limit)
        (error "Stack overflow")
        (begin
          (set! top-ptr (+ 1 top-ptr))
          (vector-set! the-stack top-ptr val)))))

(define pop-to-ptr!
  (lambda (ptr)
    (set! top-ptr ptr)))

(define stack-ref
  (lambda (ptr)
    (vector-ref the-stack ptr)))

(define decrement-ptr
  (lambda (ptr n)
    (- ptr n)))

(define extract
  (lambda (ptr n receiver)
    (letrec
      ((loop (lambda (k)
               (let ((next (decrement-ptr ptr k)))
                 (if (> k n)
                     (list next)
                     (cons (stack-ref next) (loop (+ 1 k))))))))
      (apply receiver (loop 1)))))
```

Figure 10.4.2   Top-level interpretation procedures

```
(define eval-exp/stack
  (lambda (exp)
    (variant-case exp
      (lit (datum) (apply-valcont/stack datum dummy))
      (varref (var) (apply-env/stack env-reg var))
      (proc (formals body) (apply-valcont/stack exp env-reg))
      (app (rator rands)
        (make-proc-valcont! rands env-reg)
        (eval-exp/stack rator))
      (else (error "Invalid abstract syntax:" exp)))))

(define eval-rands/stack
  (lambda (rands)
    (if (null? rands)
        (apply-proc/stack)
        (begin
          (make-first-valcont! rands env-reg)
          (eval-exp/stack (car rands))))))
```

A typical stack segment, pushed by calling *make-tag-cont!* with components *val-1 ... val-n,* has the form

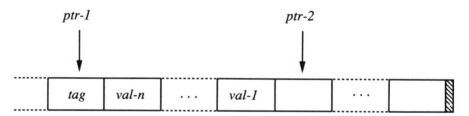

where *ptr-1* and *ptr-2* are pointers delimiting the segment. (The top of the stack is to the left.)

It will be useful to have a procedure, **extract**, that retrieves the values in a stack segment and also returns a pointer to the stack location immediately past the segment; see figure 10.4.1. In the above example, the call (extract *ptr-1 n receiver*) will result in the procedure *receiver* being called with arguments *val-n ... val-1* and *ptr-2.* Using **extract**, it is easy to code *apply-valcont/stack.* See figure 10.4.4.

```
(define make-rest-argcont!
  (lambda (val env-or-dummy)
    (push! env-or-dummy)
    (push! val)
    (push! '*rest)))

(define make-all-argcont!
  (lambda (proc proc-env)
    (push! proc-env)
    (push! proc)
    (push! '*all)))

(define make-final-valcont!
  (lambda ()
    (init-stack!)
    (push! '*final)))

(define make-first-valcont!
  (lambda (rands env)
    (push! env)
    (push! rands)
    (push! '*first)))

(define make-proc-valcont!
  (lambda (rands env)
    (push! env)
    (push! rands)
    (push! '*proc)))
```

○ *Exercise 10.4.1*

The procedure *extract* is called with *n* being 1, 2, or 3. Rewrite *extract* so that it does not use *cons* or *apply*, and thus avoid the use of heap space. □

We also have to modify *apply-env* because it deals with the internal representation of argument continuations. The argument continuation *ak* is now a stack pointer. We modify the procedure *apply-env* of figure 10.3.8 to search in the stack and rename it *apply-env/stack*. See figure 10.4.5.

We next modify the procedure *apply-proc* to obtain *apply-proc/stack*. Before doing that, however, we first consider the structure of the stack at the time this procedure is called. The stack is pictured below, where it is assumed

Figure 10.4.4 `apply-valcont/stack` (first version)

```
(define apply-valcont/stack
  (lambda (val env-or-dummy)
    (case (stack-ref top-ptr)
      ((*final)
       (if (eq? env-or-dummy dummy)
           val
           '<Procedure>))
      ((*first)
       (extract top-ptr 2
         (lambda (rands env ak)
           (pop-to-ptr! ak)
           (make-rest-argcont! val env-or-dummy)
           (set! env-reg env)
           (eval-rands/stack (cdr rands)))))
      ((*proc)
       (extract top-ptr 2
         (lambda (rands env vk)
           (pop-to-ptr! vk)
           (make-all-argcont! val env-or-dummy)
           (set! env-reg env)
           (eval-rands/stack rands)))))))
```

the called procedure is being passed n arguments, $v_1,\ldots,v_n$ and $e_1,\ldots,e_n$ represent the argument values and argument environment-or-dummy elements, respectively, *proc* is the procedure being called, and *env* is the associated environment if the procedure is a closure, or a dummy value if it is a primitive.

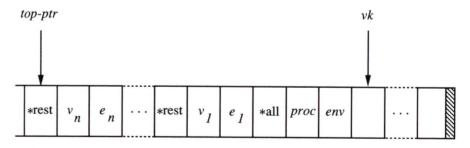

First we naively transform `apply-proc` of figure 10.3.7 to imperative form. If a primitive procedure is being called, `apply-proc/stack` extracts the argument values from the stack and calls the procedure with these values. The

Imperative Form and Stack Architecture

Figure 10.4.5 `apply-env/stack`

```
(define apply-env/stack
  (lambda (env var)
    (variant-case env
      (initial-env ()
        (apply-valcont/stack (init-env var) dummy))
      (extended-env (formals ak env)
        (if (memq var formals)
            (letrec
              ((loop (lambda (formals ak)
                       (case (stack-ref ak)
                         ((*rest)
                          (extract ak 2
                            (lambda (val env-or-dummy ak)
                              (if (eq? var (car formals))
                                  (apply-valcont/stack val
                                    env-or-dummy)
                                  (loop (cdr formals) ak)))))
                         (else (error "Invalid tag:" ak))))))
              (loop (reverse formals) ak))
            (apply-env/stack env var))))))
```

answer that is returned must be passed to the value continuation, *vk*, that is just below the *all continuation. This requires that the stack be popped until *vk* becomes the top of the stack before *apply-valcont/stack* is called. See figure 10.4.4 for our initial version of *apply-valcont/stack* and figure 10.4.7 for a new version of *find-all-argcont* that searches for *all down the stack and passes its receiver the values immediately to its right indicated by *proc, env,* and *vk* in the diagram above.

If the procedure being called is a closure, an extended environment is created that contains a reference to the argument continuation, which is the current top of the stack. The body of the called procedure is then evaluated in this environment by a call to *eval-exp/stack*; however, this procedure is expecting a value continuation, not an argument continuation, to be on the top of the stack. The value continuation *vk* that is just below the *all continuation is waiting to receive the value of the procedure call, so we are tempted to pass *vk* to *pop-to-ptr!* before calling *eval-exp/stack*, as in figure 10.4.6, but this does not work. The environment used when evaluating the body refers to the procedure's arguments via a pointer to the *rest con-

Figure 10.4.6 *apply-proc/stack* (first version)

```
(define apply-proc/stack
  (lambda ()
    (find-all-argcont top-ptr
      (lambda (proc proc-env vk)
        (variant-case proc
          (prim-1 (unary-op)
            (let ((ans (unary-op (unary-arg top-ptr))))
              (pop-to-ptr! vk)
              (apply-valcont/stack ans dummy)))
          (prim-2 (binary-op)
            (let ((ans (binary-op
                         (binary-arg-1 top-ptr)
                         (binary-arg-2 top-ptr))))
              (pop-to-ptr! vk)
              (apply-valcont/stack ans dummy)))
          (proc (formals body)
            (let ((ak top-ptr))
              (pop-to-ptr! vk)
              (set! env-reg (extend-env formals ak proc-env))
              (eval-exp/stack body)))
          (else (error "Invalid primitive operation:" proc)))))))
```

Figure 10.4.7 *find-all-argcont*

```
(define find-all-argcont
  (lambda (ptr receiver)
    (case (stack-ref ptr)
      ((*all) (extract ptr 2 receiver))
      ((*rest)
       (extract ptr 2
         (lambda (ignored ignored-env-or-dummy ak)
           (find-all-argcont ak receiver)))))))
```

tinuation that was on the top of the stack at the time that *apply-proc/stack* was called. When that evaluation of the body begins, however, the top of the stack is below the *all continuation. We may picture the environment and continuation at the time evaluation of the body begins as follows.

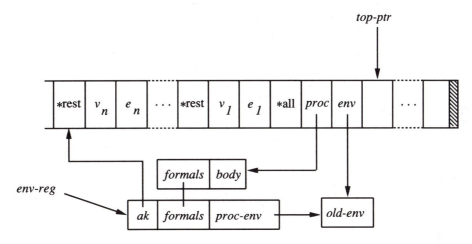

In the course of the body's evaluation, other values will likely be pushed on the stack, overwriting the procedure's arguments. The environment is said to contain a *dangling pointer*: a pointer into an invalid region of the stack (above the top of the stack or below its bottom).

This problem may be solved by pushing a new value continuation on the top, rather than popping the stack to an existing value continuation. We call this a *return value* continuation, since it is applied when a closure returns. See figure 10.4.8. When applied, a return value continuation pops the stack to the value continuation just below the *all continuation that referred to the returning procedure.

How else could dangling pointers arise? The only time that dangling pointers can be created is when we pop the stack. The problem with our first version of `apply-proc/stack` was that we popped the stack on procedure entry, thus losing the arguments. Now we have arranged things so that the stack is not popped on procedure entry but only on procedure exit. So to avoid dangling pointers, we must ensure that after a procedure returns, there will be no further references to its arguments. This can most easily be arranged by not allowing procedures to return closures or store closures in data structures. Such a returned (or stored) closure is called an *upward funarg* ("funarg" abbreviates "functional argument"). To enforce our "no upward funarg" rule, we insert a run-time check in `apply-valcont/stack` to ensure that closures are never returned. See figure 10.4.9.

- *Exercise 10.4.2*
Checking to see if a closure is being returned as in figure 10.4.9 is more restrictive than is necessary. A less restrictive test to avoid a dangling pointer

Figure 10.4.8 `apply-proc/stack` with return value continuations

```
(define apply-proc/stack
  (lambda ()
    (find-all-argcont top-ptr
      (lambda (proc proc-env vk)
        (variant-case proc
          (prim-1 (unary-op)
            (let ((ans (unary-op (unary-arg top-ptr))))
              (pop-to-ptr! vk)
              (apply-valcont/stack ans dummy)))
          (prim-2 (binary-op)
            (let ((ans (binary-op
                          (binary-arg-1 top-ptr)
                          (binary-arg-2 top-ptr))))
              (pop-to-ptr! vk)
              (apply-valcont/stack ans dummy)))
          (proc (formals body)
            (let ((ak top-ptr))
              (make-return-valcont! vk)
              (set! env-reg (extend-env formals ak proc-env))
              (eval-exp/stack body)))
          (else (error "Invalid primitive operation:" proc)))))))

(define make-return-valcont!
  (lambda (vk)
    (push! vk)
    (push! '*return)))
```

is to compare the environment pointer of the procedure with the appropriate value continuation pointer. Although this is less restrictive, language designers have avoided this test because it is more difficult to enforce using grammar rules and leads to costly run-time checks. Implement `apply-valcont/stack` using this less restrictive check and test it by passing `map` a higher-order procedure. □

Our interpreter now uses the heap only for allocating environments. We conclude by putting the environment on the stack as well. Environments are formed when closures are called. We have just seen that return value continuations are placed on the stack at this time. Thus if environments are to be put on the stack, it is natural to include them in *return continuations.

Figure 10.4.9   `apply-valcont/stack` (second version)

```
(define apply-valcont/stack
  (lambda (val env-or-dummy)
    (case (stack-ref top-ptr)
      ((*final)
       (if (eq? env-or-dummy dummy)
           val
           '<Procedure>))
      ((*first)
       (extract top-ptr 2
         (lambda (rands env ak)
           (pop-to-ptr! ak)
           (make-rest-argcont! val env-or-dummy)
           (set! env-reg env)
           (eval-rands/stack (cdr rands)))))
      ((*proc)
       (extract top-ptr 2
         (lambda (rands env vk)
           (pop-to-ptr! vk)
           (make-all-argcont! val env-or-dummy)
           (set! env-reg env)
           (eval-rands/stack rands))))
      ((*return)
       (if (eq? env-or-dummy dummy)
           (extract top-ptr 1
             (lambda (vk ak)
               (pop-to-ptr! vk)
               (apply-valcont/stack val env-or-dummy)))
           (error "Can't return procedures"))))))
```

To include an environment in a *return continuation, it is only necessary
to record the formals list and old environment. It is not necessary to include
the argument list, since it is already represented in the continuation.

```
(define make-return-valcont!
  (lambda (vk env formals)
    (push! formals)
    (push! env)
    (push! vk)
    (push! '*return)))
```

The corresponding *return case in `apply-valcont/stack` follows.

```
((*return)
 (if (eq? env-or-dummy dummy)
     (extract top-ptr 3
       (lambda (vk proc-env-ignored formals-ignored ak)
         (pop-to-ptr! vk)
         (apply-valcont/stack val env-or-dummy)))
     (error "Can't return procedures:" val)))
```

In this representation, environments, like continuations, are represented by stack pointers. When we build the return value continuation, we just push the formals and the saved environment on the stack. The extended environment is now represented by a pointer to the top of the stack. The initial environment may be represented by an illegal stack pointer; we use the integer -1. The code for `apply-env/stack` is similar to that of figure 10.4.5, except that we now test for the initial environment in a different way, and we extract the pieces of an extended environment differently. The code that searches a given contour remains the same. See figure 10.4.10.

The stack architecture we have derived is representative of the techniques that are often used in the implementation of typical block-structured programming languages. The portion of the stack containing the argument and return value continuations of a given call is called the *stack frame* or *activation record* of the call. A stack frame typically includes (1) arguments of the call, (2) a pointer to the next stack frame below on the stack, termed the *dynamic link*, and represented by the `vk` element of our return value continuations, and (3) a link to the environment at the surrounding lexical level, termed the *static link*, and represented by the `env` element of our return value continuations.

We now show a trace of a small program that utilizes all the concepts we have been discussing. The program is

```
let x = 89
in let f = proc (g) g(72)
   in f(proc (y) +(x, y))
```

which is equivalent to

```
(proc (x)
  (proc (f) f(proc (y) +(x, y)))
  (proc (g) g(72)))
(89)
```

Figure 10.4.10   Procedures for stack-allocated environments

```
(define apply-proc/stack
  (lambda ()
    (find-all-argcont top-ptr
      (lambda (proc proc-env vk)
        (variant-case proc
          (prim-1 (unary-op)
            (let ((ans (unary-op (unary-arg top-ptr))))
              (pop-to-ptr! vk)
              (apply-valcont/stack ans dummy)))
          (prim-2 (binary-op)
            (let ((ans (binary-op (binary-arg-1 top-ptr) (binary-arg-2 top-ptr))))
              (pop-to-ptr! vk)
              (apply-valcont/stack ans dummy)))
          (proc (formals body)
            (make-return-valcont! vk proc-env formals)
            (set! env-reg top-ptr)
            (eval-exp/stack body))
          (else (error "Invalid primitive operation:" proc)))))))

(define apply-env/stack
  (lambda (env var)
    (if (= env -1)
        (apply-valcont/stack (init-env var) dummy)
        (case (stack-ref env)
          ((*return)
           (extract env 3
             (lambda (ignored-vk env formals ak)
               (if (memq var formals)
                   (letrec
                     ((loop (lambda (formals ak)
                              (case (stack-ref ak)
                                ((*rest)
                                 (extract ak 2
                                   (lambda (val env-or-dummy ak)
                                     (if (eq? var (car formals))
                                         (apply-valcont/stack val env-or-dummy)
                                         (loop (cdr formals) ak)))))
                                (else (error "Invalid continuation"))))))
                     (loop (reverse formals) ak))
                   (apply-env/stack env var)))))
          (else (error "Invalid environment:" env))))))
```

and its trace is found in figure 10.4.11. In the trace, the numbers on the left are stack references. Each snapshot is concerned with what positions on the stack have changed. Stack pointers are preceded by an indicator of its type: E for environment, S for static link, D for dynamic link, and A for argument list. With the exception of the final value continuation, each tag is formed by concatenating * to the first letter of each part of the hyphenated continuation name. So, rest-argcont becomes *ra, etc. Since each procedure uses a different formal parameter list, the procedure can be identified by just referring to #(proc formals ..). Primitives are expressed by naming the primitive with a tag that indicates its arity. Operands and formal parameters are enclosed in parentheses. Lines beginning with ==> contain the four important locations that are used in apply-proc/stack.

In figure 10.4.12 we present the state of the stack at line 30-21 of figure 10.4.11. This demonstrates that static links from two activation records can reference the same location, whereas dynamic links always reference different locations. The boldface boxes that contain three items of information can be conceptually thought of as one box, so that pointers to 20, 19, and 18 can be treated as a pointer to location 20. When this is done, we can say that the static links are a subset of the dynamic links. For example, there is a dynamic link, but not a static link, that references location 20.

We have succeeded in freeing our interpreter from reliance on the heap by using stack allocation, but this has come at substantial cost. We have given up two desirable features: upwards funargs (but see exercise 10.4.2) and tail recursion.

In order to deallocate the stack safely on procedure exit, we introduced a restriction on the interpreted language: it no longer allows procedures to be returned as values from other procedures or to be stored in heap-allocated data structures. This restriction explains why most programming languages do not allow upward funargs: language designers typically assume implementors will insist on using stack-allocated environments. Of course, Scheme allows upward funargs, so environments cannot always be stack allocated in Scheme. Procedures that are passed to other procedures as arguments, termed *downward funargs*, do not pose this problem. Downward funargs must be represented as closures, but their environments may be stack allocated.

We have derived an interpreter for a language with the no-upward-funarg rule, for this rule is the norm in contemporary languages. This restriction is often unfortunate, however. We have shown many examples of the power of upward funargs, but their uses extend well beyond these. Of course, heap allocation of environments is one way of avoiding restrictions on upward funargs. We explore others in the exercises.

Figure 10.4.11 Stack trace

```
0-0: *final-v
3-1: *pv (89) E-1
3-1: *aa #(proc (x) ..) E-1
6-4: *fv (89) E-1
6-4: *ra 89 dummy
==> #(proc (x) ..) E-1 A6 D0
8-7: S-1 (x)
10-9: *rv D0
13-11: *pv (#(proc (g) ..)) E8
13-11: *aa #(proc (f) ..) E8
16-14: *fv (#(proc (g) ..)) E8
16-14: *ra #(proc (g) ..) E8
==> #(proc (f) ..) E8 A16 D10
18-17: S8 (f)
20-19: *rv D10
23-21: *pv (#(proc (y) ..)) E18
23-21: *aa #(proc (g) ..) E8
26-24: *fv (#(proc (y) ..)) E18
26-24: *ra #(proc (y) ..) E18
==> #(proc (g) ..) E8 A26 D20
28-27: S8 (g)
30-29: *rv D20
33-31: *pv (72) E28
33-31: *aa #(proc (y) ..) E18
36-34: *fv (72) E28
36-34: *ra 72 dummy
==> #(proc (y) ..) E18 A36 D30
38-37: S18 (y)
40-39: *rv D30
43-41: *pv (x y) E38
43-41: *aa #(prim-2 -) dummy
46-44: *fv (x y) E38
46-44: *ra 89 dummy
49-47: *fv (y) E38
49-47: *ra 72 dummy
==> #(prim-2 +) dummy A49 D40
40-31: *rv D30 S18 (y) *ra 72 dummy *aa #(proc (y) ..) E18
30-21: *rv D20 S8 (g) *ra #(proc (y) ..) E18 *aa #(proc (g) ..) E8
20-11: *rv D10 S8 (f) *ra #(proc (g) ..) E8 *aa #(proc (f) ..) E8
10-1: *rv D0 S-1 (x) *ra 89 dummy *aa #(proc (x) ..) E-1
0-0: *final-v
161
```

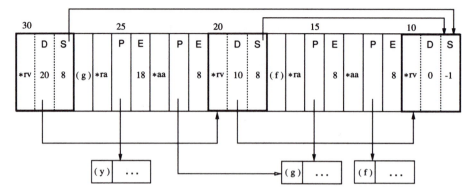

P Procedure
E Environment
S Static link
D Dynamic link

Figure 10.4.12   Static and dynamic links

Besides the exclusion of upward funargs, we have paid another price for the allocation of argument lists on the control stack: our interpreter is no longer properly tail recursive. Each time a procedure is called, even when the call is in tail position, the control stack is extended by pushing a return value continuation. Thus tail-form programs no longer exhibit iterative control behavior. We saw in chapter 8 that this is a major disadvantage. As in the case of upward funargs, there are strategies for recovering proper tail recursion when argument lists are stack allocated, though at present they are not widely used. See, for example, exercise 10.4.11.

- *Exercise 10.4.3*
  Add if, let, begin, and := to this interpreter. □

- *Exercise 10.4.4*
  Add letrecproc to the language using environments, as developed in section 5.6. □

- *Exercise 10.4.5*

Using the results of the previous two exercises, solidify your understanding of how dynamic and static links work by drawing the stack diagrams for the evaluation of the following expression.

```
letrecproc p(f, g, n) =
  if zero(n)
    then f(0)
    else let t = if even(n)
                 then proc (x) f(+(x, n))
                 else proc (x) g(+(x, n))
         in p(t, g, -(n, 1))
in p(proc (x) x, proc (x) x, 4)
```

☐

- *Exercise 10.4.6*

Finish the imperative transformation on the last interpreter of this section, so that all procedures communicate via registers, including *find-all-argcont*. ☐

○ *Exercise 10.4.7*

The argument continuation tags now serve only to allow the interpreter to search through and locate the end of an argument list. Eliminate this search in the definition of `apply-argcont` by including additional information about the total number of stack locations occupied by the arguments. Also eliminate the argument continuation tags. ☐

○ *Exercise 10.4.8*

Avoid the linear search for the *all continuation by maintaining a register (sometimes called the *base pointer*) containing a pointer to its location in the stack. ☐

○ *Exercise 10.4.9*

Is it possible to move the argument continuations to the stack without moving the value continuations to the stack at the same time, or to move the value continuations without moving the argument continuations? ☐

○ *Exercise 10.4.10*

Avoid reversing the formals list by searching upward in the stack, starting with the *all continuation. ☐

○ *Exercise 10.4.11*

It can be determined statically, that is, by analysis of program text, whether a call is in tail position. When evaluation of such a tail call begins, there will be a return value continuation for the currently executing procedure on top of the control stack. The argument continuations for the tail call will be placed on top of this return value continuation. Since control need not return to the procedure making the call, its arguments are no longer necessary. This allows the control stack to be collapsed prior to the call by copying its argument list and *return continuation down over the locations previously occupied by the argument list and *return continuation of the procedure making the call. Thus as the result of a tail call one argument list and return value continuation is created and one is destroyed, so there is no net growth in the number of return value continuations. This technique is called *tail call optimization*. (Compilers may refine this technique so that in specific instances the number of stack elements that need to be copied is reduced, or it may even be possible to eliminate copying altogether.)

Modify our interpreter to perform tail call optimization. ☐

○ *Exercise 10.4.12*

When accessing a nonlocal variable binding (one with a lexical depth greater than zero), one static link is traversed for every level of lexical depth. An alternate representation of closures allows variable references to be performed in constant time and also allows upward funargs to be supported while argument lists are stack allocated. With this representation, a closure is a vector containing, in addition to the procedure, the bindings of all its free variables. Bindings that are assignable (with `varassign`) must be represented by cells that are shared by any closures that close over them. In this way static links are avoided. Compiled code can access a nonlocal (free) variable binding by indexing into the closure's vector using an offset computed at compile time. This makes access to nonlocal variables more efficient, at the expense of less efficient closure creation.

Modify our interpreter to use this closure representation. You will first need to write a procedure to compute the free variables of a procedure. You may also need to store variable binding names as well as their values. ☐

○ *Exercise 10.4.13*

Another approach to achieving constant time variable access is to use a *display*. The idea is to collect all of the static links associated with the current environment and store them in a vector. If the lexical depth of variable references is precomputed, it is then possible to access the appropriate environment contour in constant time. Since there is only one global display, it is in general necessary to update the display when a procedure is called and to restore its previous state when the procedure returns. Thus increased efficiency of nonlocal variable access is obtained at the expense of decreased procedure call efficiency. Since most program variables typically have a low lexical depth, this tradeoff is seldom favorable, but it is still useful at times. (Also, displays do not solve the upward funarg problem as closure-vectors do, since the environment contours remain stack allocated.)

Modify our interpreter to use a display. ☐

o *Exercise 10.4.14*

Another way to solve the no-upward-funarg problem is to convert the source program to continuation-passing style. Then the only procedure that ever "returns" is the final value continuation. What is wrong with this solution? ☐

o *Exercise 10.4.15*

Just as stack allocation of environments makes it more difficult to implement upward funargs, so stack allocation of continuations makes it more difficult to implement first-class continuations, such as those provided by `callcc` of section 9.3. When control information has been captured in a first-class continuation, it is essential that it not be lost due to popping of the control stack (at least as long as the first-class continuation is accessible). A brute-force solution is to copy the entire control stack into a heap-allocated structure whenever a first-class continuation is created. This approach is acceptable only when first-class continuations are infrequently created, however, refinements of this technique allow first-class continuations to be supported along with stack allocation of control information with only a very small performance penalty.

Modify an interpreter with stack allocated continuations to support `callcc`. ☐

10.5 Summary

A program in first-order tail form can be converted easily to iterative form, in which binding is replaced by variable assignment and a procedure call is a tail call of no arguments, which is effectively a jump. Therefore a program in first-order tail form is effectively a flowchart.

If the transformation to iterative form is applied to a program obtained by converting to continuation-passing style, the continuations can be stack-allocated, rather than heap-allocated.

If this transformation is applied to an interpreter that does not support first-class continuations, then continuations can be represented using a stack, but environments are still allocated from the heap. By further transformations, the environment can also be allocated on the stack. This greatly simplifies storage management for the interpreter, at the expense of losing procedures as first-class values and of losing the proper implementation of tail-recursion. Common imperative languages have traditionally used this design strategy.

11   Scanners and Parsers

Humans generate programs as strings of characters, using rules of concrete syntax. Interpreters and compilers cannot attach meaning to programs until their characters are grouped into meaningful units. For clarity and efficiency this analysis is divided into two parts: scanning and parsing.

Scanning is the process of analyzing a sequence of characters into larger units, called *lexical items, lexemes,* or *tokens*. This process is sometimes called *lexical* scanning. Typical tokens are variables, keywords, numbers, punctuation, whitespace, and comments. The output of a scanner is a sequence of tokens. These are represented using a convenient data structure, so that later processing stages do not have to deal with the details of character codes and the like. Thus, scanning creates a token sequence that abstracts a character sequence by removing unnecessary details.

Parsing organizes a sequence of tokens into syntactic elements such as expressions, statements, and blocks. These are generally specified using BNF or some equivalent formalism. The syntactic elements are typically nested, so the output of a parser is usually called a *parse tree* or *abstract syntax tree*, and they provide convenient access to the syntactic components of a program.

11.1 Lexical Scanning Using Finite Automata

In every language, part of the design is the specification of the lexical structure of the language. Typical pieces of such a specification might be:

- Any sequence of spaces and newlines is equivalent to a single space.

- A comment begins with % and continues until the end of the line.

- An identifier is a sequence of letters and digits starting with a letter, and a variable is an identifier that is not a keyword.

These specifications serve to define the lexical items or tokens of the language. A scanner analyzes a sequence of characters and returns a sequence of corresponding tokens. One could take a specification of the tokens, such as that given above, and write from scratch a program to do scanning. Such an approach is error prone, however, and it is difficult to modify the scanner if the specification changes.

A better approach is to introduce a formal model for the specification of tokens. We can then implement this model in various ways. In this section we introduce finite automata as a model for scanning. We then show how to implement this model using a few higher-order procedures that abstract the basic actions of a scanner.

We can specify tokens in a formal way using *finite automata*, also known as *finite state machines*. A finite automaton is a machine that takes a sequence of characters and produces a result in the following way: At any given moment, a finite automaton is in one of a finite number of *states*. At each step of operation, the automaton takes a character from the sequence. Based on this character and the current state, it may do one of two things: *halt*, producing a result, or *move to a new state*, becoming ready to consume more of the sequence. These actions are sometimes called *transitions*.

A finite automaton is specified by giving a *start state,* in which it begins to process the character sequence, and a *transition function* that specifies the next state or halts with a result for various possible combinations of character and current state. As an illustration, the table in figure 11.1.1 indicates the transition function of a finite automaton with start state `start-state`. It formally specifies the identifier, comment, and whitespace tokens previously defined.

Another method of representing a transition function is to draw a graph. The nodes of the graph represent the various states and the edges the possible transitions between states. The edges are directed so that they connect each state with the possible next states. Each edge is labeled with the characters that affect the transition. See figure 11.1.2 for a graph corresponding to the above table.

Initially the automaton is in state `start-state`. Based on the first character, it enters `identifier-state`, `whitespace-state`, or `comment-state`, depending on whether the character is the beginning of an identifier, whitespace, or comment. The automaton continues in that state, collecting the characters in the token until it sees the first character that is *not* in the token at which point it halts. This signifies completion of the token.

State	Character	Next State	Result
`start-state`	any letter	`identifier-state`	
`start-state`	space or newline	`whitespace-state`	
`start-state`	`%`	`comment-state`	
`start-state`	anything else		`error`
`identifier-state`	any letter or digit	`identifier-state`	
`identifier-state`	anything else		`identifier`
`whitespace-state`	space or newline	`whitespace-state`	
`whitespace-state`	anything else		`whitespace`
`comment-state`	any except newline	`comment-state`	
`comment-state`	newline		`comment`

Figure 11.1.1   Finite automaton table for a scanner

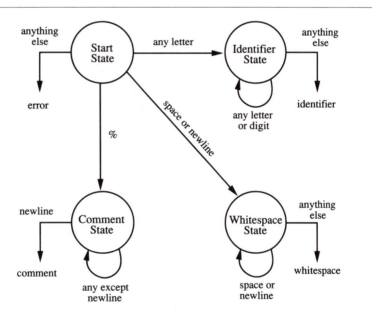

Figure 11.1.2   Finite automaton diagram for a scanner

For example, consider the action of the automaton on `foo3(bar)`.

State:	`start-state`
Character:	`f`
State:	`identifier-state`
Character:	`o`
State:	`identifier-state`
Character:	`o`
State:	`identifier-state`
Character:	`3`
State:	`identifier-state`
Character:	`(`
Result:	`identifier`

When the automaton sees the left parenthesis, it concludes that the current token is finished and returns `identifier`, signifying that an identifier has been found.

Of course, to make this into a useful language-processing tool, we need to add some additional features to our automaton. Not only should it return the symbol `identifier`, but it should report which identifier was found. To do this, we equip our automaton with a buffer in which it can collect the characters as they are seen. Furthermore, we also need to make sure that the terminating character (the left parenthesis in our example) is not lost, since it is part of the next token. We shall see how to accomplish these tasks in the next section.

11.2 Simulating a Scanning Automaton

We would like to write programs that model the behavior of such automata. Since an automaton finds only the first token, if we wish to find all the tokens, the automaton can be called repeatedly. We shall see how to do this later. Our goal, of course, is not to build a program corresponding only to the automaton we sketched but to be able to build any program of this sort. We therefore create a general design and some standard components from which such programs can be built. Using the power of functional abstraction, we represent the components of our automata as procedures.

At each state, the automaton looks at the next character and decides what action to perform. Thus we define *scanner states* to be procedures that take a character as an argument and return a scanner action. These actions correspond to the transitions, or edges, in a finite automaton.

A common scanner action is to shift a character from the sequence to the buffer of characters that have been scanned as part of a token. This suggests that scanner actions be procedures that take two arguments: a buffer and a character sequence. When the scanner detects the end of a token, it returns the token and the character sequence. Thus we define *scanner actions* to be procedures that take a buffer and a character sequence and return a token and character sequence.

When a shift action is performed, it is not known whether the current token is complete. Thus the next action is passed a new buffer, formed by adding the character at the head of the character sequence to the old buffer, and the tail of the character sequence. We express this with the `shift` procedure of figure 11.2.1, which is passed an action and returns another action. For example, (`shift` *action*) returns an action that takes the first character from a sequence, places it in a buffer, and then runs *action* on the remaining character sequence and extended buffer.

Assuming sequences are represented as lists, the behavior of the `shift` procedure may be illustrated by this equation:

```
    ((shift action) buffer          '(a b ...))
⇒ (action          (cons 'a buffer)  '(b ...))
```

Here is a slightly longer example:

```
    ((shift (shift (shift action))) '() '(a b c d ...))
⇒ ((shift (shift action))          '(a)  '(b c d ...))
⇒ ((shift action)                  '(b a)  '(c d ...))
⇒ (action                          '(c b a)  '(d ...))
```

In this example we see how elementary actions can be strung together to make complex actions, and how the behavior of the program mimics that of a machine with two registers. We also note that the characters are accumulated in the buffer in reverse order.

We have used `char-seq-head` and `char-seq-tail` instead of `car` and `cdr` so that we may represent a sequence of characters in some way other than as a list. We shall see later how this might be useful.

A second type of scanner action is to drop the first character of the sequence. This is useful, for example, when the first character is a whitespace or comment character. We express this with the procedure *drop* of figure 11.2.1. Like *shift*, *drop* is really an action maker, since it takes an action and returns an action.

Figure 11.2.1   Scanner actions

```
(define shift
  (lambda (next-action)
    (lambda (buffer char-seq)
      (next-action
        (cons (char-seq-head char-seq) buffer)
        (char-seq-tail char-seq)))))

(define drop
  (lambda (next-action)
    (lambda (buffer char-seq)
      (next-action buffer (char-seq-tail char-seq)))))

(define goto-scanner-state
  (lambda (state)
    (lambda (buffer char-seq)
      (let ((next-action (state (char-seq-head char-seq))))
        (next-action buffer char-seq)))))

(define-record scanner-answer (token unscanned))

(define emit
  (lambda (cooker)
    (lambda (buffer char-seq)
      (make-scanner-answer
        (cooker (reverse buffer))
        char-seq))))
```

The equational picture for *drop* is

$$((\text{drop } action) \; buffer \; '(a \; b \; ...))$$
$$\Rightarrow (action \qquad\qquad buffer \qquad '(b \; ...))$$

Thus we might compute as follows:

$$((\text{drop } (\text{drop } (\text{shift } action))) \; '() \; '(a \; b \; c \; d \; ...))$$
$$\Rightarrow ((\text{drop } (\text{shift } action)) \qquad '() \qquad '(b \; c \; d \; ...))$$
$$\Rightarrow ((\text{shift } action) \qquad\qquad '() \qquad\quad '(c \; d \; ...))$$
$$\Rightarrow (action \qquad\qquad\qquad '(c) \qquad\quad '(d \; ...))$$

Next we address the control behavior of our machine. To do this, let us reconsider the notion of a *state* of a finite state machine. We described the behavior of our machine as a transition function that took as inputs a state and a character and produced as output the action to be performed. If we curry this function, we get for each state a function from characters to actions. Therefore, in our simulation we model a state as a procedure that takes an input character and returns an action.

To invoke a state, we introduce the procedure *goto-scanner-state* (see figure 11.2.1), which takes a state and returns an action. Executing (goto-scanner-state *state*) applies *state* to the first character to find the next action to execute and then invokes this action on the current buffer and character sequence. The effect is to go to the given state. A typical action might be expressed by

```
(drop (drop (shift (goto-scanner-state state))))
```

Our machine finishes when the next character is not part of the current token. The current buffer is then passed to a procedure that builds a convenient data structure representing the token. We call such a procedure a *cooker* because it "cooks" the raw characters into a token. The buffer is reversed before being passed to the cooker, so that it sees the characters in their original order. The new token is then returned along with the sequence of unprocessed characters. We use a record type to return these two values. See the definition of `emit` in figure 11.2.1. Note that `char-seq` is returned as is, so that the first character in the sequence can become the first character of the next token.

Before writing cookers, we must be specific about the representation of tokens. We often need only a small amount of information about a token, such as "this token is an identifier," "this token is an assignment symbol," or "this token is a left parenthesis." We call this information the *class* of the token. For some classes of tokens we are also interested in additional information. For a variable we need to know which symbol represents the variable, and for a number we need to know what number is represented by the digits in the token. We call this additional information the *data* of the token. We therefore represent a token by a record containing its class (represented as a symbol) and its data.

The procedure *cook-punctuation* takes a symbol identifying a class and returns a cooker that ignores the buffer and produces a token of the indicated class. This is useful for parentheses, assignment symbols (:=), etc. See figure 11.2.2. The procedure *cook-number* converts the buffer to a number using the Scheme procedure *string->number*.

The procedure *cook-identifier* cooks potential program variables. We might simply record the list of characters already in the buffer as the data of

Figure 11.2.2   Cooking procedures for a scanner

```scheme
(define-record token (class data))

(define cook-punctuation
  (lambda (class)
    (lambda (buffer)
      (make-token class '*))))

(define cook-number
  (lambda (buffer)
    (make-token 'number
      (string->number (list->string buffer)))))

(define cook-identifier
  (lambda (buffer)
    (let ((symbol (string->symbol (list->string buffer))))
      (if (memq symbol keywords-list)
          (make-token symbol '*)
          (make-token 'variable symbol)))))
```

identifier tokens, but then determining whether two identifiers were the same would be time consuming. Instead, we convert each buffer into a unique value that the rest of the language processor can easily handle.

In most language processors, this is done by building a *symbol table*: a database of all the identifiers appearing in a program. An identifier is represented by a reference to a record in this database (for example, a pointer to an entry in a hash table). Whenever an identifier appears, the scanner consults the database to see if the identifier is already there. If it is, a reference to its entry is returned. If not, a new entry is created, and a reference to the new entry is returned. Then it is easy for the rest of the language processor to determine if two identifiers are the same: it just compares the references. This is easier than comparing the strings. Also, the database allows a more sophisticated language processor to keep track of other attributes of an identifier, such as its type, internal representation, etc. For our interpreters, however, all we need is a quick way of testing identifiers for equality.

Scheme maintains its own symbol table, with one entry per symbol. Scheme represents these symbols internally as pointers into this table. The Scheme reader and the procedure *string->symbol* make or find entries in this table. Thus our scanner uses *string->symbol* instead of maintaining its own table.

When *cook-identifier* has obtained the symbol corresponding to the characters in the buffer, it checks whether this symbol is in a global list of keywords. If the symbol is a keyword, it produces a token using the keyword as its class (as *cook-punctuation* does); otherwise, it produces a `variable` token. Of course, this precludes using `number` or `variable` as a keyword.

Now we have enough machinery to write a sample automaton. See figure 11.2.3 and exercise 11.2.1. Each scanner state is a procedure that takes a character and returns an action. We have four states: one for the starting state, in which we have seen no characters, and one for each of the three major classes of tokens. In *scanner-identifier-state*, for example, the machine is accumulating an identifier token. So long as the next character is alphabetic or numeric, it shifts that character into the buffer. If it is any other character (either whitespace or a delimiter), it is not part of the current token, so the machine performs an (`emit cook-identifier`) action. The offending character remains at the head of the sequence to be processed later. We choose the character `#\nul` arbitrarily to represent some character, not in the character set of the language being scanned, to act as a character sequence terminator. Similarly, we use a token of class `end-marker` to act as a token sequence terminator. Since our automaton is built as a scanner state, we start it by using *goto-scanner-state*. See the procedure *scan-once* of figure 11.2.4. Here is a simple test:

```
> (define char-seq-head car)
> (define char-seq-tail cdr)
> (define keywords-list '())
> (define raw-data
    (append (string->list "abc is 652") (list #\nul)))
> (set! x (scan-once scanner-start-state raw-data))
> x
#(scanner-answer
  #(token variable abc)
  (#\space #\i #\s #\space #\6 #\5 #\2 #\nul))
> (set! x (scan-once scanner-start-state
            (scanner-answer->unscanned x)))
> x
#(scanner-answer
  #(token variable is)
  (#\space #\6 #\5 #\2 #\nul))
> (set! x (scan-once scanner-start-state
            (scanner-answer->unscanned x)))
> x
```

Figure 11.2.3   A scanner written in functional style

```
(define scanner-start-state
  (lambda (c)
    (cond
      ((char-whitespace? c)
       (drop (goto-scanner-state scanner-start-state)))
      ((char-alphabetic? c)
       (shift (goto-scanner-state scanner-identifier-state)))
      ((char-numeric? c)
       (shift (goto-scanner-state scanner-number-state)))
      ((char=? c #\%)
       (drop (goto-scanner-state scanner-comment-state)))
      ((char=? c #\()
       (drop (emit (cook-punctuation 'lparen))))
      ((char=? c #\))
       (drop (emit (cook-punctuation 'rparen))))
      ((char=? c #\nul)
       (emit (cook-punctuation 'end-marker)))
      (else (scan-error c)))))

(define scanner-identifier-state
  (lambda (c)
    (cond
      ((char-alphabetic? c)
       (shift (goto-scanner-state scanner-identifier-state)))
      ((char-numeric? c)
       (shift (goto-scanner-state scanner-identifier-state)))
      (else (emit cook-identifier)))))

(define scanner-number-state
  (lambda (c)
    (cond
      ((char-numeric? c)
       (shift (goto-scanner-state scanner-number-state)))
      (else (emit cook-number)))))

(define scanner-comment-state
  (lambda (c)
    (cond
      ((char=? c #\newline)
       (drop (goto-scanner-state scanner-start-state)))
      (else (drop (goto-scanner-state scanner-comment-state))))))
```

Figure 11.2.4 Procedures to drive a scanner

```
(define scan-once
  (lambda (start-state char-seq)
    ((goto-scanner-state start-state) '() char-seq)))

(define scan-char-seq
  (lambda (start-state char-seq)
    (let ((next-answer (scan-once start-state char-seq)))
      (variant-case next-answer
        (scanner-answer (token unscanned)
          (make-token-seq
            token
            (lambda ()
              (if (eq? (token->class token) 'end-marker)
                  '()
                  (scan-char-seq start-state unscanned)))))))))
```

```
#(scanner-answer
 #(token number 652)
 (#\nul))
> (set! x (scan-once scanner-start-state
                (scanner-answer->unscanned x)))
> x
#(scanner-answer
 #(token end-marker *)
 (#\nul))
```

Each call of *scan-once* returns the next token and the unscanned sequence
of characters. To obtain a sequence of all the tokens corresponding to a
sequence of characters, we use a loop that recognizes the end-marker token. See the procedure *scan-char-seq* of figure 11.2.4. Here we have used
make-token-seq to build the answer. The procedure *make-token-seq* takes
a thunk as its second argument. This allows for the possibility that the token
sequence may be represented as a stream rather than as an ordinary list. For
an ordinary list, we would simply use

```
(define make-token-seq
  (lambda (token thunk)
    (cons token (thunk))))
```

as we did in section 4.5.2. In this case we could repeat our test.

```
> (scan-char-seq scanner-start-state
    (append (string->list "abc is 652") (list #\nul)))
(#(token variable abc)
 #(token variable is)
 #(token number 652)
 #(token end-marker *))
```

This completes our scanner, but we have done more than write a single scanner. We have developed a set of components that may be used to assemble any scanner.

- *Exercise 11.2.1*
  Provide a suitable definition for the procedure *scan-error* used in figure 11.2.3. The procedure *scan-error* should return an action. ☐

- *Exercise 11.2.2*
  When building large programs, it is not good programming style to clutter up the global name space with names like `scanner-identifier-state` that do not need to be known globally. Rewrite the procedures in figure 11.2.3 using `letrec` to hide all the state names except for `scanner-start-state`. ☐

- *Exercise 11.2.3*
  Extend our grammar and scanner to allow numbers to have an optional sign and decimal point (with at least one digit required before the decimal point), such as 142, 12.3, -5., and +0.9876. ☐

- *Exercise 11.2.4*
  A string begins with a double quote and ends with the next double quote that is not immediately preceded by a backslash character (\). A double quote character preceded by a backslash is interpreted as a single double quote character in the string, and a sequence of two backslash characters is interpreted as a single backslash character. (The backslash is used here as an *escape* character. Other escape characters or sequences of escape characters are frequently used to indicate nonprinting characters, such as newline and tab.) Extend our grammar and scanner with the lexical class **string**, such as "ab cd" and

  ```
  "!? % ( \\
  )\"(
  % )"
  ```

  ☐

- *Exercise 11.2.5*

  Modify `scanner-start-state` so that it produces comments as tokens rather than dropping them. Represent the datum associated with a comment token as a string. □

○ *Exercise 11.2.6*

  In most programming languages, a number or identifier must be followed by a delimiter, such as whitespace, (,), or ". Thus the character sequence 108ifcar would produce a lexical error. (In most programming languages a number of other special characters, such as +, =, and :, are also delimiters.) This rule also clarifies why ab is a single identifier, ab, and not two identifiers, a and b. Modify `scanner-start-state` so that numbers and identifiers must be followed by a delimiter. □

We have used `char-seq-head` and `char-seq-tail` to manipulate character sequences so that we have the option of representing them as something other than lists. For example, we could store the characters of the initial character sequence in a globally bound string, called `chars-to-scan`, and represent character sequences via a number that indexes a character of the string. The characters that have yet to be scanned will be the indexed character and all those that follow it in the string. For this representation we define

```
(define chars-to-scan '*)

(define char-seq-head
  (lambda (n)
    (string-ref chars-to-scan n)))

(define char-seq-tail
  (lambda (n)
    (+ n 1)))
```

We also must define `scan-string` so that the string it is passed is communicated to `char-seq-head` via `chars-to-scan`. This is one of the rare cases where an assignment is appropriate in our programs.

```
(define scan-string
  (lambda (start-state char-string)
    (set! chars-to-scan
      (string-append char-string (string #\nul)))
    (scan-char-seq start-state 0)))
```

- *Exercise 11.2.7*

  Modify the scanner so that its character and token sequences are represented as streams (cf. section 4.5.2). ☐

- *Exercise 11.2.8*

  Using the techniques of this section, produce a scanner for the concrete syntax of the interpreted language as specified in appendix C. For the list of keywords, use

  ```
  (if then else let in proc begin end letmutable letrecproc letrec
   during letdynamic letarray letproc method define definearray
   simpleclass simpleinstance class instance abort letcont callcc
   coroutine wind unwind within sum)
  ```

  An answer to this exercise may be found in appendix E. ☐

- *Exercise 11.2.9*

  We have represented automaton states as procedures, with an entire automaton being represented by its start state. Another approach would be to

  1. represent states as symbols, called *labels,*
  2. define automata to be procedures that map labels to scanner actions,
  3. define actions to be procedures whose arguments include an automaton, as well as a buffer and a character sequence, and
  4. replace goto-scanner-state by *goto-label*, which takes an automaton and a label and applies the automaton to the label.

  Implement a scanner corresponding to the automaton of figure 11.1.1 and figure 11.1.2 using this approach. ☐

- *Exercise 11.2.10*

  Make the buffer representation independent by adding the procedures *make-empty-buffer*, *buffer-extend*, and *buffer-contents* to the procedures in figure 11.2.1. Define these procedures using a global vector of bounded size. Also test the scanner with the procedures that follow. What are the advantages and disadvantages of the two representations? Why is it okay to use side-effecting procedures with the following representation?

```
(define make-empty-buffer
  (lambda ()
    (let ((c (cons '() '*)))
      (set-cdr! c c)
      c)))

(define buffer-contents car)

(define buffer-extend
  (lambda (value buffer)
    (let ((end-cell (cdr buffer))
          (new-cell (cons value '())))
      (set-cdr! end-cell new-cell)
      (if (eq? end-cell buffer)
          (set-car! buffer new-cell)
          (set-cdr! buffer new-cell))
      buffer)))
```

⬚

11.3 Constructing a Predictive Parser

We now address the problem of parsing the sequence of tokens returned by a scanner to obtain a parse tree. For each scanner or scanner/parser combination there is an associated set of character sequences that is accepted without error. Sets that can be defined in this way by finite state automata are said to be *regular*. Typically the set of character sequences that makes up a token is regular, however, the set of token sequences that correspond to the programs in a language is seldom a regular set. Programs are typically members of *context-free* sets defined by context-free grammars. Regular sets are also context free, but many context-free sets are not regular.

The property that distinguishes context-free and regular sets, and hence distinguishes parsing from scanning, is that context-free elements may be nested to arbitrary depth. For example, expressions may typically contain subexpressions, with no limit on the depth of nesting. It is possible, though awkward, for scanners (finite state automata) to recognize nested structures if there is a limit on the depth of nesting, but they cannot recognize structures with arbitrarily deep nesting.

Although the BNF grammar of exercise 11.2.8 defines a regular set, in general, BNF grammars define context-free sets. A simple programming language might be described in BNF as follows:

⟨command⟩ ::= begin ⟨command⟩ ; ⟨command⟩ end
       | while ⟨expression⟩ do ⟨command⟩
       | if ⟨expression⟩ then ⟨command⟩ else ⟨command⟩
       | ⟨variable⟩ := ⟨expression⟩

⟨expression⟩ ::= ⟨variable⟩
       | ⟨constant⟩
       | (⟨expression⟩ + ⟨expression⟩)

The job of a parser is to take a sequence of tokens and analyze it to see if it fits the form specified by a grammar. Before implementing a parser for the grammar above, we specify its input and output. The input to the parser is a sequence of tokens, so the grammar we are really working with is

⟨command⟩ ::= begin ⟨command⟩ semicolon ⟨command⟩ end
       | while ⟨expression⟩ do ⟨command⟩
       | if ⟨expression⟩ then ⟨command⟩ else ⟨command⟩
       | ⟨variable⟩ assign-sym ⟨expression⟩

⟨expression⟩ ::= ⟨variable⟩
       | ⟨constant⟩
       | lparen ⟨expression⟩ plus-sym ⟨expression⟩ rparen

where begin, end, etc., are the token classes corresponding to the keywords and semicolon, assign-sym, plus-sym, lparen, and rparen are the token classes corresponding to the various special characters or character sequences appearing in the token sequence. We assume the scanner has removed comments and whitespace.

The result from the parser must do more than indicate whether the token sequence meets the specifications of the grammar. An interpreter or compiler needs to know which portions of the token sequence are associated with which elements of the grammar. This indicates *why* the string belongs to the language defined by the grammar. As we saw in chapter 3, this knowledge is conveyed by a *parse tree* or *abstract syntax tree*. We form parse trees using records, with a distinct record type associated with each production alternative of a grammar. For our sample grammar, we use the following record types.

```
(define-record compound-command (cmd1 cmd2))
(define-record while-command (exp cmd))
(define-record if-command (exp cmd1 cmd2))
(define-record assignment-command (variable-symbol exp))

(define-record var-expression (variable-symbol))
(define-record constant-expression (number))
(define-record sum-expression (exp1 exp2))
```

There is one type of parse tree for each kind of command and expression. As an example, the program

```
begin x := foo; while x do x := (x + bar) end
```

is represented by this tree

```
#(compound-command
  #(assignment-command x #(var-expression foo))
  #(while-command
    #(var-expression x)
    #(assignment-command x
      #(sum-expression #(var-expression x) #(var-expression bar)))))
```

Abstract syntax trees do not contain entries for tokens, such as keywords and semicolons, that carry no information. The interior nodes of the syntax tree correspond to productions, whereas its leaves correspond to information-carrying tokens, such as variables and numbers.

• *Exercise 11.3.1*
In the second assignment statement of the above syntax tree, why is the first occurrence of x represented by x, but the second by #(var-expression x)? □

In this section we illustrate one way of writing parsers by hand. We do this by extending the approach used in our scanner. Our scanner took a character sequence and returned a token and a sequence of those characters remaining after scanning the characters of the token. Our parser will take a token sequence and return a parse tree displaying the structure represented by an initial series of tokens and a sequence of the remaining tokens.

We use a strategy called *predictive parsing*: the action to be performed at each step is determined by a nonterminal to be matched and the first token of the sequence. We therefore introduce the notion of a *parser state*, analogous to a scanner state, that takes a token and returns a parser action. Each state looks at the first element of the token sequence, decides which production to use, and then tries to match some leading portion of the sequence against that production.

The main difference between a parser and a scanner is that when a parser goes from one state to the next, it is always possible to retain a record of the previous state, which a scanner (a finite state automaton) cannot do. This effectively allows parsers to enter states *recursively,* since a return to the previous state is possible when the work of the new state is finished. Thus there is no limit to the depth to which structures recognized by parsers may be nested.

At a given time a parser may have matched some initial elements, say B, C, and D, of some production, say A, with other elements of the production remaining to be matched. We picture this example as follows:

$$A \longrightarrow B \ C \ D \ ? \ \ldots$$

Parsing activity will be done by *parser actions* whose functionality is similar to that of scanner actions: they take a buffer and a token sequence and return a parse tree and a token sequence. The buffer contains information corresponding to the parts of the production that have already been matched (B, C, and D in our example). The two values returned by parser actions are represented using a new record type, `parser-answer`.

The action taken by a parser at a given point in matching a production depends on the next element of the production (? in our example). There are four possibilities, each of which corresponds to an action procedure defined in figure 11.3.1.

1. The next element in the production is a token without data, like a semicolon. We need to check that the next item in the token sequence is indeed a semicolon, but we do not put the semicolon in the parse tree, because it carries no useful information. In general, we check that the next token is of the right class and then drop it. This job is performed by actions returned by the procedure *check/drop*. Once again we use a sequence ADT, including the procedures `token-seq-head` and `token-seq-tail`, to avoid committing to a particular representation of token sequences.

2. The next element in the production is a token with data, such as a variable. Again, we need to check that the next item in the token sequence is of the right class, but in this case, we need to shift its data into the buffer. This is done by actions that *check/shift* returns.

3. There are no more items in the production. In this case, we need to return a syntax tree for the production, along with the remainder of the token

Figure 11.3.1   Parser procedures

```
(define check/drop
  (lambda (class next-action)
    (lambda (buffer token-seq)
      (let ((token (token-seq-head token-seq)))
        (if (eq? (token->class token) class)
            (next-action buffer (token-seq-tail token-seq))
            (error "Syntax error: expecting a" class "not a" token))))))

(define check/shift
  (lambda (class next-action)
    (lambda (buffer token-seq)
      (let ((token (token-seq-head token-seq)))
        (if (eq? (token->class token) class)
            (next-action (cons (token->data token) buffer) (token-seq-tail token-seq))
            (error "Syntax error: expecting a" class "not a" token))))))

(define-record parser-answer (tree unparsed))

(define reduce
  (lambda (prod-name)
    (lambda (buffer token-seq)
      (make-parser-answer
        (apply (get-constructor-from-name prod-name) (reverse buffer))
        token-seq))))

(define goto-parser-state
  (lambda (state)
    (lambda (buffer token-seq)
      (let ((next-action (state (token-seq-head token-seq))))
        (next-action buffer token-seq)))))

(define process-nt
  (lambda (state next-action)
    (lambda (buffer token-seq)
      (let ((next-answer ((goto-parser-state state) '() token-seq)))
        (next-action (cons (parser-answer->tree next-answer) buffer)
          (parser-answer->unparsed next-answer))))))

(define emit-list
  (lambda ()
    (lambda (buffer token-seq)
      (make-parser-answer (reverse buffer) token-seq))))
```

sequence. For historical reasons this is called a *reduce* action, though it is similar to the `emit` action of our scanners. The syntax tree returned by a reduce action is a record whose type is associated with the production that has just been completed. This record will have a field associated with each element of information collected while parsing the production. The buffer contains precisely this information when the reduce action is performed, so all that is required is to apply the record construction procedure associated with the production to the buffer. The procedure `reduce` takes a production name and returns a parser answer record with a parse tree constructed in this way. It reverses the buffer, since the first value in the buffer contains the last piece of information provided by an element of the production. The procedure `get-constructor-from-name` is used to obtain the appropriate record-building procedure when given the production name. Although the procedures of figure 11.3.1 may be used in any parser constructed in this way, the procedure `get-constructor-from-name` is specific to each grammar, just as `keywords-list` is specific to each scanner. For our sample grammar we use

```
(define get-constructor-from-name
  (lambda (prod-name)
    (case prod-name
      ((compound-command) make-compound-command)
      ((while-command) make-while-command)
      ((if-command) make-if-command)
      ((assignment-command) make-assignment-command)
      ((var-expression) make-var-expression)
      ((constant-expression) make-constant-expression)
      ((sum-expression) make-sum-expression)
      (else (error "Invalid production name:" prod-name)))))
```

4. The last, and most interesting, case arises when the next item in the production is a nonterminal. In this case we want to parse the portion of the token sequence that matches the nonterminal. For this we need something like the *goto-scanner-state* action in the scanner. See the procedure *goto-parser-state* in figure 11.3.1, which invokes a parser state on the first token in the sequence, yielding an action that is then applied to the *entire* token sequence.

This is useful for getting states started, but it is not quite what we want because it continues to collect parse trees in the *current* buffer. What we want instead is to generate a fresh parse tree by invoking the parser *recursively,* starting with an empty buffer.

This action is performed by procedures returned by the procedure *process-nt* of figure 11.3.1. The given state is started with the current token sequence and an empty buffer. The state returns with *parser-answer* containing the parse tree for the given nonterminal and the unparsed part of the token sequence. The tree is added to the buffer, and parsing continues by performing the next action with the new buffer and unparsed token sequence.

To illustrate this, imagine that we are working on the production

$$A \longrightarrow B\ C\ D\ X\ \ldots$$

where X is a nonterminal and is the next element in the production. Assuming sequences are represented by lists, at this point the state of our parser looks like this:

```
((process-nt X next-action)
 '(D-tree C-tree B-tree)
 '(x ... y ... ))
```

The parser action returned by (process-nt X *next-action*) is applied to the buffer and the sequence. The buffer contains parse trees for the parts of the token sequence corresponding to the B, C, and D. The token sequence now consists of $(x \ldots y \ldots)$, where $x \ldots$ denotes the tokens corresponding to an X production and $y \ldots$ denotes the remaining tokens. Of course, the parser doesn't know the location of the boundary between the xs and the ys; that is what it has to determine. The procedure *process-nt* starts a parser to match an initial segment of the token sequence against X:

```
((goto-parser-state X) '() '(x ... y ... ))
```

This returns an answer consisting of the parse tree for the $x \ldots$ and the part of the token sequence that follows them:

```
#(parser-answer X-tree '(y ... ))
```

Next, *process-nt* pushes *X-tree* on the buffer and continues parsing the remaining sequence.

```
(next-action
  '(X-tree D-tree C-tree B-tree)
  '(y ... ))
```

Figure 11.3.2   A parser written in functional style

```
(define parse-command
  (lambda (token)
    (case (token->class token)
      ((begin)
       (check/drop 'begin
         (process-nt parse-command
           (check/drop 'semicolon
             (process-nt parse-command
               (check/drop 'end
                 (reduce 'compound-command)))))))
      ((variable)
       (check/shift 'variable
         (check/drop 'assign-sym
           (process-nt parse-expression
             (reduce 'assignment-command)))))
      (else (parse-error token)))))

(define parse-expression
  (lambda (token)
    (case (token->class token)
      ((variable)
       (check/shift 'variable
         (reduce 'var-expression)))
      ((number)
       (check/shift 'number
         (reduce 'constant-expression)))
      ((lparen)
       (check/drop 'lparen
         (process-nt parse-expression
           (check/drop 'plus-sym
             (process-nt parse-expression
               (check/drop 'rparen
                 (reduce 'sum-expression)))))))
      (else (parse-error token)))))
```

Figure 11.3.3   Procedures to drive a parser

```
(define parse-once
  (lambda (start-state token-seq)
    ((goto-parser-state start-state) '() token-seq)))

(define parse-token-seq
  (lambda (start-state token-seq)
    (let ((answer (parse-once start-state token-seq)))
      (variant-case answer
        (parser-answer (tree unparsed)
          (if (eq? (token->class (token-seq-head unparsed))
                   'end-marker)
              tree
              (error "Tokens left over:" unparsed)))))))
```

This accomplishes our goal of finding the parse tree, explaining an initial segment of the token sequence as an instance of production X. (We shall discuss *emit-list* later.)

Now we have enough parsing technology to write a parser for our simple grammar. We do this by writing a set of mutually recursive states. Each state is a procedure that takes a token and dispatches on its class, returning an action. See figure 11.3.2.

A scanner requires a driver loop, but a parser does not, because it only produces a single tree. It is only necessary to invoke the start state of the parser and check that there are no tokens left over when it returns. See the definition of *parse-token-seq* in figure 11.3.3.

● *Exercise 11.3.2*
Finish the parser and scanner for this language. You will have to include ;, +, and := in *scanner-start-state*; while and if commands in *parse-command*; and definitions for *token-seq-head* and *token-seq-tail*. □

In an interactive system, we do not want to produce just a single parse tree. Instead, we must take a stream of tokens and produce a stream of parse trees. A read-eval-print loop may be constructed by modifying the scanning and parsing routines so that the scanner takes a stream of characters (generated by calls to *read-char*) and produces a stream of tokens and the parser takes a stream of tokens and returns a stream of parse trees.

- *Exercise 11.3.3*

Modify the parser driver to create an interactive read-eval-print loop. This loop should call the procedure *top-level-eval*, passing it the parse tree for evaluation. Use the prompt `-->`. The loop should exit when the special token end is encountered prior to parsing a command. If *eval-print* is defined only to write, *read-eval-print* becomes a convenient device for testing the parser. For example,

```
> (read-eval-print)
--> x:=y
#(assignment-command x #(var-expression y))
--> begin x:=y ; u := (v + u) end
#(compound-command
 #(assignment-command x #(var-expression y))
  #(assignment-command u
   #(sum-expression #(var-expression v) #(var-expression u))))
--> begin x:=y ;
         uu := ((x + v) + u) end
#(compound-command
 #(assignment-command x #(var-expression y))
 #(assignment-command uu
  #(sum-expression
   #(sum-expression #(var-expression x) #(var-expression v))
   #(var-expression u))))
--> end
>
```

An answer to this exercise may be found in appendix F. ☐

Our approach to parsing can handle only grammars of a rather restricted form: those with the property that if we know what nonterminal we are looking for and what item is at the head of the token sequence, we can easily determine which production to use. Thus parsing procedures always know what to match next, and matching never fails unless there is a syntactic error in the sequence. This class of grammars is called LL(1). In general, the process of choosing the lexical classes that predict the use of a given production is far more subtle than our examples might suggest. For more details, see the references on compiler theory at the end of the book.

The grammar we used was a simple example of a grammar in this class. We can write more complicated grammars that are still in this class. For example, we often use the Kleene star in grammar rules to indicate sequences of entries, as in

⟨command⟩ ::= `begin` ⟨command⟩ {`semicolon` ⟨command⟩}* `end`

This defines a compound command as a nonempty sequence of commands separated by semicolons and surrounded by a `begin`-`end` pair. For such constructs, we want to build a parse tree that contains a list of parse trees.

```
(define-record compound-command (cmd-list))
```

For example, parsing the command

```
begin C1; C2; C3 end
```

should produce this parse tree:

```
#(compound-command (C1-tree  C2-tree  C3-tree))
```

To do this, we can add a new action, defined by the procedure *emit-list* of figure 11.3.1. This procedure returns the *list* of parse trees in the buffer, without making them into a tree. With this action, we can define compound commands as shown in figure 11.3.4. When the state *parse-command* sees a `begin`, it calls the state *parse-command-list*. The procedure *parse-command-list* parses a command and then goes to state *command-list-loop*, which continues accumulating command trees in its buffer.

For example, assume that $C1$, $C2$, and $C3$ abbreviate sequences of tokens that form commands and that token sequences are represented as lists. Then we may expand the code for *goto-parser-state*, *parse-command*, and *check-drop* to deduce that

```
((goto-parser-state parse-command)
 '()
 '(begin C1 semicolon C2 semicolon C3 end ...))
```

⇒ ```((process-nt parse-command-list next-action)
 '()
 '(C1 semicolon C2 semicolon C3 end ...))
```
```

Figure 11.3.4   Parsing lists of commands using `emit-list`

```
(define parse-command
  (lambda (token)
    (case (token->class token)
      ((begin)
       (check/drop 'begin
         (process-nt parse-command-list
           (check/drop 'end
             (reduce 'compound-command)))))
      ...)))

(define parse-command-list
  (lambda (token)
    (process-nt parse-command
      (goto-parser-state command-list-loop))))

(define command-list-loop
  (lambda (token)
    (case (token->class token)
      ((semicolon)
       (check/drop 'semicolon
         (process-nt parse-command
           (goto-parser-state command-list-loop))))
      ((end) (emit-list)))))
```

where *next-action* is (check/drop 'end (reduce 'compound-command)),

> ⇒ (let ((next-answer *recursive-call*))
>   (*next-action*
>   (cons (parser-answer->tree next-answer) '())
>   (parser-answer->unparsed next-answer)))

Via a subderivation, we compute

> *recursive-call*

> ⇒ ((goto-parser-state parse-command-list)
>   '()
>   '(*C1* semicolon *C2* semicolon *C3* end ...))

> ...

$\Rightarrow$ ((emit-list)
   '(*C3-tree C2-tree C1-tree*)
   '(end ...))

$\Rightarrow$ #(parser-answer
   (*C1-tree C2-tree C3-tree*)
   (end ...))

Continuing the main derivation,

    (let ((next-answer *recursive-call*))
     (*next-action*
      (cons (parser-answer->tree next-answer) '())
      (parser-answer->unparsed next-answer)))

$\Rightarrow$ (let ((next-answer '#(parser-answer
                   (*C1-tree C2-tree C3-tree*)
                   (end ...))))
     (*next-action*
      (cons (parser-answer->tree next-answer) '())
      (parser-answer->unparsed next-answer)))

$\Rightarrow$ (*next-action*
   '((*C1-tree C2-tree C3-tree*))
   '(end ...))

By expanding *next-action*, we continue:

$\Rightarrow$ ((check/drop 'end (reduce 'compound-command))
   '((*C1-tree C2-tree C3-tree*))
   '(end ...))

$\Rightarrow$ ((reduce 'compound-command)
   '((*C1-tree C2-tree C3-tree*))
   '(...))

$\Rightarrow$ #(parser-answer
   #(compound-command
    (*C1-tree C2-tree C3-tree*))
   (...))

Thus the call to the parser returns a compound-command with a single *list* of parse trees for *C1*, *C2*, and *C3*, as desired.

The emit-list action, in conjunction with *goto-parser-state*, is flexible enough to handle most of the repetitive lists that arise in practice.

Modify `parse-command` to accept semicolon-*terminated* compound state-ments, given by

⟨command⟩ ::= begin ⟨command⟩ ; ... ; ⟨command⟩ ; end

instead of the semicolon-separated commands used above. □

● *Exercise 11.3.5*

Using the scanner of exercise 11.2.8, prepare a parser for the interpreted lan-guage as specified in appendix C. Here is a sample program for testing your parser: (see figure 11.3.5)

```
letrecproc
  add(x, y) = if x
              then y
              else add(sub1(x), add1(y));
  mult(x, y) = if x
               then 0
               else if sub1(x)
                    then y
                    else add(y, mult(sub1(x), y))
in let x = 1;
       y = 2;
       z = proc (x, y) mult(add(3, x), y);
       w = proc () add := proc (x, y) x
    in letarray a[8];
               b[add(x, mult(y, x))]
        in begin
            b[add(x, 1)] := 17;
            y := mult(x, b[y]);
            y := add(x, y);
            w();
            z(x, y)
          end
```

□

○ *Exercise 11.3.6*

Extend the parser of exercise 11.3.5 and modify the interpreter in figure 6.1.2 so that some arguments may be passed by reference (use the abstract syntax `brvar (var)`), and others by value. Call-by-value should be the default and call-by-reference variables should be preceded by an @. For example, in

Figure 11.3.5   Sample parser output

```
#(letrecproc
   (#(procdecl add (x y)
       #(if #(varref x)
            #(varref y)
            #(app #(varref add)
                  (#(app #(varref sub1) (#(varref x)))
                   #(app #(varref add1) (#(varref y)))))))
     #(procdecl mult (x y)
        #(if #(varref x)
             #(lit 0)
             #(if #(app #(varref sub1) (#(varref x)))
                  #(varref y)
                  #(app #(varref add)
                        (#(varref y)
                         #(app #(varref mult)
                               (#(app #(varref sub1) (#(varref x)))
                                #(varref y)))))))))
   #(let (#(decl x #(lit 1))
          #(decl y #(lit 2))
          #(decl z #(proc (x y)
                        #(app #(varref mult)
                              (#(app #(varref add) (#(lit 3) #(varref x)))
                               #(varref y)))))
          #(decl w #(proc () #(varassign add #(proc (x y) #(varref x)))))))
     #(letarray (#(decl a #(lit 8))
                 #(decl b #(app #(varref add)
                               (#(varref x)
                                #(app #(varref mult) (#(varref y) #(varref x)))))))
        #(begin
           #(arrayassign #(varref b)
                         #(app #(varref add) (#(varref x) #(lit 1))) #(lit 17))
           #(begin
              #(varassign y
                 #(app #(varref mult)
                       (#(varref x) #(arrayref #(varref b) #(varref y)))))
              #(begin
                 #(varassign y #(app #(varref add) (#(varref x) #(varref y))))
                 #(begin
                    #(app #(varref w) ())
                    #(app #(varref z) (#(varref x) #(varref y)))))))))))))
```

```
--> let p = proc (@x, y)
              begin
                y := +(y, 1);
                x := +(x, 1)
              end;
        z = 5
    in begin
         p(z, z);
         z
       end;
  6
```

a new cell is created for y but not for x, so z is incremented once. □

11.4 Recursive Descent Parsers

If we are using an implementation language that does not have first-class procedures, the techniques we have described so far are not directly applicable.
We can avoid using first-class procedures by expanding the definitions of parsing actions. The result is a self-contained parsing program. Parsers of this
form are called *recursive descent parsers*.

Let us start with the parser of figure 11.3.2. Consider a typical parsing
action

```
((check/shift 'variable (check/drop 'assign-sym ...))
 buffer token-seq)
```

Expanding the definition of *check/shift*, this is equal to

```
((lambda (buffer token-seq)
   (if (eq? (token->class (token-seq-head token-seq)) 'variable)
       ((check/drop 'assign-sym ...)
        (cons (token->data (token-seq-head token-seq)) buffer)
        (token-seq-tail token-seq))
       (parse-error (token-seq-head token-seq))))
 buffer token-seq)
```

Using the fact that ((lambda (x y) ...) *e1 e2*) is the same as (let ((x *e1*)
(y *e2*)) ...), we can rewrite this as

```
(let ((buffer buffer)
      (token-seq token-seq))
  (if (eq? (token->class (token-seq-head token-seq)) 'variable)
      ((check/drop 'assign-sym ...)
       (cons (token->data (token-seq-head token-seq)) buffer)
       (token-seq-tail token-seq))
      (parse-error (token-seq-head token-seq))))
```

Since *check/drop* is also defined by a lambda expression whose bound
variables are `token-seq` and `buffer`, we can expand the application of
`(check/drop 'assign-sym ...)` into another `let`:

```
(let ((buffer buffer)
      (token-seq token-seq))
  (if (eq? (token->class (token-seq-head token-seq)) 'variable)
      (let ((buffer (cons (token->data (token-seq-head token-seq))
                          buffer))
            (token-seq (token-seq-tail token-seq)))
        (if (eq? (token->class (token-seq-head token-seq))
                 'assign-sym)
            (let ((buffer buffer)
                  (token-seq (token-seq-tail token-seq)))
              next-action-body)
            (parse-error (token-seq-head token-seq))))
      (parse-error (token-seq-head token-seq))))
```

We continue expanding *next-action-body* until it is a *reduce* action. The
procedure *reduce* was defined by

```
(define reduce
  (lambda (prod-name)
    (lambda (buffer token-seq)
      (make-parser-answer
        (apply (get-constructor-from-name prod-name)
               (reverse buffer))
        token-seq))))
```

We can then replace

```
((reduce prod-name) buffer token-seq)
```

by

```
(make-parser-answer
  (apply constructor (reverse buffer))
  token-seq)
```

where *constructor* is the procedure associated with **prod-name** by *get-constructor-from-name*.

This takes care of actions, but what about states? In our functional parser of figure 11.3.2, states were of this form:

```
(lambda (token)
  (case (token->class token)
    ((class) action)                                                  (*)
    ...
    (else (parse-error ...))))
```

States are only invoked at one point, which is in *goto-parser-state*:

```
(define goto-parser-state
  (lambda (state)
    (lambda (buffer token-seq)
      (let ((next-action (state (token-seq-head token-seq))))
        (next-action buffer token-seq)))))
```

Thus

```
(goto-parser-state state)
```

$\Rightarrow$
```
  (lambda (buffer token-seq)
    (let ((next-action (state (token-seq-head token-seq))))
      (next-action buffer token-seq)))
```

which by β-reduction

$\Rightarrow$
```
  (lambda (buffer token-seq)
    (case (token->class (token-seq-head token-seq))
      ((class) (action buffer token-seq))
      ...
      (else (parse-error ...))))
```

by substituting (*) for *state* and β-reducing again.

Similarly, recalling the definition of **process-nt**

```
(define process-nt
  (lambda (state next-action)
    (lambda (buffer token-seq)
      (let ((next-answer ((goto-parser-state state) '() token-seq)))
        (variant-case next-answer
          (parser-answer (tree unparsed)
            (next-action (cons tree buffer) unparsed)))))))))
```

we can derive the equivalence

$$((\text{process-nt } \textit{state next-action}) \textit{ buffer token-seq})$$

```
⇒ (let ((buffer buffer)
        (token-seq token-seq))
    (let ((next-answer ((goto-parser-state state) '() token-seq)))
      (variant-case next-answer
        (parser-answer (tree unparsed)
          (let ((buffer (cons tree buffer))
                (token-seq unparsed))
            next-action-body)))))
```

When we are done, the parser consists of a set of mutually recursive procedures of the following form:

```
(define parse-some-nonterminal
  (lambda (buffer token-seq)
    (case (token->class (token-seq-head token-seq))
      ((class) (action buffer token-seq))
      ...
      (else (parse-error ...)))))
```

Whenever a nonterminal appears in the right-hand side of a production, the corresponding procedure is called recursively. See figure 11.4.1 for the recursive descent translation of *parse-command* of figure 11.3.2. In this parser, we have mechanically expanded the code using the above techniques, except that we have not included any of the (else (parse-error ...)) lines. An optimized version would not contain redundant let and if expressions.

Recursive descent parsers are commonly used in situations where more sophisticated parser generation techniques, such as table-driven parsers, are unnecessary or impractical. They can be coded in almost any language that allows recursion.

Figure 11.4.1   A recursive descent version of `parse-command`

```
(define parse-command
  (lambda (buffer token-seq)
    (case (token->class (token-seq-head token-seq))
      ((begin)
        (if (eq? (token->class (token-seq-head token-seq)) 'begin)
            (let ((buffer buffer)
                  (token-seq (token-seq-tail token-seq)))
              (let ((next-answer (parse-command '() token-seq)))
                (variant-case next-answer
                  (parser-answer (tree unparsed)
                    (let ((buffer (cons tree buffer))
                          (token-seq unparsed))
                      (if (eq? (token->class (token-seq-head token-seq)) 'semicolon)
                          (let ((buffer buffer)
                                (token-seq (token-seq-tail token-seq)))
                            (let ((next-answer (parse-command '() token-seq)))
                              (variant-case next-answer
                                (parser-answer (tree unparsed)
                                  (let ((buffer (cons tree buffer))
                                        (token-seq unparsed))
                                    (if (eq? (token->class (token-seq-head token-seq))
                                             'end)
                                        (let ((buffer buffer)
                                              (token-seq (token-seq-tail token-seq)))
                                          (make-parser-answer
                                            (apply make-compound-command
                                              (reverse buffer))
                                            token-seq))))))))))))))))
      ((variable)
        (if (eq? (token->class (token-seq-head token-seq)) 'variable)
            (let ((buffer (cons (token->data (token-seq-head token-seq)) buffer))
                  (token-seq (token-seq-tail token-seq)))
              (if (eq? (token->class (token-seq-head token-seq)) 'assign-sym)
                  (let ((buffer buffer)
                        (token-seq (token-seq-tail token-seq)))
                    (let ((next-answer (parse-expression '() token-seq)))
                      (variant-case next-answer
                        (parser-answer (tree unparsed)
                          (let ((buffer (cons tree buffer)) (token-seq unparsed))
                            (make-parser-answer
                              (apply make-assignment-command (reverse buffer))
                              token-seq))))))))))
```

Figure 11.4.2   A two-argument continuation version of *parse-command*

```
(define parse-command
  (lambda (token-seq future-action)
    (case (token->class (token-seq-head token-seq))
      ((begin)
       (parse-command (token-seq-tail token-seq)
         (lambda (tree1 unparsed1)
           (if (eq? (token->class (token-seq-head unparsed1)) 'semicolon)
               (parse-command (token-seq-tail unparsed1)
                 (lambda (tree2 unparsed2)
                   (if (eq? (token->class (token-seq-head unparsed2)) 'end)
                       (future-action
                         (make-compound-command tree1 tree2)
                         (token-seq-tail unparsed2))
                       (parse-error ...))))
               (parse-error ...)))))
      ((variable)
       (let ((unparsed1 (token-seq-tail token-seq)))
         (if (eq? (token->class (token-seq-head unparsed1)) 'assign-sym)
             (parse-expression (token-seq-tail unparsed1)
               (lambda (tree2 unparsed2)
                 (future-action
                   (make-assignment-command
                     (token->data (token-seq-head token-seq))
                     tree2)
                   unparsed2)))
             (parse-error ...))))
      (else (parse-error ...)))))
```

- *Exercise 11.4.1*
  Rewrite *parse-expression* as a recursive descent parser. □

- *Exercise 11.4.2*
  The code in figure 11.4.1 is unnatural, since it was generated mechanically from the definitions given in the text. Rewrite it to be optimized in some of the ways that humans typically write programs. □

- *Exercise 11.4.3*
  The parser in figure 11.4.1 is not quite free of higher-order procedures, since it still contains instances of `apply`. Rewrite it to eliminate these instances. □

- *Exercise 11.4.4*

The parser developed in this section can be written in a continuation-passing style. For example, the buffer can be replaced by a two-argument continuation `future-action` as in figure 11.4.2. The final value continuation might be `make-parser-answer`. Write `parse-expression` using this approach. □

11.5 Table-Driven Parsers

In section 11.3, we derived a general strategy and a set of useful components for building parsers. In section 11.4, we showed how to eliminate the use of higher-order procedures in these parsers by expanding the definitions of the components; the result was a strategy for building recursive descent parsers by hand.

In this section, we shall use the techniques of section 3.6 to derive a different representation of these components that will not require first-class procedures. As in our representation of finite functions in section 3.6, we create a grammar showing the ways in which each class of procedures can be put together and then write special-purpose `apply-` procedures for each class. The result will be a single parsing program that can be customized by simply changing a table: such procedures are said to be *table driven*.

The transformation of our procedural parsers into a data structure representation is useful for several reasons. We shall have a single driver program that scans the token sequence, basing its decision on a table: a data structure that describes a specific parser. To change the syntactic specification of the language we are processing, we need only change the table. The resulting representation is declarative: it looks very much like a grammar. This eliminates an important source of coding errors. Finally, the table-driven parser avoids the use of first-class procedures, so it can be implemented in a language that does not support first-class procedures. We do this, however, at the cost of restricting ourselves to parsers built using only our six actions.

The parsers we built in section 11.3 had a very stylized form. We write a grammar that describes this form, choose an alternate representation that is more convenient, and then write special-purpose `apply-` procedures that interpret this form. The form we choose is a *parsing table*. These tables are similar to a BNF grammar, so they are easy to write.

We begin by modifying the procedures of figure 11.3.1. First we make them independent of the representation of parser actions by introducing the procedure `apply-parser-action`. Then we make the modification, as sug-

Figure 11.5.1   Parser actions in procedural representation

```scheme
(define check/drop
  (lambda (class next-action)
    (lambda (buffer token-seq grammar)
      (let ((token (token-seq-head token-seq)))
        (if (eq? (token->class token) class)
            (apply-parser-action next-action
              buffer
              (token-seq-tail token-seq)
              grammar)
            (error "Syntax error: expecting a" class "not a" token))))))

(define check/shift
  (lambda (class next-action)
    (lambda (buffer token-seq grammar)
      (let ((token (token-seq-head token-seq)))
        (if (eq? (token->class token) class)
            (apply-parser-action next-action
              (cons (token->data token) buffer)
              (token-seq-tail token-seq)
              grammar)
            (error "Syntax error: expecting a" class "not a" token))))))

(define reduce
  (lambda (prod-name)
    (lambda (buffer token-seq grammar)
      (make-parser-answer
        (apply (get-constructor-from-name prod-name)
               (reverse buffer))
        token-seq))))

(define goto-label
  (lambda (label)
    (lambda (token-seq buffer grammar)
      (let ((next-action
              (apply-parser-state
                (apply-parser-grammar grammar label)
                (token-seq-head token-seq))))
        (apply-parser-action next-action
          buffer
          token-seq
          grammar)))))
```

Figure 11.5.1   Parser actions in procedural representation (continued)

```
(define process-nt
  (lambda (label next-action)
    (lambda (buffer token-seq grammar)
      (let ((next-answer
              (apply-parser-action
                (goto-label label) '() token-seq grammar)))
        (variant-case next-answer
          (parser-answer (tree unparsed)
            (apply-parser-action next-action
              (cons tree buffer)
              unparsed
              grammar)))))))

(define emit-list
  (lambda ()
    (lambda (buffer token-seq grammar)
      (make-parser-answer (reverse buffer) token-seq))))
```

gested in exercise 11.2.9, of adding a grammar as a third register and replacing `goto-parser-state` by `goto-label`. The resulting definitions are shown in figure 11.5.1. The only substantial change is in *goto-label*. It uses *apply-parser-grammar* to find a state, applies that state to the head of the sequence to find an action, and applies that action to the current sequence, buffer, and grammar.

Proceeding along the lines suggested in section 3.6.2, our next step is a transformation to a data structure representation of parser actions. This is obtained by creating a record type for each action and moving the code for interpreting actions from the action procedures into *apply-parser-action*. Since three of our six actions take a *next-action* argument, we adopt a list of frames representation.

Each frame contains one of the following record types.

```
(define-record check/shift (class))
(define-record check/drop (class))
(define-record process-nt (label))
(define-record reduce (prod-name))
(define-record goto-label (label))
(define-record emit-list ())
```

Assuming the use of our customary representation of records as vectors, the form of our action data structures may be represented by the following grammar.

$action$ ::= (#(check/shift $class$) . $action$)
| (#(check/drop $class$) . $action$)
| (#(process-nt $label$) . $action$)
| (#(reduce $prod$-$name$))
| (#(goto-label $label$))
| (#(emit-list))

Dot notation is used in the first three productions. Thus an action is a list of frames of the form (check/shift $class$), (check/drop $class$), or (process/nt $label$), terminated by a (reduce $prod$-$name$), (goto-label $label$), or (emit-list) frame. For example:

```
(#(check/drop begin)
 #(process-nt command)
 #(check/drop semicolon)
 #(process-nt command)
 #(check/drop end)
 #(reduce compound))
```

The procedure `apply-parser-action` takes an action represented as a list of frames, a buffer, a token sequence, and a grammar. It dispatches on the type of action record and then does the same thing the action did when actions were represented as procedures. See figure 11.5.2.

This completes the representation for actions. What about states? In the original parser, states were of this form:

```
(lambda (token)
  (case (token->class token)
    ((class) action)
    ...
    (else (parse-error ...)))))
```

Figure 11.5.2   List of frames version of parser actions

```
(define apply-parser-action
  (lambda (action buffer token-seq grammar)
    (let ((first-frame (car action))
          (next-action (cdr action)))
      (variant-case first-frame
        (check/drop (class)
          (let ((token (token-seq-head token-seq)))
            (if (eq? (token->class token) class)
                (apply-parser-action next-action
                  buffer (token-seq-tail token-seq) grammar)
                (error "Syntax error: expecting a" class "not a" token))))
        (check/shift (class)
          (let ((token (token-seq-head token-seq)))
            (if (eq? (token->class token) class)
                (apply-parser-action next-action
                  (cons (token->data token) buffer)
                  (token-seq-tail token-seq)
                  grammar)
                (error "Invalid token class" class token))))
        (process-nt (label)
          (let ((next-answer (apply-parser-action
                               (apply-parser-state (apply-grammar grammar label)
                                 (token-seq-head token-seq))
                               '() token-seq grammar)))
            (variant-case next-answer
              (parser-answer (tree unparsed)
                (apply-parser-action next-action
                  (cons tree buffer) unparsed grammar)))))
        (reduce (prod-name)
          (make-parser-answer
            (apply (get-constructor-from-name prod-name) (reverse buffer))
            token-seq))
        (goto-label (label)
          (let ((next-action (apply-parser-state (apply-grammar grammar label)
                               (token-seq-head token-seq))))
            (apply-parser-action next-action buffer token-seq grammar)))
        (emit-list () (make-parser-answer (reverse buffer) token-seq))
        (else (error "Invalid frame:" first-frame))))))
```

Figure 11.5.3   List of frames version of `apply-parser-state`

```
(define apply-parser-state
  (lambda (state token)
    (letrec
      ((loop
         (lambda (alternatives)
           (if (null? alternatives)
               (error "Invalid token:" token)
               (let ((this-alternative (car alternatives)))
                 (cond
                   ((eq? (car this-alternative) 'else)
                    (cdr this-alternative))
                   ((memq (token->class token)
                          (car this-alternative))
                    (cdr this-alternative))
                   (else (loop (cdr alternatives)))))))))
      (loop state))))
```

Alternately, the information in a state may be represented by a data structure of a form indicated by the syntax

---

$state$ ::= ($alternative$ ...)

$alternative$ ::= (($class$) . $action$)
            | (else . $action$)

A state is a list of alternatives. Each alternative is a list whose first element is the list of applicable token classes (or the keyword else), followed by an action. Here are two typical alternatives

```
((variable) (check/drop variable) (reduce var-expression))
(else (goto-label command))
```

The procedure `apply-parser-state` interprets these data structures by checking each alternative in turn. See figure 11.5.3.

Figure 11.5.4   Redefinition of `parse-once`

```
(define parse-once
  (lambda (grammar token-seq)
    (let ((start-state (car (car grammar))))
      (let ((start-action (list (make-goto-label start-state))))
        (apply-parser-action start-action '() token-seq grammar)))))
```

Finally, we represent a grammar as an association list of label-state pairs:

grammar ::= ((*label* . *state*) ...)

or equivalently, by expanding *state*,

grammar ::= ((*label* *alternative* ...) ...)

The procedure `apply-grammar` is simply this:

```
(define apply-grammar
  (lambda (grammar label)
    (cond
      ((null? grammar) (error "Invalid label:" label))
      ((eq? (caar grammar) label) (cdar grammar))
      (else (apply-grammar (cdr grammar) label)))))
```

(This is essentially the same as the composition of the Scheme procedures *cdr* and *assq*.)

We now rewrite `parse-once` as in figure 11.5.4 to use the data structure representation. By convention, we assume that the first state in our grammars is the start state.

Now we can define our sample grammar in the data structure representation. Assuming the representation of records as vectors, we may use the data structure defined in figure 11.5.5. The entire grammar is a quoted list structure that can be read and interpreted by `apply-parser-state`. The table looks very much like the underlying grammar.

This completes the transformation of our procedural parsers into a data structure representation. We now have a single driver program (`parse-token-seq`) that scans the token sequence, basing its decision on a table that describes a specific parser. The table representation is declarative: it looks very much like a grammar. To change the syntactic specification, we need only change the

Figure 11.5.5   The parsing table for figure 11.3.2

```
(define command-grammar
  '((command
      ((begin)
        #(check/drop begin)
        #(process-nt command)
        #(check/drop semicolon)
        #(process-nt command)
        #(check/drop end)
        #(reduce compound-command))
      ((variable)
        #(check/shift variable)
        #(check/drop assign-sym)
        #(process-nt expression)
        #(reduce assignment-command)))
    (expression
      ((variable)
        #(check/shift variable)
        #(reduce var-expression))
      ((number)
        #(check/shift number)
        #(reduce constant-expression))
      ((lparen)
        #(check/drop lparen)
        #(process-nt expression)
        #(check/drop plus-sym)
        #(process-nt expression)
        #(check/drop rparen)
        #(reduce sum-expression)))))
```

table. Abstracting the control structure in the states eliminates an important source of coding errors. Finally, the table-driven parser avoids the use of first-class procedures, so it can be implemented in a language that does not support first-class procedures. We do this, however, at the cost of restricting ourselves to parsers built using only our six actions.

• *Exercise 11.5.1*
Rewrite the parser of exercise 11.3.5 using a parsing table. □

Figure 11.5.6 A scanner table

```
(define scanner-table
  '((start-state
      (((whitespace) #(drop) #(goto-label start-state))
       ((alphabetic) #(shift) #(goto-label identifier-state))
       ((numeric) #(shift) #(goto-label number-state))
       ((#\%) #(drop) #(goto-label comment-state))
       ((#\() #(drop) #(emit lparen))
       ((#\)) #(drop) #(emit rparen))
       ((#\nul) #(emit end-marker))
       (else #(scan-error))))
    (identifier-state
      (((alphabetic) #(shift) #(goto-label identifier-state))
       ((numeric) #(shift) #(goto-label identifier-state))
       (else #(emit identifier))))
    (number-state
      (((numeric) #(shift) #(goto-label number-state))
       (else #(emit number))))
    (comment-state
      (((#\newline) #(drop) #(goto-label start-state))
       (else #(shift) #(goto-label comment-state))))))
```

• *Exercise 11.5.2*
Transform the scanner components of section 11.2 into a table representation.
A typical scanning table might look something like figure 11.5.6. □

○ *Exercise 11.5.3*
Some people do not like using many parentheses in their programs. Choose
a representation for parsing tables that uses keywords instead of parentheses.
Write a lexical specification and a grammar for your representation. □

○ *Exercise 11.5.4*
Repeat the previous exercise for scanning tables. The concrete syntax should
look something like figure 11.1.1. □

○ *Exercise 11.5.5*
Write a program that takes a parsing table and generates the corresponding
recursive descent parser. □

11.6 Summary

Before actual processing, programs must be translated from human-readable syntax into an abstract syntax more suitable for machine manipulation. This translation is divided into two phases: scanning and parsing.

A scanner groups the characters used to express the concrete syntax and processes these groups to form tokens, such as variables, keywords, and numbers. Finite automata are used to model the scanning process. These automata may be simulated using highly stylized higher-order procedures. The resulting scanning procedure accepts a sequence of characters and returns a sequence of tokens. This includes processing tokens into forms that are more easily used in later processing; for example, forming numbers from digit strings and maintaining a symbol table.

A parser takes a sequence of tokens and returns a parse tree reflecting the syntactic structure of the program. A predictive parser can be built by extending the approach of the scanning automata to recursively start a new automaton when a non-terminal must be parsed. A parser built in this way may be transformed into a recursive descent parser, which does not rely on the existence of first-class procedures in the defining language, by expanding the definitions of the higher-order functions in the automata.

Because these programs are highly stylized, the portions that vary can be represented compactly in a table. The set of such tables is a new special-purpose programming language, which can be interpreted by a single program.

The approach to parsers illustrated in this chapter is restricted to grammars with certain properties. Although many grammars satisfy these properties, more advanced techniques are sometimes required.

Besides illustrating basic scanning and parsing techniques, the programs developed in this chapter illustrate important programming techniques that will be used again in chapter 12.

12 Compiler Derivation

We have seen that an interpreter may be viewed as a machine implemented in software that "executes" a parse tree. The process of compilation is the translation of an expression into a data representation (object code) that can be executed on a machine implemented efficiently in hardware.

In this chapter we start with a standard CPS interpreter for a small language. Through systematic transformation of this interpreter we then simultaneously derive a compiler and an idealized machine architecture for the compiler's object code. This is done in several steps. First, in section 12.1, we abstract the elementary actions performed by the interpreter and the formation of continuations. We then modify the interpreter so that instead of performing each action it generates a bit of code representing the action. The resulting code corresponds to a CPS version of the source program, where each action has an explicit continuation. We next define a procedure that takes this code and executes it. This procedure, which defines an abstract machine for the object code, is derived systematically from the actions performed by the original interpreter.

Next, in section 12.2, we transform our compiler and machine so that the object code more closely resembles typical machine language. Once more, this is accomplished by simultaneously transforming the compiler and machine to take advantage of certain patterns in the object code. In the third section we show how to make the output of the compiler look more realistic.

The source language of the compilers in the first two sections includes several forms that together present most of the object code patterns that compilers typically generate, with one important exception: procedures. Thus we conclude, in section 12.4, by adding procedure expressions to the source language and deriving a compiler and machine that support closures.

By following a methodical discipline of program development, we are assured of the correctness of the resulting programs. Each step in the development is verifiable. In effect, the original interpreter provides a semantic specification for our language, and we are proving the correctness of the compiler and machine implementation with respect to this specification.

12.1 Deriving a Compiler and Machine from an Interpreter

We begin with a simple language with literal, variable, and conditional forms, plus a form that sums the values of multiple subexpressions. As in our earlier interpreters, zero denotes false and other values denote true. We assume the literal, variable, and conditional (if) forms have the concrete syntax of the corresponding forms and the abstract syntax introduced in chapter 5. For the addition operator, we use the following concrete and abstract syntax.

⟨exp⟩ ::= sum(⟨operands⟩)   sum (rands)

See figure 12.1.1 for a CPS interpreter for this language. As usual, `apply-env` is borrowed from an environment ADT. The procedure `add-list` sums the values in a list. To test the interpreter, we define the procedure *run*.

```
(define run
  (lambda (exp)
    (eval-exp (parse exp) init-env (lambda (val) val))))
```

An identity procedure serves as the final value continuation. We assume in our sample transcripts that `init-env` is an initial environment that binds the variables five and six to the respective integers. (Since our language does not have procedures, the initial environment is the only environment. Though the environment argument is always the same, we include it to aid the later treatment of procedures.)

```
> (run "if sum(1, five) then 3 else six")
3
```

Interpreters perform several sorts of operations. For example, the operations performed by our present interpreter may be categorized as follows:

1. dispatching on the type of an expression (by `variant-case`),

2. calling itself and *eval-rands* to evaluate subexpressions,

3. forming continuations,

Figure 12.1.1   An interpreter

```
(define eval-exp
  (lambda (exp env k)
    (variant-case exp
      (lit (datum) (k datum))
      (varref (var) (k (apply-env env var)))
      (if (test-exp then-exp else-exp)
        (eval-exp test-exp env
          (lambda (test)
            (if (true-value? test)
                (eval-exp then-exp env k)
                (eval-exp else-exp env k)))))
      (sum (rands)
        (eval-rands rands env
          (lambda (sum-args)
            (k (add-list sum-args)))))
      (else (error "Invalid abstract syntax:" exp)))))

(define eval-rands
  (lambda (rands env k)
    (if (null? rands)
        (k '())
        (eval-exp (car rands) env
          (lambda (first)
            (eval-rands (cdr rands) env
              (lambda (rest)
                (k (cons first rest)))))))))
```

4. invoking continuations with the results of elementary operations,

5. making if tests, and

6. returning results when done (in the final value continuation).

Operations of type 4, 5, and 6 correspond to machine operations that must be performed at run time. We refer to them as *actions*. On the other hand, we would like operations of type 1 and 2 to be performed at compile time. The forming of continuations (type 3) corresponds to maintaining a sequential ordering of instructions in the object code.

Our goal is to modify this interpreter so that it still does dispatching on the form of expressions and recursion on subexpressions but does not perform actions at compile time. Instead, it should return object code that will perform actions at run time. The first step toward this goal is to abstract the actions by creating a procedure for each one. In general, the body of such a procedure is a subexpression of the interpreter definition that performs an action, whereas the formal parameters of the procedure are the free variables of the body that vary with program execution. Except for `halt-action` (called by the final value continuation), the free variables always include a continuation, k, that is invoked after the action has been performed.

For example, variable lookup may be abstracted as follows:

```
(define eval-exp
  (lambda (exp env k)
    (variant-case exp
      ...
      (varref (var) (varref-action var env k))
      ...)))

(define varref-action
  (lambda (var env k)
    (k (apply-env env var))))
```

For our language, this technique works in all but one case: the test action. If this transformation were applied directly to the test action in the `if` clause of the interpreter, we would obtain the following definition.

```
(define test-action
  (lambda (var then-exp else-exp env k)
    (if (true-value? var)
        (eval-exp then-exp env k)
        (eval-exp else-exp env k))))
```

The difficulty is that evaluation of a subexpression is not an elementary action. The solution is to simplify the test action by using procedures that package evaluation of the then and else expressions. Thus the test action need only invoke the appropriate procedure.

We have already seen instances in which procedures of no arguments, called thunks, have been used to delay evaluation. When CPS is used (as in our interpreter), however, a thunk must take one argument: a continuation. In the context of our interpreter, we refer to these procedures as *action thunks*. An action thunk for evaluation of an expression, *exp*, in an environment, *env*, may be created by an expression of this form:

$$(\text{lambda (k) (eval-exp } exp\ env\ \text{k))}$$

Figure 12.1.2 An interpreter that abstracts actions

```
(define eval-exp
  (lambda (exp env k)
    (variant-case exp
      (lit (datum) (lit-action datum k))
      (varref (var) (varref-action var env k))
      (if (test-exp then-exp else-exp)
        (eval-exp test-exp env
          (build-cont
            (lambda (test)
              (test-action test
                (lambda (k)
                  (eval-exp then-exp env k))
                (lambda (k)
                  (eval-exp else-exp env k))
                k)))))
      (sum (rands)
        (eval-rands rands env
          (build-cont
            (lambda (arg-list)
              (sum-action arg-list k)))))
      (else (error "Invalid abstract syntax:" exp)))))

(define eval-rands
  (lambda (rands env k)
    (if (null? rands)
        (emptyargs-action k)
        (eval-exp (car rands) env
          (build-cont
            (lambda (first)
              (eval-rands (cdr rands) env
                (build-cont
                  (lambda (rest)
                    (rest-action first rest k)))))))))))
```

See figure 12.1.2 and figure 12.1.3 for the resulting interpreter, which abstracts actions. Each action is called at only one point. Figure 12.1.3 also includes a new version of the `run` procedure that invokes the procedure `halt-action` to return a result. The procedure `build-cont` is introduced in anticipation of a subsequent code transformation. At this point, it is trivial.

An interpreter executes actions in some appropriate sequence, and a compiler generates code that reflects the same sequence. Before we can modify our interpreter to perform compilation, we must abstract this sequencing behavior. Since continuations control the sequencing of execution, our next step is to abstract the creation of continuations.

We are now prepared to transform our interpreter into a compiler. Since we have abstracted actions, the core of the interpreter, in figure 12.1.2, is unchanged by this transformation. The transformation is performed by redefining the actions and continuation-building procedures of figure 12.1.3. For the procedures' names to make sense, *eval* now means "compile," rather than "execute," and *action* means "generate code," rather than "perform an action."

Thus `eval-exp` no longer returns a final result. Instead it returns code that may be viewed as a symbolic (data structure) representation of the result. The environment and continuation passed to `eval-exp` must also be represented symbolically. After we complete the transformation of `eval-exp` into a compiler, we then derive an abstract machine that interprets compiled code to obtain final values.

First, we create a record type for each action. Each action procedure, with one exception, is then redefined to be the record creation procedure of its record type. Thus the work to be performed by each action is postponed by creating a data structure with all the necessary information. See figure 12.1.4. The exception is `test-action`, which invokes the then and else thunks before invoking its record creation procedure. This allows the then and else expressions to be compiled. It is possible to invoke these thunks at compile time because they call `eval-exp`, which returns actions that delay final evaluation.

The remaining step is to create continuations that are represented symbolically, rather than as procedures. We use a single record type named cont.

```
(define-record cont (reg code))
```

The first field corresponds to the formal parameter of a continuation procedure. The symbol in this field denotes a *register,* since the locations in which continuations receive values will correspond to registers in our target machine.

Figure 12.1.3 Action procedures, with *build-cont* and *run*

```
(define halt-action
  (lambda (val)
    val))

(define lit-action
  (lambda (datum k)
    (k datum)))

(define varref-action
  (lambda (var env k)
    (k (apply-env env var))))

(define test-action
  (lambda (test then-action-thunk else-action-thunk k)
    (if (true-value? test)
        (then-action-thunk k)
        (else-action-thunk k))))

(define sum-action
  (lambda (sum-args k)
    (k (add-list sum-args))))

(define emptyargs-action
  (lambda (k)
    (k '())))

(define rest-action
  (lambda (first rest k)
    (k (cons first rest))))

(define build-cont
  (lambda (k)
    (lambda (v)
      (k v))))

(define run
  (lambda (exp)
    (eval-exp (parse exp) init-env
      (build-cont
        (lambda (val)
          (halt-action val))))))
```

Figure 12.1.4   Action construction procedures

```
(define-record halt-instruc (val-reg))
(define halt-action make-halt-instruc)

(define-record lit-instruc (datum k))
(define lit-action make-lit-instruc)

(define-record varref-instruc (var env-reg k))
(define varref-action make-varref-instruc)

(define-record sum-instruc (arg-list-reg k))
(define sum-action make-sum-instruc)

(define-record emptyargs-instruc (k))
(define emptyargs-action make-emptyargs-instruc)

(define-record rest-instruc (first-reg rest-reg k))
(define rest-action make-rest-instruc)

(define-record test-instruc (test-reg then-code else-code))
(define test-action
  (lambda (test then-action-thunk else-action-thunk k)
    (make-test-instruc test
      (then-action-thunk k)
      (else-action-thunk k))))
```

We call this the *formal register* of the continuation, by analogy with the formal parameter of a lambda expression. It is important not to confuse these registers with variables in the source program or variables in the interpreter itself. The second field of a cont record contains code representing the body of the corresponding continuation procedure.

Since a register is simply a machine location, we must be sure that the register we choose will not be in use (contain needed information) at the time its continuation is invoked. Thus when forming a continuation, we must allocate a suitable register to receive its argument. For simplicity, we initially assume the existence of an unlimited number of registers named r1, r2, ... A new register is allocated for each continuation by the procedure allocate-reg. In section 12.2 we introduce a more practical register allocator that reuses registers.

Thus continuations are represented by records generated by calling *make-cont* with a newly generated register and an action that refers to that register. To create these continuation records, we redefine *build-cont*.

```
(define build-cont
  (lambda (action-generator)
    (let ((reg (allocate-reg)))
      (make-cont reg
        (action-generator reg)))))
```

Here *action-generator* refers to a procedure that takes a register and returns an action that may use this register. Thus the lambda expressions of figure 12.1.2 that once defined continuations now define action generators, and their formal parameters are now bound to register names, rather than values.

When invoking *eval-exp*, we use the *symbol* env-reg to represent the register that will contain the initial environment. Here is a simple test.

```
> (define compile
    (lambda (exp)
      (eval-exp (parse exp) 'env-reg
        (build-cont
          (lambda (reg)
            (halt-action reg))))))
> (compile "six")
#(varref-instruc six env-reg
 #(cont r0
  #(halt-instruc r0)))
```

To better understand the code returned by *eval-exp*, it may be translated into a corresponding Scheme expression. Each -instruc record is replaced by an application to the corresponding -action procedure, and each cont record is replaced by a corresponding lambda expression. Thus (compile "six") returns the code

```
(varref-action 'six init-env
  (lambda (r0)
    (halt-action r0)))
```

Some of the language's literals and all of its variables, such as six, must be quoted, since operands are evaluated, and references to env-reg must be replaced by init-env.

Next we try a more complicated example.

```
> (compile "sum(five, 9)")
#(varref-instruc five env-reg
 #(cont r2
  #(lit-instruc 9
   #(cont r4
    #(emptyargs-instruc
     #(cont r5
      #(rest-instruc r4 r5
       #(cont r3
        #(rest-instruc r2 r3
         #(cont r1
          #(sum-instruc r1
           #(cont r0
            #(halt-instruc r0)))))))))))))))
```

When executed, this code does the following:

1. loads the value of the variable five in the initial environment into r2,

2. loads the literal 9 into r4,

3. loads the empty list into r5,

4. starts forming a list of arguments by making a pair from the contents of registers r4 and r5 and places the result in r3,

5. completes the argument list by consing the contents of r2 onto the list in r3 and places the result in r1,

6. sums the elements of the list in r1 and places the result in r0, and

7. halts, returning the result in r0.

The Scheme expression corresponding to this code follows:

```
(varref-action 'five init-env
 (lambda (r2)
  (lit-action 9
   (lambda (r4)
    (emptyargs-action
     (lambda (r5)
      (rest-action r4 r5
       (lambda (r3)
        (rest-action r2 r3
         (lambda (r1)
          (sum-action r1
           (lambda (r0)
            (halt-action r0)))))))))))))
```

Observe that these Scheme expressions corresponding to code are in continuation-passing style. This CPS differs from the CPS of chapter 8 in the granularity of the actions for which continuations are created. Here each action is very small, corresponding to a single machine instruction. In chapter 8, on the other hand, continuations were only created for procedure calls.

There is another important relationship between our code and lambda expressions. We say that a register r *occurs free* in code C if C contains a use of r that is not contained within a cont record in which r is the formal register. Thus register r occurs free in C if and only if the variable r occurs free in the Scheme expression corresponding to C.

The next example illustrates the compilation of conditional code.

```
> (compile "if 0 then sum(3, 4) else sum(five, six)")
#(lit-instruc 0
 #(cont r1
   #(test-instruc r1
     #(lit-instruc 3
       #(cont r3
         #(lit-instruc 4
           #(cont r5
             #(emptyargs-instruc
               #(cont r6
                 #(rest-instruc r5 r6
                   #(cont r4
                     #(rest-instruc r3 r4
                       #(cont r2
                         #(sum-instruc r2
                           #(cont r0
                             #(halt-instruc r0)))))))))))))))
     #(varref-instruc five env-reg
       #(cont r8
         #(varref-instruc six env-reg
           #(cont r10
             #(emptyargs-instruc
               #(cont r11
                 #(rest-instruc r10 r11
                   #(cont r9
                     #(rest-instruc r8 r9
                       #(cont r7
                         #(sum-instruc r7
                           #(cont r0
                             #(halt-instruc r0))))))))))))))))))
```

Figure 12.1.5   A machine

```
(define eval-code
  (lambda (code)
    (variant-case code
      (halt-instruc (val-reg) (get-reg val-reg))
      (lit-instruc (datum k) (apply-cont k datum))
      (varref-instruc (var env-reg k)
        (apply-cont k (apply-env (get-reg env-reg) var)))
      (sum-instruc (arg-list-reg k)
        (apply-cont k (add-list (get-reg arg-list-reg))))
      (emptyargs-instruc (k) (apply-cont k '()))
      (rest-instruc (first-reg rest-reg k)
        (apply-cont k
          (cons (get-reg first-reg) (get-reg rest-reg))))
      (test-instruc (test-reg then-code else-code)
        (if (true-value? (get-reg test-reg))
            (eval-code then-code)
            (eval-code else-code)))
      (else (error "Invalid code:" code)))))

(define apply-cont
  (lambda (k v)
    (variant-case k
      (cont (reg code) (set-reg! reg v) (eval-code code))
      (else (error "Invalid continuation:" k)))))

(define goto-cont
  (lambda (k)
    (variant-case k
      (cont (reg code) (eval-code code))
      (else (error "Invalid continuation:" k)))))

(define build-cont
  (lambda (action-generator)
    (let ((reg (allocate-reg)))
      (make-cont reg
        (action-generator reg)))))

(define run
  (lambda (exp)
    (eval-code (compile exp))))
```

The notion of "simple" expressions was introduced to assure that continuations were not created for simple actions.

• *Exercise 12.1.1*
Translate the preceding code into a corresponding Scheme expression and trace its evaluation by hand. Use care in translating `test-instruc`. ☐

○ *Exercise 12.1.2*
Define a procedure *code->scheme* that takes code generated by *eval-exp* and returns a corresponding Scheme expression. For example,

```
> (code->scheme (compile "sum(five, 9)"))
(varref-action 'five init-env
  (lambda (r2) ...))
> (varref-action 'five init-env
    (lambda (r2) ...))
14
```
☐

Finally, we create a procedure, *eval-code*, for executing code produced by *eval-exp*. This procedure is in effect a machine for executing the object code produced by our compiler.

Since each type of code record represents a different action, it is only necessary for *eval-code* to dispatch on the code record type and perform the corresponding action. We systematically derive *eval-code* from the definitions of the action procedures in figure 12.1.2. (This is analogous to the transformation from procedural to data structure representation introduced in section 3.6.) It is necessary to allow for the representation of continuations as data structures by introducing the procedure *apply-cont*. To account for the use of registers, we also use the procedure *get-reg* to obtain the values of registers associated with continuations. We also assume that the current environment is recorded in a register that is always named `env-reg`. Register values are assigned using the procedure *set-reg!* in *apply-cont*. When no register should be set, we use *goto-cont*. Although *goto-cont* will not be used until we discuss the interpretation of compiled procedures, we include it here to show just how similar it is to *apply-cont*. See figure 12.1.5, which also includes the latest definition of *build-cont* and a *run* procedure that performs parsing, compilation, and execution. Before testing, we must define the register ADT. This is simplified by using the finite function ADT from chapter 3 and the cell ADT from chapter 4. See figure 12.1.6.

Figure 12.1.6   Implementation of a register allocation ADT

```
(define reg-file
  (extend-ff 'env-reg (make-cell init-env) (create-empty-ff)))

(define get-reg
  (lambda (sym)
    (cell-ref (apply-ff reg-file sym))))

(define set-reg!
  (lambda (sym val)
    (cell-set! (apply-ff reg-file sym) val)))

(define reg-counter 0)

(define allocate-reg
  (lambda ()
    (let ((reg (string->symbol
                 (string-append
                   (symbol->string 'r)
                   (number->string reg-counter)))))
      (set! reg-file (extend-ff reg (make-cell '*) reg-file))
      (set! reg-counter (+ reg-counter 1))
      reg)))
```

12.2 Register Allocation

In this section we modify the compiler of the last section to employ a more
realistic register allocation algorithm. This algorithm reuses registers when
they no longer contain useful information.

To better understand the register allocation problem, suppose the same
register, r0, were used for every continuation returned by

```
(build-cont
  (lambda (first) ...))
```

We might then observe the following.

```
> (compile "sum(five, 9)")
#(varref-instruc five env-reg
 #(cont r0
  #(lit-instruc 9
   #(cont r0
    #(emptyargs-instruc
     #(cont r3
      #(rest-instruc r0 r3
       #(cont r2
        #(rest-instruc r0 r2
         #(cont r1
          #(sum-instruc r1
           #(cont r0
            #(halt-instruc r0)))))))))))))))
```

This code is (up to renaming) the same as that of the sum(five, 9) example in the last section, except that r2 and r4 have both been replaced by r0. In the two rest-instruc lines reference is made to the same register, r0. At the time these lines are executed, r0 will contain 9 (the value of the second argument), while the reference to r0 in the second rest-instruc line should have referred to 5 (the value of the first argument).

In the last section we avoided this problem by allocating a new register for each continuation. This is impractical because the registers that are referred to by most instructions are those in the CPU, and their number is strictly limited. The register allocation performed by compilers should make the best possible use of the available CPU registers, while assuring that a register is not reused as long as it still contains needed information.

When allocating a register for a new continuation, we may select any register that does not occur free in any of the pieces of code from which the body of the new continuation is being constructed. It is precisely these free registers that contain needed information. Thus the register allocation problem is analogous to the lexical variable capture problem of chapter 4 in that we can choose any register that does not occur free in the code representing the continuation's body.

To allocate a new register, we use a modified version of *allocate-reg*. This procedure now takes a list of registers that are in use and returns a register that is not in use, selected from a list of general registers. We define *reg-names* to contain the list of registers named r0 through r5 and redefine *reg-file* to include these new registers.

```
(define reg-names '(r0 r1 r2 r3 r4 r5))
```

```
(define reg-file
  (extend-ff*
    reg-names
    (map (lambda (x) (make-cell '*)) reg-names)
    (extend-ff 'env-reg (make-cell init-env) (create-empty-ff))))

(define allocate-reg
  (lambda (used-regs)
    (letrec
      ((loop
         (lambda (avail)
           (cond
             ((null? avail) (error "No more registers"))
             ((memq (car avail) used-regs) (loop (cdr avail)))
             (else (car avail))))))
      (loop reg-names))))
```

All the continuation construction procedures (except the final value continuation created by *compile*) take a continuation as an argument and use this continuation to create the body of the new continuation. Since registers that occur free in the argument continuation will appear free in the body, we must have a way of determining which registers occur free in a continuation. This is easiest if we determine the free variables in a new continuation at the time we build it and record this information in the record representing the continuation. Thus we extend the cont record type.

```
(define-record cont (reg free-regs code))
```

Given a list of free registers, it is now easy to build a new continuation.

```
(define build-cont
  (lambda (free-regs action-generator)
    (let ((reg (allocate-reg free-regs)))
      (make-cont reg free-regs (action-generator reg)))))
```

The evaluation (compilation) procedures of figure 12.2.1 are the same as those of figure 12.1.2 except that *build-cont* now receives a list of free registers as well as an action generator. In the final value continuation built by *compile* this list is empty, whereas in other cases it is obtained using *cont->free-regs*. In the continuation of the call of *eval-rands* on the cdr of the operand list, the register *first* occurs free as well as the free registers

Figure 12.2.1   A compiler with register allocation

```
(define compile
  (lambda (exp)
    (eval-exp (parse exp) 'env-reg
      (build-cont '()
        (lambda (final) (halt-action final))))))

(define eval-exp
  (lambda (exp env k)
    (variant-case exp
      (lit (datum) (lit-action datum k))
      (varref (var) (varref-action var env k))
      (if (test-exp then-exp else-exp)
        (eval-exp test-exp env
          (build-cont (cont->free-regs k)
            (lambda (test)
              (test-action test
                (lambda (k)
                  (eval-exp then-exp env k))
                (lambda (k)
                  (eval-exp else-exp env k))
                k)))))
      (sum (rands)
        (eval-rands rands env
          (build-cont (cont->free-regs k)
            (lambda (arg-list)
              (sum-action arg-list k)))))
      (else (error "Invalid abstract syntax:" exp)))))

(define eval-rands
  (lambda (rands env k)
    (if (null? rands)
        (emptyargs-action k)
        (eval-exp (car rands) env
          (build-cont (cont->free-regs k)
            (lambda (first)
              (eval-rands (cdr rands) env
                (build-cont (cons first (cont->free-regs k))
                  (lambda (rest)
                    (rest-action first rest k)))))))))))
```

in **k**. This is accounted for by adding *first* to the free register list when building this continuation.

The list of registers that is maintained in each continuation should, of course, be removed from the output of our compiler, but we take care of that later. Here is the code produced for "sum(five, 9)".

```
#(varref-instruc five env-reg
  #(cont r0 ()
   #(lit-instruc 9
    #(cont r1 (r0)
     #(emptyargs-instruc
      #(cont r2 (r1 r0)
       #(rest-instruc r1 r2
        #(cont r1 (r0)
         #(rest-instruc r0 r1
          #(cont r0 ()
           #(sum-instruc r0
            #(cont r0 ()
             #(halt-instruc r0)))))))))))))))
```

• *Exercise 12.2.1*

Modify the interpreter for the language of this section to use the following version of eval-rands:

```
(define eval-rands
  (lambda (rands args env k)
    (if (null? rands)
        (k args)
        (eval-exp (car rands) env
          (lambda (first)
            (eval-rands (cdr rands) (cons first args) env k))))))
```

Next use the resulting interpreter to derive a compiler similar to the one in figure 12.2.1. Now observe that for this compiler, register allocation may be simplified by assigning a distinct register to each continuation construction procedure that uses a register. For example, *first* could always be r3, provided r3 was not used for other purposes. Modify the procedures that construct continuations accordingly. □

In some cases it may be necessary to maintain more intermediate results than will fit the available CPU registers. Our `allocate-reg` procedure issues an error message in such cases. A practical compiler would arrange for the excess results to be stored in main memory. This is called *register spilling* and occurs rarely if there are a reasonable number of general-purpose CPU registers (say a dozen or more).

○ *Exercise 12.2.2*
Modify the compiler of this section to perform register spilling. Use a register file with only four registers, a vector of 100 elements to simulate the portion of memory used for spilled registers, and a new action, called `move`, that copies a spill-vector element indicated by an index to a given register. □

12.3 Obtaining More Realistic Object Code

Traditional object code consists of a sequence of machine instructions. Although actions are analogous to typical machine instructions in the functions they perform, the nesting of a continuation within each action is not typical. The next step in the evolution of our compiler is to simply "flatten" the code representation so that it becomes a list of actions, without nesting of continuations.

To derive this change in code representation, it helps to view the present code structure (without free register lists) using a BNF grammar.

⟨code⟩ ::= #(halt-instruc ⟨reg⟩)
    | #(lit-instruc ⟨datum⟩ ⟨cont⟩)
    | #(varref-instruc ⟨var⟩ ⟨reg⟩ ⟨cont⟩)
    | #(sum-instruc ⟨reg⟩ ⟨cont⟩)
    | #(emptyargs-instruc ⟨cont⟩)
    | #(rest-instruc ⟨reg⟩ ⟨reg⟩ ⟨cont⟩)
    | #(test-instruc ⟨reg⟩ ⟨code⟩ ⟨code⟩)

⟨cont⟩ ::= #(cont ⟨reg⟩ ⟨code⟩)

Since there is only one production for ⟨cont⟩, we can substitute its right-hand side for each appearance of ⟨cont⟩, obtaining the following grammar.

$$\langle \text{code} \rangle ::= \texttt{\#(halt-instruc } \langle \text{reg} \rangle \texttt{)}$$
$$| \quad \texttt{\#(lit-instruc } \langle \text{datum} \rangle \texttt{ \#(cont } \langle \text{reg} \rangle \texttt{ } \langle \text{code} \rangle \texttt{)))}$$
$$| \quad \texttt{\#(varref-instruc } \langle \text{var} \rangle \texttt{ } \langle \text{reg} \rangle \texttt{ \#(cont } \langle \text{reg} \rangle \texttt{ } \langle \text{code} \rangle \texttt{)))}$$
$$| \quad \texttt{\#(sum-instruc } \langle \text{reg} \rangle \texttt{ \#(cont } \langle \text{reg} \rangle \texttt{ } \langle \text{code} \rangle \texttt{)))}$$
$$| \quad \texttt{\#(emptyargs-instruc \#(cont } \langle \text{reg} \rangle \texttt{ } \langle \text{code} \rangle \texttt{)))}$$
$$| \quad \texttt{\#(rest-instruc } \langle \text{reg} \rangle \texttt{ } \langle \text{reg} \rangle \texttt{ \#(cont } \langle \text{reg} \rangle \texttt{ } \langle \text{code} \rangle \texttt{)))}$$
$$| \quad \texttt{\#(test-instruc } \langle \text{reg} \rangle \texttt{ } \langle \text{code} \rangle \texttt{ } \langle \text{code} \rangle \texttt{)}$$

Now each form of code, except for test-instruc and halt-instruc, contains a single embedded code (the "normal" continuation). This suggests a list of frames representation, which avoids unnecessary nesting (See section 10.2.).

$$\langle \text{code} \rangle ::= \texttt{(\#(halt-instruc } \langle \text{reg} \rangle \texttt{))}$$
$$| \quad \texttt{(\#(lit-instruc } \langle \text{datum} \rangle \texttt{ } \langle \text{reg} \rangle \texttt{) . } \langle \text{code} \rangle \texttt{)}$$
$$| \quad \texttt{(\#(varref-instruc } \langle \text{var} \rangle \texttt{ } \langle \text{reg} \rangle \texttt{ } \langle \text{reg} \rangle \texttt{) . } \langle \text{code} \rangle \texttt{)}$$
$$| \quad \texttt{(\#(sum-instruc } \langle \text{reg} \rangle \texttt{ } \langle \text{reg} \rangle \texttt{) . } \langle \text{code} \rangle \texttt{)}$$
$$| \quad \texttt{(\#(emptyargs-instruc } \langle \text{reg} \rangle \texttt{) . } \langle \text{code} \rangle \texttt{)}$$
$$| \quad \texttt{(\#(rest-instruc } \langle \text{reg} \rangle \texttt{ } \langle \text{reg} \rangle \texttt{ } \langle \text{reg} \rangle \texttt{) . } \langle \text{code} \rangle \texttt{)}$$
$$| \quad \texttt{(\#(test-instruc } \langle \text{reg} \rangle \texttt{ } \langle \text{code} \rangle \texttt{) . } \langle \text{code} \rangle \texttt{)}$$

Except for test code, the code now has the form of a list of simple instructions terminated by a halt instruction.

It is easy to modify our previous code to use this new representation: we simply redefine the code construction procedures of figure 12.1.4. The new procedures add a record representing the new action to a list that represents its continuation. Since these records closely resemble standard machine instructions, we give them names that would be familiar to assembly language programmers: stop, fetch, sum-list, move-imm (move immediate), and brz (branch on zero). There are also instructions, cons-3 (cons with three arguments, one being a destination register) and cons-1 (corresponding to placing the empty list into a destination register) that would be unfamiliar to most assembly language programmers, since machines typically do not maintain lists. It is possible to eliminate list operations from the machine by representing the argument list on a stack, rather than in a heap.

See figure 12.3.1 for the new code construction procedures. While we are defining these procedures, we have the opportunity to remove the list of free registers from the object code (though of course not from the internal representation of continuations).

Figure 12.3.1   Action construction procedures for flat code

```
(define-record stop (reg))
(define halt-action
  (lambda (val)
    (cons (make-stop val) '())))

(define-record move-imm (datum reg))
(define lit-action
  (lambda (datum k)
    (cons (make-move-imm datum (cont->reg k))
          (cont->code k))))

(define-record fetch (var env reg))
(define varref-action
  (lambda (var env k)
    (cons (make-fetch var env (cont->reg k))
          (cont->code k))))

(define-record sum-list (sum-args reg))
(define sum-action
  (lambda (sum-args k)
    (cons (make-sum-list sum-args (cont->reg k))
          (cont->code k))))

(define-record cons-1 (reg))
(define emptyargs-action
  (lambda (k)
    (cons (make-cons-1 (cont->reg k))
          (cont->code k))))

(define-record cons-3 (first rest reg))
(define rest-action
  (lambda (first rest k)
    (cons (make-cons-3 first rest (cont->reg k))
          (cont->code k))))

(define-record brz (test else-instruc))
(define test-action
  (lambda (test then-action-thunk else-action-thunk k)
    (cons (make-brz test (else-action-thunk k))
          (then-action-thunk k))))
```

Figure 12.3.2 Machine for flat object code

```
(define eval-code
  (lambda (code)
    (let ((ir (car code)) (pc (cdr code)))
      (variant-case ir
        (stop (reg) (get-reg reg))
        (move-imm (datum reg)
          (set-reg! reg datum)
          (eval-code pc))
        (fetch (var env reg)
          (set-reg! reg (apply-env (get-reg env) var))
          (eval-code pc))
        (sum-list (sum-args reg)
          (set-reg! reg (add-list (get-reg sum-args)))
          (eval-code pc))
        (cons-1 (reg)
          (set-reg! reg '())
          (eval-code pc))
        (cons-3 (first rest reg)
          (set-reg! reg (cons (get-reg first) (get-reg rest)))
          (eval-code pc))
        (brz (test else-instruc)
          (if (zero? (get-reg test))
              (eval-code else-instruc)
              (eval-code pc)))
        (else (error "Invalid code:" code)))))))
```

A simple test demonstrates that (in the absence of `brz` instructions) our object code now has the usual form of a sequence of simple instructions.

```
> (compile "sum(five, 9)")
(#(fetch five env-reg r0)
 #(move-imm 9 r1)
 #(cons-1 r2)
 #(cons-3 r1 r2 r1)
 #(cons-3 r0 r1 r0)
 #(sum-list r0 r0)
 #(stop r0))
```

The continuation of each instruction is the sequence of instructions that follows it.

Since we have changed the object code representation, a new machine (*eval-code* procedure) is required to execute our code. This machine begins by binding the first instruction of its code to the variable `ir` and binding the code representing the continuation of the first instruction to the variable `pc`. These variables correspond to the instruction register and program counter of typical hardware machines. Our machine then dispatches on the record type of `ir`, which corresponds to instruction decoding in hardware. Execution of each instruction (except `stop` and possibly `brz`) concludes with the recursive call `(eval-code pc)`, which corresponds to repetition of the fetch-execute cycle in hardware. See figure 12.3.2.

The procedure *eval-code* can be made to resemble hardware more closely by transforming it to imperative form in the style chapter 10. The result is displayed in figure 12.3.3. We have introduced two more variables, `done` and `result`, which model additional machine states and allow us to use a single recursive call to *eval-code/reg*.

It would be even more realistic if we represented object code as a *vector* of instructions, rather than as a *list* of instructions. The machine procedure would then use `(set! pc (+ pc 1))`, instead of `(set! pc (cdr pc))`, to update the program counter. This more closely resembles the program counter increment operation of a traditional fetch-execute cycle. The code vector is also more realistic in that it embodies the random access character of a typical machine's main memory. This allows absolute code addresses to be represented by vector indices.

Our list-of-instructions object code is not entirely flat, since the else branch code of a `brz` instruction is contained within the instruction itself. See the top portion of figure 12.3.4.

Using the vector-of-instructions code representation, we can place the else code at the end of the code vector. A `brz` instruction then includes a vector index (absolute address) referring to the else code, instead of the code itself. The code is now completely flat. See the lower portion of figure 12.3.4.

Many compilers output *relocatable code* in which structure such as that introduced by conditional statements is represented by *symbolic addresses*. A system software utility called a *linker* is then used to read this code file and write a code file in which these symbolic addresses are replaced by numeric memory addresses.

o *Exercise 12.3.1*

Write a procedure `link` that takes list-of-instructions code and returns flat vector-of-instructions code. Modify *eval-code/reg* to execute vector-of-instructions code. □

Figure 12.3.3   Register machine for flat object code

```
(define ir '*)
(define pc '*)
(define done '*)
(define result '*)

(define eval-code
  (lambda (code)
    (set! pc code)
    (set! done #f)
    (eval-code/reg)))

(define eval-code/reg
  (lambda ()
    (set! ir (car pc))
    (set! pc (cdr pc))
    (variant-case ir
      (stop (reg)
        (set! done #t)
        (set! result (get-reg reg)))
      (move-imm (datum reg)
        (set-reg! reg datum))
      (fetch (var env reg)
        (set-reg! reg (apply-env (get-reg env) var)))
      (sum-list (sum-args reg)
        (set-reg! reg (add-list (get-reg sum-args))))
      (cons-1 (reg)
        (set-reg! reg '()))
      (cons-3 (first rest reg)
        (set-reg! reg (cons (get-reg first) (get-reg rest))))
      (brz (test else-instruc)
        (if (zero? (get-reg test)) (set! pc else-instruc)))
      (else (error "Invalid instruction:" ir)))
    (if done result (eval-code/reg))))
```

Figure 12.3.4   Comparison of compiled code

```
> (compile "if 0 then sum(3, 4) else sum(five, six)")
(#(move-imm 0 r0)
 #(brz r0 (#(fetch five env-reg r0)
           #(fetch six env-reg r1)
           #(cons-1 r2)
           #(cons-3 r1 r2 r1)
           #(cons-3 r0 r1 r0)
           #(sum-list r0 r0)
           #(stop r0)))
 #(move-imm 3 r0)
 #(move-imm 4 r1)
 #(cons-1 r2)
 #(cons-3 r1 r2 r1)
 #(cons-3 r0 r1 r0)
 #(sum-list r0 r0)
 #(stop r0))

> (compile "if 0 then sum(3, 4) else sum(five, six)")
#(#(move-imm 0 r0)
  #(brz r0 9)
  #(move-imm 3 r0)
  #(move-imm 4 r1)
  #(cons-1 r2)
  #(cons-3 r1 r2 r1)
  #(cons-3 r0 r1 r0)
  #(sum-list r0 r0)
  #(stop r0)
  #(fetch five env-reg r0)
  #(fetch six env-reg r1)
  #(cons-1 r2)
  #(cons-3 r1 r2 r1)
  #(cons-3 r0 r1 r0)
  #(sum-list r0 r0)
  #(stop r0))
```

A shortcoming of our compiler is that conditional expressions can lead to multiple copies of code. For example, the code for

```
"sum(f(x), if z then x else y)"
```

will contain two copies of the addition. Modify the compiler so that conditional expressions never duplicate code. □

• *Exercise 12.3.3*

Add the form `greater`(exp_1, exp_2), which is nonzero if the value of exp_1 is greater than the value of exp_2, to the source language, and derive an associated compiler and machine. □

• *Exercise 12.3.4*

Add `begin` and `:=` forms to the source language, and derive an associated compiler and machine. □

12.4 Compiling Procedures

The techniques introduced so far may be used with minor variations to enrich the source language of our compiler with a great many language features, such as additional primitive operators and control structures. However, there is one especially important extension that requires new techniques: the addition of procedures. In this section we introduce these techniques.

We begin by extending the CPS interpreter of figure 12.1.1 to interpret forms for creation and application of procedures. See figure 12.4.1. All procedural values are closures, since in our small language there are no first-class primitives. (Primitives, such as `sum`, are special forms.)

The next step in the transformation of our interpreter is to define procedures that abstract actions and use `build-cont` to abstract continuations, as in section 12.1. We also use the register allocation technique of section 12.2. A naive approach to this transformation would result in the following definitions.

Figure 12.4.1   Interpreter for a language with procedures

```
(define-record closure (formals body env))

(define eval-exp
  (lambda (exp env k)
    (variant-case exp
      (proc (formals body)
        (k (make-closure formals body env)))
      (app (rator rands)
        (eval-exp rator env
          (lambda (closure)
            (eval-rands rands env
              (lambda (args)
                (apply-closure closure args k))))))
      ...)))

(define apply-closure
  (lambda (closure args k)
    (variant-case closure
      (closure (formals body env)
        (eval-exp body (extend-env formals args env) k)))))
```

```
(define eval-exp
  (lambda (exp env k)
    (variant-case exp
      (proc (formals body)
        (close-action formals body env k))
      (app (rator rands)
        (eval-exp rator env
          (build-cont
            (lambda (closure)
              (eval-rands rands env
                (build-cont
                  (lambda (args)
                    (apply-closure closure args k)))))))
      ...)))

(define close-action
  (lambda (formals body env k)
    (k (make-closure formals body env))))
```

If we try to write `apply-closure` with this approach, however, we run into two difficulties. First, the body of a closure is not passed to `eval-exp` until the closure is invoked (at run time). This defeats the purpose of compilation. Second, even if the body were represented in some form such that `apply-closure` did not have to call `eval-exp`, it would still be necessary to (1) extend the environment, (2) evaluate the body with the argument list, environment, and current continuation, and then (3) return a result to the caller. Since in most machines environment extension, procedure call (code invocation), and procedure return are performed by separate instructions, we would like to break the work of `apply-closure` down into more primitive actions.

To avoid these difficulties, we first introduce a new type of object, called an *exec*, that executes a procedure's body given an environment, argument list, and continuation and returns the result. A closure then contains only an exec and an environment:

```
(define-record closure (exec env)).
```

Initially we represent execs as procedures. When an exec is invoked with an environment, argument list, and continuation, it extends the environment. The extended environment is then passed to a continuation that executes the body of the associated procedure with a continuation that returns the result. We abstract these actions and continuations with the following procedures.

```
(define build-exec
  (lambda (formals body)
    (lambda (env args k)
      (extend-env-action formals args env
        (lambda (extended-env)
          (eval-exp body extended-env
            (lambda (val)
              (return-action val k)))))))))

(define extend-env-action
  (lambda (formals args env k)
    (k (extend-env formals args env))))

(define return-action
  (lambda (v k)
    (k v)))
```

We begin evaluation of an application by evaluating its operator with a continuation that accepts the value of the operator, which must be a closure. This continuation then evaluates the operands by calling `eval-rands` with a continuation that applies the closure's exec to the closure's environment, the argument list, and the continuation of the application. This may be expressed by extending the interpreter of figure 12.2.1 as follows.

```
(define eval-exp
  (lambda (exp env k)
    (variant-case exp
      (proc (formals body)
        (close-action (build-exec formals body) env k))
      (app (rator rands)
        (eval-exp rator env
          (build-cont (cont->free-regs k)
            (lambda (closure)
              (eval-rands rands env
                (build-cont (cons closure (cont->free-regs k))
                  (lambda (args)
                    (apply-closure-action closure args k)))))))))
      ...)))

(define close-action
  (lambda (exec env k)
    (k (make-closure exec env))))

(define apply-closure-action
  (lambda (closure args k)
    (variant-case closure
      (closure (exec env) (exec env args k)))))
```

The full interpreter employs the action procedures of figure 12.1.3 in addition to those above.

We are now ready to transform the interpreter into a compiler and derive a machine that interprets the compiler's object code. This object code is composed of data structures that symbolically represent actions, continuations, and execs.

Once more, the transformation from an interpreter to a compiler is accomplished by redefining the action procedures, without further modification of `eval-exp`. We add the record type and action procedure definitions of figure 12.4.2 to those of figure 12.1.4.

Figure 12.4.2   Actions to support procedures

```
(define-record extend-env-instruc (formals args-reg env-reg k))
(define extend-env-action make-extend-env-instruc)

(define-record return-instruc (return-reg k))
(define return-action make-return-instruc)

(define-record close-instruc (exec env-reg k))
(define close-action make-close-instruc)

(define-record save-instruc (reg-list k))
(define save-action make-save-instruc)

(define-record restore-instruc (k))
(define restore-action make-restore-instruc)

(define-record apply-closure-instruc (closure-reg args-reg k))
(define apply-closure-action
  (lambda (closure-reg args-reg k)
    (variant-case k
      (cont (reg free-regs code)
        (save-action
          (append '(save-regs k-reg env-reg) free-regs)
          (make-cont 'ignore-reg '()
            (make-apply-closure-instruc closure-reg args-reg
              (make-cont reg '()
                (restore-action
                  (make-cont 'ignore-reg '() code))))))))
      (else (error "Invalid continuation:" k)))))
```

These transformations have been entirely straightforward. The interesting transformation is that of *build-exec*. The naive approach would be to define an *exec* record type as follows.

```
(define-record exec (formals body))
(define build-exec make-exec)
```

The difficulty with this approach is that the body will not be compiled (passed to *eval-exp*) until the exec record is interpreted at run time. Since *eval-exp* now accepts environments and continuations symbolically, it should be possible to compile the body of a closure prior to run time. At compile time we do not know what the environment, argument list, or continuation will be when an exec is invoked, but it is enough to know what registers they will be in. It is common practice for the environment, argument list, and continuation to be recorded in standard locations prior to a procedure call. Thus, by convention, we assume that these values are conveyed to a called procedure in registers named `env-reg`, `args-reg`, and `k-reg`, respectively. It follows that execs may be represented simply as the code generated by an `extend-env-action`. This code creates an extended environment for a procedure call with a continuation that invokes a procedure in the new environment. We use *make-cont* instead of *build-cont* because we want to name the register ourselves.

```
(define build-exec
  (lambda (formals body)
    (extend-env-action formals 'args-reg 'env-reg
      (make-cont 'env-reg '()
        (eval-exp body 'env-reg
          (build-cont '()
            (lambda (val)
              (return-action val 'k-reg)))))))))
```

A simple example illustrates that an application compiles to a `close-instruc` command that forms a closure containing an `extend-env-instruc` command and the current environment. This closure is then passed to a continuation that evaluates the operands of the application and then applies the closure to the argument list, with the continuation of the application (in this case the final value continuation). We leave the free register lists in the following code.

```
> (compile "(proc (x) x)(17)")
#(close-instruc
 #(extend-env-instruc (x) args-reg env-reg
  #(cont env-reg ()
   #(varref-instruc x env-reg
    #(cont r0 ()
     #(return-instruc r0 k-reg)))))
 env-reg
 #(cont r0 ()
  #(lit-instruc 17
   #(cont r1 (r0)
    #(emptyargs-instruc
     #(cont r2 (r1 r0)
      #(rest-instruc r1 r2
```

```
             #(cont r1 (r0)
              #(save-instruc (save-regs k-reg env-reg)
               #(cont ignore-reg ()
                #(apply-closure-instruc r0 r1
                 #(cont r0 ()
                  #(restore-instruc
                   #(cont ignore-reg ()
                    #(halt-instruc r0)))))))))))))))))))
```

This corresponds to the following Scheme CPS code.

```
(close-action
 (lambda (env-reg)
  (lambda (args-reg k-reg)
   (extend-env-action '(x) args-reg env-reg
    (lambda (env-reg)
     (varref-action 'x env-reg
      (lambda (r0)
       (return-action r0 k-reg)))))))
 init-env
 (lambda (r0)
  (lit-action 17
   (lambda (r1)
    (emptyargs-action
     (lambda (r2)
      (rest-action r1 r2
       (lambda (r1)
        (save-action '(save-regs k-reg env-reg)
         (lambda ()
          (apply-closure-action r0 r1
           (lambda (r0)
            (restore-action
             (lambda ()
              (halt-action r0)))))))))))))))))))))

(define save-action
  (lambda (lst goto)
    (goto)))

(define restore-action
  (lambda (goto)
    (goto)))
```

Figure 12.4.3   Interpreter for procedure code

```
(define eval-code
  (lambda (code)
    (variant-case code
      (close-instruc (exec env-reg k)
        (apply-cont k
          (make-closure exec
            (get-reg env-reg))))
      (extend-env-instruc (formals args-reg env-reg k)
        (apply-cont k
          (extend-env formals (get-reg args-reg) (get-reg env-reg))))
      (save-instruc (reg-list k)
        (set-reg! 'save-regs
          (map (lambda (reg)
                 (cons reg (get-reg reg)))
               reg-list))
        (goto-cont k))
      (apply-closure-instruc (closure-reg args-reg k)
        (set-reg! 'k-reg k)
        (set-reg! 'args-reg (get-reg args-reg))
        (set-reg! 'env-reg (closure->env (get-reg closure-reg)))
        (eval-code (closure->exec (get-reg closure-reg))))
      (restore-instruc (k)
        (for-each (lambda (file-entry)
                    (set-reg! (car file-entry) (cdr file-entry)))
                  (get-reg 'save-regs))
        (goto-cont k))
      (return-instruc (return-reg k)
        (apply-cont (get-reg k) (get-reg return-reg)))
      ...)))
```

In converting code to such Scheme expressions, it is necessary to create thunks for continuations when the corresponding machine instruction invokes *goto-cont* instead of *apply-cont*. These machine instructions are save-instruc and restore-instruc. The associated actions, *save-action* and *restore-action*, are included for completeness.

Next, we extend the *eval-code* procedure in figure 12.1.5 to support the new action codes. See figure 12.4.3. In the apply-closure-instruc clause, the continuation register, k-reg, is set to the continuation of the procedure call. This corresponds to saving the program counter before jumping to a procedure in conventional architectures. The first argument of *set-reg!* is the *name* of a register, so it must be quoted. The argument list must also be moved from the register in which it is currently stored to the standard register, named `args-reg`, in which the exec expects to find it. Finally, the environment stored in the closure is moved to `env-reg` and the exec is executed. Derivation of the other clauses of *eval-code* from the corresponding action procedures is straightforward.

Before running code, we create a register file not only to contain r0, r1, r2, r3, r4, r5, and env-reg, but also to include args-reg, k-reg, and save-regs.

```
(define reg-file
  (extend-ff*
    reg-names
    (map (lambda (x) (make-cell '*))
         (append '(args-reg k-reg save-regs) reg-names))
    (extend-ff 'env-reg (make-cell init-env) (create-empty-ff))))
```

- *Exercise 12.4.1*
  Modify the definitions of *eval-exp* and *eval-code* in this section for list-of-instruction code representation. []

- *Exercise 12.4.2*
  Modify the definitions of *eval-exp* and *eval-code* in this section for vector-of-instruction code representation. []

- *Exercise 12.4.3*
  Modify the definitions of *eval-exp*, *eval-code*, and *init-env* to support primitive procedures, such as +, -, and *. []

- *Exercise 12.4.4*
  Extend the compiler and machine to handle letrecproc. []

- *Exercise 12.4.5*
  Modify the compiler so that it uses labels and goto instructions in place of procedure call instructions whenever possible. []

- *Exercise 12.4.6*
  One way of verifying the correctness of our compiler is to show that for any source expression *exp*

```
(eval-code (compile exp))  ⇒  (eval-exp exp env-reg k-reg)
```

where *eval-exp* is an evaluator, not the compiler. Verify, by induction on the structure of *exp*, that this relation holds. Note that *env-reg* and *k-reg* do not appear explicitly on the left-hand side of this equation, but they appear in the code generated by (compile *exp*). Be careful about this in your proof.

□

o *Exercise 12.4.7*
Modify the compiler and machine to use lexical addresses as in exercise 2.3.10. To do this, give the compiler a second argument, symbol-table, a map from variables to lexical addresses (pairs of integers). In the machine, env-reg will hold a *lexical environment*: a map from lexical addresses to values. Then varref-instruc is replaced by an instruction of the form (lex-varref-instruc ⟨integer⟩ ⟨integer⟩ ⟨register⟩ ⟨code⟩), so that program variables no longer appear in compiled code. □

o *Exercise 12.4.8*
To relate the lexical scope compiler of the preceding exercise to the interpreter, we must relate the symbol table and lexical environment used in this compiler and machine to the ordinary environments used in the interpreter. This can be done by reconstructing the interpreter environment as the composition of these two maps. The compiler must obey the specification below. Verify, by induction on *exp*, that this relation holds.

```
    (eval-code (compile exp symbol-table))
 ⇒ (eval-exp exp (compose env-reg symbol-table) k-reg)
```
□

o *Exercise 12.4.9*
The compiler and machine of this section do not properly handle tail recursion, because the implementation of *build-exec* specifies that a new continuation is built every time a procedure is entered. Figure 12.4.4 contains an implementation of a compiler that generates code that runs tail recursively. It does this by using a special-case compiler, *tr-eval-exp*, to compile code in tail position. Notice how *tr-eval-exp* calls *eval-exp* on the subexpressions (in nontail position) of an application.

First, implement this compiler. Then verify that it produces code that executes tail-recursive procedures iteratively. To do this, modify the machine to keep track of the length of the continuation (the contents of k-reg). Then write a tail-recursive program in the source language and confirm that when

Figure 12.4.4   Properly tail-recursive compiler

```
(define tr-eval-exp
  (lambda (exp env free-regs k)
    (variant-case exp
      (lit (datum) (tr-lit-action datum free-regs k))
      (varref (var) (tr-varref-action var env free-regs k))
      (proc (formals body)
        (tr-close-action (build-exec formals body) env free-regs k))
      (app (rator rands)
        (eval-exp rator env
          (build-cont free-regs
            (lambda (closure)
              (eval-rands rands env
                (build-cont (cons closure free-regs)
                  (lambda (args)
                    (tr-apply-closure-action closure args free-regs k)))))))))
      (if (test-exp then-exp else-exp)
        (eval-exp test-exp env
          (build-cont free-regs
            (lambda (test)
              (tr-test-action test
                (lambda (free-regs k)
                  (tr-eval-exp then-exp env free-regs k))
                (lambda (free-regs k)
                  (tr-eval-exp else-exp env free-regs k))
                free-regs
                k)))))
      (sum (rands)
        (eval-rands rands env
          (build-cont free-regs
            (lambda (arg-list)
              (tr-sum-action arg-list free-regs k)))))
      (else (error "Invalid abstract syntax: " exp)))))

(define tr-return-to
  (lambda (free-regs k-reg)
    (build-cont (cons k-reg free-regs)
      (lambda (new-var)
        (return-action k-reg new-var)))))
```

Figure 12.4.4   Properly tail-recursive compiler (continued)

```
(define tr-lit-action
  (lambda (datum free-regs k-reg)
    (make-lit-instruc datum (tr-return-to free-regs k-reg))))

(define tr-varref-action
  (lambda (var env-reg free-regs k-reg)
    (make-varref-instruc var env-reg
      (tr-return-to free-regs k-reg))))

(define tr-sum-action
  (lambda (arg-list-reg free-regs k-reg)
    (make-sum-instruc arg-list-reg (tr-return-to free-regs k-reg))))

(define tr-close-action
  (lambda (exec env-reg free-regs k-reg)
    (make-close-instruc exec env-reg
      (tr-return-to free-regs k-reg))))

(define-record tr-apply-closure-instruc (closure-reg args-reg k-reg))
(define tr-apply-closure-action
  (lambda (closure-reg args-reg free-regs k-reg)
    (make-tr-apply-closure-instruc closure-reg args-reg k-reg)))

(define build-exec
  (lambda (formals body)
    (extend-env-action formals 'args-reg 'env-reg
      (make-cont 'env-reg '()
        (tr-eval-exp body 'env-reg '() 'k-reg)))))

(define eval-code
  (lambda (code)
    (variant-case code
      (tr-apply-closure-instruc (closure-reg args-reg k-reg)
        (set-reg! 'k-reg (get-reg k-reg))
        (set-reg! 'args-reg (get-reg args-reg))
        (set-reg! 'env-reg (closure->env (get-reg closure-reg)))
        (eval-code (closure->exec (get-reg closure-reg))))
      ...)))
```

it runs, the size of the continuation is independent of the number of iterations of the program. □

○ *Exercise 12.4.10*
Extend the compiler of exercise 12.4.9 to handle :=, `begin`, and `letrecproc`. □

● *Exercise 12.4.11*
Here is a somewhat different approach to compiling. In this approach, the compiled code is regarded as acting on a machine with four registers: an accumulator, a buffer, a lexical environment, and a continuation. Such a machine can be modeled as we did in chapter 11, by writing the actions as procedures that take the values of the registers as their arguments. See figure 12.4.5 for the definition of such a machine, in a procedural representation.

The compiler takes four arguments: a boolean flag (true if the source expression is in tail position), a source expression, a symbol table, and machine code, and produces another code. See figure 12.4.6. A suitable top-level procedure might be

```
(define run
  (lambda (exp)
    ((compile-exp #t (parse exp)
       initial-symbol-table restore-code)
     '*
     '()
     initial-lex-env
     (lambda (x) x))))
```

a. Write the rest of the auxiliary functions to implement the compiler of figure 12.4.6 and the machine of figure 12.4.5.

b. Confirm that it executes tail-form programs iteratively, as you did for the `tr-eval-exp` compiler of exercise 12.4.9.

c. Add :=, `begin`, and `letrecproc` to this compiler.

d. Modify the compiler and machine so that it emits useful trace information on every procedure call.

e. Add `callcc` to the initial lexical environment.

f. Add dynamically-scoped globals to the language; these should behave like Scheme procedures defined using `define`. □

Figure 12.4.5 Actions of the four-register machine

```
(define lit-action
  (lambda (datum code)
    (lambda (acc val* lex-env k)
      (code datum val* lex-env k))))

(define varref-action
  (lambda (lex-addr code)
    (lambda (acc val* lex-env k)
      (code (lookup-lex-env lex-env lex-addr) val* lex-env k))))

(define if-action
  (lambda (then-code else-code)
    (lambda (acc val* lex-env k)
      (if acc
          (then-code acc val* lex-env k)
          (else-code acc val* lex-env k)))))

(define proc-action
  (lambda (code-of-body code)
    (lambda (acc val* lex-env k)
      (code
        (lambda (args new-k)
          (code-of-body '* '() (extend-lex-env args lex-env) new-k))
        val*
        lex-env k))))

(define restore-code (lambda (acc val* lex-env k) (k acc)))

(define invoke-code (lambda (acc val* lex-env k) (acc val* k)))

(define save-action
  (lambda (code1 code2)
    (lambda (acc val* lex-env k)
      (code1 '* '() lex-env
        (lambda (v) (code2 v val* lex-env k))))))

(define push-action
  (lambda (code)
    (lambda (acc val* lex-env k)
      (code acc (cons acc val*) lex-env k))))
```

Figure 12.4.6   Compiler for the four-register machine

```
(define compile-exp
  (lambda (tail-pos? exp symbol-table next-code)
    (variant-case exp
      (lit (datum) (lit-action datum next-code))
      (varref (var)
        (varref-action
          (lexical-addr symbol-table var)
          next-code))
      (if (test-exp then-exp else-exp)
        (compile-exp #f test-exp symbol-table
          (if-action
            (compile-exp tail-pos? then-exp
              symbol-table
              next-code)
            (compile-exp tail-pos? else-exp
              symbol-table
              next-code))))
      (proc (formals body)
        (proc-action
          (compile-exp #t body
            (extend-symbol-table formals symbol-table)
            restore-code)
          next-code))
      (app (rator rands)
        (let ((app-code (compile-rands rands
                          symbol-table
                          (compile-exp #f rator symbol-table invoke-code))))
          (if tail-pos?
              app-code
              (save-action app-code next-code)))))))

(define compile-rands
  (lambda (rands symbol-table next-code)
    (if (null? rands)
        next-code
        (compile-exp #f (car rands) symbol-table
          (push-action
            (compile-rands (cdr rands) symbol-table next-code))))))
```

• *Exercise 12.4.12*

In this exercise we shall prove the correctness of the compiler of figure 12.4.6. Because the compiler and machine are functional, the correctness criterion is simpler than that of exercise 12.4.6, although the proof is somewhat more complicated because it is necessary to account for tail recursion. The correctness criterion requires three statements:

```
    ((compile-exp #f exp symbol-table next-code) acc val* lex-env k)
 ⇒ (eval-exp exp (compose lex-env symbol-table)
      (lambda (z) (next-code (cons z val*) lex-env k)))


    ((compile-exp #t exp symbol-table next-code) acc '() lex-env k)
 ⇒ (eval-exp exp (compose lex-env symbol-table) k)


    ((compile-rands rands symbol-table next-code) acc val* lex-env k)
 ⇒ (eval-rands rands (compose lex-env symbol-table)
      (lambda (w)
        (next-code (append (reverse w) val*) lex-env k)))
```

We can explain each of these statements as follows:

1. The goal of the code for *exp* in nontail position is to evaluate *exp* in a continuation that pushes the value of *exp* onto the buffer and then performs the next action.

2. The goal of the code for *exp* in tail position is to evaluate *exp* and pass the value to the continuation *k*. Note that in this case, val* will always be empty, and *next-code* is ignored. This accounts for the '* in run above.

3. The goal of the code for a list of operands is to accumulate the values in reverse order on the top of the stack val* and then to perform the next action.

Prove, using induction on the structure of *exp*, that each of these three relations is true. ☐

• *Exercise 12.4.13*

The compiler uses a four-register machine in much the same way as the scanner of chapter 11 uses a two-register machine. Careful attention to the use of acc and val* makes it clear that it is acting in the same way as the buffer, if we think about acc being consed onto val*. Rewrite the compiler so that it combines the uses of acc and val* and hence uses just three registers. ☐

12.5 Summary

An interpreter can be modified to become a translator from the defined language to the defining language by introducing an ADT of interpreter actions, and then redefining the action-building procedures to emit code rather than perform actions.

If the interpreter is a CPS interpreter, the output from the translator is CPS code that strongly resembles ordinary assembly language. Variables in the CPS code correspond to machine registers, and the binding patterns in the CPS code correspond to the setting of those registers.

Because the CPS output code is stylized, it is possible to build an interpreter that is specialized for this code. The resulting interpreter is analogous to the microprogram of a conventional machine.

The CPS output code can be transformed into a sequence of machine instructions by a simple regrouping of its components, or by changing the action procedures to emit this syntax initially.

Appendix A Record Implementation

Standard Scheme does not support records, though most implementations provide some such mechanism (sometimes called structures). Here we provide an implementation of the record facility used in this book.

In order to introduce the new special forms `define-record` and `variant-case`, some syntactic extension (or "macro") facility is required. See figure A.1 and figure A.2 for an implementation of `define-record` and `variant-case` using `extend-syntax`. See Dybvig [1987] for details of this `extend-syntax` mechanism.

Figure A.1   Auxiliaries for `define-record` and `variant-case`

```
(define record-proc-names
  (lambda (name fields)
    (let ((name-str (symbol->string name)))
      (cons (string->symbol (string-append (symbol->string 'make-) name-str))
            (cons (string->symbol (string-append name-str "?"))
                  (map (lambda (field)
                         (string->symbol (string-append name-str
                                                         "->"
                                                         (symbol->string field))))
                       fields))))))

(define record-indices
  (lambda (vec-len)
    (letrec ((loop (lambda (i)
                     (if (= i vec-len) '() (cons i (loop (+ i 1)))))))
      (loop 1))))

(define make-unique-name
  (lambda (names)
    (string->symbol (apply string-append (map symbol->string names)))))
```

Figure A.2 Implementation of `variant-case` and `define-record`

```
(extend-syntax (variant-case else)
  ((variant-case var) (error "variant-case: no clause matches" var))
  ((variant-case var (else exp1 exp2 ...)) (begin exp1 exp2 ...))
  ((variant-case exp clause ...)
   (not (symbol? 'exp))
   (with ((var (gensym)))
     (let ((var exp)) (variant-case var clause ...))))
  ((variant-case var (name (field ...) exp1 exp2 ...) clause ...)
   (with (((make-name name? name->field ...)
          (record-proc-names 'name '(field ...))))
     (if (name? var)
         (let ((field (name->field var)) ...) exp1 exp2 ...)
         (variant-case var clause ...)))))

(extend-syntax (define-record)
  ((define-record name (field ...))
   (with (((make-name name? name->field ...) (record-proc-names 'name '(field ...)))
          (unique-name (make-unique-name '(name field ...)))
          (vec-len (+ 1 (length '(field ...)))))
     (with (((i ...) (record-indices 'vec-len)))
       (begin
         (define make-name
           (let ((unique-name vector))
             (lambda (field ...)
               (unique-name 'name field ...))))
         (define name?
           (lambda (obj)
             (and (vector? obj)
                  (= (vector-length obj) vec-len)
                  (eq? (vector-ref obj 0) 'name))))
         (define name->field
           (lambda (obj)
             (if (name? obj)
                 (vector-ref obj i)
                 (error "name->field: bad record" obj))))
         ...)))))
```

Appendix B Abstract Syntax

In this book, although we present syntax for a character string language, we also support a list structure language. Both of the languages parse to identical parse trees, using the record declarations given here. This way the program processing programs all have the same abstract view, regardless of the choice of language.

Figure B.1   Abstract syntax record declarations for chapter 5

```
(define-record define (var exp))
(define-record varref (var))
(define-record lit (datum))
(define-record app (rator rands))
(define-record if (test-exp then-exp else-exp))
(define-record let (decls body))
(define-record decl (var exp))
(define-record proc (formals body))
(define-record varassign (var exp))
(define-record letmutable (decls body))
(define-record begin (exp1 exp2))
(define-record letrecproc (procdecls body))
(define-record procdecl (var formals body))
(define-record letrec (decls body))
(define-record dynassign (var exp body))
(define-record letdynamic (decls body))
```

Figure B.2   Abstract syntax record declarations for chapter 6

```
(define-record definearray (var dim-exp))
(define-record letarray (arraydecls body))
(define-record arrayref (array index))
(define-record arrayassign (array index exp))
(define-record letproc (procdecls body))
(define-record local (decls))
(define-record keydecl (var exp))
```

Figure B.3   Abstract syntax record declarations for chapter 7

```
(define-record super-meth-app (name rands))
(define-record meth-app (name rands))
(define-record i-varref (var))
(define-record c-varref (var))
(define-record i-varassign (var exp))
(define-record c-varassign (var exp))
(define-record method (formals body))
(define-record new-simpleinst (class-exp))
(define-record new-simpleclass (c-vars i-vars methdecls init-exp))
(define-record new-class (parent-exp c-vars i-vars methdecls init-exp))
(define-record new-instance (class-exp parent-exp i-vars methdecls))
```

Figure B.4   Abstract syntax record declarations for chapter 9

```
(define-record abort (exp))
(define-record letcont (var body))
(define-record callcc (exp))
(define-record coroutine (exp))
(define-record wind (pre body post))
```

Figure B.5   Abstract syntax record declaration for chapter 12

```
(define-record sum (rands))
```

Appendix C Character String Syntax

The tokens of the language are defined by the following grammar.

$$\begin{aligned}
\langle\text{identifier}\rangle &::= \langle\text{nondigit-id-char}\rangle \, \{ \, \langle\text{nondigit-id-char}\rangle \ | \ \langle\text{digit}\rangle \, \}^* \\
& \ | \ \texttt{+} \ | \ \texttt{-} \ | \ \texttt{*} \\
\langle\text{integer-literal}\rangle &::= \langle\text{digit}\rangle \, \{ \langle\text{digit}\rangle \}^* \\
\langle\text{whitespace}\rangle &::= \{ \, \langle\text{space}\rangle \ | \ \langle\text{newline}\rangle \, \}^+ \\
\langle\text{comment}\rangle &::= \texttt{\%} \, \{ \langle\text{any-char-but-newline}\rangle \}^* \\
\langle\text{assign-sym}\rangle &::= \texttt{:=} \\
\langle\text{ampersand}\rangle &::= \texttt{\&} \\
\langle\text{double-ampersand}\rangle &::= \texttt{\&\&} \\
\langle\text{lparen}\rangle &::= \texttt{(} \\
\langle\text{rparen}\rangle &::= \texttt{)} \\
\langle\text{lbracket}\rangle &::= \texttt{[} \\
\langle\text{rbracket}\rangle &::= \texttt{]} \\
\langle\text{comma}\rangle &::= \texttt{,} \\
\langle\text{eqsign}\rangle &::= \texttt{=} \\
\langle\text{semicolon}\rangle &::= \texttt{;} \\
\langle\text{colon}\rangle &::= \texttt{:} \\
\langle\text{dollar-sign}\rangle &::= \texttt{\$}
\end{aligned}$$

The letters are the 52 upper and lower case letters; the digits are the ten decimal digits; a "nondigit-id-char" is any letter.

The language is defined by the following concrete and abstract syntax.

⟨form⟩ ::= `define` ⟨var⟩ `=` ⟨exp⟩	`define (var exp)`
| `definearray` ⟨var⟩ `[`⟨exp⟩`]`	`definearray (var dim-exp)`
| ⟨exp⟩	
⟨exp⟩ ::= ⟨integer-literal⟩	`lit (datum)`
| ⟨varref⟩	
| ⟨operator⟩ ⟨operands⟩	`app (rator rands)`
| `if` ⟨exp⟩ `then` ⟨exp⟩ `else` ⟨exp⟩	`if (test-exp then-exp else-exp)`
| `let` ⟨decls⟩ `in` ⟨exp⟩	`let (decls body)`
| `proc` ⟨varlist⟩ ⟨exp⟩	`proc (formals body)`
| ⟨var⟩ `:=` ⟨exp⟩	`varassign (var exp)`
| `letmutable` ⟨decls⟩ `in` ⟨exp⟩	`letmutable (decls body)`
| `begin` ⟨exp⟩ ⟨compound⟩	`begin (exp1 exp2)`
| `letrecproc` ⟨procdecls⟩ `in` ⟨exp⟩	`letrecproc (procdecls body)`
| `letrec` ⟨decls⟩ `in` ⟨exp⟩	`letrec (decls body)`
| ⟨var⟩ `:=` ⟨exp⟩ `during` ⟨exp⟩	`dynassign (var exp body)`
| `letdynamic` ⟨decls⟩ `in` ⟨exp⟩	`letdynamic (decls body)`
| `letarray` ⟨arraydecls⟩ `in` ⟨exp⟩	`letarray (arraydecls body)`
| ⟨array-exp⟩ `[`⟨exp⟩`]`	`arrayref (array index)`
| ⟨array-exp⟩ `[`⟨exp⟩`]` `:=` ⟨exp⟩	`arrayassign (array index exp)`
| `letproc` ⟨procdecls⟩ `in` ⟨exp⟩	`letproc (procdecls body)`
| `local` ⟨decls⟩ `in` ⟨exp⟩	`local (decls body)`
| ⟨instance-var⟩	
| ⟨class-var⟩	
| ⟨instance-var⟩ `:=` ⟨exp⟩	`i-varassign (var exp)`
| ⟨class-var⟩ `:=` ⟨exp⟩	`c-varassign (var exp)`
| `method` ⟨varlist⟩ ⟨exp⟩	`method (formals body)`
| `$`⟨var⟩ `(`⟨exps⟩`)`	`meth-app (name rands)`
| `simpleinstance` ⟨exp⟩	`new-simpleinst (class-exp)`
| `simpleclass` ⟨varlist⟩ ⟨varlist⟩ ⟨methdecls⟩ ⟨exp⟩	`new-simpleclass (c-vars i-vars methdecls init-exp)`
| `class` ⟨exp⟩`,` ⟨c-vars⟩ ⟨i-vars⟩ ⟨methdecls⟩ ⟨exp⟩	`new-class (parent-exp c-vars i-vars methdecls init-exp)`
| `$`⟨var⟩ ⟨super-rands⟩	`super-meth-app (name rands)`
| `instance` ⟨exp⟩`,` ⟨exp⟩`,` ⟨varlist⟩ ⟨methdecls⟩	`new-instance (class-exp parent-exp i-vars methdecls)`
| `abort` ⟨exp⟩	`abort (exp)`

| letcont ⟨var⟩ in ⟨exp⟩   letcont (var body)
| callcc ⟨exp⟩   callcc (exp)
| coroutine ⟨exp⟩   coroutine (exp)
| wind ⟨exp⟩ within ⟨exp⟩   wind (pre body
      unwind ⟨exp⟩   post)
| sum ⟨operands⟩   sum (rands)

```
          ⟨var⟩ ::= ⟨identifier⟩
     ⟨operator⟩ ::= ⟨varref⟩
                  |  (⟨exp⟩)
      ⟨operand⟩ ::= ⟨exp⟩
       ⟨varref⟩ ::= ⟨var⟩                        varref (var)
        ⟨decls⟩ ::= ⟨decl⟩ {;⟨decl⟩}*
         ⟨decl⟩ ::= ⟨var⟩ = ⟨exp⟩               decl (var exp)
      ⟨varlist⟩ ::= ( )
                  |  (⟨vars⟩ {,⟨keydecl⟩}*)
                  |  (⟨keydecls⟩)
         ⟨vars⟩ ::= ⟨var⟩ {,⟨var⟩}*
    ⟨compound⟩ ::= {;⟨exp⟩}* end
    ⟨procdecls⟩ ::= ⟨procdecl⟩ {;⟨procdecl⟩}*
    ⟨procdecl⟩ ::= ⟨var⟩ ⟨varlist⟩ = ⟨exp⟩     procdecl (var formals body)
   ⟨array-exp⟩ ::= ⟨exp⟩
   ⟨arraydecls⟩ ::= ⟨arraydecl⟩ {;⟨arraydecl⟩}*
   ⟨arraydecl⟩ ::= ⟨var⟩ [⟨exp⟩]               decl (var exp)
     ⟨keydecls⟩ ::= ⟨keydecl⟩ {,⟨keydecl⟩}*
      ⟨keydecl⟩ ::= :⟨var⟩ = ⟨exp⟩             decl (var exp)
     ⟨operands⟩ ::= ( )
                  |  (⟨exps⟩ {,⟨keydecl⟩}*)
                  |  (⟨keydecls⟩)
         ⟨exps⟩ ::= ⟨exp⟩ {,⟨exp⟩}*
⟨instance-var⟩ ::= &⟨var⟩                       i-varref (var)
    ⟨class-var⟩ ::= &&⟨var⟩                      c-varref (var)
    ⟨methdecls⟩ ::= ( )
                  |  ( ⟨decls⟩ )
⟨super-rands⟩ ::= (super)
                  |  (super, ⟨exps⟩)
```

Appendix D Character String Parser

This appendix is composed of nine figures. In order to run programs from chapter 5, you must include the record declarations from appendix B, the scanner from appendix E, and all of figures D.1 through D.4. Once chapter 5 works, it is very easy to add either chapter 6, section 6.6, chapter 7, chapter 9, or chapter 12. To run chapter 6, section 6.6, chapter 7, chapter 9, or chapter 12, include figure D.5, figure D.6, figure D.7, figure D.8, or figure D.9, respectively. These are modular, so for example, to run chapter 9, include everything necessary to run chapter 5, plus figure D.8. The definitions of figure D.6 redefine *parse-rands* and *parse-varlist* and they are needed only when the defined language supports section 6.6.

If you choose to use the interactive capabilities of appendix F, you will want to add those definitions and thus override some of these. This design is intentional. Often it is better to get the character string parser working smoothly before making it run interactively with unbounded character streams.

The code of this appendix is explained in chapter 11. The procedures *parse-loop∗* and *parse-loop+* are not presented in that chapter. Once that chapter is understood, their use will become clear. The ∗ and the + correspond to Kleene star and Kleene plus, respectively. They are useful when parsing expressions that have an arbitrary number of items, such as argument and parameter lists.

The procedure *error* is not part of Scheme, but virtually every Scheme system supports it. Here is the definition we used throughout the book:

```
(define error
  (lambda args
    (for-each (lambda (x) (display x) (display " ")) args)
    (newline)
    (reset)))
```

```
(define check/drop
  (lambda (class next-action)
    (lambda (buffer token-seq)
      (let ((token (token-seq-head token-seq)))
        (if (eq? (token->class token) class)
            (next-action buffer (token-seq-tail token-seq))
            (error "Syntax error: expecting a" class "not a" token))))))

(define check/shift
  (lambda (class next-action)
    (lambda (buffer token-seq)
      (let ((token (token-seq-head token-seq)))
        (if (eq? (token->class token) class)
            (next-action (cons (token->data token) buffer)
                         (token-seq-tail token-seq))
            (error "Syntax error: expecting a" class "not a" token))))))

(define goto-parser-state
  (lambda (state)
    (lambda (buffer token-seq)
      (let ((next-action (state (token-seq-head token-seq))))
        (next-action buffer token-seq)))))

(define reduce
  (lambda (prod-name)
    (lambda (buffer token-seq)
      (make-parser-answer
        (apply (get-constructor-from-name prod-name) (reverse buffer))
        token-seq))))

(define process-nt
  (lambda (state next-action)
    (lambda (buffer token-seq)
      (let ((next-answer ((goto-parser-state state) '() token-seq)))
        (next-action
          (cons (parser-answer->tree next-answer) buffer)
          (parser-answer->unparsed next-answer))))))

(define emit-list
  (lambda ()
    (lambda (buffer token-seq)
      (make-parser-answer (reverse buffer) token-seq))))
```

```
(define-record parser-answer (tree unparsed))
(define token-seq-head car)
(define token-seq-tail cdr)

(define character-string-parser
  (lambda (a-string)
    (parse-token-seq parse-form
      (character-string-scanner a-string))))

(define parse-token-seq
  (lambda (start-state token-seq)
    (let ((answer (parse-once start-state token-seq)))
      (variant-case answer
        (parser-answer (tree unparsed)
          (if (eq? (token->class (token-seq-head unparsed)) 'end-marker)
              tree
              (error "Tokens left over:" unparsed)))))))

(define parse-once
  (lambda (start-state token-seq)
    ((goto-parser-state start-state) '() token-seq)))

(define parse-loop*
  (lambda (terminator separator action)
    (letrec
      ((more (lambda (token)
               (let ((class (token->class token)))
                 (cond
                   ((eq? class terminator) (emit-list))
                   ((eq? separator class)
                    (check/drop separator
                      (action (goto-parser-state more))))
                   (else (error "Invalid separator token:" token))))))
       (lambda (token)
         (let ((class (token->class token)))
           (if (eq? class terminator)
               (emit-list)
               (action (goto-parser-state more)))))))))
```

Figure D.1   Parser procedures (continued)

```
(define parse-loop+
  (lambda (terminator separator action)
    (letrec
      ((more (lambda (token)
               (let ((class (token->class token)))
                 (cond
                   ((eq? class terminator) (emit-list))
                   ((eq? separator class)
                    (check/drop separator
                      (action (goto-parser-state more))))
                   (else (error "Invalid separator token:" token)))))))
        (lambda (token)
          (action (goto-parser-state more)))))))
```

Figure D.2   Parser globals needed for all chapters

```
(define parse-form
  (lambda (token)
    ((case (token->class token)
       ((define) seen-define)
       ((definearray) seen-define)
       (else parse-exp))
     token)))

(define parse-exp
  (lambda (token)
    ((case (token->class token)
       ((number) seen-number)
       ((variable) seen-variable)
       ((lparen) seen-lparen)
       ((if) seen-if)
       ((let) seen-let)
       ((proc) seen-proc)
       ((begin) seen-begin)
       ((letmutable) seen-letmutable)
       ((letrecproc) seen-letrecproc)
       ((letrec) seen-letrec)
```

```
      ((letdynamic) seen-letdynamic)
      ((letarray) seen-letarray)
      ((letproc) seen-letproc)
      ((local) seen-local)
      ((dollar-sign) seen-dollar-sign)
      ((ampersand) seen-ampersand)
      ((double-ampersand) seen-double-ampersand)
      ((method) seen-method)
      ((simpleclass) seen-simpleclass)
      ((simpleinstance) seen-simpleinstance)
      ((class) seen-class)
      ((instance) seen-instance)
      ((abort) seen-abort)
      ((letcont) seen-letcont)
      ((callcc) seen-callcc)
      ((coroutine) seen-coroutine)
      ((wind) seen-wind)
      ((sum) seen-sum)
      (else (error "Invalid parse-exp token:" token)))
    token)))

(define parse/var
  (lambda (token)
    (case (token->class token)
      ((lparen) (seen-var&lparen token))
      ((assign-sym) (seen-var&assign-sym token))
      ((lbracket) (seen-var&lbracket token))
      (else (reduce 'varref)))))
```

Figure D.3   Constructors

```scheme
(define get-constructor-from-name
  (lambda (prod-name)
    (case prod-name
      ((chain) (lambda (x) x))
      ((lit) make-lit)
      ((app) make-app)
      ((app/var) (lambda (var rands) (make-app (make-varref var) rands)))
      ((begin) (letrec ((loop (lambda (exps)
                                (if (null? (cdr exps))
                                    (car exps)
                                    (make-begin (car exps) (loop (cdr exps)))))))
                 loop))
      ((define) make-define)
      ((varref) make-varref)
      ((if) make-if)
      ((proc) make-proc)
      ((let) make-let)
      ((letmutable) make-letmutable)
      ((letrecproc) make-letrecproc)
      ((letrec) make-letrec)
      ((decl) make-decl)
      ((procdecl) make-procdecl)
      ((varassign) make-varassign)
      ((dynassign) make-dynassign)
      ((letdynamic) make-letdynamic)
      ((definearray) make-definearray)
      ((arrayref) make-arrayref)
      ((arrayref/var) (lambda (var index)
                        (make-arrayref (make-varref var) index)))
      ((arrayassign) make-arrayassign)
      ((arrayassign/var) (lambda (var index val)
                           (make-arrayassign (make-varref var) index val)))
      ((letarray) make-letarray)
      ((letproc) make-letproc)
      ((local) make-local)
```

```
((stuff-and-keydecls) append)
((keydecl) make-keydecl)
((i-var) make-i-varref)
((c-var) make-c-varref)
((method) make-method)
((letcont) make-letcont)
((i-varassign) make-i-varassign)
((c-varassign) make-c-varassign)
((new-simpleinst) make-new-simpleinst)
((new-simpleclass) make-new-simpleclass)
((new-class) make-new-class)
((instance) make-new-instance)
((meth-app) (lambda (var rands)
              (if (null? rands)
                  (error "Invalid method rands:" rands)
                  (let ((rand (car rands)))
                    (if (and .(varref? rand)
                             (eq? (varref->var rand) 'super))
                        (make-super-meth-app var (cdr rands))
                        (make-meth-app var rands))))))
((abort) make-abort)
((letcont) make-letcont)
((callcc) make-callcc)
((coroutine) make-coroutine)
((wind) make-wind)
((sum) make-sum)
(else (error "Bad production name:" prod-name)))))
```

Figure D.4   Chapter 5 parsing procedures

```
(define seen-define
  (lambda (token)
    (check/drop 'define
      (check/shift 'variable
        (check/drop 'eqsign
          (process-nt parse-exp (reduce 'define)))))))

(define seen-number
  (lambda (token)
    (check/shift 'number (reduce 'lit))))

(define seen-variable
  (lambda (token)
    (check/shift 'variable (goto-parser-state parse/var))))

(define seen-lparen
  (lambda (token)
    (check/drop 'lparen
      (process-nt parse-exp
        (check/drop 'rparen
          (goto-parser-state parse-proc))))))

(define seen-if
  (lambda (token)
    (check/drop 'if
      (process-nt parse-exp
        (check/drop 'then
          (process-nt parse-exp
            (check/drop 'else
              (process-nt parse-exp (reduce 'if)))))))))

(define seen-proc
  (lambda (token)
    (check/drop 'proc
      (check/drop 'lparen
        (process-nt parse-varlist
          (check/drop 'rparen
            (process-nt parse-exp (reduce 'proc))))))))
```

Figure D.4   Chapter 5 parsing procedures (continued)

```
(define seen-begin
  (lambda (token)
    (check/drop 'begin
      (process-nt parse-compound
        (check/drop 'end (reduce 'begin))))))

(define seen-let
  (lambda (token)
    (check/drop 'let
      (process-nt parse-decls
        (check/drop 'in (process-nt parse-exp (reduce 'let)))))))

(define seen-letmutable
  (lambda (token)
    (check/drop 'letmutable
      (process-nt parse-decls
        (check/drop 'in
          (process-nt parse-exp (reduce 'letmutable)))))))

(define seen-letrec
  (lambda (token)
    (check/drop 'letrec
      (process-nt parse-decls
        (check/drop 'in (process-nt parse-exp (reduce 'letrec)))))))

(define seen-letrecproc
  (lambda (token)
    (check/drop 'letrecproc
      (process-nt parse-procdecls
        (check/drop 'in (process-nt parse-exp (reduce 'letrecproc)))))))

(define seen-letdynamic
  (lambda (token)
    (check/drop 'letdynamic
      (process-nt parse-decls
        (check/drop 'in (process-nt parse-exp (reduce 'letdynamic)))))))
```

```
(define seen-var&lparen
  (lambda (token)
    (check/drop 'lparen
      (process-nt parse-rands
        (check/drop 'rparen (reduce 'app/var))))))

(define seen-var&assign-sym
  (lambda (token)
    (check/drop 'assign-sym
      (process-nt parse-exp
        (goto-parser-state parse-assign-or-dynassign)))))

(define parse-proc
  (lambda (token)
    (case (token->class token)
      ((lparen)
       (check/drop 'lparen
         (process-nt parse-rands (check/drop 'rparen (reduce 'app)))))
      (else (reduce 'chain)))))

(define parse-assign-or-dynassign
  (lambda (token)
    (case (token->class token)
      ((during)
       (check/drop 'during (process-nt parse-exp (reduce 'dynassign))))
      (else (reduce 'varassign)))))

(define parse-varlist
  (parse-loop* 'rparen 'comma
    (lambda (action) (check/shift 'variable action))))

(define parse-compound
  (parse-loop* 'end 'semicolon
    (lambda (action) (process-nt parse-exp action))))

(define parse-rands
  (parse-loop* 'rparen 'comma
    (lambda (action)
      (process-nt parse-exp action))))
```

Figure D.4   Chapter 5 parsing procedures (continued)

```
(define parse-decls
  (parse-loop+ 'in 'semicolon
    (lambda (action) (process-nt parse-decl action))))

(define parse-procdecls
  (parse-loop+ 'in 'semicolon
    (lambda (action) (process-nt parse-procdecl action))))

(define parse-decl
  (lambda (token)
    (case (token->class token)
      ((variable)
       (check/shift 'variable
         (check/drop 'eqsign
           (process-nt parse-exp (reduce 'decl)))))
      (else (error "Invalid parse-letdecl token:" token)))))

(define parse-procdecl
  (lambda (token)
    (case (token->class token)
      ((variable)
       (check/shift 'variable
         (check/drop 'lparen
           (process-nt parse-varlist
             (check/drop 'rparen
               (check/drop 'eqsign
                 (process-nt parse-exp (reduce 'procdecl))))))))
      (else (error "Invalid parse-procdecl token:" token)))))
```

Figure D.5   Chapter 6 parsing procedures

```
(define seen-var&lbracket
  (lambda (token)
    (check/drop 'lbracket
      (process-nt parse-exp
        (check/drop 'rbracket
          (goto-parser-state
            parse-arrayassign-or-arrayref/var))))))

(define seen-definearray
  (lambda (token)
    (check/drop 'definearray
      (check/shift 'variable
        (check/drop 'lbracket
          (process-nt parse-exp
            (check/drop 'rbracket (reduce 'definearray))))))))

(define seen-letarray
  (lambda (token)
    (check/drop 'letarray
      (process-nt parse-arraydecls
        (check/drop 'in (process-nt parse-exp (reduce 'letarray)))))))

(define seen-letproc
  (lambda (token)
    (check/drop 'letproc
      (process-nt parse-procdecls
        (check/drop 'in (process-nt parse-exp (reduce 'letproc)))))))

(define seen-local
  (lambda (token)
    (check/drop 'local
      (process-nt parse-decls
        (check/drop 'in (process-nt parse-exp (reduce 'local)))))))

(define parse-arrayassign-or-arrayref
  (lambda (token)
    (case (token->class token)
      ((assign-sym)
       (check/drop 'assign-sym
         (process-nt parse-exp (reduce 'arrayassign))))
      (else (reduce 'arrayref)))))
```

Figure D.5   Chapter 6 parsing procedures (continued)

```
(define parse-arrayassign-or-arrayref/var
  (lambda (token)
    (case (token->class token)
      ((assign-sym)
       (check/drop 'assign-sym
         (process-nt parse-exp (reduce 'arrayassign/var))))
      (else (reduce 'arrayref/var)))))

(define parse-arraydecls
  (parse-loop+ 'in 'semicolon
    (lambda (action) (process-nt parse-arraydecl action))))

(define parse-arraydecl
  (lambda (token)
    (case (token->class token)
      ((variable)
       (check/shift 'variable
         (check/drop 'lbracket
           (process-nt parse-exp
             (check/drop 'rbracket (reduce 'decl))))))
      (else (error "Invalid parse-arraydecl token:" token)))))
```

Figure D.6   Section 6.6 parsing procedures

```
(define parse-vars-until-optdecls
  (parse-loop* 'rparen 'comma
    (lambda (action)
      (goto-parser-state
        (lambda (token)
          (case (token->class token)
            ((colon) (emit-list))
            ((variable) (check/shift 'variable action))
            (else (error "Invalid parse-vars-until-optdecls:" token))))))))

(define parse-optdecls
  (parse-loop* 'rparen 'comma
    (lambda (action) (process-nt parse-optdecl action))))
```

```
(define parse-optdecl-var
  (lambda (token)
    (case (token->class token)
      ((variable)
       (check/shift 'variable
         (check/drop 'eqsign
           (process-nt parse-exp (reduce 'keydecl)))))
      (else (error "Invalid parse-optdecl-var token:" token)))))

(define parse-optdecl
  (lambda (token)
    (case (token->class token)
      ((colon) (check/drop 'colon
                 (goto-parser-state parse-optdecl-var)))
      (else (error "Invalid parse-optdecl token:" token)))))

(define parse-exps-until-keydecls
  (parse-loop* 'rparen 'comma
    (lambda (action)
      (goto-parser-state
        (lambda (token)
          (case (token->class token)
            ((colon) (emit-list))
            (else (process-nt parse-exp action))))))))

(define parse-keydecls
  (parse-loop* 'rparen 'comma
    (lambda (action) (process-nt parse-keydecl action))))

(define parse-keydecl
  (lambda (token)
    (case (token->class token)
      ((colon)
       (check/drop 'colon
         (check/shift 'variable
           (check/drop 'eqsign
             (process-nt parse-exp (reduce 'keydecl))))))
      (else (error "Invalid parse-opts token:" token)))))
```

Figure D.6   Section 6.6 parsing procedures (continued)

```
(define parse-varlist
  (lambda (token)
    (process-nt parse-vars-until-optdecls
      (process-nt parse-optdecls (reduce 'stuff-and-keydecls)))))

(define parse-rands
  (lambda (token)
    (process-nt parse-exps-until-keydecls
      (process-nt parse-keydecls (reduce 'stuff-and-keydecls)))))
```

Figure D.7   Chapter 7 parsing procedures

```
(define seen-dollar-sign
  (lambda (token)
    (check/drop 'dollar-sign
      (check/shift 'variable
        (check/drop 'lparen
          (process-nt parse-rands
            (check/drop 'rparen (reduce 'meth-app))))))))

(define seen-ampersand
  (lambda (token)
    (check/drop 'ampersand
      (check/shift 'variable (goto-parser-state parse/ivar)))))

(define seen-double-ampersand
  (lambda (token)
    (check/drop 'double-ampersand
      (check/shift 'variable (goto-parser-state parse/cvar)))))

(define seen-method
  (lambda (token)
    (check/drop 'method
      (check/drop 'lparen
        (process-nt parse-varlist
          (check/drop 'rparen
            (process-nt parse-exp (reduce 'method))))))))
```

```
(define seen-simpleinstance
  (lambda (token)
    (check/drop 'simpleinstance
      (process-nt parse-exp (reduce 'new-simpleinst)))))

(define seen-simpleclass
  (lambda (token)
    (check/drop 'simpleclass
      (check/drop 'lparen
        (process-nt parse-varlist
          (check/drop 'rparen
            (check/drop 'lparen
              (process-nt parse-varlist
                (check/drop 'rparen
                  (check/drop 'lparen
                    (process-nt parse-methdecls
                      (check/drop 'rparen
                        (process-nt parse-exp
                          (reduce 'new-simpleclass)))))))))))))))

(define seen-class
  (lambda (token)
    (check/drop 'class
      (process-nt parse-exp
        (check/drop 'comma
          (check/drop 'lparen
            (process-nt parse-varlist
              (check/drop 'rparen
                (check/drop 'lparen
                  (process-nt parse-varlist
                    (check/drop 'rparen
                      (check/drop 'lparen
                        (process-nt parse-methdecls
                          (check/drop 'rparen
                            (process-nt parse-exp
                              (reduce 'new-class)))))))))))))))))
```

Figure D.7   Chapter 7 parsing procedures (continued)

```
(define seen-instance
  (lambda (token)
    (check/drop 'instance
      (process-nt parse-exp
        (check/drop 'comma
          (process-nt parse-exp
            (check/drop 'comma
              (check/drop 'lparen
                (process-nt parse-varlist
                  (check/drop 'rparen
                    (check/drop 'lparen
                      (process-nt parse-methdecls
                        (check/drop 'rparen (reduce 'instance)))))))))))))))

(define parse/ivar
  (lambda (token)
    (case (token->class token)
      ((assign-sym)
       (check/drop 'assign-sym
         (process-nt parse-exp (reduce 'i-varassign))))
      (else (reduce 'i-var)))))

(define parse/cvar
  (lambda (token)
    (case (token->class token)
      ((assign-sym)
       (check/drop 'assign-sym
         (process-nt parse-exp (reduce 'c-varassign))))
      (else (reduce 'c-var)))))

(define parse-methdecls
  (parse-loop* 'rparen 'semicolon
    (lambda (action) (process-nt parse-decl action))))
```

Figure D.8   Chapters 9 parsing procedures

```
(define seen-abort
  (lambda (token)
    (check/drop 'abort
      (process-nt parse-exp (reduce 'abort)))))

(define seen-letcont
  (lambda (token)
    (check/drop 'letcont
      (check/shift 'variable
        (check/drop 'in (process-nt parse-exp (reduce 'letcont)))))))

(define seen-callcc
  (lambda (token)
    (check/drop 'callcc
      (process-nt parse-exp (reduce 'callcc)))))

(define seen-coroutine
  (lambda (token)
    (check/drop 'coroutine
      (process-nt parse-exp (reduce 'coroutine)))))

(define seen-wind
  (lambda (token)
    (check/drop 'wind
      (process-nt parse-exp
        (check/drop 'within
          (process-nt parse-exp
            (check/drop 'unwind
              (process-nt parse-exp (reduce 'wind)))))))))
```

Figure D.9   Chapter 12 parsing procedure

```
(define seen-sum
  (lambda (token)
    (check/drop 'sum
      (check/drop 'lparen
        (process-nt parse-rands (check/drop 'rparen (reduce 'sum)))))))
```

Appendix E Character String Scanner

This appendix gives a complete implementation of a scanner that supports
the character string syntax of the defined language. The character #\nul
represents some character, not in the language being scanned.

Figure E.1   Character string scanner

```
(define shift
  (lambda (next-action)
    (lambda (buffer char-seq)
      (next-action (cons (char-seq-head char-seq) buffer) (char-seq-tail char-seq)))))

(define drop
  (lambda (next-action)
    (lambda (buffer char-seq)
      (next-action buffer (char-seq-tail char-seq)))))

(define goto-scanner-state
  (lambda (state)
    (lambda (buffer char-seq)
      ((state (char-seq-head char-seq)) buffer char-seq))))

(define emit
  (lambda (cooker)
    (lambda (buffer char-seq)
      (make-scanner-answer (cooker (reverse buffer)) char-seq))))

(define-record token (class data))

(define-record scanner-answer (token unscanned))
```

Figure E.1   Character string scanner (continued)

```
(define char-seq-head car)

(define char-seq-tail cdr)

(define cook-punctuation
  (lambda (class)
    (lambda (buffer) (make-token class '*))))

(define cook-number
  (lambda (buffer)
    (make-token 'number (string->number (list->string buffer)))))

(define cook-identifier
  (lambda (buffer)
    (let ((symbol (string->symbol (list->string buffer))))
      (if (memq symbol keywords-list)
          (make-token symbol '*)
          (make-token 'variable symbol)))))

(define scan-once
  (lambda (start-state char-seq)
    ((goto-scanner-state start-state) '() char-seq)))

(define scan-char-seq
  (lambda (start-state char-seq)
    (let ((next-answer (scan-once start-state char-seq)))
      (variant-case next-answer
        (scanner-answer (token unscanned)
          (make-token-seq token
            (lambda ()
              (if (eq? (token->class token) 'end-marker)
                  '()
                  (scan-char-seq start-state unscanned)))))))))

(define character-string-scanner
  (lambda (a-string)
    (scan-char-seq scanner-start-state
      (string->list (string-append a-string (string #\nul))))))

(define make-token-seq
  (lambda (token thunk)
    (cons token (thunk))))
```

Figure E.2   Finite state automaton

```
(define scanner-start-state
  (lambda (c)
    (cond
      ((char-whitespace? c)
       (drop (goto-scanner-state scanner-start-state)))
      ((char-alphabetic? c)
       (shift (goto-scanner-state scanner-identifier-state)))
      ((char-numeric? c)
       (shift (goto-scanner-state scanner-number-state)))
      ((char=? c #\%)
       (drop (goto-scanner-state scanner-comment-state)))
      ((char=? c #\()
       (drop (emit (cook-punctuation 'lparen))))
      ((char=? c #\))
       (drop (emit (cook-punctuation 'rparen))))
      ((char=? c #\[)
       (drop (emit (cook-punctuation 'lbracket))))
      ((char=? c #\])
       (drop (emit (cook-punctuation 'rbracket))))
      ((char=? c #\,)
       (drop (emit (cook-punctuation 'comma))))
      ((char=? c #\=)
       (drop (emit (cook-punctuation 'eqsign))))
      ((char=? c #\;)
       (drop (emit (cook-punctuation 'semicolon))))
      ((char=? c #\&)
       (drop (goto-scanner-state scanner-ampersand-state)))
      ((char=? c #\$)
       (drop (emit (cook-punctuation 'dollar-sign))))
      ((char=? c #\:)
       (drop (goto-scanner-state scanner-assign-state)))
      ((or (char=? c #\+) (char=? c #\-) (char=? c #\*))
       (shift (emit cook-identifier)))
      ((char=? c #\nul)
       (emit (cook-punctuation 'end-marker)))
      (else (error "Invalid character to scan:" c)))))
```

```
(define scanner-identifier-state
  (lambda (c)
    (cond
      ((char-alphabetic? c)
       (shift (goto-scanner-state scanner-identifier-state)))
      ((char-numeric? c)
       (shift (goto-scanner-state scanner-identifier-state)))
      (else (emit cook-identifier)))))

(define scanner-number-state
  (lambda (c)
    (cond
      ((char-numeric? c)
       (shift (goto-scanner-state scanner-number-state)))
      (else (emit cook-number)))))

(define scanner-comment-state
  (lambda (c)
    (cond
      ((char=? c #\newline)
       (drop (goto-scanner-state scanner-start-state)))
      (else (drop (goto-scanner-state scanner-comment-state))))))

(define scanner-assign-state
  (lambda (c)
    (cond
      ((char=? c #\=)
       (drop (emit (cook-punctuation 'assign-sym))))
      (else (emit (cook-punctuation 'colon))))))

(define scanner-ampersand-state
  (lambda (c)
    (cond
      ((char=? c #\&)
       (drop (emit (cook-punctuation 'double-ampersand))))
      (else (emit (cook-punctuation 'ampersand))))))

(define keywords-list
  '(if then else let in proc begin end letmutable letrecproc letrec
     during letdynamic letarray letproc method define definearray
     simpleclass simpleinstance class instance abort letcont callcc
     coroutine wind unwind within sum))
```

Appendix F A Read-Eval-Print Loop

Here is an implementation of the read-eval-print loop for the character string syntax of the interpreted language. The interactive nature of the read-eval-print loop and the side effect of reading a character require us to introduce a somewhat unorthodox stream ADT.

Figure F.1   A stream ADT for interactive computing

```
(define stream-car
  (lambda (s)
    (car (s))))

(define stream-cdr
  (lambda (s)
    (cdr (s))))

(define make-stream
  (lambda (car-val th)
    (lambda ()
      (cons car-val (let ((cdr-val #f))
                      (lambda ()
                        (if (pair? cdr-val)
                            cdr-val
                            (begin (set! cdr-val ((th))) cdr-val))))))))

(define the-null-stream
  (make-stream 'end-of-stream (lambda () the-null-stream)))

(define stream-null?
  (lambda (s)
    (eq? (stream-car s) 'end-of-stream)))
```

```
(define stream-for-each
  (lambda (proc stream)
    (letrec
      ((loop
         (lambda (stream)
           (if (not (stream-null? stream))
               (begin
                 (proc (stream-car stream))
                 (loop (stream-cdr stream)))))))
      (loop stream))))

(define make-input-stream
  (lambda ()
    (let ((char (read-char)))
      (if (eof-object? char)
          the-null-stream
          (make-stream char make-input-stream)))))
```

Figure F.3   Interface to the parser

```
(define make-char-seq make-stream)

(define char-seq-head stream-car)

(define char-seq-tail stream-cdr)

(define make-token-seq make-stream)

(define token-seq-head stream-car)

(define token-seq-tail stream-cdr)
```

Each expression is thought of as if it were placed in a begin expression, and hence each must be followed by a ;. When the last expression is entered, it must be followed by end to match the implied begin. As the sequence of parse trees is consumed, each tree is evaluated and the result of the evaluation is usually written, followed by a new prompt. The procedure *eval-print* reflects the desired form of evaluation and whether or not printing should occur. Below are two versions: one for testing the parser, which just writes the tree, and the other for making calls to *eval-exp* using an initial environment. Other versions are possible as the arguments to *eval-exp* vary.

Figure F.4   An eval loop for interactive computing

```
(define eval-print
  (lambda (tree)
    (write tree)))

(define eval-print
  (lambda (tree)
    (let ((result (eval-exp tree init-env)))
      (if (not (or (define? tree)
                   (definearray? tree)
                   (varassign? tree)
                   (arrayassign? tree)))
          (write result)))))

(define read-eval-print
  (lambda ()
    (display "--> ")
    (stream-for-each
      (lambda (tree)
        (eval-print tree)
        (newline)
        (display "--> "))
      (parse-token-seq parse-semicolon-terminated-form
        (scan-char-seq scanner-start-state (make-input-stream)))))))
```

If **end** is entered after the last expression to be evaluated, the read-eval-print loop terminates.

Figure F.5   Token sequence parser

```
(define parse-semicolon-terminated-form
  (lambda (token)
    (process-nt parse-form
      (goto-parser-state parse-terminated-by))))

(define parse-terminated-by
  (lambda (token)
    (case (token->class token)
      ((semicolon)
       (check/drop 'semicolon (reduce 'chain)))
      ((end)
       (reduce 'chain))
      (else (error "Invalid terminator:" token)))))

(define parse-token-seq
  (lambda (start-state token-seq)
    (let ((token (token-seq-head token-seq)))
      (if (or (eq? (token->class token) 'end)
              (eq? (token->class token) 'end-marker))
          the-null-stream
          (variant-case (parse-once start-state token-seq)
            (parser-answer (tree unparsed)
              (make-stream tree
                (lambda ()
                  (parse-token-seq start-state unparsed)))))))))
```

Appendix G List Structure Syntax

The list structure language is defined by the following concrete and abstract syntax.

⟨form⟩ ::= (define ⟨var⟩ ⟨exp⟩)	define (var exp)
| (definearray ⟨var⟩ ⟨exp⟩)	definearray (var dim-exp)
| ⟨exp⟩	
⟨exp⟩ ::= ⟨integer-literal⟩	lit (datum)
| ⟨varref⟩	
| (⟨operator⟩ ⟨operands⟩)	app (rator rands)
| (if ⟨exp⟩ ⟨exp⟩ ⟨exp⟩)	if (test-exp then-exp else-exp)
| (let ⟨decls⟩ ⟨exp⟩)	let (decls body)
| (proc ⟨varlist⟩ ⟨exp⟩)	proc (formals body)
| (varassign ⟨var⟩ ⟨exp⟩)	varassign (var exp)
| (letmutable ⟨decls⟩ ⟨exp⟩)	letmutable (decls body)
| (begin ⟨exp⟩ ⟨compound⟩)	begin (exp1 exp2)
| (letrecproc ⟨procdecls⟩ ⟨exp⟩)	letrecproc (procdecls body)
| (letrec ⟨decls⟩ ⟨exp⟩)	letrec (decls body)
| (dynassign ⟨var⟩ ⟨exp⟩ ⟨exp⟩)	dynassign (var exp body)
| (letdynamic ⟨decls⟩ ⟨exp⟩)	letdynamic (decls body)
| (letarray ⟨arraydecls⟩ ⟨exp⟩)	letarray (arraydecls body)
| (arrayref ⟨array-exp⟩ ⟨exp⟩)	arrayref (array index)
| (arrayassign ⟨array-exp⟩ ⟨exp⟩ ⟨exp⟩)	arrayassign (array index exp)
| (letproc ⟨procdecls⟩ ⟨exp⟩)	letproc (procdecls body)
| (local ⟨decls⟩ ⟨exp⟩)	local (decls body)

| (i-varref ⟨var⟩)	i-varref (var)
| (c-varref ⟨var⟩)	c-varref (var)
| (i-varassign ⟨var⟩ ⟨exp⟩)	i-varassign (var exp)
| (c-varassign ⟨var⟩ ⟨exp⟩)	c-varassign (var exp)
| (method ⟨varlist⟩ ⟨exp⟩)	method (formals body)
| (meth-app ⟨var⟩ ⟨operands⟩)	meth-app (name rands)
| (simpleinstance ⟨exp⟩)	new-simpleinst (class-exp)
| (simpleclass ⟨varlist⟩ ⟨varlist⟩ ⟨methdecls⟩ ⟨exp⟩)	new-simpleclass (c-vars i-vars methdecls init-exp)
| (class ⟨exp⟩ ⟨c-vars⟩ ⟨i-vars⟩ ⟨methdecls⟩ ⟨exp⟩)	new-class (parent-exp c-vars i-vars methdecls init-exp)
| (meth-app ⟨var⟩ super ⟨operands⟩)	super-meth-app (name rands)
| (instance ⟨exp⟩ ⟨exp⟩ ⟨varlist⟩ ⟨methdecls⟩)	new-instance (class-exp parent-exp i-vars methdecls)
| (abort ⟨exp⟩)	abort (exp)
| (letcont ⟨var⟩ ⟨exp⟩)	letcont (var body)
| (callcc ⟨exp⟩)	callcc (exp)
| (coroutine ⟨exp⟩)	coroutine (exp)
| (wind ⟨exp⟩ ⟨exp⟩ ⟨exp⟩)	wind (pre body post)
| (sum ⟨operands⟩)	sum (rands)

⟨varref⟩ ::= ⟨var⟩	varref (var)
⟨var⟩ ::= ⟨symbol⟩	
⟨decls⟩ ::= (⟨decl⟩ {⟨decl⟩}*)	
⟨decl⟩ ::= (⟨var⟩ ⟨exp⟩)	decl (var exp)
⟨varlist⟩ ::= ({⟨var⟩}*{⟨keydecl⟩}*)	
⟨compound⟩ ::= { ⟨exp⟩}*	
⟨procdecls⟩ ::= (⟨procdecl⟩ {⟨procdecl⟩}*)	
⟨procdecl⟩ ::= (⟨var⟩ ⟨varlist⟩ ⟨exp⟩)	procdecl (var formals body)
⟨arraydecls⟩ ::= (⟨arraydecl⟩ {⟨arraydecl⟩}*)	
⟨arraydecl⟩ ::= (⟨var⟩ ⟨exp⟩)	decl (var exp)
⟨array-exp⟩ ::= ⟨exp⟩	
⟨keydecls⟩ ::= ⟨keydecl⟩ {⟨keydecl⟩}*	

Appendix G List Structure Syntax

⟨keydecl⟩ ::= (: ⟨var⟩ ⟨exp⟩)   `decl (var exp)`
⟨methdecls⟩ ::= ( ) | ⟨decls⟩
⟨operands⟩ ::= {⟨exp⟩}* {⟨keydecl⟩}*
⟨operator⟩ ::= ⟨exp⟩

Appendix H List Structure Parser

This appendix contains a list structure parser for the language of appendix G. The assumption here is that the argument to *parse* has been read by Scheme's *read* procedure. With this, we have given up some of the flexibility that comes with a character string parser, since we are basically letting Scheme do the scanning for us. This allows us to ignore the character structure of a program and focus in on its tree structure. Use the record declarations of appendix B for building the actual abstract syntax. The form table for chapter 5 is stored in `form-table`. When you wish to extend the form table to include chapter 6, 7, 9, or 12, just append one table to another and redefine `form-table`. For example, to add the special forms of chapter 7, simply

```
(define form-table (append form-table form-table-for-chapter-7))
```

There is an additional test in the procedure *parse-with-keys* that is only of use when running section 6.6.

We have defined the predicate *approve?* to always return true. This means that the parser is quite willing to accept illegal programs, such as `if` expressions with too many parts. It is a worthwhile exercise to implement your own version of *approve?* Use an `approve-table` like the `form-table` that associates each symbol with a procedure of the form `(lambda (exp) ...)`. For example, the `approve-table` entry for `if` is `(lambda (exp) (= (length exp) 4))`.

Figure H.1   List structure parser

```
(define parse
  (lambda (exp)
    (if (form? exp)
        (parse-form exp)
        (parse-exp exp))))

(define form?
  (lambda (x)
    (and (pair? x) (memq (car x) '(define definearray)))))

(define parse-form
  (lambda (form)
    (let ((form-pair (assq (car form) form-table)))
      (if (and (pair? form-pair) (approve form))
          (apply (cdr form-pair) (cdr form))
          (error "Invalid top-level form:" form)))))

(define parse-exp
  (lambda (exp)
    (cond
      ((symbol? exp) (make-varref exp))
      ((number? exp) (make-lit exp))
      ((and (pair? exp) (not (form? exp))) (parse-pair exp))
      (else (error "Invalid expression:" exp)))))

(define parse-pair
  (lambda (exp)
    (let ((x (car exp)))
      (if (symbol? x)
          (let ((form-pair (assq x form-table)))
            (if (and (pair? form-pair) (approve exp))
                (apply (cdr form-pair) (cdr exp))
                (make-app (parse-exp (car exp)) (parse-rands (cdr exp)))))
          (make-app (parse-exp (car exp)) (parse-rands (cdr exp)))))))
```

Figure H.1   List structure parser (continued)

```
(define approve
  (lambda (x) #t))

(define parse-decl
  (lambda (decl)
    (make-decl (car decl) (parse-exp (cadr decl)))))

(define parse-procdecl
  (lambda (triple)
    (make-procdecl (car triple) (cadr triple) (parse-exp (caddr triple)))))

(define parse-with-keys
  (lambda (proc)
    (letrec ((loop (lambda (exps)
                     (cond
                       ((null? exps) '())
                       ((and (pair? (car exps)) (eq? (car (car exps)) ':))
                        (map (lambda (decl)
                               (make-keydecl (cadr decl) (parse-exp (caddr decl))))
                             exps))
                       (else (cons (proc (car exps)) (loop (cdr exps))))))))
      loop)))

(define parse-rands (parse-with-keys parse))
(define parse-formals (parse-with-keys (lambda (x) x)))
```

Figure H.2   Form tables for language of appendix G

```scheme
(define form-table
  (list
    (cons 'define
      (lambda (var exp)
        (make-define var (parse-exp exp))))
    (cons 'definearray
      (lambda (var exp)
        (make-definearray var (parse-exp exp))))
    (cons 'if
      (lambda (test-exp then-exp else-exp)
        (make-if (parse-exp test-exp) (parse-exp then-exp) (parse-exp else-exp))))
    (cons 'let
      (lambda (decls body)
        (make-let (map parse-decl decls) (parse-exp body))))
    (cons 'proc
      (lambda (formals body)
        (make-proc (parse-formals formals) (parse-exp body))))
    (cons 'varassign
      (lambda (var body)
        (make-varassign var (parse-exp body))))
    (cons 'letmutable
      (lambda (decls body)
        (make-letmutable (map parse-decl decls) (parse-exp body))))
    (cons 'begin
      (letrec ((loop (lambda (exps)
                       (if (null? (cdr exps))
                           (parse-exp (car exps))
                           (make-begin (parse-exp (car exps)) (loop (cdr exps)))))))
        (lambda exps
          (loop exps))))
    (cons 'letrecproc
      (lambda (procdecls body)
        (make-letrecproc (map parse-procdecl procdecls) (parse-exp body))))
    (cons 'letrec
      (lambda (decls body) (make-letrec (map parse-decl decls) (parse-exp body))))
    (cons 'dynassign
      (lambda (var exp body)
        (make-dynassign var (parse-exp exp) (parse-exp body))))
    (cons 'letdynamic
      (lambda (decls body)
        (make-letdynamic (map parse-decl decls) (parse-exp body))))))
```

```
(define form-table-for-chapter-6
  (list
    (cons 'letarray
      (lambda (arraydecls body)
        (make-letarray (map parse-decl arraydecls) (parse-exp body))))
    (cons 'arrayref
      (lambda (array index)
        (make-arrayref (parse-exp array) (parse-exp index))))
    (cons 'arrayassign
      (lambda (array index exp)
        (make-arrayassign (parse-exp array) (parse-exp index) (parse-exp exp))))
    (cons 'letproc
      (lambda (procdecls body)
        (make-letproc (map parse-procdecl procdecls)
          (parse-exp body))))
    (cons 'local
      (lambda (decls body)
        (make-local (map parse-decl decls) (parse-exp body))))))

(define form-table-for-chapter-7
  (list
    (cons 'i-varref
      (lambda (var) (make-i-varref var)))
    (cons 'c-varref
      (lambda (var) (make-c-varref var)))
    (cons 'i-varassign
      (lambda (var exp) (make-i-varassign var (parse-exp exp))))
    (cons 'c-varassign
      (lambda (var exp) (make-c-varassign var (parse-exp exp))))
    (cons 'method
      (lambda (formals body)
        (make-method (parse-formals formals) (parse-exp body))))
    (cons 'meth-app
      (lambda args
        (let ((name (car args)) (rands (cdr args)))
          (if (and (pair? rands) (symbol? (car rands)) (eq? (car rands) 'super))
              (make-super-meth-app name (parse-rands (cdr rands)))
              (make-meth-app name (parse-rands rands))))))))
```

```
      (cons 'simpleinstance
        (lambda (class-exp)
          (make-new-simpleinst (parse-exp class-exp))))
      (cons 'simpleclass
        (lambda (c-vars i-vars methdecls init-exp)
          (make-new-simpleclass c-vars i-vars
            (map parse-decl methdecls)
            (parse-exp init-exp))))
      (cons 'class
        (lambda (parent-exp c-vars i-vars methdecls init-exp)
          (make-new-class (parse-exp parent-exp) c-vars i-vars
            (map parse-decl methdecls)
            (parse-exp init-exp))))
      (cons 'instance
        (lambda (class-exp parent-exp i-vars methdecls)
          (make-new-instance (parse-exp class-exp) (parse-exp parent-exp)
            i-vars
            (map parse-decl methdecls))))))

(define form-table-for-chapter-9
  (list
    (cons 'abort
      (lambda (exp) (make-abort (parse-exp exp))))
    (cons 'letcont
      (lambda (var body) (make-letcont var (parse-exp body))))
    (cons 'callcc
      (lambda (exp) (make-callcc (parse-exp exp))))
    (cons 'coroutine
      (lambda (exp) (make-coroutine (parse-exp exp))))
    (cons 'wind
      (lambda (pre body post)
        (make-wind (parse-exp pre) (parse-exp body) (parse-exp post))))))

(define form-table-for-chapter-12
  (list
    (cons 'sum
      (lambda rands
        (make-sum (parse-rands rands))))))
```

Appendix I Scheme Procedures Used

Figure I.1 is a list of the Scheme procedures used in the book. This list does not include arithmetic operations or combinations of car and cdr, such as cadr. Those procedures that are not in the IEEE Scheme standard are marked with a dagger (†). Of these, eval and gensym are discussed in the text; the others should be self-explanatory.

append	eval†	number?	string-length
apply	for-each	pair?	string-ref
assq	gensym†	positive?	string?
boolean?	length	procedure?	symbol->string
car	list	read	symbol?
cdr	list->string†	read-char	vector
char-alphabetic?	list->vector	remainder	vector->list†
char-numeric?	list-ref	reverse	vector-length
char-whitespace?	make-vector	reverse!	vector-ref
char=?	map	set-car!	vector-set!
char?	member	set-cdr!	vector?
cons	memq	string	write
display	memv	string->list†	zero?
eof-object?	newline	string->number	
eq?	not	string->symbol	
equal?	null?	string-append	

Figure I.1   Scheme procedures used in the book

For Further Reading

This book is an analytic study of programming language concepts, not a survey or a history. Therefore, we do not list all the relevant references. To find such a list, start with any good survey book (say Sethi [1989]) and chase a few pointers, and you will have enough references to last a lifetime.

What we have decided to do instead is share with you a list of papers and books that have given us the most hours of enjoyment. In some instances the hours of enjoyment came because we were the authors, and in other instances it came because the excitement of learning a new idea gave us such exhilaration.

The most important books are those that change the way you look at the world. So we will begin our reading list with two books in this category. The first is *Structure and Interpretation of Computer Programs,* by Hal Abelson and Gerry Sussman with Julie Sussman [1985]. This is a challenging introduction to programming that emphasizes general problem-solving techniques and uses Scheme throughout. We often list this book as a required text in our courses, just because every computer scientist and programmer should read it. A second mind-expanding book is *Godel, Escher, Bach: an Eternal Golden Braid* by Douglas R. Hofstadter [1979]. If you have not read this, take some time off and get acquainted with it. It is a joy to read and will open your mind to new and exciting ways to think about recursion, especially as it occurs in the real world, and the meaning of symbols. We hope our book will have as deep an effect on you as these books did on us.

If you are new to recursive programming and symbolic computation, then we suggest you look at *The Little Lisper* by Friedman and Felleisen [1989]. Another good choice is Springer and Friedman's *Scheme and the Art of Programming* [1989]. This introduction to programming using Scheme is less ambitious than *Structure and Interpretation of Computer Programs*.

Scheme was introduced in Sussman and Steele [1975]. Its development is recorded in Steele and Sussman [1978] and Rees and Clinger [1986]. The specification of Scheme is the IEEE standard [1991]. Dybvig [1987] provides a short introduction to Scheme along with a complete reference manual that includes some features specific to the Chez Scheme implementation. It also includes a number of insightful examples.

We learned a great deal about the use of higher-order procedures for programming from Burge [1975]. A more recent text on functional programming is Reade [1989]. The technical reports by Steele and Sussman, listed in the references, are extremely instructive on many topics.

Almost any text on discrete mathematics for computer science contains additional material on induction and Backus-Naur Form.

Most implementations of languages that are dialects of Lisp provide a syntactic abstraction mechanism, traditionally called *macros,* for extending the language with new special forms. Kohlbecker [1986] reviews traditional approaches to macros and proposes mechanisms for conveniently specifying syntactic transformations and avoiding the unintended capture of variables through such transformations.

The idea of data abstraction was a prime innovation of the 1970's, and has a large literature, from which we mention only Parnas [1972] on the importance of interfaces as boundaries for information-hiding.

We learned about the representation of sets of procedures as data structures from Reynolds [1972]. This technique was formalized under the name of *supercombinators* by Hughes [1982]. For more detail, see Peyton Jones [1987].

The lambda calculus was introduced by Alonzo Church [1941] to study mathematical logic. More introductory treatments of the lambda calculus may be found in Peyton Jones [1987] or Stoy [1977]. Barendregt [1981] provides an encyclopedic reference.

Refinements of the lambda calculus that give sound rules for reasoning about programs using call-by-value were studied by Plotkin [1975]. Felleisen and Friedman *et al.* [1987,1989] extend this to include assignment and control operations. Techniques for reasoning about imperative programs were pioneered in Floyd [1967] and Hoare [1969], which started a large literature in the 1970's.

Streams are discussed at length in Springer and Friedman [1989] and Abelson and Sussman [1985].

Chapters 5–7

When we wrote the first interpreter that used if in the defining language to explain if in the defined language, we wrote a *meta-circular interpreter*. Metacircular interpreters were used in McCarthy [1960] to show the power of Lisp. See also McCarthy [1965]. Smith [1984] took that concept to its limit by imagining an infinite tower of interpreters.

Denotational semantics allows the definition of languages in terms of the lambda calculus, rather than depending on another programming language. See Stoy [1977], Gordon [1979], Schmidt [1986], or the encyclopedic Milne and Strachey [1976]. Our use of Scheme allows most of the formal precision of denotational semantics in an executable form. The idea that the expressed and denoted values of a language determined a great deal of its structure was stressed by Strachey [1973].

Object-oriented languages first appeared with Simula 67 (Birtwistle et al. [1979]). The object-oriented metaphor was extended by Smalltalk (Goldberg and Robson [1980]) and Carl Hewitt's Actors (Hewitt [1977]). Both used human interaction and sending and receiving messages as the metaphor for explaining their ideas. Scheme grew out of Sussman and Steele's attempts to understand Hewitt's work. Springer and Friedman [1989] and Abelson and Sussman [1985] both provide further examples of object-oriented programming in Scheme and discuss when functional and imperative programming styles are most appropriate. Steele [1990] and Keene [1989] describe CLOS, the powerful object-oriented programming facility of Common Lisp. A later arrival, gaining rapid popularity at the time of this writing, is C++ (Stroustrup [1986], Ellis and Stroustrup [1990]), which trades some of the generality of Smalltalk or Actors for run-time efficiency.

Chapters 8–10

The current interest in continuation-passing style is commonly dated from Strachey and Wadsworth [1974]. Reynolds [1972] shows how transforming an interpreter into CPS eliminates some of the difficulties of metacircular interpreters. Plotkin [1975] gives a very clean version of the CPS transformation and studies its theoretical properties. The translation of programs in tail form to imperative form dates back to McCarthy [1962].

Steele's RABBIT compiler (Steele [1978]) uses CPS conversion as the basis for a compiler. In this compiler, the source program is converted into CPS and then into iterative form; it can then be compiled easily. This line of development led to the ORBIT compiler (Kranz *et al.* [1986]), and to the Standard ML of New Jersey compiler (Appel and Jim [1989]).

Our treatment of coroutines is based on Haynes, Friedman, and Wand [1986]. An introduction to using first-class continuations can be found in Springer and Friedman [1989]. The discussion of dynamic wind is based on Baker [1978].

Continuations may be used for a variety of purposes beyond those discussed in the text. The use of continuations as a model of lightweight processes and as program transformations are explored in Wand [1980a,b]. The efficient implementation of continuations is treated in Hieb, Dybvig, and Bruggeman [1990].

Chapters 11–12

The theory of scanner and parser design is well developed. It provides systematic techniques for dealing with a wide range of programming language grammars that do not satisfy the properties required by the techniques of chapter 11. Parsing theory relies in turn on the extensive theory of formal grammars, which studies general classes of grammars and the types of automata that are required for parsing their languages. A compiler textbook, such as Aho, Sethi, and Ullman [1986] or Fisher and LeBlanc [1988], should be consulted for details.

Our treatment of compiler derivation is motivated by Appel and Jim [1989] and Kelsey and Hudak [1989], who treat CPS code as an assembly language. Exercise 12.4.12 is based on Clinger [1984].

General Readings

A rich source of material on the early history of programming languages is Wexelblat [1981]. Braffort and Hirschberg [1963] and Steel [1966] contain several seminal papers. Horowitz [1983] anthologizes many classic papers on programming language design.

The major professional organizations in computing, the Association for Computing Machinery (ACM) and the IEEE Computer Society, are rich sources for learning more about programming languages. They sponsor major conferences and publish several journals that cover this field. Some of the major conferences are the ACM Symposium on Principles of Programming Languages, ACM Symposium on Programming Language Design and Implementation. ACM Symposium on Lisp and Functional Programming, and ACM Symposium on Functional Programming Languages, and Computer Architecture. For details, see the listings that are published regularly in the *Communications of the ACM* and IEEE Computer.

Some of the journals that publish important papers in programming languages are *ACM Transactions on Programming Languages and Systems, IEEE Software, Journal of Computer Languages, Software: Practice and Experience, Lisp and Symbolic Computation*, and the *Journal of Functional Programming*.

References

Abelson, H., Sussman, G.J., with Sussman, J. [1985] *Structure and Interpretation of Computer Programs*, Cambridge, MA: The MIT Press.

Aho, A.V., Sethi, R., and Ullman, J.D. [1986] *Compilers: Principles, Techniques, and Tools*, Reading, MA: Addison-Wesley.

Appel, A.W., and Jim, T. [1989] "Continuation-Passing, Closure-Passing Style," *Conf. Rec. 16th ACM Symp. on Principles of Programming Languages*, 293–302.

Backus, J. [1973] "Programming Language Semantics and Closed Applicative Languages," *Proc. 1st ACM Symp. on Principles of Programming Languages*, Boston, 71–86.

Baker, H. [1978] "Shallow Binding in Lisp 1.5" *Comm. ACM 21*, 565–569.

Barendregt, H.P. [1981] *The Lambda Calculus: Its Syntax and Semantics*, North-Holland, Amsterdam.

Birtwistle, G.M., Dahl, O.J., Myhrhaug, B., and Nygaard, K. [1979] *Simula Begin*, Studentlitteratur, Box 1717, S-221 01 Lund, Sweden.

Braffort P., and Hirschberg D. (eds.) [1963] *Computer Programming and Formal Systems*, Amsterdam: North-Holland.

Burge, W.H. [1975] *Recursive Programming Techniques*, Reading, MA: Addison-Wesley.

Church, A. [1941] *The Calculi of Lambda Conversion*, Princeton University Press; reprinted 1963 by University Microfilms, Ann Arbor, MI.

Clinger, W. [1984] "The Scheme 311 Compiler: An Exercise in Denotational Semantics," *Conf. Rec. 1984 ACM Symposium on Lisp and Functional Programming*, 356–364.

Dybvig, K. [1987] *The Scheme Programming Language*, Prentice-Hall, Englewood Cliffs, NJ.

Ellis, M.A. and Stroustrup, B., [1990] *The Annotated C++ Reference Manual*, Reading, MA: Addison-Wesley.

Felleisen, M., Friedman, D.P., Kohlbecker, E., and Duba, B. [1987] "A Syntactic Theory of Sequential Control," *Theoret. Comp. Sci. 52*, 205–237.

Felleisen, M., and Friedman, D.P. [1989] "A Syntactic Theory of Sequential State," *Theoret. Comp. Sci. 69*, 243–287.

Fischer, C.N., and LeBlanc, R.J. [1988] *Crafting a Compiler*, Menlo Park, CA: Benjamin/Cummings.

Floyd, R.W. [1967] "Assigning Meanings to Programs," *Proc. Symp. on Applied Mathematics*, Amer. Math. Soc., 19–32.

Friedman, D.P., and Felleisen, M. [1989] *The Little LISPer* (third edition), New York, NY: Macmillan.

Goldberg, A., and Robson, D. [1983] *Smalltalk-80: The Language and its Implementation*, Reading MA: Addison-Wesley.

Gordon, M.J.C. [1979] *The Denotational Description of Programming Languages*, Springer, Berlin.

Haynes, C.T., Friedman D.P., and Wand, M. [1986] "Obtaining Coroutines with Continuations," *Computer Languages 11*, 143–153.

Hewitt, Carl [1977] "Viewing Control Structures as Patterns of Passing Messages," *Artificial Intelligence 8*, 323–364.

Hieb, R., Dybvig, K., and Bruggeman, C. [1990] "Representing Control in the Presence of First-Class Continuations" *Proc. ACM SIGPLAN 1990 Conference on Programming Language Design and Implementation*, 66–77.

Hoare, C.A.R. [1969] "An Axiomatic Basis for Computer Programming," *Comm. ACM 12*, 576–580, 583.

Hofstadter, D.R. [1979] *Gödel, Escher, Bach: An Eternal Golden Braid*, New York: Basic Books.

Horowitz, E. [1983] *Programming Languages: A Grand Tour*, Rockville, MD: Computer Science Press.

Hughes, R.J.M., [1982] "Super Combinators: A New Implementation Method for Applicative Languages," *Proc. 1982 ACM Symp. on Lisp and Functional Programming*, 1–10.

For Further Reading

IEEE Computer Society [1991] *IEEE Standard for the Scheme Programming Language*, IEEE Std 1178-1990, New York: IEEE.

Keene, S.E. [1989] *Object-Oriented Programming in Common Lisp*, Reading, MA: Addison-Wesley.

Kelsey, R., and Hudak, P. [1989] "Realistic Compilation by Program Transformation," *Conf. Rec. 16th Ann. ACM Symp. on Principles of Programming Languages*, 281–292.

Kohlbecker, E.M. [1986] *Syntactic Extensions in the Programming Language Lisp*, PhD thesis, Indiana University. Portions published as: Kohlbecker, E., Friedman, D.P., Felleisen, M., and Duba, B. "Hygienic Macro Expansion," *Proc. 1986 ACM Conference on Lisp and Functional Programming*, 151–161, and Kohlbecker, E.M., and Wand, M., "Macro-by-Example: Deriving Syntactic Transformations from their Specifications" *Conf. Rec. 14th ACM Symp. on Principles of Prog. Lang.* (1987), 77–84.

Kranz, D.A., Kelsey, R., Rees, J.A., Hudak, P., Philbin, J., and Adams, N.I. [1986] "Orbit: An Optimizing Compiler for Scheme," *Proc. SIGPLAN '86 Symp. on Compiler Construction, SIGPLAN Notices 21*, 7, 219–223.

McCarthy, J. [1960] "Recursive Functions of Symbolic Expressions and their Computation by Machine, Part I," *Comm. ACM 3*, 184–195. Also reprinted in Horowitz [1983].

McCarthy, J. [1962] "Towards a Mathematical Science of Computation," *Information Processing 62* (Popplewell, ed.) Amsterdam: North-Holland, 21–28.

McCarthy, J. *et al.* [1965] *LISP 1.5 Programmer's Manual*, Cambridge, MA: The MIT Press. Portions reprinted in Horowitz [1983].

Milne, R. and Strachey C. [1976] *A Theory of Programming Language Semantics*, Chapman & Hall, London, and Wiley, New York.

Parnas, D.L. [1972] "A Technique for Module Specification with Examples," *Comm. ACM 15*, 330–336.

Peyton Jones, S.L. [1987] *The Implementation of Functional Programming Languages*, Englewood Cliffs, NJ: Prentice-Hall International.

Plotkin, G.D. [1975] "Call-by-Name, Call-by-Value and the λ-Calculus," *Theoret. Comp. Sci. 1*, 125–159.

Reade, C. [1989] *Elements of Functional Programming*, Reading, MA: Addison-Wesley.

Rees, J., and Clinger, W., eds. [1986] "Revised[3] Report on the Algorithmic Language Scheme," *SIGPLAN Notices 21*, 12, 37–79.

Reynolds, J.C. [1972] "Definitional Interpreters for Higher-Order Programming Languages," *Proc. ACM Nat'l. Conf.*, 717–740.

Schmidt, D.A. [1986] *Denotational Semantics: A Methodology for Language Development*, Boston: Allyn and Bacon.

Sethi, R. [1989] *Programming Languages: Concepts and Constructs*, Reading, MA: Addison-Wesley.

Smith, B.C. [1984] "Reflection and Semantics in Lisp," *Conf. Rec. 11th ACM Symp. on Principles of Programming Languages*, 23–35.

Springer, G., and Friedman, D.P. [1989] *Scheme and the Art of Programming*, Cambridge MA: The MIT Press, and New York: McGraw-Hill.

Steel, T.B. (ed.) [1966] *Formal Language Description Languages for Computer Programming*, Amsterdam: North-Holland.

Steele, G.L. [1976] "LAMBDA: The Ultimate Declarative," MIT AI Memo #379, Cambridge, MA.

Steele, G.L. [1978] "Rabbit: A Compiler for Scheme," MIT AI Lab TR 474, Cambridge, MA.

Steele, G.L. [1990] *Common Lisp: the Language* (2nd edition), Burlington MA: Digital Press.

Steele, G.L. Jr. and Sussman, G.J. [1976] "LAMBDA: The Ultimate Imperative," MIT AI Memo #353, Cambridge, MA.

Steele, G.L. and Sussman, G.J. [1978] "The Revised Report on SCHEME," MIT AI Memo #452, Cambridge, MA.

Steele, G.L. Jr. and Sussman, G.J. [1978a] "The Art of the Interpreter or, the Modularity Complex (Parts Zero, One and Two)," MIT AI Memo #453, Cambridge, MA.

Steele, G.L. and Sussman, G.J. [1980] "Design of a LISP-Based Microprocessor," *Comm. ACM 23*, 628–645.

Stoy, J.E. [1977] *Denotational Semantics: The Scott-Strachey Approach to Programming Language Theory*, The MIT Press, Cambridge, MA.

Strachey, C. [1973] "The Varieties of Programming Language," Oxford University Computing Laboratory, Technical Monograph PRG-10.

Strachey, C. and Wadsworth, C.P. [1974] "Continuations: A Mathematical Semantics for Handling Full Jumps," Oxford University Computing Laboratory Technical Monograph PRG-11.

Sussman, G.J. and Steele, G.L., Jr. [1975] "SCHEME: An Interpreter for Extended Lambda Calculus," MIT AI Memo #349, Cambridge, MA.

Wand, M. [1980a] "Continuation-Based Multiprocessing" *Proc. 1980 LISP Conference* (J. Allen, ed.), Palo Alto, CA: The Lisp Company, pp. 19–28.

Wand, M. [1980b] "Continuation-Based Program Transformation Strategies," *J. ACM 27*, 164–180.

Wexelblat, R.L. [1981] *History of Programming Languages*, New York: Acadmic Press.

Index